# LANDSCAPE AND FILM

Previously published in the AFI Film Readers series
Edited by Charles Wolfe and Edward Branigan

*New Media*
Anna Everett and John T. Caldwell

*Authorship and Film*
David A. Gerstner and Janet Staiger

*Westerns*
Janet Walker

*Masculinity*
Peter Lehman

*Violence and American Cinema*
J. David Slocum

*The Persistence of History*
Vivian Sobchack

*Home, Exile, Homeland*
Hamid Naficy

*Black Women Film and Video Artists*
Jacqueline Bobo

*The Revolution Wasn't Televised*
Lynn Spigel and Michael Curtin

*Classical Hollywood Comedy*
Henry Jenkins and Kristine Brunovska Karnick

*Disney Discourse*
Eric Smoodin

*Black American Cinema*
Manthia Diawara

*Film Theory Goes to the Movies*
Jim Collins, Ava Preacher Collins, and Hilary Radner

*Theorizing Documentary*
Michael Renov

*Sound Theory/Sound Practice*
Rick Altman

*Fabrications*
Jane M. Gaines and Charlotte Herzog

*Psychoanalysis and Cinema*
E. Ann Kaplan

*East European Cinemas*
Anikó Imre

# LANDSCAPE AND FILM

EDITED BY

## MARTIN LEFEBVRE

Routledge
Taylor & Francis Group
New York London

Routledge is an imprint of the
Taylor & Francis Group, an informa business

Published in 2006 by
Routledge
Taylor & Francis Group
270 Madison Avenue
New York, NY 10016

Published in Great Britain by
Routledge
Taylor & Francis Group
2 Park Square
Milton Park, Abingdon
Oxon OX14 4RN

© 2006 by Taylor & Francis Group, LLC
Routledge is an imprint of Taylor & Francis Group

Printed in the United States of America on acid-free paper
10 9 8 7 6 5 4 3 2 1

International Standard Book Number-10: 0-415-97554-9 (Hardcover) 0-415-97555-7 (Softcover)
International Standard Book Number-13: 978-0-415-97554-4 (Hardcover) 978-0-415-97555-1 (Softcover)

Taylor & Francis Group
is the Academic Division of Informa plc.

Visit the Taylor & Francis Web site at
http://www.taylorandfrancis.com

and the Routledge Web site at
http://www.routledge-ny.com

# contents

# illustrations

illustrations

# acknowledgments

I would like to warmly thank Santiago Hildago, Charlotte Selb, Brian Crane, Adam Rosadiuk, and Kevin Shelton for helping out with several tasks during the preparation of the manuscript. I am grateful to Dean Christopher Jackson of the Faculty of Fine Arts at Concordia University for his generous support to the University Research Chair in Film Studies. My gratitude also goes to AFI series editors, Edward Branigan and Charles Wolfe, for their kind support of this project.

Thanks to Jacques Aumont for permission to translate his essay published initially in French in *A quoi pensent les films* (Paris: Séguier, 1996) and to Jean Mottet for permission to translate his essay first published in French in *L'invention de la scène américaine. Cinéma et paysage* (Paris: L'Harmattan, 1998). Portions of Katie Russell's essay previously appeared as part of "Twilight in the Image Bank," in *David Rimmer: Films & Tapes 1967–1993*, ed. Jim Shedden (Toronto: Art Gallery of Ontario, 1993). A different version of my essay was published in French in *Poétique* 130 (April 2002).

Finally, I owe a very special debt of gratitude to Claire Dutil and Vincent Dutil-Lefebvre for their constant love and support. Their presence in all of the various landscapes of my life is an endless source of joy.

**Martin Lefebvre**

# introduction

Martin  Lefebvre

It is well known that one of the first wonders the cinema offered its viewers was that of images of the natural world in movement. Early spectators enjoyed the sights of crashing waves and tree leaves rustling in the wind. Not surprisingly, travel films quickly became popular—the famous "Hale's Tours of the World," for instance, is testimony to this interest for sightseeing that the cinema was catering to in its early years. Cinema, of course, developed at a time when our relation to space was undergoing important changes: nineteenth century colonialism; the development of ethnography in the context of Darwinism; the emergence of a traveling leisure class and of tourism (the word comes from the *Grand Tour* young European aristocrats were expected to take during their formative years); new and faster means of locomotion; and the "discovery" and aesthetic appreciation of novel locations such as mountainous terrains, ocean shorelines, etc.

Travel films were certainly a way for the less wealthy classes to see what otherwise was only accessible to them in still form through painting or photography. While the appeal for sightseeing is certainly understandable, one interesting aspect is the way it precedes the grand scale development and domination of narrative cinema. In fact, it is almost as if the *décor* had been set first and the cinema was simply waiting for the players to arrive and turn it into the setting for some unfolding drama. And in this respect, the cinema was inverting the process often regarded as the one giving birth to landscape in Western art: the slow emancipation of space from the demands of eventhood and narrative. But this is less paradoxical when we consider that cinematic landscapes came on the scene of "visuality" at the end of a century that saw the landscape genre flourish in an unprecedented degree in painting.

It is obvious that landscape as such is not a *genre* in the dominant cinema, as it is in still visual media; the institution of cinema prefers generic categories that revolve around narrative. Of course, specific landscapes (or cityscapes) may belong to the iconography of various genres, such as Westerns, road movies, and gangster and science fiction films. As such, they often appear to be somewhat peripheral material; after all, the telling of a story always requires a setting of some sort. This apparently peripheral role is perhaps what led Sergei Eisenstein, in the final section of his *Nonin-*

*different Nature*, to compare film landscapes with film music. Indeed, for the great Soviet filmmaker and theorist, both film landscape and film music share the ability to express, in cinematic form (i.e., on the image track or the soundtrack), what is otherwise inexpressible. In short, landscape was to silent film what music is to sound film: "landscape is a complex bearer of the possibilities of a plastic interpretation of emotions."[1]

But if landscape can fulfil this function, according to Eisenstein, it is because—like music—it is "the freest element of film, the least burdened with servile, narrative tasks, and the most flexible in conveying moods, emotional states, and spiritual experiences" (Eisenstein 1987, 217). Part of the value of this definition lies in how it throws into relief landscape's conflictual or tense relationship with narrative. And within the overall context offered by Eisenstein's film theory, this aligns landscape with a host of other conceptions that also challenge narrative's empire over all aspects of a film, of which the best known is undoubtedly the concept of "attraction." Though clearly distinct in strict Eisensteinian parlance and belonging to different phases of his theoretical output, both landscape and attraction nonetheless share important traits. In effect, both pertain to Eisenstein's interest in representing (on film) and inducing (in spectators) emotional states and both imply a certain freedom or autonomy from narrative. Of course, for landscape to fulfil the function Eisenstein conceived for it, it must obviously distinguish itself from mere background space or subservient setting where action and events take place. Eisenstein's own answer to this question was what he called the "musicality" of the emotional landscape, the key example for this being the "fog" sequence from his own *Battleship Potemkin* (1925), which, as early as 1929, he had likened to musical composition with his notion of "tonal montage."[2]

I mention Eisenstein in introducing this volume on landscape and film not because the essays found here directly address his films or theories, but because, in a sense, most of them start from the general understanding that the kinds of issues raised by landscape imply something like the tension between it and narrative found in the Soviet director's discussion of the matter. In other words, the authors of this volume agree that in investigating landscape in film one is considering an object that amounts to much more than the mere spatial background that necessarily accompanies the depiction of actions and events. The actual nature of that object which, in fiction films, lies in excess of its narrative function as setting, and which can also be found in other regimes of filmmaking (early cinema's "system of attractions," experimental cinema, and "home movies"), constitutes the real subject matter of this collection. How, then, are landscapes etched into films? What sort of role do they play? How do they relate to the still landscapes of the pictorial tradition and notions such as the picturesque or the sublime? What is their ideological or symbolic function?

Landscape is a multifaceted and pluridisciplinary spatial object whose meanings and representations extend from real-life environments to art. It is "practiced" or studied by, among others, architects (landscape architecture), artists (painting, "land art"), art historians, writers and literary critics, geographers, historians, urban planners, ecologists and environmentalists, and, of course, filmmakers and film scholars. Furthermore, it is relevant in aesthetics as well as in economic and political debates over land development and exploitation, tourism, and national identity and sovereignty. Yet despite all this attention, and perhaps because it is so widely spread among different knowledge formations and disciplines, landscape remains notoriously difficult to define, having apparently no single set of fixed criteria outside of its spatial nature. For instance, J. B. Jackson (the founding editor of *Landscape* magazine whose pioneering work on ordinary landscapes beginning in the 1950s—influenced in part by the French movement of *géographie humaine*—inspired a whole generation of American cultural geographers to "read" landscapes) admitted as much when he wrote

> For more than 25 years I have been trying to understand and explain that aspect of the environment that I call the landscape. I have written about it, lectured about it, travelled widely to find out about it; and yet I must admit that the concept continues to elude me. Perhaps one reason for this is that I persist in seeing it not as a scenic or ecological entity but as a political or cultural entity, changing in the course of history.[3]

Cultural geographers insist that landscapes do not exist independently of human investment toward space, which is one way of distinguishing them from the idea of "nature." For nature is that which we usually conceive of as existing independently from us, whereas it is our (real and imaginary) interaction with nature and the environment that produces the landscape. In other words, should humans and all things human disappear from the face of the earth tomorrow, nature as we conceive of it would likely continue to exist (and even possibly thrive!), which is more than we could say for landscapes. This much is obvious, in fact, when we consider the emergence of landscape painting in the West during the late Renaissance.

The first autonomous landscape paintings in Europe were produced during the sixteenth and seventeenth centuries at the hands of artists such as El Greco, Joachim Patinir, Albrecht Altdorfer, Annibale Carracci, Jan Joseph van Goyen, Jacob von Ruisdael, and Claude Lorrain. These works were produced after centuries of using nature as a backdrop to paintings. Like most historians of landscape painting, the philosopher Edward S. Casey observes that

It is a remarkable fact that what we now call routinely "landscape painting" was unknown in the ancient world of the West. Nothing like the broad vistas, the commodious scenes that we consider to be the sine qua non of landscape painting, is to be found in the art of earlier times. At the most, this art included a schematic landscape vista that served as a literal background for the myth or story that was the subject matter and the primary focus of the scene.[4]

But why this change of attitude from artists after centuries of representing the natural environment as a mere place-setting and not, as the "primary focus," or the Argument of a work? There can be no simple answer to this question, which has haunted art historians at least since Ruskin.[5] For instance, one would surely wish to consider factors that concern art, such as changes in its social function during the Renaissance, or the rise of the modern persona of the Artist and of artistic individuality through style, or again the development of linear perspective. But several other factors would also need to be taken into account that affected the European sensibility toward the natural world during that period. Thus, for instance, the translation into the vernacular tongues of works by Theocritus, Ovid, Virgil, Pliny, and Horace participated in a revival of pastoral literature—from Boccaccio to Milton. But the development of landscape painting also benefited from a more favourable philosophical and religious context. While the Church had long been suspicious of the contemplation of earthly, sensual, things,[6] Renaissance Humanists began (at the peril of their lives!) developing the idea that God was in everything—including nature. Moreover, in the Northern countries, Reformation iconoclasm led artists, who could no longer find religious commissions, to adopt secular subject matters.

Of course, the Renaissance was also a time of great scientific discoveries (heliocentrism), social changes (development of capitalism and, with it, new forms of land management and changing relations between city and country), and travel (discovery of the New World; establishment of new commercial routes to the Orient and to Africa; improvements in topography and cartography) that profoundly transformed European conceptions and experience of space and environment. When we conceive of the emergence of landscape painting in the West as related to all these changes we are obviously committing ourselves to the idea that landscape, as Malcolm Andrews puts it, "is already an artifice before it has become the subject of a work of art."[7] But this is not to say that landscape art is a simple mirror reflection of that artifice, for art is a place where the "artifice of landscape" develops and transforms itself, a place where human beings not only recognize their investment in space but also redefine it.

Difficulty in pinning down the entity that we call "landscape" can be traced back to the term's origin. The word itself only entered into the English lexicon in the seventeenth century as "landskip" (or sometimes "landtskip") and was borrowed either from the Middle Dutch "*landschap*" or "*landscap*," the Flemish "*lantskip*," or the German "*landschaft*." Old English equivalents to the German suffix "-*shaft*" include "-scipe" (the modern form of which is "-ship"), which was related to "gesceap" or "gescape" and to Middle English words in the family of the verb "ishapen," all of which mean to give *form* or *shape* (in the sense of creating something). Of course, the current suffix "-ship" may be understood to carry part of that meaning if one is ready to concede that a noun like "friendship," in denoting a state or a condition of being, also stands for the *form* of the relation that unites people who are friends. But what sort of "form" is implied by the "*landschap*" or "land-shape"?

There is something that happens when, say, hiking in some wildlife reserve or looking down from the window of a airplane or even driving on some stretch of highway, we look at the natural environment *as if* it were framed.[8] This purely mental activity can also be reproduced—even more forcefully so—by looking through a camera's *viewfinder*. The term itself betrays the process involved: that of finding a view by creating or shaping it through the framing.[9] What happens in such circumstances can be understood as the construction (or replication) of a form: suddenly the view becomes organized, it "holds" together as a whole, there is either balance or imbalance in the composition, etc. It can now become a landscape. Form now reigns where previously there stood only the "formlessness" of pure (spatial) continuity. The origins of that frame and of its shaping powers are lost to us today as we cannot extirpate ourselves from some 500 years of Western landscape imagery. The form of landscape is thus first of all the form of a view, of a particular gaze that requires a frame. With that frame nature turns into culture, land into landscape. But though it may be foundational for the emergence of landscape—and especially for landscape art—geographers and other landscape scholars often remind us that the view itself cannot be divorced from other experiential aspects that accompany it. It follows that the form of a landscape also corresponds to the form of our experience of it, with the latter including representations of the different personal, cultural, and social functions it can associate to or serve.

Thus it is, for instance, that the historian Simon Schama, in *Landscape and Memory*, has worked at unearthing the various mythical sediments that layer and *frame* our interaction with landscapes. Schama's argument is that "landscapes are culture before they are nature; constructs of the imagination projected onto wood and water and rock"[10] and that furthermore these often ancient constructs, whose origins are sometimes forgotten, continue nonetheless to haunt our interactions with and representations of land as landscapes. Others, such as geographers Denis Cosgrove and Jay Appleton, have opted for Marxist and anthropological perspectives, respectively. Cosgrove sees landscape as an "ideological concept" that "represents a way in which certain classes of people have signified themselves and their world through their imagined relationships with nature, and through which they have underlined and communicated their own social role and that of others with respect to external nature."[11] As for Appleton, he has argued that what usually stands as the preferred forms of landscape in art are really views of space that offer strategic or tactical advantage as prospect ("unimpeded opportunity to see") or refuge ("an opportunity to hide"), thus relating aesthetic forms to spatial forms expressing group survival.[12] Whether we agree with the various perspectives offered by these (and many other) landscape scholars, all of them have followed J. B. Jackson's call to study landscape as something anchored in human life.

Now, there can be no doubt that film contributes to this "anchorage" of landscape in human life and participates in the process of "imaginative projection" discussed by Schama, all the while being haunted as well by layers of past landscape projections. Nowhere is this more obvious perhaps than in those landscapes that have become such an integral part of the iconography of Western films. When I travel through that part of Navajo land that straddles Utah and Arizona known as Monument Valley, I cannot but help think of Hollywood Westerns, especially John Ford's films. My own "framing" of the land, the photos I take, are all "contaminated" by my experience and memory of these films, of what that stretch of land has come to stand for symbolically. The cinema has thus dramatically transformed the experience that we have of that land—and in this regard, readers will not be surprised to find that several essays in this volume refer to the Western and to Ford's Monument Valley. But this, as mentioned earlier, is only the most obvious case of cinematic projection onto landscape.

In presenting what he regards as three "symbolic landscapes" in America (the New England Village; Main Street of Middle America; and California Suburbia), geographer Donald W. Meinig hinted at the importance of film when considering how "actual landscapes become symbolic landscapes."

> For the past 60 years the cinema has been widely assumed to have had a powerful impact on popular attitudes toward many things. It has displayed an enormous range of landscapes to millions of people, and within those myriad scenes there have been some which were obviously meant to convey settings representative of some concept of the ordinary good and happy life in America. An efficient beginning for an investigation of these would be a study of the character of the outdoor sets which the major motion-picture

companies maintained on their lots during the peak of the Hollywood era circa 1920s–1950s. One suspects, for example, that "small town America" was filmed time and again on essentially the same set in which the facades of an idealized "typical" Main Street, church, and a few residences had been created. A logical extension of such an inquiry would be an inventory of the actual towns which were used for on-location filming of similar kinds of shows.[13]

And yet, film scholars have been slow in responding to invitations such as Meinig's or, more recently, that of W. J. T. Mitchell, whose revisionist approach to landscape as a "dynamic medium" acting out on the political stage of identity formation is, he tells us, greatly influenced by the existence of *moving* cinematic landscapes—as opposed to the motionless landscapes of still media.[14] As a result, the present volume is, at the time of writing these lines, the first English language collection devoted to this topic.[15]

The aim of this book is twofold. First, it seeks to offer the reader a series of views of cinematic landscapes produced from varying perspectives. As a result, *auteur* studies and textual analyses will be seen standing next to regional or national approaches to landscape; historical research on early cinema landscapes next to generic studies; narrative next to non-narrative forms; formal considerations over *mise-en-scène* next to ideological considerations regarding the national landscape; and so on. The goal, however, is not to produce a complete or integrative overview of the issues raised by landscape with regard to the different sites of interests of the discipline of film studies—something no single collection of essays could presumably ever hope to achieve—but to offer instead a group of variegated intellectual *"vedute"* in order to underscore the vastness of the terrain that needs to be represented. Second, and in a related vein, the goal is also to showcase views taken from both sides of the Atlantic by selecting authors whose works represent the different film studies traditions of North America and Europe as well as other disciplines concerned with landscape representation (art history, literature, geography), and whose interests, in some instances, take them well beyond the borders of either Western or narrative filmmaking.

An outline of the various sections of the volume and of each essay's main arguments should make clear the adopted trajectory for the book and provide readers with a map to help them navigate through the various issues and points of view that find expression in the thirteen chapters that follow. The essays have been divided into four sections. These, however, should not be conceived as air-tight and readers will most likely find several overlaps between chapters in the different sections.

The first section, Space, Setting, Landscape, takes up the issue of the representation of space on film by way of comparisons with two other artistic media, the stage (theatre or opera) and painting. Jacques Aumont's "The Invention of Place: Danièle Huillet and Jean-Marie Straub's *Moses and Aaron*" investigates the cinematic adaptation of Arnold Schoenberg's opera by the two avant-garde filmmakers. Devoid of clear stage directions, Schoenberg's libretto locates the narrative in nondescript biblical locations (the Burning Bush, Mount Sinai, the Desert) that suggest abstract metaphysical space more than real physical space. And indeed, Aumont observes that most stage productions of the opera have avoided attempts at rendering a "realist" space, adopting instead a more symbolic representation. With a film adaptation, however, the opposite might seem tempting, as it was with Joseph Losey's *Don Giovanni* or Francesco Rosi's *Carmen,* both of which opted for a Hollywood-like strategy of spatial realism in their choice and screen treatment of locations. Aumont shows that nothing could be further from Straub's and Huillet's intention in choosing to set the first two acts of *Moses and Aaron* in the amphitheatre at Alba Fucens, situated near Rome and dating back to the first century. The intricacies of the *mise-en-scène,* camera framing, and editing of this space, with its architecture and surrounding landscape, are painstakingly examined by Aumont's textual analysis of a film that avoids classical cinema's procedures for constructing filmic space. In the process, we discover how much a film can gain in complexity from the use of an historically and culturally layered *real* landscape, such as the ancient amphitheatre of Alba Fucens. With the help of the *mise-en-scène*—"the human figures of the drama, costume, postures, and gestures"—the landscape comes to evoke what Aumont calls an implicit "underground reservoir" of meaning, memory, history, and death—a process he sees as an authorial signature in most of the works of Straub and Huillet. In the end, Aumont argues that film can be made to expressively reveal the subsoil of a landscape and project it symbolically onto the narrative by allowing "the spectator to engage in the mental—and affective—work of gaining access to the film's location, at once as a substratum of the filming and as an imaginary framework for the drama."

In the second chapter, "Between Setting and Landscape in the Cinema," I examine "landscape" in film as a spatial *predicate* distinct from "setting" or "territory." All three terms are understood as different ways we have developed for representing space to ourselves: as the location for some unfolding action (setting); as a space of aesthetic contemplation and spectacle (landscape); and as a *lived* space that we possess—or would like to possess (territory). The essay seeks mostly to distinguish landscape from setting in the context of narrative cinema and on the grounds of the Western art of landscape painting. Drawing from works as diverse as Laura Mulvey's famous "Visual Pleasure and Narrative Cinema" essay[16] or Tom Gunning and André Gaudreault's equally well-known description of a "system of monstrative attractions" at work in early cinema,[17] I argue that we need to distinguish, *within* what Gunning and Gaudreault have called the "system of narrative cinema," between "narrative" and "spectacular" modes of spectatorship. I then try to show how landscape relates to the second of these modes and how it relies on a certain type of gaze whose earliest manifestations seem to be traceable to the Renaissance. Through this gaze natural space finally emancipated itself from its role as mere narrative setting in Western painting. This historically constructed gaze may be active in filmmakers and in film spectators as well. This idea leads to distinguishing between "two paradigms that define the poles of an interpretive spectrum: in one case, the spectator imputes to the film (or to its director) the intention to present a landscape…in the other, the spectator must assume the he/she is the source of the cinematic landscape." The proposition is then fleshed out by considering examples from both interpretive paradigms.

The volume's second section, entitled National Landscapes and Cultural Identities and Traditions, is concerned with the function film landscapes play in identity formation either by way of ideology or their connection to national traditions in the fine arts and cultural matters at large.

As indicated by the titles of the first two chapters in this section, Jean Mottet's "Toward a Genealogy of the American Landscape: Notes on Landscapes in D. W. Griffith (1908–1912)" and Maurizia Natali's "The Course of the Empire: Sublime Landscapes in the American Cinema," both authors attend to American film landscapes. Jean Mottet's contribution concerns Griffith's work during his days at Biograph, which he sees as being an important source in the development of American cinema's use of landscape imagery at a time when the new medium was attempting to create and share its vision of America and its worldview. Situating Griffith within what was already an established tradition toward nature in American philosophy (Emerson, Thoreau, Crevecoeur) and fine arts (the Hudson River School, the American Impressionists, Winslow Homer), Mottet examines three Griffithian landscapes: the ideal country homestead, the seashore, and the West.

The first of these landscapes is set in the mythical tradition of the pastoral into which Americans introduced new sets of concerns as they sought to provide themselves with their own sense of national identity. The second, the ocean shoreline, argues Mottet, offers a different view of Griffith's approach to landscape, one closer in spirit to the paintings of Winslow Homer after his return to America. "One gets the impression," writes Mottet, "that, in Griffith's work, the sea encourages a rupture with ordinary experience in favor of a more spiritual quest." Finally, Mottet considers Griffith's representation of America's Southwestern landscape. Although none of the filmmaker's early work can properly be considered to fall into the generic category of the western, Mottet demonstrates that in those films which are set in the Southwest, Griffith abandoned his usual landscape references (from painting and literature) and instead adopted a new approach that showcased several "primitive functions" of the soon to be classical Western film landscape. More specifically, by referring to the work of Jay Appleton, Mottet shows that, combined with the use of long shots, Griffith's use of the age-old distinction between prospect and refuge in a narrative context of embattled space constitutes the cornerstone of what will become the American Western's use of landscape.

In "The Course of the Empire: Sublime Landscapes in the American Cinema," Maurizia Natali also considers the key role played by American painters of the nineteenth century in the depiction of a national landscape expressing the political ambitions of the young nation. The trajectory Natali charts goes from Hudson River School founder Thomas Cole's *The Course of Empire*—a series of five canvases, first exhibited in 1836, showing the transformations undergone by a single landscape over the "course of empire": from the *Savage State*, to the *Pastoral or Arcadian State*, the *Consummation of Empire*, *Destruction*, and *Desolation*—to the live television images of the destruction and ruins of the World Trade Center following the terrorist attacks of September 11, 2001. Between these two sets of images, Natali places 100 years of American cinematic landscapes which she considers as forming an immense "wall of screens" or theatre of memory addressed to the world.

According to Natali, what unites these American landscapes—those of nineteenth century painters such as Cole and Frederic Church, of Hollywood movies, and the ruins of 9/11—are ideological and iconological scenarios (*pathos formulae* to use Aby Warburg's term) having to do with "sublime imperial fantasies," i.e., with "*the primary U.S. fantasy* of being (or behaving as) an Empire":

> like *pathos formulae*, Hollywood's dramatic "figures in the landscape" are iconological and political compositions that display uncanny likenesses, survivals and returns from past U.S. history and ideology. Film landscapes are never purely narrative backgrounds nor simply distracting spectacular settings. They bear the traces of political projects and ideological messages. They press onto viewers' senses, memories, and fears and become part of their memory, carrying the subliminal strength of a past, even archaic, worldview ready to come back as future progress. Like the footprints left on the surface of the moon by U.S. astronauts, Hollywood landscapes bear the footprints of the United States' recurrent manifest destiny.

Natali concludes her essay with a survey of Hollywood's own "Course of Empire" from E. S. Porter's *The Great Train Robbery* to Roland Emmerich's *The Day After Tomorrow*.

In "Asphalt Nomadism: The New Desert in Arab Independent Cinema," Laura U. Marks examines the "desert" landscapes of contemporary Arabic independent films. The desert, of course, has long been an important part of life in the Middle East, around which nomadic and sedentary cultures have had to "position" themselves. And though the desert is first of all a *real* space—a space that, Marks's claims, has been increasingly left behind by Arabs in past decades—it is also a *figural* space, a space that exists relationally with regards to what Gilles Deleuze and Félix Guattari call "the smooth and the striated." Of course, as Marks observes, there is no such thing as a purely smooth space: "Once you explore it [smooth space], it springs into complex life on scales both micro and macro." At best, the desert as perfectly smooth is an "outsider's fantasy." And yet, *relatively* speaking, there is an important part of smoothness in the desert. Marks's understanding of the desert is further characterized by the *mu'allaqat*, the odes of pre-Islamic nomads. Accordingly, the desert, as concept, shares with the odes a number of properties: "nomadic, nonteleological, self-organized, embodied, and concrete." But as Islam made more converts in the Middle East, it affected the nomadic life of the desert. "Monotheism," writes Marks, "cannot tolerate nomads."

Islam, however, is only one of the factors that bears on sedentarisation in the Middle East. Another one is oil. And in that regard, one of the ironies that underpins Marks's analysis of contemporary independent Arabic road movies is the bond that exists in the Middle East between the desert and the road. Indeed, both spaces come to mirror each other—literally, i.e., as inverted images—through their connection to oil: the desert being the place where oil is found and produced, and the asphalt road—made from petroleum—the place where it is consumed. This inversion carries over to the structural relation between smooth and striated spaces. For as Marks notes, oil exploitation in the Middle East is the "final" and "decisive" striation of the desert whereby the "Arab world was incorporated into the global economy at expense of place." Oil exacerbated the pressure on nomadic populations to accept a sedentary lifestyle: "Some Bedouins," writes Marks, "got airconditioned cars and became sedentary and fat; others simply became immiserated." And yet, perversely, it is on the roads built for those very machines for which oil is extracted—the Land Cruisers and Maximas of films such as Abdallah al Junaibi's *When?*, Joana Hadjithomas' and Khalil Joriege's *Rounds*, Rehab Omar Ateeq's *The Car or the Wife*, or Hani el Shibani's *A Warm Winter Night*—that the new asphalt nomadism of independent films emerges.

Catherine Russell's "The Inhabited View: Landscape in the Films of David Rimmer" explores the work of the celebrated Canadian experimental filmmaker. Russell situates Rimmer's "structural" films in the context of political and philosophical debates in Canadian aesthetics in such a way as to challenge accepted ideas regarding the notion of nationalist art practice. English Canadian writers such as George Grant, Northrop Frye, Harold Innis, Marshall McLuhan, Margaret Atwood, and Gaile McGregor have all attempted to define the Canadian national character with regards to how Canadians interact with nature and technology, either in real life or in the imaginary worlds of fiction and art. Most often, the goal is to distinguish Canadian identity from American identity. In that context, a critical idiom has arisen which sees landscape art as a representation of alienation toward and recoil from nature and thus as an outgrowth of what Northrop Frye has called the "garrison mentality"[18]: a view of nature and of the Northern Frontier as so oppressive, threatening, and alien that it requires being kept at bay by the building of fortified walls and mental garrisons. Gaile McGregor has called this the "Wacousta Syndrome" in reference to Major John Richardson's 1832 novel *Wacousta*.[19] Russell offers close study of several films by Rimmer, examining framing and composition, in order to contest the claim that his work is exemplary of McGregor's Wacousta Syndrome. Indeed, through structural cinema's foregrounding of off-screen space—the space occupied by the filmmaker—the films suggest instead an "inhabited" or "domesticated" view of the Canadian landscape. The natural world of *Canadian Pacific I and II* and *Landscape*, writes Russell, "far from being 'monstrous'…it becomes a home for the eye, a restful and welcoming sight that reaches forward to the vanishing points of perspective, completing a structure of representation that includes and is predicated on the viewing subject-position." Landscape, here, is not so much "nature" (the wild and threatening fantasy screen of so many Canadian cultural critics), but a cultural production in its own right.

In the process, Russell critiques McGregor's work for mimicking "the worst features of the American mythology it aims to counter." She then goes on to propose a less totalizing, and more "local" and historical, context to investigate the films of Rimmer by considering his involvement in the Vancouver artistic community. The point of this critique is to dispute the notion that one can look at landscape or art through a totalizing nationalistic gaze and to offer instead a more ecological perspective that considers the specific geo-historical context of production as well as the specificity of the medium used. As shown by the example of Zacharius Kunuk's Inuit-produced feature *Atanarjuat*, Russell argues that one's uninhabitable landscape can easily be integrated into another's "visual culture of everyday life."

The move toward a more local understanding of landscape is echoed in Heather Nicholson's consideration of amateur filmmakers' landscape imagery—a popular subject matter for nonprofessional filmmakers since the beginning of hobby cinematography during the 1920s. In "Sites of Meaning: Gallipoli and other Mediterranean Landscapes in Amateur Films (c. 1928–1960)," Nicholson investigates some of the reasons that led amateur filmmakers to include landscape imagery in their "home movies" and how this practice allowed for the formation and circulation of landscape meanings. More specifically she examines the footage produced by a retired British army officer, Lt. Colonel James Fitzwilliam O'Grady, who had served during World War I and fought the Turks at Gallipoli, on the western shore of the Dardanelles. Almost 20 years later, in 1934, O'Grady returned to the battlefields of the Dardanelles armed this time with a 16 mm camera. Nicholson explains how the resulting film, *Gallipoli Revisited, 1934. A Pilgrimage Cruise,* "documents on 16 mm black and white silent film stock with intertitles a commemorative tour of the different battlefield sites and war memorials associated with the Gallipoli campaign." Nicholson observes that the landscapes included in home movies and nonprofessional travel films generally participate in deliberate "memorializing acts" that "approximate the diaries, notebooks, and image making of earlier commentators." As such, home movies, much like nonprofessional photography, can help us better understand how individuals and families "mediate, negotiate, and circulate specific identities in public spaces." Thus, because of O'Grady's own personal connection to the sites where he had fought, been wounded, and lost many of his comrades in arms, his "filmic framing of landscape features," Nicholson notes, "convey a poignancy that is associated with his own acts of remembrance."

In "The Presence (and Absence) of Landscape in Silent East Asian Films," Peter Rist investigates the use of exterior locations in Chinese, Korean, and Japanese silent cinema and questions the possible ties that exist among them and the Asian scroll landscape painting tradition. The chapter begins by briefly outlining the history, period styles, and aesthetic principles of Oriental landscape painting, lamenting in passing how poorly Asian art is represented in Western art history textbooks. Rist points out the importance this pictorial tradition has given to the ability of artists to use landscape for evoking mood and atmosphere, and for producing what Alexander Soper calls "animation through spirit consonance." Moving on to film, Rist observes that "during the silent film era…there was very little aesthetic use made of the landscape and even less in the way of allusion to landscape painting." Rather, exterior locations tended mostly to be used as settings for narrative action and special effects. There were nonetheless important exceptions to the rule, as Rist points out. These were films where landscape shots were used poetically and pictorially instead of simply serving the narrative.

Whereas Eisenstein saw Asian scroll landscapes as an early form of pictorial representation that was to eventually evolve into cinematic montage,[20] Rist is more concerned with connecting *horizontal scrolls* to the figure of the lateral moving camera and with examining how the moods the latter create compare with the feel of Asian landscape paintings. Indeed, Rist shows how, in the absence of direct references to the landscape tradition, formal features such as camera movements and parallel editing of shots with a landscape component managed nonetheless to capture some of the basic principles of Oriental landscape painting in the way they pertain to "resonant visual and emotional correspondences." After an overview of the use of landscape imagery in the work of many of the most important Asian filmmakers of the silent period, including Ozu Yasujiro and Mizoguchi Kenji, Rist concludes by turning to the relatively little-known silent films of Japanese director Shimizu Hiroshi, whom he considers to be "East Asia's first truly original 'landscape' filmmaker" and "the first important director of 'road movies' in world cinema history."

The penultimate section of this volume, Early Film Landscapes, is devoted to landscape in early cinema. In some sense, this was perhaps the golden age of cinematic landscapes, the age of the "cinema of attractions" and of non-narrative "landscape" genres such as "scenics" and travel films. But if travel films were popular, how did the notion of a "moving landscape," a notion so different from the fixed-point views long associated with the picturesque in painting and even photography, ever come to be naturalized in visual media? What are its sources? In their chapter, "From Flatland to Vernacular Relativity: The Genesis of Early English Screenscapes," David B. Clarke and Marcus A. Doel investigate the origins of this transformation by way of some of the various devices produced for the capture and exhibition of images that accompanied the new regime of vision introduced by the nineteenth century. This new regime was marked by what the authors portray as a "democratization of spectatorship" in that it challenged the fixed centrality of classical perspective through mobility and depth and eventually "transformed the picturesque notion of landscape." Clarke and Doel examine how the ground for this transformation which culminated with the arrival of film was laid by pre-cinematic apparatuses such as the panorama, the diorama, and the stereograph. But this process of transformation in visual culture culminating with the cinema did not always progress smoothly. Indeed, Clarke and Doel's essay also documents some of the tensions that accompanied it and that were responsible, in their view, for the failure of the British film industry in the early years of filmmaking. British directors, they claim, simply succumbed to a pre-cinematic conception of the picturesque under the weight of a landscape art tradition deeply connected to English national identity.

In "Landscape and Archive: Trips Around the World as Early Film Topic (1896–1914)," Antonio Costa reminds us of the importance of the "trip around the world" theme in the first two decades of the cinema, that is, from the moment the Lumière brothers sent out their operators to capture moving images from the four corners of the globe. The theme itself, the interest it managed to arouse in early film viewers, must be conceived in the context of the new culture of time and space that was ushered in by the nineteenth century and which fully expressed itself in such events as the Paris World Fair of 1900 or the Pan-American Exposition of Buffalo the following year, both of which prominently featured film exhibits and world travel themes. Throughout the essay, Costa discusses the Lumière catalogue (the world's first archive to include moving images of landscapes) as well as other films and projects concerned with showing views taken from around the world. These principally include a film by documentary pioneer Luca Comerio, *Dal Polo all'Equatore* (*From the Pole to the Equator*), that was rediscovered during the mid-1980s through the work of Italian avant-garde filmmakers Yervant Gianikian and Angela Ricci Lucchi; Albert Khan's fantastic "Archives de la planète" project which used film along with world gardens to document and even "reproduce a...scale model of the unceasing process of transformation, of the evolution of life, from the infinitely small to the infinitely big"; and Marcel Fabre's 1914 adaptation of Albert Robida's famous novel *Voyages très extraordinaires de Saturnin Farandoul dans les 5 ou 6 parties du monde et dans tous les pays connus et même inconnus de M. Jules Verne* (*Saturnin Farandoul's Most Extraordinary Trips in the 5 or 6 Parts of the World and in All the Known and Even Unknown Countries of Mr. Jules Verne*), a spoof of the Vernian novel which, adapted to the screen, parodies early cinema's trip around the world *topos* and its "implications in terms of adventure, knowledge, and conquest." All of these productions and projects offer variations on the same theme, which Costa describes. But the heart of the matter, writes Costa in his conclusion, is really to illustrate "that there is no single or unique landscape-function in early cinema, instead, various functions are distributed along several paths."

The final section, Landscape *Auteurs*, takes a look at the work of three directors who have made landscape a key part of their *oeuvre*: Peter Greenaway, Anthony Mann, and Michelangelo Antonioni.

In "A Walk Through Heterotopia: Peter Greenaway's Landscapes by Numbers," Bridget Elliott and Anthony Purdy step into the labyrinth—or, better yet, the hall of mirrors—of Peter Greenaway's cinema by way of an abandoned project for a television series entitled *Fear of Drowning* whose nine episodes were outlined by the filmmaker in a book he published in 1988, shortly after the release of *Drowning by Numbers*.[21] The episodes of increasing length were to act as a prequel of sorts to *Drowning by Numbers*. Landscape elements play an important role in Greenaway's description of the episodes and Elliott and Purdy recognize in them the influence of British Land Art. Following the trail of allusions, resonances, analogies, and rhymes that leads from *Fear of Drowning* to Greenaway's early films as well as the allusions, resonances, analogies, and rhymes that one finds between them (for instance, the "H" of *A Walk Through H* and *H is for House*, or the recurring use of the number 92, etc.) Elliott and Purdy come to see the "heterotopian" nature of Greenaway's films, including *Drowning by Numbers*—the focus of the second part of the essay.

Moreover, for Elliott and Purdy, *Drowning by Numbers'* treatment of space, and of landscape in particular, can also be seen as a commentary of sorts on the similitudes and differences that exist between narrative cinema and painting. The film, they write, reveals narrative cinema's "limitations as a genre capable of adequately representing the complexities of landscape...the emphasis on the highly contrived nature of the landscape [being] a way of drawing the viewer's attention to the filmmaker's dilemma" in that regard. On the other hand, Greenaway's film continually quotes from paintings—including landscape paintings. But he does so in ways opposite to the classical narrative cinema's traditional approach to figure/ground relations with regards to natural settings. Particular attention is then given to Greenaway's treatment of a painting by William Holman Hunt which is seen to reverse "the typical Hollywood practice of making the landscape serve the narrative by situating it, authenticating it, and reflecting human emotions and psychological states." In the end, the authors claim that "Greenaway's approach to film and to landscape is... that of a painter" as well as that of a literary "allegorist." However, much will be lost, they argue, if one fails as well to recognize in the director's work the influence of Land Artists such as Richard Long.

The next chapter in this section, Tom Conley's "Landscape and Perception: On Anthony Mann," offers close readings of two of Mann's famous 1950s Westerns, *Winchester 73* and *The Man from Laramie*. Conley begins by considering a metaphor once used by Christian Metz to portray cinematic enunciation. In *L'énonciation impersonelle ou le site du film*, Metz argues that, unlike verbal language, the source of filmic discourse doesn't lie in real persons but in the (imaginary) space, or geography, of the "depersonalized" image (or *text*) where remains only a trace of the film's source or target.[22] The absence—*invisibility* or *lack*—of "persons" leads Metz to characterize this textual space as a "landscape." But what if we are to take this "landscape" metaphor literally as a way of investigating the "real" landscapes of the cinema? This is precisely what Conley sets out to do with the help of the concept of "perspectival object" borrowed from the work of French psychoanalyst Guy Rosolato.

As Conley points out, "for Rosolato, the task of psychoanalysis entails the exploration of our perception of the unknown." In some sense, the perspectival object is to the subject what the "vanishing point" is to painting: that which organizes the space and makes it visible while being absent from it, unknown to it. In film, argues Conley, the perspectival object appears in moments (or rather landscapes) when "speech becomes textual," and the image becomes "legible."

One example will suffice here to give readers a sense of Conley's landscape hermeneutic. Looking at *Winchester 73*, Conley notices how much the shape of the giant cactuses seen in the landscape resembles that of a repeating rifle with its barrel stuck into the earth: "We see a world of spiked and spurred gun-cactuses that proliferate the very enigma that inhabited the film since the inscription of the title on [a] hillside. 'Winchester 73s' are frozen everywhere in the landscape, but the hero, bent on finding the object of his quest, gallops forward, entirely blind to its presence." Such blindness is the counterpart to the hero's fetishistic relation to the prized rifle that the embattled brothers both seek to own. But since the cactuses also resemble "fossilized dejections," they also *make visible* the nature of the hero's drive and render more complex the relations that exist between the rifle and the landscape which are first made legible—quite literally so— through the credit sequence (the title of the film, which also happens to be the name of the rifle, is first seen written onto a hillside, espousing the hill's shape). "From the overlay of interpretations," writes Conley, "it can be deduced that the perspectival object, a point spotting the visibility and invisibility of what is known and unknown, is made manifest whenever the decor is both a landscape *and* a field of textual images which both the hero and spectator are impelled to decrypt." These are moments where the visual regime of a film may be referred to what Deleuze has called the "perception-image," a style of image that often characterizes long shots and *a fortiori* classical Western films, and where the "interval" between visibility and invisibility, or insight and blindness, comes to manifest itself. Conley uses these concepts to explore the "pictogrammatic" fields of Mann's two films, which he sees as foregrounding the cinema's ability to turn the image into a legible and language-like surface able to "address" viewer and character alike.

In the final chapter, "The Cinematic Void: Desert Iconographies in Michelangelo Antonioni's *Zabriskie Point*," Matthew Gandy takes a new look at the most overtly political—and often neglected—film by the famous Italian director. Because Antonioni's best known work is what Seymour Chatman has dubbed "the great tetralogy,"[23] he is often thought of as an exclusively urban filmmaker who uses city and industrial landscapes to give resonance to his critique of the emotional decay of modern life. Yet, in the 30-year period between *Del gente del Po* and *The Passenger*, Antonioni has often integrated natural landscape settings to his films. Gandy, in fact, observes that one "can trace a shift within Antonioni's films from the neo-realist 'urban deserts' portrayed in earlier features such as *La notte* and *L'eclisse* toward a gradual engagement with real deserts as powerful metaphors for social and cultural redemption in *Zabriskie Point* and *The Passenger*."

Gandy is particularly interested in the way the desert is used in *Zabriskie Point* as the centrepiece of Antonioni's critique of American culture and of its landscapes of violence (university campus), consumption (the giant billboards), and waste. But he is equally concerned with situating this critique within the discourses of modernity, and therefore with historicizing Antonioni's approach to landscape. Refuting recent claims according to which Antonioni's desert landscapes share important similarities with the early postmodernism of North American Land Art during the late 1960s, Gandy situates instead *Zabriskie Point*'s allegorical landscape squarely within the "high modernist" tradition as it integrates into the filmmaker's "largely teleological, dualistic, and hierarchical conception of modern culture." In such a context, Death Valley's desert appears as a "primitivist" and even Romantic denunciation of the film's modern, consumer capitalist culture. However, it also connects with certain forms of sublime high modernist abstraction in art: the desert's emptiness possibly suggesting the "empty canvases" of Abstract-Expressionist–inspired colour field painting, for instance. These various strands come together in what Gandy sees as the universalist conception of nature that the film manifests, a conception where "the perceived antinomy between nature and culture is never seriously challenged." The issue, however, is not to question whether this conception of nature is flawed or not (it is according to Gandy) but to situate it historically as a discursive artifact in relation to the discourses of modernity—something that has hardly been done with regards to Antonioni's work. Only then does it become possible to see Antonioni's desert as a "powerful tableau for the enactment of a particular form of cultural critique framed within the teleological discourses of modernist thought."

Part of my journey through cinematic landscapes ends here as that of new readers of these essays begins. I can only hope that their own travels through them will be as rewarding as mine have been. I equally hope that the map provided by these introductory notes will have been helpful to those interested in surveying the territory before them prior to directly moving into it—and being moved by it—at their own pace. Though natural settings in cinema have long been overlooked (the other side of the Eisensteinian comparison of film landscapes with film music is that both risk "invisibility"), they are far from being irrelevant with regards to the way we experience films, as illustrated by the various essays gathered here. Landscape connects film both to the world and to the various traditions and reasons for representing it. If anything, I hope that this volume will encourage others to further explore this highly complex relation. Finally, readers on both sides of the Atlantic will notice that the language used in essays written by American, British, and Canadian scholars has not been standardised and therefore reflects each collaborator's geographic point of origin.[24] Indeed it was felt that, rather than unify the text in this way, a volume devoted to landscape should be sensitive to geographic specificity. Now on to the sights!

# notes

1. Sergei M. Eisenstein, *Nonindifferent Nature*, trans. Herbert Marshall (Cambridge: Cambridge University Press, 1987), 355; hereafter cited in text.

2. See "The Fourth Dimension in Cinema," in S. M. Eisenstein, *Selected Works. Vol. I, Writings, 1922-34*, ed. and trans. Richard Taylor (London: BFI, 1988), 181–194. This, of course, is not the only example of "musical landscape" in Eisenstein. Indeed, a stunning—though conceptually flawed—example can be found in his account of a scene from Alexander Nevsky in the essay entitled "Vertical Montage." There, Eisenstein argues that shots can be perceived in a linear and temporal fashion such that the shape of their "contents" can be transposed to music. The (failed) analogy works on the premise that the image will be "read"—or visually scanned—from left to right with the eyes following the contours of the bi-dimensional shapes in much the same way that one "reads" a musical score with the succession of notes forming a similar visual outline. The point that matters here is that Eisenstein chooses a portion of the film where landscape is dominant in the composition of the shots and where the "action" has come to a halt (this is the moment before the battle when everyone waits). See "Vertical Montage," in S. M. Eisenstein, *Selected Works. Vol. II, Towards a Theory of Montage*, eds. Michael Glenny and Richard Taylor, trans. Richard Taylor (London: BFI, 1991), 327–399. As Anne Nesbet recently observed, "Eisenstein reads the landscape as if it were a musical score; he reads the score as if it were a landscape. He discovers in this peculiarly synaesthetic landscape its essential 'gesture', its bones, the way music and landscape animate and inhabit each other." *Savage Junctures. Sergei Eisenstein and the Shape of Thinking* (London: I. B. Taurus, 2003), 177. Finally, Eisenstein's conception of the "emotional landscape" must be grasped in the context of his understanding of nature as "nonindifferent," as (already) dialectical, and in his attempt to use art as a way of insuring the communion of Man and Nature through an affect characterized as the subjective experience of the laws of nature. See S. M. Eisenstein's *Nonindifferent Nature*, as well as my essay "Eisenstein, Rhetoric and Imaginicity: Towards a Revolutionary Memoria," in *Screen* 41, no. 4 (Winter 2000): 349–368.

3. J. B. Jackson, "The Order of Landscape," in *The Interpretation of Ordinary Landscapes*, ed. D. W. Meinig (New York: Oxford University Press, 1979), 153.

4. Edward S. Casey, *Representing Place. Landscape Painting and Maps* (Minneapolis: Minnesota University Press, 2002), 3.

5. John Ruskin, *Modern Painters, Vol. III* (New York: E. P. Dutton & Co., 1906).

6. Kenneth Clark, *Landscape into Art* (London: John Murray, 1976), cites Petrarch's self-reproach for having taken pleasure at contemplating the view from atop a mountain after he had feasted his eyes for a few minutes on the distant prospect of the Alps, the Mediterranean, and the Rhône at his feet, it occurred to him to open at random his copy of St. Augustine's *Confessions*. His eyes fell upon the following passage: "And men go about to wonder at the heights of the mountains, and the mighty waves of the sea, and the wide sweep of rivers, and the circuit of the ocean, and the revolution of the stars, but themselves they consider not." "I was abashed, and asking my brother (who was anxious to hear more) not to annoy me, I closed the book, angry with myself that I should still be admiring earthly things, who might long ago have learned from even

the pagan philosophers that nothing is wonderful but the soul, which when great itself, finds nothing great outside itself. Then, in truth, I was satisfied that I had seen enough of the mountain; I turned my inward eye upon myself, and from that time not a syllable fell from my lips until we reached the bottom again." (10)

7. Malcolm Andrews, *Landscape and Western Art* (Oxford: Oxford University Press, 1999), 1.

8. Of course, both the airplane's window and the car's windshield already offer us a framed view.

9. Before the invention of photographic cameras, the Claude glass (or mirror), named in honour of the seventeenth century painter Claude Lorrain, offered eighteenth century painters and landscape sightseers a tool for framing a unified and picturesque visual field. The glass consisted of a darkened convex mirror that would frame a view in a way that approximated the effect of a Claude landscape painting. The reflected image would reduce the field of vision to a manageable size—though still wide because of the mirror's curvature—while the tinting of the glass ensured that the various elements of the "composition" would be agreeably uniform in terms of color scheme, reproducing the desired effect. Interestingly, the Claude glass requires that sightseers turn their backs to the real landscape in order to enjoy the framed (or cultured) view offered by the mirror.

10. Simon Schama, *Landscape and Memory* (New York: Vintage, 1996), 61.

11. Denis E. Cosgrove, *Social Formation and Symbolic Landscapes*, Paperback ed. (Madison: University of Wisconsin Press, 1998).

12. Jay Appleton, *The Experience of Landscape* (London: John Wiley, 1975), 73.

13. D. W. Meinig, "Symbolic Landscapes. Some Idealizations of American Communities," in The Interpretation of Ordinary Landscapes, op. cit., 175.

14. In the introduction to his *Landscape and Power* collection, Mitchell writes that "although [the] collection does not contain any essays on cinematic landscapes, it should be clear why moving images of landscape are, in a very real sense, the subtext for these revisionist accounts of traditional motionless landscape images in photography, painting, and other media." W. J. T. Mitchell, "Introduction," in *Landscape and Power,* ed. W. J. T. Mitchell (Chicago: University of Chicago Press, 1994), 2.

15. There have been nonetheless several important and noteworthy English language contributions to the study of landscape and film. Worth mentioning here are Scott MacDonald, *The Garden in the Machine: A Field Guide to Independent Films about Place* (Berkeley: University of California Press, 2001); Bart Testa, *Spirit in the Landscape* (Toronto: Art Gallery of Toronto, 1989); P. Adams Sitney, "Landscape in the Cinema: the Rhythms of the World and the Camera," in *Landscape, Natural Beauty, and the Arts*, eds. Salim Kemal and Ivan Gaskel (Cambridge: Cambridge University Press, 1993), 103–126; Ian Christie, "Landscape and 'Location': Reading Filmic Space Historically," in *Rethinking History*, 4, no. 2 (2000): 165–174. Several publications on the topic also exist in French, including two collections edited by Jean Mottet: *Les paysages du cinéma* (Seyssel: Champ Vallon, 1999) and *L'arbre dans le paysage* (Seyssel: Champ Vallon, 2002). See also: Jean Mottet, *L'invention de la scène américaine. Cinéma et paysage* (Paris: l'Harmattan, 1998); Maurizia Natali, *L'image-paysage* (Paris: Presses universitaires de Vincennes, 1996);

Antonio Costa also edited an issue of *CINéMAS* devoted to film and landscape, "Le paysage au cinéma," *CINéMAS* 12, no. 1 (Automne 2001).

16. Laura Mulvey, "Visual Pleasure and Narrative Cinema," in *Visual and Other Pleasures* (Bloomington: Indiana University Press, 1989), 14–26.

17. André Gaudreault and Tom Gunning, "Le cinéma des premiers temps: un défi à l'histoire du cinéma?", in *L'Histoire du cinéma: nouvelles approches*, eds. J. Aumont, A. Gaudreault, and M. Marie (Paris: Publications de la Sorbonne Nouvelle-Colloque de Cerisy, 1989), 49–63.

18. Northrop Frye, "Conclusion to a Literary History of Canada," in *The Bush Garden: Essays on the Canadian Imagination* (Toronto: House of Anansi Press, 1971).

19. Gaile McGregor, *The Wacousta Syndrome. Explorations in the Canadian Landscape* (Toronto: University of Toronto Press, 1985). *Wacousta* is an historical novel, à la Fennimore Cooper, set during Chief Pontiac's rebellion in the 1760s.

20. Eisenstein (1987, op. cit., 243) writes

> The tradition of the picture scroll has largely been preserved for a long period in Japanese engraving, especially since this engraving is not limited at all by the edges of a single sheet, but very often consists of several sheets—diptychs and triptychs—that can exist completely separately, but the full picture of the mood and subject are produced only when they are placed next to each other. In this sense the montage method of cinematography, where, in the process of shooting, one stream of events is broken up into separate shots and by the will of the film editor is again collected into a whole montage sequence, repeats completely this stage of the general evolutionary course of the history of painting.

21. Peter Greenaway, *Fear of Drowning By Numbers / Règles du jeu* (Paris: Dis Voir, 1988).

22. Christian Metz, *L'énonciation impersonnelle ou le site du film* (Paris: Klincksieck, 1991), 34.

23. These are: *L'avventura, La notte, L'eclisse,* and *Deserto Rosso.* See Seymour Chatman, *Antonioni or the Surface of the World* (Berkeley: University of California Press, 1985).

24. All French language citations are translated by myself unless otherwise indicated; whenever English translations were available I have used and cited them; when existing translations were faulty I offered new translations.

# the invention of place

danièle huillet and

one        jean-marie straub's

*moses and aaron*

j a c q u e s   a u m o n t

*translated by kevin shelton and martin lefebvre*

We know a great deal about the origins of this film, *Moses and Aaron*. The premise, like many other films by Straub and Huillet, remains a desire to confront the medium of film with a preexisting text that somehow resists it. Such as the text of *Othon*, by Pierre Corneille, which resisted being captured on film with its highly compact intrigue and the essentially foreign character of its seventeenth century language, Arnold Schoenberg's opera poses its own difficulties. It resists being captured on film by the density of its politico-theological debate, by the violence of its intrigues around power, not to mention its strange musical composition, with its technique of twelve tones that forces us to deal with a musical language we are not accustomed to hearing. In each case, the filmmakers' preoccupation was to superimpose a film script over the drama of the text—because film is not theatre—without, however, altering the nature of the drama specific to the text.

Scripting, in this case, is not an exercise of *adaptation*, nor is it a narratological or compositional analysis. In classical theatre, the most obvious elements of scripting, from the very first reading of the text, are the entrances and exits indicated in the stage directions, often underscored in the text itself (e.g., "Leave!" "Here she is!"). In the filming of *Othon*, Straub and Huillet constantly make use of these natural dramatic articulations of the text, more often than not, by emphasizing them cinematically (for example, ensuring that the character remains invisible to the camera before suddenly appearing with a twist of the camera, or the reverse, by including the receding footsteps for a long time after the character has left the image). This technique is sometimes used in *Moses and Aaron*; at least once, when the Hebrews see the two brothers arrive from afar, they comment on their almost supernatural allure; and when finally the choir sings "See Aaron! See Moses! They have come at last!", the panoramic camera roams to show them, motionless in the middle of the set. And yet, the libretto by Schoenberg seldom uses this type of dramatic scripting; the transitions are rarely marked by an entrance or an exit. Moreover, the Schoenberg style is based on—and this is perhaps one of the few constants in the diversity of his works—the absence of clear scripting into parts, movements, or sections. The scripting, in the case of the film, therefore, needs to be ensured through other means.

In the filming of *Othon*, another technique was tried and developed: the use of a visually impressive location, at once dramatically practical (perhaps even capable of proposing its own unique solutions for *découpage* and *mise-en-scène*), and historically charged. In their treatment of the opera *Moses and Aaron*, Huillet and Straub underscored the work's segmentation by either introducing or uncovering a number of transitions by shifts in framing. However, if the film was able to maintain its own strength as a film, while confronted with that of the text of the opera, it is in large part due to the filmmakers' careful selection and use of location. The locations in the text by Schoenberg are only sketchy biblical locations. They act as a support for the primary episodes: the place of the revelation; the place where Moses meets Aaron; as well as places for the long public address for two voices before the people, for the encounter with God, for the pagan orgy, and, finally, for the punishment of Aaron. Even more than the purely theoretical palaces of Corneille's or Racine's emperors, these are symbolic locations, almost entirely coinciding with their specific names. It is therefore not at all surprising that practically every *mise-en-scène* of *Moses and Aaron* in the theatre retained only the first term of the specific names. The tension created between the abstract power of these names (the Burning Bush, Mount Sinai, the Desert) and their concrete configuration, which they must exhibit to effectively serve as a support for the drama, follows the emphasis suggested by the text and the music of an underscored *metaphysical abstraction*: no landscape, no geography. In the theatre, they are usually rendered purely as symbolic spaces, almost as if they were being staged for Wagner.

Naturally, the setting for the film of this opera is confronted by a similar question, but with completely different means. Whatever scenic option is chosen, the film has a real difficulty escaping the possibility of the emphasis being placed at the other pole, that of documentary realism, where the apparently singular, concrete determinations of the locations become dominant. An adaptation in the Hollywood spirit would not have hesitated to multiply the sets and settings, preferably picturesque ones as was the case with Joseph Losey's *Don Giovanni* or Francesco Rosi's *Carmen* which, even though shot in Europe, were driven by the same interest in the spectacular. Straub and Huillet's remarkable solution is entirely different: manifestly dialectic, it neither renounces visibility, i.e., concrete, singular, and historical existing space, nor abstract symbolism. Indeed, for the first two acts of the opera—the part that was actually composed by Schoenberg, the third act never having been completed[1]—the filmmakers chose a striking and astonishing location: a Roman amphitheatre from the first century, situated in the middle of the Apennines, about 50 miles (80 kilometers) east of Rome (Figure 1.1).

There is little to add to the very precise and lucid comments made by the filmmakers about the choice of this location.[2] The decision to film everything in one location does however multiply the constraints (i.e., reduces the choice of possibilities). The location had to be practical: accommodate two characters as well as a whole chorus, a caravan of different animals as well as the imprecations of the prophet, not to mention the dance before the golden calf. Moreover, it had to be out of the way

Figure 1.1

The amphitheatre of Alba Fucens. Production still.

of tourists and sheltered from onlookers, especially inopportune noises; it should be in a location with little threat of rain. It had to be historically and symbolically congruous: preferably an ancient site (and, given our relation to Antiquity, a monumental site). Its geography needed to be striking: it is a plateau. Finally, since it was to accommodate a representation of a semitheatrical nature, it should also have certain intrinsic visual and acoustic qualities, and more fundamentally, retain some trace of the work's origin in the theatre (not to mention in music). We know the solution for this multifaceted problem: everything except for the third act was filmed in the amphitheatre of Alba Fucens, close to the city of Avezzano, in the Abruzzi region.

This decision brought with it innumerable problems, both materially and intellectually, not to mention some very real headaches. But it surely manifests a desire not to forget the theatre, incarnated once and for all in the film's scenography. It is also, perhaps more indirectly, an effect of taking very seriously the documentary nature of what is called the *cinématographe*. If the latter is capable of rendering a location—and not simply, as in theatre, the constructing of a dramatic space or a functional substitute for it; but if the film is to exploit the vividness, the very *smell*[3] of a place—then it is necessary to find a setting whose strong visual and symbolic presence imposes itself as such, so that the filming can bring these concrete qualities to light.

There to be read in the amphitheatre of Alba Fucens are the layers of History. It was built in the year 40 of our calendar, just a few years after the death of the prophet Jesus, also known as Christ, under the brief rule of Caligula, marked, amongst other things, by the mad emperor's penchant for festivities and exotic religions. The choice of this site for framing a *biblical* action is, in itself, a powerful image that links together the Old and New Testaments, in much the same manner as the *figural* interpretation of the Bible proposed by the Church Fathers[4] (e.g., St. Augustine sees Moses as a *figura Christi*, and the Ministry of Aaron as an *umbra* and a *figura* of the eternal Ministry).[5] Such an amphitheatre, in a province of the Roman Empire, probably served for games (though its architecture does not seem to suggest this), but certainly for religious, civil, and sacrificial festivities. Caligula had reestablished the Egyptian cult of Isis, banned by Tiberius, and his immediate successor, Claudius, was the first to chase the Jews from Rome.[6] Of course, Moses and Aaron is a Jewish story, not a Christian or pagan narrative. Choosing this amphitheatre to stage it both contradicts the story and adds new elements to it: it lets Roman history and Christian history break into biblical history. Furthermore, innumerable similar amphitheatres have figured in numerous genre films such as ancient epics (with gladiators) and Christian epics (with lions); these have acquired a particular iconographic weight, which Alba Fucens implicitly evokes in our memory.

This idea of an implicit evocation, of an underground reservoir (of meaning, of memory, of history, of death) whose task it is for the landscape to conjure, is an eminently recognizable one, for it constitutes within Straub and Huillet's cinema a quasi-authorial thematic trait.[7] In almost every one of their films, the landscapes are immense tombs, cenotaphs, or monuments to some anonymous martyrology. For instance, *Fortini Cani* has long panoramic shots of the villages of the Alpuan Alps, where some Oradour-like Nazi massacres took place. These shots are silent, only supported by the sentence that precedes them and which offers the key to understanding them. There is nothing in these shots, only beautiful, ancient, and austere homes; or again, in another village, brand new low-income housing (yet already showing their wear and tear), where children play and trucks roll by on the road in the distance (there is an irresistible feeling of war); and from time to time, a marble slab makes an appearance, *ex voto*. The Italian countryside, as the character of the second part (*De la nuée à la résistance*) finds out, is soaked in the blood of its partisans; while the *Dialogues* of the first part tell us that this countryside was, in a time before our own, in the time of myths, populated with gods and when men were once like the gods (*eritis sicut Dei*: another infraction, of Christianity into paganism this time). As well, we can think of the adaptation of Stéphane Mallarmé's *Coup de dés* situated in Père-Lachaise, in front of the Wall of the Federates; or again, of *Othon*, which begins with a shot of the opening of a cave where, during World War II, the Communists had hidden their weapons. Or even again, the landscapes of *Lothringen!* which exude their historical weight (the weight of massacres and exploitation) as they are seen through both long and medium shots.

But how can we come to know all that which the image can never sufficiently say? (After all, the flip-side of the image's strength and also its limit is that it can only show.) The most expedient way is to verbally state the necessary information: theories of facts (Marzabotto in *Fortini Cani*), or litanies of numbers (the commentaries of Engels about the French landscapes in *Trop tôt, trop tard!*). The most expressive is, perhaps, to create a filmic figure, where something from in and under the ground is brought to light. In the great confrontation scene between Galba and Camille, in act II of *Othon*, this chthonic subsoil manifests itself through an immense cavity that we see—a gaping hole in the background at the right behind Galba, in the shot where he appears for the first time. The inscription of the bodies of the "actors" or "models" into these locations needs to be taken literally; after all, each shot institutes a particular relationship between each of them and the site from which they either stand out or are embedded. Consequently, at the mysterious cave, opening beside Galba, which is made visible through a slight reframing of the image, we need to add, for example, the triple historical setting that delimits the space that Camille occupies (on the left, the baroque palaces; on the right, antique stone walls in ruin; in the back and lower than her face, the carriages).

There is no voiceover in *Moses and Aaron* to tell us what haunts this location that we see: the implicit evocation is consummated, so to speak, by the fact that everything, from in and under the ground, is channelled through the human figures of the drama, in their costumes, postures, and gestures, as if they had just sprung up there, like flowers (like a Valerian marine cemetery, where "*le don de vivre est passé dans les fleurs*" [the gift of life is passed down in the flowers]). This is why such a location must be treated with care, if not a particular meticulousness—even if it is not a piece of nature that needs to be respected on principle or by devotion. In both, *Empedocles* and in *Antigone* as well, Straub and Huillet have pushed to the limit the art of walking on, without stepping on, a location so that it is not flattened or changed by the mere act of being filmed.[8] This extremely similar treatment of the amphitheatre of Alba Fucens, albeit far less fragile than the brush on the slopes of Etna, demonstrates that the approach is not just an obsession; nor is it inspired by some desire for cleanliness or even some moral desire ("ecological," as some commentators have smirked), but remains an aesthetic decision that is simultaneously a political decision. By refusing to leave any visible traces of their filming, Straub and Huillet enjoin themselves to not add any visible stratum, either to the history or the visibility, of their locations. Their locations are forever marked by having played host to a film—but this mark should never be conspicuous: it must become another subterranean mark, identical to the nature of all the other marks that each film evokes. The location should have been transformed, not in its appearance, but in its being (Figure 1.2).

Once this relationship of intimacy, of an essential connivance as it were, has been established with a location, the question of whether it

Figure 1.2

The amphitheatre of Alba Fucens. Production still.

can be considered an effective ground for the *mise-en-scène* as well needs to be addressed. The arena of Alba Fucens possesses properties common to all such amphitheatres that are remarkably useful: its form is hollow, focusing the drama more than enclosing it. It allows, without any artifice (beyond the one of its selection), framing the drama and preventing it from becoming dispersed. The oval shape of the arena is good, conjoining the rounded—which closes—and the elongated—that orients, providing a clean, marked axis. Everything is incessantly brought back to the ground, where the red dust covers the surface of the elliptic-shaped interior; on this, the barest imaginable background, the characters stand in draped clothing (a stylized antiquity) and seem to emerge from the soil. Alba Fucens is like the Monument Valley of this film, a way to make the bodies surge up from the setting or disappear into it, much like John Ford's Indians who seem to meld with the rock and sand.[9]

Logically, this location, presented with such a quiet insistence as real, infrangible, inalterable, and unadulterated, does not need to be constructed in the film according to the usual methods of spatial composition and suturing. Classical cinema, which seldom sets its dramas in real locations, but creates composite spaces by cheating on just about everything, needs to compensate by finding ways to guarantee the coherence of these imaginary spaces. This is the function of the match-cut: whether the chosen vector is the gaze or the dialogue, it always functions to suture the images in order to create the effect of continuity. Hollywood classicism—to which we owe so many popular epics—introduced yet another supplemental guarantee, that of the establishing or "master" shot. This is a wider shot providing a stable and large enough view of the entire setting at least once, so that each of the other shots that compose the scene may be referred to it as one its fragments. Freed by this double guarantee from the need to construct a truly coherent space, classical cinema is led to produce very abstract spaces that resemble those of literature: that which is given appears as certain (nothing unforeseen can emerge from such a space); that which is not given must be supplied by the spectator (who is invited to find it in the most immediately available of reservoirs, that of verisimilitude and of common places).

The work of framing and montage in *Moses and Aaron* takes us far away from these classical procedures. Not that there is nothing akin to match-cutting or establishing shots, but what requires "matching" is of a completely different nature. Each framing is clearly affirmed, more often than not by an element that marks it as distinct from classical norms such as centring, symmetry, and horizontality. Instead we find a de-centring of the characters which leaves little or not enough space on the side of the frame, the systematic use of high-angle framing (indicating a point of view that mimics no possible diegetic gaze), or all of a sudden a low-angle framing (shot 32, on Moses and Aaron, when leprosy appears[10]), faces in profile (the most rare point of view, emphasized in the meeting between the two protagonists in the desert: left profile of Aaron in shot 13, right profile in shot 15, front view of Moses in between the two). Even when eye-line matches and general address codes are obvious from one shot to another, they are never constructed according to the rules of transparency; each framing continues, in part, to exist for itself as if disconnected from those that precede and follow it. Many shots in act I function like a "master shot";[11] they undoubtedly allow us to mentally reconstruct a geometry or a topology, but they do not naturalize these by making them immediate or transparent; it all seems to remain at the level of construction, and is continuously felt as such, especially due to the extreme abruptness of camera movements, more so with the film's last one, which only allows us, and with lightning speed, a brief glimpse of Moses and Aaron.

There lies a single purpose behind these various refusals of classicism: to avoid using the traditional means for representing "filmic" space (in the sense Eric Rohmer uses the term in his essay on F. W. Murnau [12]), to clearly and expressively forgo these means in order to allow the spectator to engage in the mental—and affective—work of gaining access to the film's location, at once as a substratum of the filming and as an imaginary framework for the drama.

When we set out to study the representation of space, it is because we wish to find some principles that account for the relations between man and his surroundings. When we try to define, for a given era, the notion of what a place is, we try to determine the conventional rule by which a certain understanding of space embodies itself in a system of thought and of representation.[13]

This distinction, put forward by Pierre Francastel, between space as a transhistorical category, which is always more or less considered in a Kantian spirit, and place as a profoundly historical form that relates to the imaginary and symbolizing accents of an age, is the ground for any description of *Moses and Aaron*. Basically, by segmenting and editing the film in such a jarring manner, the filmmakers move away from a naturalizing effect to underscore the fact that the scenography has a meaning of its own.

The first meaning, or first determination, as I mentioned earlier, is that of a subsoil: that which emerges and evokes lightly or heavily. The second, of a related nature, yet more frankly conventional and therefore easier to decipher, is metaphorical and affects the luminous and the atmospheric phenomena. In the middle of a lengthy shot of Moses hearing the voices attributing him his mission of prophecy and proselytism, and after about four minutes of a fixed frame on the neck of the singer, the camera is slightly raised and a pan begins that will take it almost full circle, only stopping as it comes to frame a mountain which lies behind Moses' head. Physically present in the landscape, this mountain has a remarkable shape: its pecks are like two regular breasts, separated by rounded clefts (Figure 1.3). Between the two mountaintops, a light falls over the valley, diffusely piercing the layer of clouds with a certain brightness. At the end of this shot, which at first obstinately showed only the back of the actor's head, and then slowly swept across the meagre vegetation clinging to the sides of the theatre, there appears something akin to splendour[14] like that of the Burning Bush, i.e., the voice of God (all the while the voices chant and speak, "Like this bush of needles, obscure before the light of truth had fallen upon it, so it is you will hear my voice in each thing"). And yet this light does not go just anywhere: it comes from the sky, striking between these two protuberances that rise up toward it. From the second meeting between Moses and God, that of the Decalogue, nothing will be shown; but on two occasions—when the horsemen arrive (shot 59) and when the sentinel announces the return of Moses (shot 72)—we can see in the background, starkly marked against a blue sky this time, the same double mountain. Now, it is well known that the traditional representations of Moses show him with two small horns on his forehead, which stand for—by deforming them—the divine rays that fall on him at Mt. Sinai.[15] What is more, at the other end of the film, at the end of act II, Moses reproaches Aaron for the column of fire and the column of clouds that guide the Hebrews, and in which he sees "images of idols"; Aaron defends himself: they are the "signs of God,"[16] and a camera pan (shot 79) sweeps one side of the amphitheatre, showing us, on the shrubs and on the ground, a column—not of fire or clouds, but of light emerging from between the clouds. These images turn a particular Italian landscape, in a particular moment of a particular day—geographic and meteorological

Figure 1.3

The mountains surrounding the amphitheatre.

phenomena—into a complex configuration, where multiple metaphoric figures come together, either taken from tradition or newly made, but always pregnant with meaning.

Straub and Huillet's films are filled with such images, with such examples of figurality, which are almost carved out from the representation of the landscapes. In *Fortini Cani*, for instance, there is a shot of a summit; slowly, the camera describes mountains of marble; slowly still it dips, hovers like a silent plane over the villages at the bottom of the valley, lifts up, continues to turn slowly, so high that we continue to think we are still airborne (on a plane or a helicopter)—suddenly, without any acceleration, the tips of a few trees enter into the camera's field of vision: the movement ends, and we realize there is no airplane, that all of this was seen from the summit, with a telephoto lens. It is almost the same sensation of not really knowing whether we are floating, or taking off, or landing, that is expressed at the end of shot 10 of *Moses and Aaron*. (A little later, a young man asks himself, "I wonder what he looks like, this new God? He hovers, no doubt, because Aaron hovered as well.") The same effect again appears in the second shot of Egypt (shot 43), where the valley of the Nile is flown over from high up, and where at the end of the panoramic, it is the mountain that surges up. In all these images, the effect is the same, a perplexity caused by the need to abruptly change from one visual register—the omniscient sight from the air—to another—the arrested sight from a stationary point. In each shot, the figures make sense, but differently: in this film, the sky is the site from which God sees; the mountain, especially when seen with a certain equality of height, is that which contradicts it.

Besides the evocative power of the land and its history, beyond the metaphoric power of the landscape, a place is also determined by the way in which bodies and figures are inscribed in it. There are a number of bodily figures in the film of unequal importance: the two main protagonists, the two "title roles" as we say in the language of opera; the "people"; and the intermediaries and representatives of the "people." The first two are stable, underscoring by contrast the diversity of the others. Moses is figured as a block: his rigid stance, his massiveness, accentuated by the volume of his robe, evokes a stone-like substance, more like a monolith (like the stone on which the Law will be written) than a statue. The first framing of the film, one of the most stunning, shows his neck, highlighting the massiveness of his shoulders, the solidity of the attachment between head and body, encircled with curls of hair befitting the Oracle of Delphi. His speeches with his brother stress the verticality of his stature, in opposition to the wavy figure of Aaron, whose hands wave figures of snakes in the air—before actually making one "really" appear by magic. Even their mouths—constantly the centre of attention because they sing—are as dissimilar as possible; the thin, horizontally stretched mouth of Günter Reich; the sinuous mouth of Louis Devos, always on the verge of laughter or sarcasm. (Even the names of the actors seem to follow this line: *Reich*, the German substantive for empire; while Devos derives from *vos*, the Flemish word for fox, therefore connoting the cunning of that animal. A mere coincidence?)

The people, for their part, have two major figurative registers that are extremely dissimilar (they could be metonymically associated with each of the two protagonists). In the first act, the people are ideologically opposed to Moses or at least reticent before him. Yet figuratively, they are on his side. Like Moses, the people appear as a block, squarely set in the middle of the frame, which they never exceed. This last point is important: not only does this figurative register eliminate any vague or generic off-screen evocation, not only does the composition confirm the statuary block of the people by highlighting the clean angles of a parallelepiped, but it also indicates that the people are not just a mass, at least not a *natural*, wide-open mass. "[The closed mass] refuses to expand and insists on persisting. What strikes us most about it is its limit. The closed mass ensures its foundations. It takes its place by limiting itself; the space it will occupy is already assigned."[17]

Throughout the first act, the position of the camera, its axis and height, varies a great deal, but all the positions give views of the people-chorus as an indivisible unit (Figure 1.4). Moreover, the choir, composed of amateurs, "so as not to have people with ideas about staging and who try to express more than just the music" (Straub and Huillet, 1987), do not gesticulate and do not pose as if they are on stage; the individual bodies that constitute this individuated mass have no really expressive gestures, no *interesting* movements. Rather, they translate through unconscious move-

Figure 1.4

The chorus.

ment the passage of their breath and voices in ways that betray the violence of the music and the concentration of this sculptural mass, situated at the centre of the oral space.

Here we find one of those figurative (and in this case, figural) inventions most consciously used by the filmmakers: the panoramic. The panoramic is always a figure in film, if only in a rhetorical sense, because it always serves as a metaphor for a gaze even when it does not signify a given subjectivity. Its use is quite remarkable in *Moses and Aaron* because it pushes to the limit this metaphorical value. Every pan during the first act—without exception whatsoever—is made to stand for the people (not so much their subjective gaze as their overall attention—they all have to listen quite a bit—as well as their connection to their leaders). This is accomplished at the expense of creating an assumed arbitrariness that actually makes the camera movement work in this way "even before the people are visible" (thus only making sense after the fact for the spectator). This arbitrary and deliberate figure unifies a number of pan shots whose individual value can be quite different. When, in shot 30, we go from the chorus to their three representatives, after which the camera pans upward and moves across their heads onto the bushes and the sky, repeating the same movement from shot 10 (the shot of Moses' vocation), the first pan is justified by the drama (we move to the three as they begin to sing); the second, however, is justified symbolically (the camera lifts when the people and their three representatives have accepted God, while one voice sings "hmmm" with a closed mouth). However, several times during the long negotiation between the people and the two messengers of God, pan shots punctuate the reaction of the people (e.g., in shot 24, after the would-be devastating retort of Aaron, "Who do not see are lost," the people burst out laughing); from this perspective, the most telling example is the lateral pan which captures Moses and Aaron, in the same shot 24, and literally visualizes the circumspection of the people by an unexpected *obraznost* effect.[18] On other occasions, we find an almost "normal" usage of the pan, designed to translate a gaze and its focalization (shot 36, the camera goes from the chorus to Aaron who exhibits the healed hand of Moses).

Herein lies the paradox. By completely playing out its figurative value, the film gives back to the panoramic (an old and tired figure if ever there was one) its figurative power: the panoramic shots, taken together, create a system that structures the space in depth (better yet, we could say it gives it a certain thickness) and breadth, without needing to worry about naturalizing the *découpage*, all the while drawing a material connection between the people-block, its two leaders, and the intermediate link among the three of them. A concrete, material, and visible movement, the panoramic figures an abstract relationship, rendering it visible, albeit in a way which requires that spectators relate together a succession of movements through an act of imagination: but this work is not at all that different—in the way it calls on memory and abstraction—from that which is simultaneously required by the music.

In the second act, the figure of the block is fissured and falls apart. The act opens with the consternation of the people, who question Moses's long absence: the screen goes black (for two minutes). Suddenly, bright sunshine, and Aaron alone in the image, de-centred so as to allow us to see a disquieting black opening—where we cannot but *read* the absence of the prophet, but also, for the spectator who remembers a little of the biblical text, the complete and equally stupefying absence from the drama of any mention of Pharaoh or Exodus.[19] Aaron listens, downcast, to the recriminations of the people's elders. In the next shot (46), the people make their entrance, yet only off-screen; we only hear the hurried feet of the choirists. Then comes a series of more tightly framed shots: on Aaron, then the chorus, and finally on the elders. It is only then (shot 49) that the first and only pan in this sequence happens, at the moment when, bowing down to the pressure, both of the people and the elders, Aaron agrees to do another miracle, and builds the golden calf (Figure 1.5). This dissociation of the people into small subgroups only increases throughout the rest of the act.

A succession of animals passes before the idol (donkeys, camels, oxen), as well as dancers, butchers, a stretcher bearing an ill person, men and women beggars, elderly people, as well as the twelve princes of the tribes, young virgins to be sacrificed by the priests, and a young naked couple. There is no common rule covering all these figures, if only their identical reference to the idol, toward which all the actions are oriented (this is particularly obvious during the dance, where the necessity of facing the

Figure 1.5

Aaron (Louis Devos) and the Golden Calf.

golden calf forces the dancers to have, more often than not, their back to the film's spectators). Moreover, although up until now the people have been represented by the unified parallelepiped block of the chorus, they are now broken down into a collection of numerous individual figures, drinking, kissing, giving gifts, and later, jumping off a cliff. Throughout the segment, the geometry has disappeared as has Moses and, with him, the Idea (the golden calf proposed by Aaron for adoration by the Hebrews is a metaphor—that of a changing form in the eternal material—but not an idea in the theological sense). Everything is bereft of regulation: the people, Aaron, the multiplied figures of the people, as well as the camera angles.

The end of the second act, i.e., after the return of Moses, after the destruction of the golden calf (which the film—and this is the only special effect—dissolves before our eyes in a milky white of overexposure by opening the diaphragm of the camera), offers itself as a confrontation between the two protagonists, who now embody, more rigidly than ever, two theoretical and political positions: Moses is a kind of anti-Zionist before the letter, opposed to the mirage of the earth "where milk and honey spill forth" (which alone made the people accept the God All-Mighty), opposed to any image of the immaterial and to any sensorial manifestation of the Idea; while Aaron identifies with the people, their joy, their suffering, their emotions, and finally their temperament, prefiguring the image of the Jew for whom it is forbidden to be like the peoples with which he will be obliged to mingle ("this people shall be preserved"). There is no more connection between framings, and the last panoramic, showing the bushes and a bit of sky, exactly corresponds with the last entrance of the chorus, singing.

Other than the panoramic, another formal technique is quite obvious in the *mise-en-scène* proposed by Straub and Huillet: the incline of the camera's axis and the system of high and low angles it creates. Though it is impossible for us to establish as strict a correlation between this formal trait and some significance—as was the case with the pan—still, we are struck by the presence of large-scale articulations that are clearly meaningful. The two acts open with segments exclusively shot in high angles,[20] from shots 11 through 23 and from shots 46 through 49. Without a doubt, this choice is in part motivated by technical considerations of feasibility and readability. Certainly, the chorus could be shown from a horizontal position (shots 30, 36, 37), but it was decided to do so only once it had been shown a number of times from above; this is the only way to show each of the singers distinctly—each body, in its unconscious gesticulations, and the differences among them. *A fortiori*, the individualized characters could be shown from any angle, but in these pivotal moments of the drama, which are violent confrontations among several roles and a number of conceptions (regarding power, ideas, the relation with the divine), the continued use of the view from above emphasizes the geometry, or the topography, of these confrontations and negotiations.

What is more, this insistence to film from above—at the expense of a simple but cumbersome camera set-up, as clearly seen in photos taken of the shooting—leads to a second and obvious consequence, both formal and semiotic, which is to sharply stress, by way of differentiation, the abandoning of this point of view. After almost a quarter of an hour of high-angle shots (I'm not counting shot 10, where Moses hears voices), the transition to shots filmed horizontally is noticeable, more so since shot 24, that of the *circumspection* around Moses and Aaron is so remarkable in its own right. Again, and perhaps even more spectacular, is shot 32, where after almost ten minutes of film shot horizontally (shots 24 through 31, with a reprieve view of the sky in shot 30), an extreme low-angle view violently separates Moses and Aaron against the sky (this is the first low-angle shot and is quite noticeable). All the rest—the miracles of the leprosy and the blood[21]—is filmed less systematically, the camera point of view alternating between horizontal and, toward the end, a final low-angle shot of Aaron, alone this time, at the moment when he announces to the Hebrews their *election* (shot 41, the last of act I filmed in the amphitheatre; the next two are shots of the Nile).

Attributing the panoramic a figural value, like the one announced by the filmmakers, may simply seem like calling on a long tradition that associates this camera movement to a gaze (with movement, the potentiality for focalization that lies in all framings seems to materialize itself). This said, one would have to argue that this figure is no less arbitrary than any other: quite the opposite, in fact—especially since the viewpoint "of the people" does not have a single point of origin, a single focus, or a single shot set-up [22](Eisenstein, 1991); it is precisely this relative arbitrariness that authorizes an equivalence between an abstract signifier—the movement—and a generic signified. The inclined axis of the camera, the formal play between high- and low-angle shots, does not necessarily have an equivalent figural value, despite the fact that we might be tempted, in this case, to conceive of it as a sort of metaphysical or theological counterpart to the figure of the panoramic—one that might be more political. For if the entire beginning of the film, from the encounter between Moses and God up until the first confrontation (a *frontal* confrontation) between Moses and the people, is filmed from above, is it not to suggest, even if only obscurely, a sort of divine, or at least transcendent, "gaze"? Inversely, doesn't the low angle become, from this perspective, the image of either the abandoning of this point of view "of God," or the adoption of a chthonic point of view, thereby making the subsoil reappear, reemerge?

As it can be seen, the description of the film, engaged here according to a clearly delimited parameter that of the spatial constructions and the making of a location at once diegetic, dramatic, and symbolic—now ends

15

with an interpretation, a terrain I will not investigate further. Of course, it makes no doubt that this film, which, for the two filmmakers consists in an attempt at staging Schoenberg's libretto (and music) for the camera, can and should be understood as a reading, an interpretation of the Schoenbergian text. No less indubitable is the fact that the preferred material-signifying procedures for the *mise-en-scène*—namely, the panoramic shot and the high angle, if one considers framing—lie at the core of this interpretation. In one case as in the other, the operation requires that one take a position about what the film, following the opera, is about: confronting different conceptions of the political, Jewishness, and faith. By staying merely on the threshold of interpretation, the description presented here attempts to be the minimal, though exact, gesture that delivers this meaning, without increasing it, and therefore without betraying it.

## notes

1. The four stage productions that preceded the making of the film (Zurich, Berlin, London, Düsseldorf) all omitted using the extant fragment from the third act. Straub and Huillet opted instead to keep it, perhaps in part out of a desire to be faithful toward Schoenberg's opera, but more fundamentally, because the choice to stage it or not affects the tone and meaning of the work. The second act ends with Moses' admission of his helplessness—*O Wort! Du Wort! Das mir fehlt*—and this could indeed serve as a possible ending ("The end of the second act, where Moses searches in vain for the words that fail him, is certainly one of the most beautiful pages of the libretto as well as a convincing and highly moving ending." René Leibowitz, *Schoenberg* [Paris: Seuil, 1969], 126.) However, such an ending leaves the confrontation between the two charismatic guides on highly theoretical ground (the power of images and propaganda vs. the power of the word and of thought). The third act, however fragmented it may be, has the advantage of presenting the confrontation in geopolitical terms: Should the people of Israel seek to exercise political power by colonizing a territory or should they instead accept their role as the chosen people in spirit alone and adopt a nomadic life? (Clearly Schoenberg preferred the second option, for he spoke against Zionism in 1935.)
2. See especially Danièle Huillet, "Notes sur le Journal de travail de Gregory Woods," *Cahiers du cinéma* 260–261 (October–November 1975): 7–47.
3. "One realizes that without even chasing around after the flavor [the smells] of Egypt, the whole of CAPITAL could be 'constructed' on a set." Sergei M. Eisenstein, "Notes for a Film of '*Capital*'," trans. Maciej Sliwowski, Jay Leyda, and Annette Michelson, *October* 2 (1976), 14.
4. See Erich Auerbach, "Figura," in *Scenes from the Drama of European Literature* (Minneapolis: Minnesota University Press, 1984), especially 28–49.
5. Saint Augustine, *De civitate Dei* (The City of God) (Turholti: Typographie Brepols, 1955), respectively, 10:6, 18:11, and 17:6.
6. "He banished from Rome all the Jews, who were continually making disturbances at the instigation of one Chrestus." Suetonius Tranquillus, "Claudius," *The Lives of the Twelve Caesars*, Alexander Thomson, trans. (New York: R. Worthington, 1883), 25. (This is the first mention of the Christians in a Roman text.)

7. Serge Daney, "Un tombeau pour l'œil," *Cahiers du cinéma* 258–259 (1975); Jean Narboni, "Là," *Cahiers du cinéma* 275 (1977); Gilles Deleuze, *Cinéma 2. L'image-temps* (Paris: Les éditions de Minuit, 1985), 332–334.

8. "Coming to understand a location is like understanding anything else…. The technicians did not have the right to set foot on the space, except for the actual filming and in specific cases, such as when a boom was needed, and then, they went carefully, and I always watched them from the corner of my eye so that they didn't crush any of the plants." J. M. Straub and D. Huillet, interview by Anne-Marie Faux and Jacques Aumont, *Art press* 117 (September 1987): 50; hereafter cited in text.

9. See Luc Vancheri, *Figuration de l'inhumain. Essai sur le devenir-accessoire de l'homme filmique* (Paris: Presses universitaires de Vincennes, 1993), 30–33.

10. The numbering of the shots is taken from the shot breakdown published in *Cahiers du cinéma* 260–261 (October–November, 1975): 69–84; and *Cahiers du cinéma* 262–263 (January 1976): 79–94 (which also offers many illustrations). I should add that the shot breakdown includes the credits; the drama itself starts at shot 10 (the vocation of Moses).

11. Shot 19 pans from the priest to the choir, and then to the group of three and again to the choir; shot 20 describes the other half of the circle, from the priest to the choir, by passing over the empty space in front of the choir; shot 22 takes up and completes these movements by furtively ending on Moses and Aaron, who have finally arrived.

12. Eric Rohmer, *L'organisation de l'espace dans le Faust de Murnau* (Paris: UGE, 1977).

13. Pierre Francastel, *La Figure et le Lieu* (Paris: Gallimard, 1967), 145.

14. Or the "goodness of God," which man cannot look upon, and that God must hide with his hand when he gives Moses the second tablets of the Law (Exodus 33:18–23).

15. The biblical text (Exodus 34:29) attributes a radiance to the face of Moses that the Hebrews cannot look upon—a reflection of the divine radiance. Translating this passage for the Latin Vulgate, St. Jerome confounded the Hebrew word signifying "radiance" with another similar Hebrew word and wrote, "*cornuta facies*" (horned face); this resulted in a long iconographic tradition of taking this literally.

16. According to the Bible, he is the one who is right (Exodus 13:21–22).

17. Elias Canetti, *Masse et puissance* (Paris: Gallimard, 1966), 13.

18. See the theory of the *obraznost* ("imaginicity" or "image-concept") in Eisenstein, "Montage 1937," *Izbrannyé pro-iszvédéniya v chesti tomakh* 2 (Moscow: Iskousstvo, 1964): 329–484. English version in Michael Glenny and Richard Taylor, eds., *S. M. Eisenstein. Selected Works, Vol. II, Towards a Theory of Montage* (London: BFI, 1991), 11–58. See especially the examples of shots made literally by using words or expressions in the framing, notably on "aversion" (p. 345 in Russian; p. 22 in English trans.) and the "overturning" of a barricade (pp. 347–349 in Russian; pp. 23–26 in English trans.).

19. The episode of the Burning Bush happens when Moses, still young, is watching over the herds of his stepfather Jethro. Before arriving at the foot of Mt. Sinai, the Hebrews had to convince Pharaoh to let them leave (the episode of the 10 plagues of Egypt), cross the Red Sea, almost die of thirst (the episode of Moses striking the rock—which, in Schoenberg's libretto, Aaron is accused of doing!) and hunger (episode with the celestial manna) in the desert, and so on. All of this is simply omitted in the opera, while the film, on this point, is more explicit: we catch a glimpse

of Egypt and of its "smells" at the end of act I, and this blackness is opportune to allow us to remember and reconstitute our memory, if only vaguely.

20. Or almost exclusively: shot 18, the first appearance of the people under the sign of the "three," is taken at human height.

21. The text by Schoenberg actualizes what the biblical text presupposes, Yahweh having announced to Moses these three "proofs" as being of a nature to convince the people (Exodus 4).

22. See the section entitled "Montage in single set-up cinema" in *S. M. Eisenstein. Selected Works, Vol. II, Towards a Theory of Montage* (London: BFI, 1991).

# between setting and
# landscape in the cinema

t w o

m a r t i n   l e f e b v r e

Rather than begin my investigation by studying a particular film's use of
landscape (its symbolism, function, etc.), I have chosen instead to query
the very notion of cinematic "landscape." Why? Quite simply, because on
reflection it seems to me that there is nothing obvious about landscape
when it comes to the cinema—at least in the sense that the term assumes
in the other visual arts. This last qualification is necessary, I would add,
because "landscape" has so many different meanings, a fact that compli-
cates matters a great deal.

At first glance it may seem surprising to assert that landscape cannot
be taken for granted in the art of film. After all, what are we to make of
the icy expanses in *Nanook of the North* (Robert Flaherty, 1922), the mountains in Arnold Fanck's *Bergfilme* of the 1920s, or the panoramic views
of Monument Valley in John Ford's Westerns, if they do not constitute
"landscapes"? This question strikes at the heart of the matter, but we are
ill-equipped to answer it until we have taken the time to consider some of
*landscape*'s various meanings.

The word "landscape," which only entered the English lexicon during the seventeenth century and was borrowed from the languages of northern European countries (its origin may be Dutch, German, or Flemish[1]), is used today in various contexts where it refers to different objects (e.g., in painting, architecture, geography—not to mention the various metaphorical meanings: *intellectual* landscape, *cultural* landscape, etc.). For the purpose of this chapter, however, it will suffice to begin by distinguishing between two common meanings of the term. Indeed, one characteristic of this term is its double sense. It can refer to a pictorial genre (and the individual works that comprise it), but it can also refer to actual views of a "real," natural, exterior space. In other words, it refers at times to the pictorial *representation* of a space and at other times to the real *perception* of a space. As a result, it is not incorrect to say that Ford's Monument Valley or *Nanook*'s ice fields are landscapes. One could also claim with some confidence that the concept of "landscape" applies to all exterior and natural spaces viewed on the cinema screen as long as it would also be applied to the same space should it be seen in the world or, in other words, when perceived *in situ*. However, this usage defines landscape by virtue of the "thing itself" rather than by its representation and therefore does not do justice to the meaning of the term within the visual arts. Within this realm, not every depiction of exterior or natural space is a *landscape*. However, to make sense of this distinction we must first differentiate between *setting* and *landscape*.

## setting and landscape

In her book, *L'Invention du paysage,* French art historian Anne Cauquelin notes the absence of the term and the notion of landscape in Ancient Greece: "for the ancient Greeks, there is neither word nor object that closely or distantly resembles what we call 'landscape'."[2] There are, however, *settings*: "Herodotus and Xenophon are not miserly in their descriptions of 'settings.' Yet these descriptions do not constitute what we call 'landscapes': instead they constitute the basic material conditions of an event, a war, an expedition or a legend, to which they remain subordinate" (Cauquelin, 39). The same occurs in Aristotle's *Poetics*: "Just as the setting (*topos*), following the Aristotelian definition, is the envelope of the bodies which it boarders, so too the supposed 'landscape' (small setting: *topion*) would be nothing without the active bodies which occupy it. Narrative comes first; its location in space is but an effect of reading" (Cauquelin, 39–40). Cauquelin's commentary thus encourages us to distinguish between two different representations of space: *setting* and *landscape*.

The setting, according to Cauquelin, is above all else the space of story and event: it is the scenery of and the theatre for what will happen. No representation or discourse recounting action or events can be made without a setting, even if that setting can been understood and interpreted by spectators in a variety of ways. Setting refers to spatial features that are necessary for all event-driven films—whether fiction or documentary. This does not, however, reduce a film's setting to a mere given. Every unit of meaning in a film—whether an action, a view of an object, etc.—implies a setting (or settings). This space is constructed by the spectator from audio-visual cues (framing, editing, sound volume, echo, etc.) and from the knowledge he/she already possesses of the spatial characteristics of our world. Setting may be precise and highly detailed or it may remain rather vague and more or less undetermined. In either case, it still serves the same discursive function: it is the place where the action or events occur. Thus, simple black backgrounds (such as those found in the early Edison films shot in the *Black Maria*) constitute a setting just as much as the prairies seen in an establishing shot in a Western.

Defining narrative space may prove more difficult than it first appears, however. This is because setting, like action, constitutes an *entirely variable conceptual construction*. In other words, setting is usually devoid of fixed boundaries; or at least, any such boundaries are indefinitely divisible, somewhat in the manner of Zeno's famous arrow paradox. In film this difficulty is compounded by the presence of duration and montage. Montage, of course, can fragment space, break down the setting of the action, and thereby expand it (at least numerically). What's more, a film's setting may always be incorporated into other, larger scale settings. Consider, for instance, Pierre Perrault's renowned documentary *La Bête lumineuse* (1982): What is its setting? Is it the province of Québec? The woods near Maniwaki? Or is it the sequence of places revealed by the discrete moments of the film: the forest, then the lake, then the cabin, and so on? Generally speaking, we might say that in the average film (fictional or documentary), the setting though precise in some aspect (forest, city, neighborhood, etc.)

(a) may also be incorporated into larger—often unseen—spaces (e.g., Québec in *La Bête lumineuse*) whose relevance can only be established through analysis or interpretation

(b) can be segmented into an indefinite number of smaller settings: the setting of each action but also of each shot or even each frame

In this sense, a film's setting, even if it is initially established as a *function of* the camera's framing(s), cannot be wholly defined by it; setting cannot, in other words, be reduced exclusively to what is seen on screen. (The use of off-screen sounds and glances are only two of several ways in which what is left "unseen" in a given film may indicate setting.) The result, as alluded to earlier, is that setting is not a given and often must be *inferred* from what is depicted. To take a well-known example, one can describe the setting of *La Sortie des usines Lumière* (Lumière brothers, 1895) as the Lumière factory. Thanks to what we see of the factory through the framing, one might also more precisely *and with equal validity* describe it as a specific point within the factory's architecture: namely, the exit where Lumière employees leave the factory after their work. *In addition*, the setting is also and quite obviously Lyon, France, Europe, and even the world!—locations whose relevance naturally rests on how we *use* the film but which are nonetheless represented even if only as mere potentialities. We thus find ourselves with a series of locations which, *according to the uses that we make of the film*, expand and contract, fitting inside one another like Russian nested dolls. They run at least potentially from the specific (the location of the employees' exit from the factory—defined by the film's framing) to the more general (Lyon, France, the world), according to the semiotic principle of *pars pro toto*. As a result, it would be sufficient to program this Lumière film in a retrospective on "Lyon at the turn of the century" for its setting to suddenly "exceed" the cinematic frame and to "encompass" not only the Lumière factory but the city of Lyon as well, even though the latter is hardly depicted at all in the film (to say the very least). Such a use of the film is, however, entirely plausible.

In this sense, to speak of a setting is already to offer an interpretation and to assert a property (a *predicate*[3]) of the filmic space presented in the frame. To speak of it is to invoke a particular way we have of *representing* a given filmic space to ourselves, of *interpreting* it. It implies reference to some way of *using* a film—be it simply trying to make sense of a narrative.

Over the years, several film theorists have examined some of the formal and stylistic principles that preside over the construction and comprehension of narrative space, especially with regard to classical cinema. Yet since this issue falls beyond the scope of this chapter, it will suffice to direct the reader to the different studies on the subject.[4]

The issue of landscape is more complicated. To begin with, we could say that landscape is, in a certain sense, the inverse of setting, that it is an "anti-setting" of sorts. Of course, I will need to be more precise. For the moment, though, the essential question is: How is landscape distinct from setting? The passage quoted earlier from Anne Cauqelin's book on painting sketches out a useful starting point: landscape, at least in the visual arts, is *space freed from eventhood* (e.g., war, expeditions, legends).

Of course, art historians have long been interested in the question of landscape, which constitutes a significant component of more general pictorial productions. They often remind us of the late "birth" of landscape painting in the West. Indeed, it would appear that landscape did not emerge in any important way in European painting until the end of the seventeenth century after a long process of emancipation whose origin may be found in part in the adoption of linear perspective and the rendering of space it allowed. Of course, such an assertion demands caution since any understanding of the "birth" of landscape will be relative to the conception of landscape one has to start with. What is clear, nonetheless, is that this periodisation is based on the conjunction of at least two criteria. The first is the distinction between *parergon* and *ergon*, which is to say between (a) landscape as spatial "accessory" to a painted scene (the scene—not the scenery—being the principal subject matter or argument of a painting) or as a simple element accompanying a larger ensemble (illuminated manuscripts, decorative frescoes, back faces of triptych panels, etc.); and (b) landscape as the primary and independent subject matter of a work (scenery as the main focus of the work). The second criterion concerns the distinction between the major artistic forms (in particular, oil painting) and the minor ones (watercolours, drawing, engraving, etc.). In this regard, it would appear that landscape was introduced into the minor forms well before the major ones. Landscape works are found, for example, in woodcuts or watercolours by Dürer from the late fifteenth century. This second distinction between major and minor forms seems to me (though I am no art historian) less useful and perhaps less important than the first, which opposes landscape as *parergon* to landscape as *ergon*. What this first distinction brings forth—at least in the context of painting—is nothing less than the emancipation of landscape from its supporting role as background or setting to events and characters; as a result, it establishes the condition of its emergence as a completely distinct aesthetic object. Therefore, even though "realist" depictions of exterior scenes have always presupposed the presence of some kind of "landscape," these depicted exteriors were conceived as *marginalia* (*parergon*) next to the true subject matter of the work, i.e., the illustrated events or characters (*ergon*). In this sense, Western painting possessed representations of natural spaces well before the seventeenth century, but not as *autonomous landscapes*. It only knew exterior, natural *settings*. As Kenneth Clark emphasizes,

> In the west landscape painting has had a short and fit-
> ful history. In the greatest age of European art, the age
> of the Parthenon and the age of Chartre's Cathedral,
> landscape did not and could not exist; to Giotto and
> Michelangelo it was an impertinence. It is only in the
> seventeenth century that great artists take up land-
> scape painting for its own sake, and try to systematize
> the rules. Only in the nineteenth does it become the
> dominant art, and create a new aesthetic of its own.[5]

Only recently, then, have painters concerned themselves with land-scape in its proper and modern sense, that is, with the autonomous landscape. Pictorial art had to free itself from earlier demands of representation (such as the depiction of events or actions) for landscape painting to emerge. Freedom from *landscape-as-setting* in favour of *autonomous landscape* is what made landscape painting as we know it today. In great measure, it has determined the general idea or concept that we now have of land-scape, and which has since come to exhibit itself through the different pictorial styles of Poussin, Lorrain, Gainsborough, Constable, Turner, Corot, Monet, Tom Thompson, etc.

At this point, the reader may better understand the basis for my initial reluctance to take for granted the idea of "filmic landscape." Indeed, in mainstream cinema, natural or exterior spaces tend to function as setting rather than landscape in the vast majority of cases. It is the place where something happens, where something takes place and unfolds. This holds for John Ford's Westerns as much as for the mountain films starring Leni Riefenstahl. Of course, this should not surprise us for we know that dominant cinema is foremost a narrative cinema based on the depiction of actions and events. Typically, from the perspective of a film's narrative or event-based economy—in other words, *from the narratological point of view*—exterior space frames the action and is subordinate to it. Should we therefore conclude that narrative cinema is incompatible with the idea of landscape? Before answering, it will prove useful to return to the question of the autonomy of landscape in art.

*autonomy and interpretation*

If we now have an idea of what distinguishes landscape from setting, it remains to be seen how this distinction actually becomes apparent. Despite the boundary line traced by the seventeenth century, which so often serves as landscape's "official" date of birth, the preceding period here offers precious insight for understanding the conditions of possibility for this birth.

In a general way, we know that in painting "landscape" is confined to the role of setting or scenery prior to the seventeenth century. It is simply the natural exterior context for an action or event, though it may also interact with it symbolically in important ways. One exceptional case among sixteenth century painters seems to be that of Albrecht Altdorfer (c. 1480–1538), whom Christopher Wood describes as painting "the first independent landscape in the history of European art."[6] Certainly there is no denying the singularity of Altdorfer's landscapes or their "autonomous" status. (Wood describes them as "narrative compositions from which the subject-matter has been removed or allowed to melt into setting and dissipate" [49]). However, though Altdorfer is exceptional, it is important to stress that similar observations could be made about a fair number of sixteenth century paintings in which landscape plays a considerable role. Two well-known examples are "The Tempest," an enigmatic work by Giorgione (c. 1477–1510); and the works of Antwerp master, Joachim Patinir (c. 1480–1524), which have received widely divergent assessments by various art historians. The cases of Giorgione and Patinir are interesting to the extent that they problematise landscape's autonomy by calling into question its development.

In light of what has been said up to this point, Patinir's works would not constitute landscapes in the full sense of the term (autonomous, independent landscapes) because characters, biblical events, or mythological themes are usually situated in these natural surroundings. But it is important to note how numerous commentators and art historians—beginning with Goethe—have noted that Patinir's scenes are peculiar. They are composed so as to invert the until then usual relationship between setting and character. Indeed, in them, the characters become accessory. Must we for this reason see these works as landscape in the modern sense of the term? In asking this, we arrive back to the initial point of inquiry: Is this a setting or a landscape? Yet what interests me here is not so much to rule on this question regarding Patinir but rather to see how his works have led to different responses or *interpretations*, whether the spectator's gaze has been drawn to the characters or to the landscape.

The argument that Patinir is a landscape painter is based on several assumptions. In his *Diary of a Journey to the Netherlands*, none other than Albrecht Dürer describes Patinir as a "good landscape artist."[7] Documentary sources also show that in at least one case Patinir hired master painters in Antwerp—notably Quinten Massys—to paint the characters in some of his paintings, preferring for his part to paint the landscapes.[8] But it is especially the composition of his works which attracts the attention of commentators. In Patinir's work it often happens that characters are literally dominated by landscapes that occupy practically the entire surface of the painting (Figure 2.1). From here, it takes only one step to arrive

25

Figure 2.1

Joachim Patinir, *Martyrdom of St. Catherine* (before 1515, 27 x 44 cm). Kunsthistorisches Museum, Vienna, Austria. (Photo credit: Erich Lessing/ Art Resource.)

at the conclusion that they constitute "autonomous" landscapes. André Piron noted this, remarking that Patinir was the "the first of the landscape artists proper."[9] Piron was not alone in noticing this,[10] but in the absence of a real landscape tradition in the sixteenth century, certain historians have trouble accepting the autonomy of landscape in Patinir's work. This attitude is well summarized by Malcolm Andrews: "But because it is so early in date for an 'independent' landscape, we are anxiously on our guard against a naive or teleologically biased interpretation of it. The virtual non-existence of an independent landscape tradition at the beginning of the sixteenth century exerts formidable pressure over our reception of these pictures, which we feel ought to have a narrative or hagiographical *raison d'être*."[11] Another good example of this attitude toward Patinir is provided by Reindert Falkenburg:

> Patinir's landscapes have constantly been measured by the yardstick of an aesthetic conception of landscape, and have been regarded as embodying a "modern" experience of landscape no longer governed by the medieval, religious world view. In that sense they have been held to represent an "aesthetic autonomy". As a result, one sometimes gets the idea that an author is talking not about a 16th-century landscape but a 19th-century one based on those notions of the aesthetic landscape experience that one reads in the letters of Schiller and Carus. In the descriptions of the origins of the 16th-century "autonomous landscape" there is not the slightest questioning of the validity of a conception of landscape which can only be called 19th-century. Art historians have evidently started from the premise that all landscape belonging to the genre are based on one and the same conception—one which they believe embodies *a priori* an exclusively aesthetic approach. This, then, tends to be the axiomatic point of departure for discussions of Patinir's paintings, which are regarded as the first "autonomous" treatments of landscape, although not always "perfect" ones.[12]

Challenging the remarks of some of his predecessors, Falkenburg maintains that Patinir's landscapes have no autonomy and are linked to the whole of events and characters depicted in the painting, even if only in a game of metaphor and complex subterranean symbolism. Consequently, and despite the importance that Falkenburg accords to them, Patinir's landscapes are once more relegated to the role of accessory in pictorial economy dominated by eventhood or narrativity. Despite this note of caution and Falkenburg's exhaustive iconographic analyses of the flora and other elements of the landscapes, doubt remains. "We still have the impression," writes Malcolm Andrews, "that the real purpose of these pictures, of the superfluous scale of their landscapes in relation to their narrative functions, consists of celebrating the immense beauty of the natural world" (Andrews, 48).

This debate over Patinir is of interest at this point because it exemplifies the ambiguity of the relation between *ergon* and *parergon*. In fact, it illustrates the difficulties of neatly distinguishing between these two concepts. What serves as the picture's subject here? What serves as the accessory? It is precisely such difficulties that lead Jacques Derrida in his study of Kant's *Critique of Judgment* to understand the relationship between *ergon* and *parergon* in terms of *différance*. This calls into question and even dissolves the opposition between them and brings to light their interconnectedness: "That which constitutes [the] *parerga* is not simply their exteriority of excess ('*surplus*'), it is the internal structural link which binds them to the lack within the *ergon*. And this lack would be constitutive of the unity of the *ergon*. Without this lack, the *ergon* would not need the *parergon*. The lack of the *ergon* is the lack of the *parergon*."[13]

In effect, however, this ambiguity ends up resolving itself in an *interpretive* enterprise, that is to say, a usage—whether it be Patinir's usage, that of his contemporaries, or that of more modern critics whose gaze has been definitively influenced by the existence of autonomous landscapes since the seventeenth century. In this sense, the birth of landscape should really be understood as the birth of a way of seeing, the birth of a gaze (that of the painter, the collector, or the critic) by which what was once in the margin has now come to take its place at the centre. One art critic who adopted such a position was Ernst Gombrich who claimed that the birth of landscape is to be defined by the way sixteenth century Italian collectors gazed at the paintings they acquired, including Flemish paintings: "We do not know, if they [the Flemish paintings] were pure landscapes—probably they were not—but for the Italian connoisseur, they were only interesting as landscapes." Regarding Giorgione's *The Tempest*, Gombrich immediately adds: "Whatever else the painting may illustrate, for the great Venetian connoisseur it belonged in the category of landscape painting."[14]

The movement from setting to landscape through the transformation of the gaze thus charts a passage from the periphery to the centre. But a gaze always presupposes a subject. In this sense, the difficulty art historians face in dating the birth of landscape painting rests in large part in identifying the subject of this (original) gaze. Is it the painter (whomever it may be: Giorgone, Patinir, Altdorfer, or any others not named here) who first frees setting, turning it into a landscape; or is it rather the connoisseur (collector, commentator, critic) who is fond of what is initially for others only accessory and supplemental? It is not my place to answer— this is first and foremost a subject for art historians. Still, it is important to recognize that the question alone clearly delimits the dual gaze and dual use on which the work of art, and therefore landscape, depends. For both the artist and the critic share—each in their own way—the power to transform a setting into a landscape, which is to say, to move the setting away from the margin and into the centre. The artist who paints an autonomous landscape thus places at the centre that which otherwise rests at the periphery, subordinated to eventhood. This is the case with Altdorfer's work, as has been admirably shown elsewhere by Christopher Wood.[15] Yet, as seen with the Italian connoisseurs discussed by Gombrich as well as with certain commentaries on Patinir's work, it is obvious that critics (spectators) too can pull setting from out of the margin at least in so far as it is seen to possess, if only in the critics' gaze, the required autonomy.

### cinema and "autonomous" landscape

There is of course no reason why the gaze by which landscape emerges in painting would not manifest itself in the work of filmmakers. Moreover, numerous filmmakers have already appropriated this gaze and freed the film's setting from its service to story, thus granting it the status of autonomous landscape. This is notably the case with several experimental films made by Canadian directors, including Michael Snow (*La région centrale*, 1971), David Rimmer (*Canadian Pacific*, 1974, and *Migration*, 1969), Jim Anderson (*Moving Bicycle Picture*, 1972–1975), Jack Chambers (*Circle*, 1968–1969), and Rick Hancox (*Landfall*, 1983).[16] We can also add the celebrated films of Walter Ruttmann (*Berlin: Symphony of a City*, 1927), Ralph Steiner (*H2O*, 1929), or Joris Ivens (*Rain*, 1929), all which stand midway between experimental films and documentaries.

But what about landscape in narrative fiction films that focus on events and action? We are familiar with the accepted golden rule of classical cinema: everything must be subordinated to the narrative. In principle, each element of the film ought to be able to be integrated into the narrative process. This is especially true for the setting (including exteriors) which situates the action and events related by the film.

Though at times we tend to forget or at least neglect the fact, it is evident that in addition to telling stories or relating events, the cinema offers a visual *spectacle*.[17] However, the amalgamation of story with spectacle unavoidably generates ambiguity, as certain film theorists have already pointed out. Everyone is familiar with the immense success achieved by Laura Mulvey who, in the political context of 1970s feminism, proposed the use of these terms to describe strategies for representing the masculine and the feminine in classical cinema: while men advance the story through their action, women threaten to arrest its development in so far as their presence onscreen can introduce moments of contemplation.[18] Despite everything, these observations still retain their pertinence today, even if one would not want to treat them as dogma. More importantly from our point of view, they throw into sharp relief both the distinction between story and spectacle and the tension that it generates. Obviously, the locus of this tension is the spectator who can either invest in the film's narrative development by way of what Paul Ricoeur terms "narrative intelligence"[19]; or invest in a contemplative attitude that produces mainly aesthetic "forms"—on which cinematic landscape depends, as we shall see. Accordingly, we can speak of two modes of spectatorial activity: a *narrative mode* and a *spectacular mode*.[20]

In the act of watching films, these two modes likely come into play at different moments. Thus spectators watch the film at some points in the narrative mode and at others in the spectacular mode, allowing them both to follow the story *and*, whenever necessary, to contemplate the filmic spectacle. It is necessary, however, to emphasize that one cannot watch the same filmic passage through both modes at the exact same time, i.e., in a way that employs both modes *absolutely* simultaneously. This is why it can be said that the spectacle halts the progression of narrative for the spectator. Thus, the tension noted above results from a tug-of-war within the spectator between the narrative and spectacular modes. When I *contemplate* a piece of film, I stop following the story for a moment, even if the narrative does not completely disappear from my consciousness—to which I may add that it is precisely because the narrative does not disappear from my consciousness that I can easily pick it up again. The interruption of the narrative by contemplation has the effect of *isolating* the object of the gaze, of momentarily freeing it from its narrative function. Said differently, the contemplation of filmic *spectacle* depends on an "autonomising" gaze. *It is this gaze which enables the notion of filmic landscape in narrative fiction (and event-based documentary) film; it makes possible the transition from setting to landscape.* The contemplation of the setting frees it briefly from its narrative function (but perhaps, in some cases, only for the length of a thought); for one instant, the natural, outdoor setting for the action is considered in its own right, as a landscape. As a result, we are made to acknowledge a characteristic of filmic landscapes which distinguishes them from pictorial landscapes: duration. In effect, landscape in narrative film possesses the peculiar ability to appear and disappear before the spectator's very eyes in accordance with the tug-of-war described above. As a result, we might describe filmic landscape as a *doubly temporalised landscape*. In other words, it is subjected simultaneously to the temporality of the cinematographic medium[21] and to that of the spectator's gaze, which is given to shifting from the narrative to the spectacular mode and back again from one moment to the next. This doubled temporal existence results in the precariousness of a landscape that more or less vanishes when the narrative mode takes over and the cinematic space resumes its narrative function as setting.

To illustrate this ephemeral landscape, simultaneously like crystal and smoke, I would like to consider a passage from the beginning of *Barry Lyndon* (Stanley Kubrick, 1975). The young Redmond, a man driven by jealousy, reproaches his cousin Nora for having danced with an English captain five times. The scene takes place on a tree-lined path (Figure 2.2). This space clearly serves as the setting for the unfolding action (a lover's quarrel), which will have repercussions throughout the film (a duel between Redmond and Captain Quinn; the exile of Redmond; etc.). But independent of its narrative function, whoever pays attention to the setting itself—and not to the action—will succeed in making the landscape emerge.[22] Of course, in this particular case, "to make the landscape emerge" means to relate the image to certain historical conventions of landscape painting that the spectator must know beforehand. In other words, it is precisely because I am sensitive to landscape in art and because I know its conventions that I am inclined to grant to the space in question the value of landscape.[23]

One might wonder at this stage if the importance accorded the spectator and his/her mode of spectatorship does not simply reduce filmic landscape to the idiosyncrasies of individual spectators? Does the camera's gaze do nothing? To understand the respective roles of the spectator and the film in the emergence of landscape, it is important to examine several examples of existing conditions that can produce—or at least encourage—viewing in the spectacular mode.

It seems possible to agree on the existence of two paradigms that define the poles of an interpretive spectrum: in one case, the spectator imputes to the film (or to its director) the intention to present a landscape—this I call the "intentional" landscape; in the other, the spectator must assume that he/she is the source of the cinematic landscape—this I call the

Figure 2.2

Still from *Barry Lyndon*.

"spectator's" landscape or, taking a cue from Gombrich, "impure" landscape. These two situations assume innumerable forms, too many in fact to present them all here. Nevertheless, it is possible to cite a few of their manifestations.

### the "intentional" landscape

Among those examples which best illustrate the first paradigm are films that quote specific paintings, such as Vincent Minnelli's *Lust for Life* (1956) or Akira Kurosawa's *Dreams* (1990).[24] Using different strategies, both films visually reproduce famous Van Gogh landscapes. Minnelli's film repeatedly shows the artist at work transforming a "real" landscape into a pictorial landscape (Figure 2.3). While such space is offered as a setting—from a narrative point of view it serves to situate the action of a scene (the action of painting)—its quotation of a well-known landscape painting shown while it is being painted by the artist *encourages* the emergence of landscape in the film,[25] assuring the autonomy of the exterior space from the narrative—even if only momentarily. Clearly, the film provides the spectator with the necessary means to contemplate the landscape and even compare it with a famous landscape painting whose creation is depicted by the narrative. While different from the example drawn from *Barry Lyndon*, the cinematic landscape here is still dependent on pictorial landscape. The difference lies in the fact that the spectator recognizes now a direct pictorial citation which is entirely attributable to the film. This process is identical to the "tableau-shot" (*plan tableau*) identified some time ago by Pascal Bonitzer with the difference that the spectator does not necessarily invest the *whole* shot, i.e., the shot in its entire duration, as a landscape.[26] This process, however, as Bonitzer emphasizes, is given to numerous variations.

One such variation is found in Kurosawa's film, in the segment entitled "Crows." Here, a character literally penetrates the universe of Van Gogh paintings after contemplating some of them in a museum.

Figure 2.3

Still from *Lust for Life*.

The passage from the museum to the world represented by the paint-ings inaugurates a brief, minimal narrative that consists of a character's quest to meet the famous Dutch painter. Yet this story, as simple is it is, continually risks fading out and being replaced by the contemplation of landscape according to a continual ebb and flow in the spectator's mind between narrative and spectacular modes under the pressure, or aesthetic "contamination," of the presence of Van Gogh's works and the character's physical integration into them. This integration manifests itself in two ways: first, the character enters into "real" landscapes (some of them hav-ing been the subject of Van Gogh's paintings) which the story situates in Van Gogh's time—as if the protagonist was travelling back in time from the museum. Second, he enters into the paintings themselves, *literally*. The latter strategy dominates the central part of the segment where special effects enable the character to pass through seven successive Van Gogh landscapes. This results in a hybrid product midway between painting (or drawing) and cinema, which even suggests animated film. Because of the presence of narrative elements, because we are following a character moving from one landscape painting to another, it could be argued that the space depicted acquires here a certain value as *setting* which it lacks as landscape art. Yet the use of famous landscape paintings—quite a *spectacu-lar* use at that—enables the spectator to restore to each of these settings their value as landscape though they are now subject to cinematic dura-tion: they have become cinematic landscapes. A different, less "techno-logical" method is used at the beginning and end of the segment. We can see the protagonist pass from the Langlois Bridge in Arles to the wheat fields of Auvers-sur-Oise, the magic of montage rendering moments and spaces that are in reality disjointed seem contiguous within the fiction.[27] The transition from the canvases on the wall of the museum to the "real" landscapes[28] (a transition from the pictorial to the filmic) is accomplished through a deliberate mimetic game: a shot of the painting (the *Pont de Lan-glois*) is followed by its "real"-life filmic "reproduction." The transition is operated by a straight-cut and a brief pause where the camera stays immo-bile, reproducing the painting's framing (Figure 2.4). The same process, though this time backwards, closes the episode: we pass from a "real"-life composition tracing the design of *Wheat Field Under Threatening Skies* (which integrates the crows by superimposition, in the manner of Hitchcock's *The Birds, 1963*)[29] to the actual canvas on the wall of the museum. In both cases, the film itself gives us the means with which to assure the emergence of filmic landscape through the co-presence of Van Gogh's works and their filmic reproduction. However, the rise of the filmic landscape does not solely concern those spaces directly connected to Van Gogh's paintings. In fact, the intertextual game of pictorial citations—together with other formal elements found throughout the segment, such as the repeated use of long shots, a montage that favours *temps morts*, and a narrative thread so

Figure 2.4

Still from *Dreams*.

simple that it can be abandoned and resumed with ease[30]—can be seen to encourage the spectator in switching back and forth between setting and landscape with regards to much of the segment's exteriors.

Of course, there can be no doubt that directors have at their disposal a great number of strategies for making the spectator experience a film (or portions thereof) in the spectacular mode and for directing their attention toward space in such a way as to free it from its subservience to narrative. As we have seen in *Lust for Life*, these strategies may even be integrated into the story itself. For instance, the presence of a character enraptured by the natural space offered to their gaze can lead the spectator to contemplate the same space as an autonomous landscape. Among the numerous examples of this, we can cite a scene from *The Misfits* (John Huston, 1961), where, in front of a wide Nevada vista, the character played by Marilyn Monroe cries, "It's like a dream!" followed by a subjective long shot of the landscape. Here, the segment's narrative construction (subjective shot showing the object of the character's comment) and its visual construction (the long shot) can lead the spectator to pay attention to the space taken in by his/her gaze, thus facilitating setting's transformation into landscape. In short, *any strategy for directing the spectator's attention toward the exterior space rather than toward the action taking place within it (regardless of whether the strategy is motivated diegetically) can be attributed to an intention to emphasize landscape.* This is the case, for example, with certain transition shots (common in classical films), or even certain *temps morts* (typical of more "modern" cinema). Of course, the more the strategy in question is made part of the diegesis— i.e., the more the landscape's spectacle is legitimized or recuperated by the unfolding of the action—the less violent the interruption of the story feels. This is the case with various transition shots in classical cinema.[31] By "transition shots," I mean those shots which indicate in the narrative a spatio-temporal change in the action; they are sometimes accompanied by an optical effect (fade-in, lap dissolve, etc.) but can be made just as well with a straight cut. They can occur at various points in the film, including at the beginning and at the end where they may serve to indicate the spatial boundaries of the diegesis. This is notably the case in *Barry Lyndon*, where Kubrick uses images of Lady Lyndon's residence, Hackton House, as a leitmotif to introduce different segments that take place there (Figure 2.5). The minimal narrative function of these shots consists of assuring the transition between two segments and in presenting the new setting for the action. This function, however, easily gives way to what may be felt as an intention to depict landscapes. In *Barry Lyndon*, it is quite tempting to impute this intention to the director since the compositions in question recall famous landscapes—for example, *Malvern Hall* painted by Constable in 1809 (Figure 2.6). The transitional shot of classical film in which the action is generally absent or reduced to a minimum can thus be used to draw the spectator's attention toward the space. Despite a purely narrative pretext legitimized by the narrative economy (the movement from one segment to another and the introduction of a new setting), this renders the setting available to be transformed into a landscape.

Finally, in so far as filmic landscape manifests a level of detachment from the story in the eyes of the spectator—i.e., it acts precisely as an *autonomous* landscape—it cannot avoid flirting with a kind of modernity. This is foremost the modernity of the cinematographic spectacle: the modernity of attractions, fragmentation, and heterogeneity. And this is why, even in the most classical narrative films (say, in some of D. W. Griffith's transitional shots, e.g., in *Way Down East*, 1921), the filmic landscape participates in modernity, if only for our gaze. This could explain why classical cinema continually tries to contain it through technical and narrative functions

Figure 2.5

Still from *Barry Lyndon*.

Figure 2.6

John Constable, *Malvern Hall* (1809; oil on canvas, 51 x 77 cm). Tate Gallery, London.

such as subjective points of view or transitional shots. It should not come as a surprise, therefore, to see landscape being incorporated in the visual language of several modernist directors or into the avant-garde aesthetic of numerous experimental filmmakers.

This modern character of landscape is related to its autonomy, to its detachment from narrative, whenever this is achieved intentionally. The connection, however, needs some explaining, especially if we identify landscape primarily with its manifestation in "classical" painting. Indeed, are we to conclude that it is the cinema that has transformed into something "modern" what was not "modern" at first? The problem here arises, one suspects, from the use of the adjective "modern." While this is not the place for a full-scale reconsideration of modernity in the arts, and in particular in film and painting, still we can highlight certain aspects of landscape painting that, from the start, have entangled it within a web of issues and problems that are resolutely modern. I take up only two: the question of style; and the relation between the emergence of landscape and certain transformations in the European sensibility toward space at the time of the birth of capitalism during the Renaissance.

With regards to style, Christopher Wood has pointed out how, ever since the Renaissance, landscape has offered artists an ideal context for emphasizing a personal style: "Outdoor settings were especially susceptible to the self-aggrandizing and self-advertising devices of the authorial persona. Landscape was a hospitable venue for pungent colouristic effects. Trees and mountain-ranges encouraged eccentric details and calligraphic line. Several Renaissance texts on pictorial randomness actually associate landscape with freedom from rule" (63). Wood also reminds us that Botticelli would paint the "landscape" part of his frescoes by throwing sponges against a wall (a gesture whose offhandedness shocked da Vinci.) Examining a sketch drawn by Dürer entitled *Quarry*, Wood then wonders about the possibility of some sort of lineage between landscape and the "abstract" line of doodling: "Perhaps linear whimsy and thoughtlessness naturally drifted toward landscape" (64). What "modern" traits! In effect, Wood's argument asks us to conceive of "early" landscape as a pictorial practice whose work consists of making style visible, which is to say of making visible that which is by definition detached and relatively autonomous from what is figuratively depicted. As a result, its work is also to inscribe the presence of the artist within the artwork's "signifying material." In fact, it is as if a continuum existed between the landscape's autonomy— from events, action, and characters, i.e., from the "subject," *ergon*—and the autonomy of art, of representation. Of course, such comment is not meant to turn the Renaissance into the birthplace of modernism in the arts. Its purpose, rather, is to alert us to a possible lineage between land- scape painting and modernism (in painting) as it developed with Impres- sionism, a movement which, as is well known, was much concerned both with the representation of landscape and with that of the artist. It is in this sense that I read Kenneth Clark's comment, drawn from the conclusion of his work *Landscape into Art*: "The painting of landscape cannot be considered independently of the trend away from imitation [of nature] as the *raison d'être* of art."[32]

The second aspect concerns the relation between emergent landscape painting and specific transformations in the way space was conceived and experienced during the Renaissance. These transformations were overdetermined by diverse cultural, economic, and scientific factors. These include, among other things, new practices of management and use of land that appear in Europe with the birth of capitalism, especially those that concern the changing relationships between the city and the country in the fifteenth and sixteenth centuries (particularly in Italy); new conceptions of space and the new cosmology that result from the establishment of commercial routes to Africa and Asia; the conquest of the New World; the improvement of cartography; as well as the scientific discoveries of Copernicus and Galileo. The geographer Denis Cosgrove has explained how in the vast context of the transition toward capitalism, the social function of the "idea" of landscape consisted of uniting—even if unstably—two opposed conceptions of the natural world: a "natural" pre-capitalist tie to the land, and an "alienated," capitalist relationship to it. He writes that

> The idea of landscape holds both types of relationship
> in an unstable unity, forever threatening to lapse into
> either the unreflexive subjectivism of the insider where
> the feeling for the land is incommunicable through
> the artificial language of art; or the objectification of
> land as property pure and simple, the outsider's view,
> where alienation is complete and a statistical weighting

can be placed upon the "landscape value" of a piece of land which can be entered into a cost/benefit analysis against the value that the land might have as an industrial site. The origin of the landscape idea in the West and its artistic expressions have served in part to promote ideologically an acceptance of the property relationship while sustaining the image of an unalienated one, of land as use. The history of the landscape idea is one of artistic and literary exploration of the tensions within it until, with the hegemonic establishment of urban industrial capitalism and the bourgeois culture of property, landscape lost its artistic and moral force and became a residual in cultural production regarded either as an element of purely individual subjectivity or the scientifically-defined object of academic study, particularly in geography.[33]

Essentially, Cosgrove's argument is in agreement with those of numerous commentators who see in the history of landscape as well as in the principle of autonomy underpinning it, the larger narrative of the reification and alienation of nature in the modern era, a narrative for which modernism has most often supplied the critique.[34]

Perhaps these stylistic and cultural problematics can serve to explain—at least in part—the marked presence of landscape in the work of so many modern directors (Pasolini, Antonioni, Godard, Wenders, Tarkovsky, for example). For in the films of these filmmakers, it finds fertile ground indeed.

This is the case, for instance, in *Teorema* (Pier Paolo Pasolini, 1968) where images of a volcanic desert repeatedly interrupt the narrative flow. This desert is an extra-diegetic space lacking narrative function: it is never the setting for the action belonging to the diegetic universe of the film; its connection to the diegesis is instead purely symbolic. Insofar as this leitmotif is autonomous in regards to the narrative, this space evokes the organizing presence of the director and assures (along with other traits such as a refusal of psychological realism, a refusal of classical causality, the use of elliptical montage, unusual framing, stylistic heterogeneity, distanciation) the modernist film aesthetic. But if the absence of diegetic motivation serves this aesthetic project, it also risks favouring the emergence of an autonomous landscape. It might be objected that the autonomy in question is not absolute and that the images of the volcanic desert participate in the (modern) thematic of bourgeois alienation elaborated by the film's narrative. In effect, the desert (which appears for the first time in the opening credits[35]) can be taken as neither more nor less than a metaphor for the spiritual aridity of the modern world laid bare. This interpretation is made possible by, among other things, the false match-

37

cut which connects the desert with the platform in the Milanese train station (the narrative setting for the scene) toward the end of the film. As a result, this relationship institutes a "symbolic" continuity between the two spaces.[36] And in this sense, the last shots of the film which show a naked man wandering in the desert allow us to see this space as a symbolic *setting*, which is to say as the setting of a symbolic nondiegetic action: just as the man stands naked, this (the desert) is Milan (the modern bourgeois world in general) made bare. Now, part of the ambiguity disappears if we recall that "setting" and "landscape" constitute two ways that we have of conceiving or representing filmic space and that both are dependent on modes of spectatorship which ebb and flow in time. Nevertheless, the question remains: What is it in the film that directs the spectator's gaze toward the desert landscape? I have already mentioned the desert's autonomy from the diegesis. Another element that can be added to this is the pictorial composition, which proceeds above all through long shots. But in them, we find an additional dimension which, paradoxically, over-determines the autonomy of the desert all the while reconnecting it to the rest of the film: its "symbolic" status.

One of the characteristics of numerous modern works is their tendency to flaunt their interpretability and their hermeneutical depth through a refusal of transparency and of "realism." Obviously, the desert of *Teorema* participates in this aesthetic, in part by its refusal to integrate itself into the diegesis of the film. Consequently, it requires hermeneutic work to discover how the space offered to the spectator is linked to the other elements of the film. Only through this work is it possible to see in the desert a symbolic or metaphoric representation of Milan and, by extension, of the modern world. *To do this, however, it is first necessary to "stop" on the desert, to arrest our gaze and to take it in as it is—which is to say, to contemplate it as a landscape—before moving on to interpret other elements of the film.* It perhaps goes without saying that this task is made easier by the desert's detachment from the story.

Though not a rule by any stretch, we can say that with many modern directors, the intentionality for landscape manifests itself according to two distinct strategies: landscapes either appear during lulls in the story (*temps morts*); or they appear in moments free of any diegetic motivation. In the first case, it is the story's space, the setting, which becomes autonomous and acquires the value of landscape; in the second, the story's space gives way to another space, a space that is "displaced" or arbitrary in terms of the narrative progress.

In Michelangelo Antonioni's work the first approach dominates his concerns with landscape. (It is the same with Wenders, another director whose films give importance to space.) At moments, Antonioni's stories seem to evaporate, letting the landscape emerge: his stories are somewhat like the character of Anna in *L'avventura* (Antonioni, 1959), who mysteriously disappears from a desert island and from the film itself; or like

Thomas, the main character in *Blow-Up* (Antonioni, 1966), who literally slips away from the image in the last shot of the film, leaving his place to the green lawn of a London park. We know that Antonioni proceeds here by de-centring: in *L'avventura*, the de-centring of Anna's disappearance permits a re-centring of the narrative around Claudia and Sandro's relationship; and in *Blow-Up*, the de-centring of the murder in the park privileges a reflection on art, representation, and reality through the character of the photographer. In other words, what would be made the object of the narrative in the classical mode (a disappearance and a questionable death to explain) is given a secondary importance. From a formal point of view, this inversion of the *ergon* and of the *parergon* is analogous to the procedure that, as we have seen, gave rise to landscape in European painting. Should we therefore be surprised to see landscapes springing up in Antonioni's films?[37] *L'avventura*, we remember, was awarded a prize at Cannes in 1960 for "the beauty of its images," as if these images could be *detached* or rendered *autonomous* from the other elements of the film—elements which clearly include the story. Since then, legions of commentators have stressed the predominance of the image in Antonioni's films.[38] To return to the two films cited earlier, it is important to realize just how difficult it can be to watch *L'avventura* without our gaze lingering (even if only for a moment) on the rocky island where Anna disappears; or likewise, to watch *Blow-Up* without seeing the park—and the photos of the park—independently of what's going on in them. Of course, if we can ascribe to Antonioni the intention of presenting a landscape, it is because the filmic treatment can lead us to see the space as autonomous and to detach it from its narrative function.

In *L'avventura*, for example, the long segment on the island after the disappearance of Anna increases the number of *temps morts*. Certain critics have already observed the importance of this stylistic trait with Antonioni, which is created simultaneously by the montage, the *mise-en-scène* and the camerawork. Seymour Chatman sees in this trait, "Antonioni's most characteristic stylistic effect." He describes it as the presentation of either "prediegetic" space (the view of a space *before* the arrival of characters and the advancement of the action) or "postdiegetic" space (the view of a space *after* the characters have left it and the action has occurred). The following quote makes explicit the link between the diegetic space and the pre- or post-diegetic space put into play by these *temps morts* (I have italicized the passages which appear to me to be the most pertinent with regard to landscape).

> The goal is not to present "the same place" but the possibility that it is in reality "another place," perhaps even an extradiegetic place. The scene is made portentous by a delay that challenges the whole tissue of fictionality. The film says not that "this is such-and-such a place,

in which event X occurs" but rather that "this place is important quite *independently* of the immediate exigencies of plot, and you will sense (if not understand) its *odd value* if you scrutinize it carefully. This is why I give you time to do so." This kind of shot does not set the stage for some other shot…, it is itself the scene. *Not that the simple space as stasis is turned into an event or action.* It is rather that the camera's lingering makes the place pregnant with significance. We *contemplate* intently, in a way parallel to but separate from the characters. We are engaged, even before they arrive or after they leave, in a scrutiny that we do not quite understand but that seems nonetheless urgent. (Chatman, 125–126)

If Chatman speaks here of *temps morts* in Antonioni's work, his description shows that these *temps morts* are equally a *spatial* concern. Essentially, *temps morts* are a way of rendering space, a way of taking it out of the film's continuity and narrative development, in order to distinguish it and to make it autonomous in the eyes of the spectator. As a result, space during these *temps morts* is clearly distinct from the setting of the action (or in Chatman's slightly different sense, from the "diegetic space"). That said, I do not aim to make these *temps morts* and their space synonymous with landscape: not all cinematic *temps morts* involve landscape, far from it. Rather, I merely intend to bring to light the affinity that exists between these *temps morts* and filmic landscapes, and which results from the way in which they can single out space.

A striking thing about Antonioni's films and their use of *temps morts* is how well they can demonstrate, within a modernist context, the changing status of filmic space, the back-and-forth movement between setting and landscape. Perhaps nowhere is this better illustrated than in *Blow-Up*, a film that incorporates the issue of landscape art into its narrative in a way that contributes to the numerous reflexive aspects of the film. Moreover, *Blow-Up* uses *temps morts* and the setting/landscape relation it sets up in such a way as to underscore the cinema's double status as both a narrative (i.e., temporal) and visual (i.e., spatial) art. The principal locus of slippage between setting and landscape is the London park where Thomas, a professional photographer, takes a series of photos. It is never clear what drives the photographer to come to the park in the first place, but it is worth noting that before venturing into it the young man stops at an antique shop and asks to see . . . some landscapes! Does this desire for landscape motivate his sudden interest in the park? Whatever else it may indicate, this brief disclosure is likely to predispose the spectator for the emergence of filmic landscapes. Furthermore, several of the photos taken by Thomas in the park qualify as landscape art, which does not, however, prevent their status—and the status of the park—from changing, as we shall see. To get a clear understanding of the situation, however, it is important to consider, if only briefly, the park's two pictorial modes of appearance in the film: the filmic and the photographic.

From the point of view of its filmic appearances, the park is undoubtedly the setting for a series of actions and events concerning Thomas: he takes photos, he interacts with a young woman, a corpse is discovered and disappears, he interacts with a mime troupe, etc. But the park is also a landscape. Each spectator is free of course to consider and see this space as landscape on his own[39]; but—and this is what concerns us for the moment—one can also impute to Antonioni the intention to depict landscape based on the visual treatment the park receives (especially in his use of *temps morts*). One example of many occurs at the end of the first segment in the park when the young woman (played by Vanessa Redgrave) wanders slowly down the path toward the bottom of the frame and then steps out of the image (Figure 2.7). The camera remains stationary and offers a long shot of a section of the park, which allows the contemplation of the landscape for a brief moment. In short, thanks to the *temps mort* following the young woman's disappearance ("postdiegetic" time according to Chatman), the story seems to fade away: all that is left is the park, a landscape embraced by the camera's gaze. Later, in the most famous segment of the film, the park reappears in the form of photos which Thomas looks at, scrutinizes, studies, blows up, and organizes. As I have already mentioned, some of these photos seem, generically, to be landscape photographs. For the most part, they recall images from the first scene in the park *intratextually*; here, however, the images of the park are presented in the form of autonomous photographic works which, by definition, are *temps morts*. The usage of the photograph is interesting in this context because it reproduces and materializes the process of autonomisation—of "arresting" the image—which is necessary for the filmic landscape's emergence in the mind of the spectator. This is likewise the case in certain photos of

Figure 2.7

Still from *Blow-Up.*

the couple framed in long shot, which are "de-narrativized" by the photographic treatment they undergo. Still, the narrative does not quite disappear: for as soon as it is partly chased off by the photographic it surges back to life through the cinematic camerawork, *découpage*, and montage in a segment that evokes Chris Marker's *La jetée* (1962).

Here, two processes are used which make the landscape fade away. First, Thomas's blow-ups (as well as Antonioni's reframings and camerawork) introduce a variation in the shot scale of the photos. What was originally a full shot becomes a medium shot, a medium close-up, a close-up, and even an extreme close-up. This movement *toward* the people photographed and *toward* the represented action has the effect of pushing the landscape back toward the margin and into the accessory role of setting. Landscape thus seems to conceal a narrative: a comment which must be taken literally since the enlargements show a man brandishing a revolver hidden in a bush and a corpse lying just outside of it. Then, there is the montage. In placing his images side by side, the photographer becomes an editor: following in part Eisenstein's lesson, he tries to give meaning to the images by juxtaposing them. And it is at this moment that montage, in the strict sense of the term, appears. Paraded before our eyes in full frame, the enlarged, reframed photos reintroduce temporality (the sequence of images) and suggest plot, eventhood. But the result is a largely elliptical story about which we will basically know nothing; it is (to use a term borrowed from the semiotics of C. S. Pierce) a sort of narrative *rheme*, i.e., a sign interpreted as that of a mere possibility and nothing more. Marie-Claire Ropars, who has analyzed this segment well, speaks of "another possible, unknowable story" written within the temporality of *Blow-Up*'s narrative.[40] Whatever we make of this possibility, the "spatial" effect of the segment is to push the landscape to give up its place to the setting. In other words, the landscape gives way to the action in the mind of the spectator. Moreover, once subjected to filmic manipulation (variations in the frame, camera movement, editing), what appears initially as a calm and tranquil image (typical adjectives for describing the art of landscape) is able to present exactly the contrary: violence and death.[41] With these enlargements, Antonioni thus offers a path leading from the *temps morts* of the visual representation to the death inscribed in them. He does this through the mediation of narrative.

But there is more. At the two extremes of the narrative chain formed by the photos, there are two images: a photo of the park and an enlargement (of an enlargement) of this same photo. The composition of the first image is (almost) identical to the long shot which shows the young woman running away and disappearing from the frame in the segment discussed earlier: it is a landscape photo (Figure 2.7). The second image (Figure 2.8), which ends the cycle of enlargements, enlarges a detail from the first to the point where nothing appears but the grain; all figuration

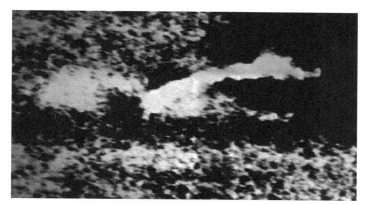

Figure 2.8

Still from *Blow-Up*.

disappears, and the photo takes on the look of an abstract painting—as Thomas's female friend later correctly points out. The passage from one photo to the other is assured by two intermediary prints (Figures 2.9 and 2.10) which enlarge the initial image of the park, showing unequivocally a man's corpse, a fact introduced immediately into the developing (rhematic) narrative of the photos. This path from one photo to the other as well as the technical process employed (i.e., enlargement) clearly suggest the existence of a continuum between the two images: one is generated by the other. Between the two lies the vague narrative of a death. Numerous possible interpretations of these elements and their relationships to each other exist; yet, there is one of particular interest to me here because it constitutes the sequence of enlargements as a kind of allegory: an allegory of a history—that of art and, more precisely, the death of figurative art—accomplished in the passage from the representation of landscape to

Figure 2.9

Still from *Blow-Up*.

Figure 2.10

Still from *Blow-Up.*

abstraction. Commenting on the work of Kenneth Clark, W. J. T. Mitchell observes that for him and many other art historians, "abstract painting constitutes...one of the results of the history of landscape."[42] An analogy between the role of *temps morts* in Antonioni's work and the role of landscape in the history of representation follows from this: thus, to whatever extent the *temps morts*—which cause Antonioni's landscape to appear—contribute to the death of the filmic narrative, to just such an extent, landscape has contributed to the death of figurative art.[43]

Now, concerning the second approach modernist filmmakers have toward landscape, it could suffice to say that we have already encountered an example with the volcanic deserts of *Teorema* were it not for the importance this approach has in the work of Jean-Luc Godard. It thus merits a (too) brief commentary. Though present since the 1960s (e.g., *Pierrot le fou*, 1965), landscape has occupied a particularly important place in Godard's *oeuvre* over the past 20 years. This is the case with films such as *Passion* (1982), *Prénom Carmen* (1993), *Je vous salue Marie* (1985), *King Lear* (1987), *Nouvelle vague* (1990), *Allemagne année 90* (1991), and *Hélas pour moi* (1993). Occasionally, Godard makes landscape emerge from the diegetic space through the use of *temps morts* or by simply shifting the camera's gaze. For example, at the start of the section titled "Incipit Lamentation" in *Nouvelle vague*, Godard obstinately films a tree (as well as the bits of sky visible between its branches) and in this way shifts the camera's gaze (and, with it, our own) away from the action occurring several feet away. From a narrative point of view, the camerawork and editing are thus "unmotivated." The result is a redistribution of the classical functions of *ergon* and *parergon*. For this moment, it is the setting-becomes-landscape—not the event (an accident on the side of the road)—that occupies the camera's attention and constitutes the image's center of gravity. From that point on, the action seems secondary. In the second part of the film, a character's remark calls attention to this process: "You become visible," Elena says to Lennox, "in the place where I disappear" (*"Tu deviens visible à la place où je disparais"*). In this example, setting and landscape still share a certain spatial contiguity. Godard's typical approach, however, consists in brutally rupturing all contiguity between the two. To achieve this, Godard calls on one of his preferred editing strategies: the "displaced" or nondiegetic insert. For example, he introduces a shot (usually static) showing the sea, a lake, the sky, a forest, or a clearing, either in the middle of a segment or between two segments. In contrast to classical transition shots, which establish the setting of a new scene, Godard's landscape inserts are in no way motivated by the action. Quite to the contrary, they interrupt or disrupt the flow of the action. If, as Chatman explains, *temps morts* give the *impression* of "another place," then this is what is offered literally by landscape inserts in Godard's films. Shots of this type abound in most of the films he has directed since the 1980s. Their presence links transcendence (even if only in relation to the story) and contemplation and contributes to the elaboration of an aesthetic tending increasingly to the expression of the sublime. As much as these landscape inserts offer an image of material reality, these "elsewheres" of the story also suggest that which cannot be represented because it overflows the image and the imagination. It is not surprising that, after his unceasing ruminations on the status of the image, Godard eventually comes to thematise—in *Je vous salue Marie* or *Hélas pour moi*—the problem of the incarnation of the divine and the analogy of Being. This is a problem simultaneously philosophical, theological, and aesthetic and goes to the heart of debates over images in Western culture. It is also a problem raised by Godard's landscapes with an insistence bordering on obsession.

Up to this point, we have examined some of the strategies filmmakers use to make landscapes visible and to introduce them into fiction films. There are undoubtedly others, and my discussion does not seek to offer an exhaustive inventory. Rather, it is important to highlight once again that these strategies can be *interpreted* without too much equivocation as indicating the intention to show a landscape. As a result, they carry the risk—or, depending on the situation, the advantage—of narrative being overwhelmed by spectacle or events being overwhelmed by autonomous images. All this will occur to the extent that these strategies encourage viewing a film in the spectacular mode. But it is equally necessary to recognize that this mode of spectatorship is not always attributable to what might be seen as an intention on the part of the filmmaker. There are cases where the spectator of the work is responsible for the emergence of landscape. This is the second paradigmatic situation noted earlier, to which we now turn before concluding.

*the spectator's landscape, or "impure" landscape*

Even if our goal here is to consider the spectator/landscape relationship in film, it will be useful to return briefly to the history of landscape in painting. Among other things, this will provide a better justification for my refusal to consider the presence of landscape in film on the basis of formal considerations alone.

Indeed, if we go back to the issues raised by art historians regarding Patinir's work, it should become clear that landscape cannot be defined solely through formal characteristics. For this reason, I have emphasized an interpretive approach: one where both landscape and setting require interpretation. However, such an interpretive bias is neither methodologically nor historically obvious.

On the one hand, as we have seen earlier, Patinir's commentators—whichever side of the debate they find themselves—traditionally look to justify their interpretation through formal characteristics proper to the works themselves (some also take into account the history of ideas and of forms). As I mentioned earlier, those who see Patinir as the first landscape artist initially rest their conviction on the composition of his paintings. In this type of argument, however, "interpretation" tends to be neglected in favour of an "objective" formal (and sometimes historical) analysis that goes together well with certain conceptions of science and knowledge. Yet, by overemphasizing form we risk losing sight of interpretation. On the other hand, it is necessary to recognize that the classical tradition of landscape painting, precisely because it is a tradition and it displays formal habits, *masks* the condition of landscape's existence as *predicate*. In other words, through these habits—whether they are artistic habits (the practice of landscape) or cultural habits (the practice of art criticism)—landscape risks appearing as a given, subjected to the "law" of genre which is now applied by all (artists and critics) without much hesitation. Yet, what the case of Patinir or that of the sixteenth-century Italian connoisseurs Gombrich discusses (and to which I referred earlier) perfectly illustrates is the necessity of *interpreting* the formal characteristics of works. Landscape must be seen as a *sign*; in other words, it must be a way of conceiving (or representing to oneself), seeing, and, therefore, interpreting a pictorial work. *The history of landscape painting is the history of this sign, the history of its various occurrences in the eyes of painters and critics (and other spectators) since the Renaissance.* In a strict sense, this history is not therefore a history of artworks (material things), even though these artworks remain a privileged site for understanding the different manifestations of landscape (especially those depending upon the painter's gaze). In fact, the importance of this clarification is revealed when we turn our attention toward works that have contested status in the history of landscape art. This is the case, for example, with the Flemish paintings mentioned by Gombrich in the passage cited earlier. It is regarding these paintings, which the Venetian collectors of the sixteenth century categorised as landscapes (*paese*), that Gombrich writes: "We do not know if they [the Flemish paintings] were *pure landscapes—probably they were not*—but for the Italian connoisseur they were interesting as landscapes only" (Gombrich, 119; italics added).

Here, Gombrich, as we can see, feels the obligation of discussing two kinds of landscape: the "pure" landscape and the Italian *paese* which one could by way of contrast name "impure" landscape. Why create this distinction? Apparently, Gombrich wants to make his readers understand that the *paese* of the Venetian collectors does not match, *in terms of its form*, the landscape painting that became "institutionalized" as a genre in the seventeenth century and whose history is usually confused with that of the artworks that fall under its banner. The confusion, at first glance, is inconsequential, as least when artworks unequivocally show the painter's gaze to be one that is formative for landscape. However, and here is the rub, replacing the gaze—the sign—with the artworks which exhibit occurrences of it leads to the adoption of an exclusively formal and reifying approach. On principle, this approach excludes the *paese* or "impure" landscape both from its field of reference and from its (generic) definition of landscape. Now, Gombrich's discussion establishes that the Italians saw landscape where others—including the Flemmish artists who painted the works—saw something else. Thus, it is clear that we cannot reduce landscape to its "pure" institutional form. Furthermore, this is why the history of painting should make room for paintings that will be seen (or interpreted) as landscapes even if these paintings do not correspond formally to "pure" landscape. In these paintings, it is the spectator's gaze which makes the natural space autonomous, transforms it into landscape, and relegates the other pictorial elements to the margin. And all this regardless of the painter's verifiable intentions regarding the landscape. To summarize, "pure" landscape is the object of a consensus among painters and spectators so strong we establish it as an institutional and generic "law," forgetting that interpretation underpins it. Conversely, the space of "impure landscape" directly stresses its ambiguity through the different interpretations and different uses to which we subject it.

Finally, even though Gombrich is not as convincing when it comes to identifying the sundry factors that have determined the "gaze" of "impure" landscape (his explanations, as interesting as they are, neglect the cultural, scientific, and economic transformations of the Renaissance mentioned earlier), he does suggest its influence on "pure" landscape and even goes so far as to see the genre as originating with it. Furthermore, he claims that this genre, once established, would become the source of our "landscaping gaze" (our sensibility to landscape) in the world: "Thus, while it is usual to represent the 'discovery of the world' as the underlying motive for the development of landscape painting, we are almost tempted to reverse the formula and assert the priority of landscape painting over landscape 'feeling'" (119). It is as if by first directing his gaze toward the paintings' margins, toward the *parergon*, western modern man succeeded in developing a feeling for landscape.[44]

After four centuries of development, landscape today constitutes a cultural habit and a sensibility revealing itself not only in our capacity to see real landscapes *in situ*, but also in our capacity to bring a "landscaping gaze" to bear on images that do not immediately derive from the genre (e.g., obviously, filmic images). In these cases, it is the cultural context that makes it possible to direct the "landscape gaze" onto the narrative spaces of fiction films despite the absence of strategies or intentions to make them autonomous. It rests on the spectator to assure the movement from setting to landscape and, when possible, to make the space autonomous by interrupting for a moment its connection to the narrative. Landscape appears when, rather than following the action, I turn my gaze toward space and contemplate it in and of itself. This is cinema's "impure" landscape, whose existence we cannot clearly attribute to a director's intention. If certain formal traits encourage its emergence (e.g., the long shot or the extreme long shot), these cannot be described as rules or fixed norms: they depend on factors which vary from one spectator to another; they also vary with the spectator's degree of interest in the narrative (or a particular moment in the narrative) or their sensibility for certain kinds of landscape (mountains, the sea, forests, the plains of the American West, etc.) filtered through their pictorial culture. This is landscape's principal mode of existence in cinema and it plays an important role in our experience of films.[45]

Dominique Chateau writes that: "Not only is it rare [that landscapes] appear without narrative necessity, but even their principal function proceeds from this necessity. Moreover, this function is secondary in terms of the narrative. In general, landscape isn't a sufficient function."[46] If we consider the question from the point of view of the films themselves (which is to say if we adopt a point of view which privileges immanence) this is quite true. We can cite, for example, the films John Ford shot in Monument Valley, such as *My Darling Clementine* (1946) or *The Searchers* (1956), for which Chateau's discussion would be entirely appropriate and where, at first glance, the space is formally subordinate to the story. But such a perspective neglects the multiple ways the spectator can use a film and, by extension, the predicative (or interpretive) aspect of landscape (as a result of which it constitutes a representation). As every fan of Ford (or the Western) knows, Monument Valley—Ford country *par excellence*—has been the object of much commentary.[47] For example, in *Géographies du Western*, J. Mauduy and G. Henriet see this "harmonious, immutable and gigantic setting, capable of enclosing the quest of the Fordian heroes in the midst of gigantic murals and pillars that unite the earth and the sky"[48] as a universal "archetype" (65) and a "cliché" (67). It is a universal "mystery" (69)

48

as well as a "tragic setting nothing like the conventional geography of the West and that recalls ancient tragedy in its abstraction" (69). Such commentary testifies, if only by its existence, to the ability of spectators to contemplate the filmic space and to bring out landscape by looking at it with an autonomising gaze. This way of gazing at images of the natural world (whether they be Ford's or someone else's), the sensibility that it attests to, is the source of our desire to speak of them, to analyze and interpret them either with regard to the qualities they exhibit on their own or in the way that we project them onto the narrative in order to connect them with themes or symbolic concerns, that is, to find some meaning in them that goes way beyond their narrative function as setting.

The case of Ford is all the more interesting because one finds with him certain ambiguities in his use of Monument Valley. Ford used this panorama nine times, beginning with *Stagecoach* (1939). Straddling the border between Utah (to the north) and Arizona (to the south), Ford constantly distorts its actual geography: in *Stagecoach*, for example, Monument Valley is used to stand for southern Arizona and southern New Mexico; in *My Darling Clementine*, he puts Tombstone there, though the city is actually situated in southern Arizona; in *The Searchers*, Ford uses Monument Valley to represent Texas. Of course, it is common knowledge that a director need not respect the natural geography. That said, Monument Valley is an easily identifiable setting and is recognizable from film to film despite representing different diegetic spaces in each film. Its recurrence thus creates an unusual situation which strongly risks pushing the spectator of Ford's films to arrest their gaze on the space despite its strong diegetic incorporation in each of the films and the absence of formal strategies to render it autonomous. Moreover, the decision to set the action of *The Searchers* in Monument Valley leads to more than referential and geographic incoherencies. Indeed, in the film, the settlers (including Aaron Edwards, the brother of the hero) have established their farm and cattle on Texan soil. But Monument Valley—which here represents the diegetic place—is a desert! As a result, what is plausible in the script and on the level of the diegetic space (Texas) is no longer plausible in the image. Evidently, Ford was ready to risk implausibility in order to set his film's action in Monument Valley. So, why speak of the "impure" landscape in such a case? Don't these comments imply Ford's interest in the natural space having a level of autonomy from the story? As a result, isn't the story subservient to the space and to the landscape, not the other way around? To say it another way, isn't this the undeniable sign of his intention to show us landscape rather than mere setting? But rather than a clear response, what these questions bring out is the ambiguity of Monument Valley in Ford's films. Thus, despite the desire to respond affirmatively to these three questions, it is important to recognize that such a claim does violence to the way that numerous (most?) spectators watch *The Searchers*. For instance, how many of them have noted the absence of pastures and the resulting implausibility? Yet, to the extent that Ford avoids, from a formal point of view, the strategies of autonomization (such as *temps morts*, extra-diegetic or displaced landscape inserts, etc.) it falls to the spectator to bring about the emergence of landscape—as is the case in front of Patinir's canvases. Simply stated, the landscape of Monument Valley in *The Searchers* is not a given—it is a predication of space which requires interpretive work on the part of the spectator.

The analogy between Flemish art of the sixteenth century and John Ford will perhaps surprise those who see from the start formal correspondences between Ford's use of Monument Valley (or other natural spaces of the West) and the paintings or illustrations of the "far west." After all, don't Ford's long shots of the desert resemble certain western landscapes as painted by Frederic Remington or Alfred Jacob Miller, or photographed by E. S. Curtis? We know, from elsewhere, that Ford is aware of this corpus of work. But it is important to clearly understand the difference between Ford and Curtis. *Indeed, although the painters, illustrators, and photographers of the West produced works within the well-established genre of pictorial landscape, Ford's films participate in a cinematic narrative genre: the Western.* This difference implies a different spatial economy and spatial functionality, as I have attempted to demonstrate throughout this chapter. What the experience of landscape in Ford's films underscores is the need for those spectators for whom certain filmic shots appear analogous to landscape paintings to rely on their pictorial culture and on the landscape sign—or gaze—in order to interpret them. In short, it is not *because* Ford uses the long shot to illustrate a cavalcade in the desert that we invoke landscape to account for the experience we have of the desert. That would not suffice. Instead, it is because, for spectators, various shots evoke the pictorial art of landscape (and its gaze), which serves as a *mediation* between the film and the landscape. In other words, it is landscape art which makes certain spectators work in the spectacular mode when they could just as well remain in the narrative mode. The painting effect, unlike when a canvas is cited, no longer needs to be interpreted as the result of the director's intention (although it remains an option). Finally, when you think about it, there is a curious circularity here which permits us to distinguish the Italian connoisseurs of the sixteenth century from Ford's spectators. If, as Gombrich suggests, the "pure" landscape later institutionalized as a pictorial genre began as "impure" landscape, it is clearly this "pure" landscape which is in large part responsible for the "impure" landscape of cinema! But this circularity is not paradoxical insofar as landscape as pictorial genre only renders manifest the landscape gaze (which makes the genre possible) in the institution of pictorial art (which, as I have explained, includes but is not reducible to the artworks themselves). This gaze has not been institutionalized in the work of fiction film directors. We know why: landscape is not, and would not be, a cinematic genre in the same sense as the Western or the gangster film. This does not however prevent the landscape gaze from manifesting itself in the spectator's activity.

Consequently, we would not write, as do David Bordwell and Kristin Thompson in their introductory textbook for film studies, *Film Art*, that the long shot or extreme long shot is, in cinema, "the framing for landscapes."[49] If this type of framing offers a view which tends to predispose the spectator to conceive a landscape because of the distance which separates the camera from the filmed object, we ought to avoid seeing this framing as the principal "cause" of this conception. On the one hand, it is necessary to note that what works for landscape works equally well for anything likely to occupy a large space. Examples include, among others, the battle scenes in *Birth of a Nation* (Griffith, 1914) and in numerous Westerns, the chariot race in *Ben Hur* (Wyler, 1959), the crowd scenes in *October* (Eisenstein, 1928), or the procession in *Ivan the Terrible* (Eisenstein, 1943). Therefore, it is not simply landscape that can benefit from long shots; representation of action and of events can also be shown by them. On the other hand, and in a more important way, the discussion of Bordwell and Thompson links the landscape back to formal traits without worrying about the interpretation of these traits. A cinematic view of an exterior space would no more constitute a landscape at first glance than a painting would. But, that said, what is produced when, instead of following the battle raging on the plains and which is clearly the object of the camera's gaze, my own gaze embraces the space and makes landscape emerge in my consciousness? From the evidence of moments where the natural space and story components (e.g., the action) exist side by side, it appears obvious that the long shot is an insufficient condition for the emergence of the cinematic landscape. *The first condition is elsewhere, in the spectator's gaze, which is to say, in their cultural knowledge and their sensibility.*

## concluding remarks

Landscape, we have seen, is a representation of space. It is a form of spatial predicate. Another way of saying it would be to say that landscape is a *form of being* of external space in our minds. This representation, or sign, manifests itself in different ways. It manifests itself in the way that human beings visually apprehend some stretch of real space; in the way that they have of apprehending the space depicted in pictorial works of art; and in the way that some of these works have of "translating" this sign into specific pictorial compositions. In the domain of art, landscape is not so much the result of a work; rather, it is the work itself which is the result of the landscape. Thus, landscape manifests itself in an interpretive gaze. More specifically, it manifests itself in the attempts by artists to translate this gaze into their work and by spectators to either interpret this translation or provide their own interpretive landscape gaze. In this chapter, we have seen that these semiotic strategies can work in the cinema and that they pertain both to spectatorship (especially through what I have called the "spectacular mode") and to a dual form of temporality (that of the film medium and the spectator's activity).

Let us now return briefly to this temporal aspect to better define its implications. Landscape in the cinema, as we know, requires that space acquire some autonomy from narrative. As we have seen, this is a likely result of the use of *temps morts* which, notwithstanding the name, often has consequences on our experience of space as well. Thus, despite the continued movement of the film through the projector and the passage of screen time, we have the impression in such moments that time itself (the film, the story) is arrested in order to deliver to our view a space. Now, a roughly similar effect is produced when the spectator's "landscape gaze" seizes what otherwise is merely a setting for the narrative: the spectator mentally arrests the unfolding of the film and internally holds the space for contemplation until returning to the narrative mode. Of course, it would be impossible to quantify this "internal *temps morts*." But its felt presence certainly renders useless any attempt at conceptualising film spectating on the sole ground of projection time (the time that it takes for the film to run through the projector). Roland Barthes, though with a different purpose in mind, recognized so much when, influenced by Eisenstein, he called for a theory of photograms (or film frames) in cinema in order to understand that which escapes the fixed temporality of both the film's transport through the projector and of narrative. "The photogram," wrote Barthes, "by instituting a reading which is at once instantaneous and vertical disregards logical time (which is only an operative time); it teaches us to dissociate technical constraint (the 'filming') from the authentically filmic, which is the 'indescribable' meaning."[50] This is not to say, however, that film landscape belongs to what Barthes calls "obtuse meaning," nor is it to imply that it need be cast in photogrammatic terms; it merely signals instead the need to grasp the emergence of landscape outside of narrative, outside of what Barthes considered to be the "informative" or communicational level of the film, and therefore as something which—*like* obtuse meaning—functions *somewhat freely* from projection and diegetic time.

52

Finally, while a great deal more remains to be said about landscape in cinema (the purpose of this essay was merely to investigate some of its conditions of emergence), it is necessary to recognize that "setting" and "landscape" are not the only predicates which account for our experience of either real or depicted space. While setting concerns narrative representation, and landscape aesthetic representation, it is equally possible to represent space in more "anthropological" terms. Indeed, space may be represented as pertaining to lived experiences other than narrative or aesthetic. This is the case, for instance, with "identity" and "belonging" and the myriad ways of engaging with space that both can entail (defending it against invaders, for example). This is where the notion of "territoriality," of space represented as a territory, becomes useful. For territory is space seen from the "inside," a subjective and lived space. This sort of space is associated more with cartographers, geographers, conquerors, hunters, but also with farmers or anyone inhabiting or having a claim on a stretch of land, than it is with the artist (although they are not mutually exclusive). When the geographer writes, "Landscape is anchored in *human life*, not something to look at but to live in, and to live in socially. Landscape is a *unity* of people and environment which opposes in its reality the false dichotomy of man and nature.... Landscape is to be judged as a *place for living and working* in terms of those who actually do work and live there. All landscapes are *symbolic*" (Cosgrove, 35),[51] he returns the landscape to its territoriality. Indeed, beyond the study of the morphology of a region, geographers, especially cultural geographers, now describe landscape as a set of relations which are woven between human beings and the land: agriculture, hunting, fishing, navigation and shipping, forestry, etc. These relations are themselves reliant on vast economic and political stakes and possess otherwise imaginary and identifying aspects whose importance cannot be overstated. When these relations describe the ways one has of inhabiting the land, owning it, fighting for it, or working on it, the land tends to be represented in terms of territory. Territoriality, in other words, becomes the dominant predicate. Hence Swiss geographer Claude Raffestin defines territoriality as "the 'sum' [in the sense of totality] of the relations maintained by a subject [or a collectivity] with *their* environment."[52] The definition has the advantage of illustrating the "possessive" character of territory which contrasts with the experience that one can make of space in terms of aesthetic contemplation.

Indeed, possession is not a required trait for representing space as a landscape, insofar as we understand it in aesthetic terms; whereas it is required when space is represented as "territory." That landscape and territory imply different modes of relation to the spatial environment, different ways of representing it, may be further evidenced by the work of E. T. Hall who defined territory—at least, in some of its important aspects—through proxemics.[53] Of course, any single stretch of land may at any point be represented as a setting, a landscape, and a territory. These semiotic divisions are not exclusive and there may even be cases of contamination between them. For instance, echoing the work of Jay Appleton,[54] French geographer Yves Lacoste has observed that, in the West at least, what are said to be the most "beautiful" landscapes tend also to be the ones that are the most advantageous for tactical and military purposes, that is, for defending or conquering a territory.[55] If Lacoste is correct, then what I've been calling the "landscape gaze" can easily overlap with a more territorial gaze, such as that of the military. According to

Lacoste, both the "aesthetic gaze" and the "tactical gaze" share a common investment in observation and in panoramic views. There is no reason, therefore, why "landscape" and "territory" could not coexist as predicates for representing the same portion of space. Whatever representation is privileged at any given moment will depend on such pragmatic considerations as the observer's relation to the land and how the observation is to be used (e.g., aesthetic enjoyment vs. an attack plan). This connection between landscape and territory can also be examined by looking at the relations that exist between mapmaking and landscape illustrations. Thus, long before the widespread use of maps, the military often used drawings which, though they were meant to serve territorial and tactical purposes, may also be looked at aesthetically; and maps, of course, may equally be used aesthetically or may be integrated into works of art.[56]

As we can imagine, the interconnections between setting, landscape, and territory may at times be quite intricate. Moreover, any depiction of space—in the cinema as elsewhere—may call on any of these representations at any given time and overlap them according to aesthetic, narrative, social, anthropological, or political purposes. However, the three predicates identified here are in no way meant to be exhaustive. The fact is that space is a complex reality that we keep discovering according to the different ways we have of relating to it and of representing it. Unravelling the tangled web of these relations and representations is the best that we can wish for.

## notes

1. See the Introduction to this volume.
2. Anne Cauquelin, *L'Invention du paysage* (Paris: Plon, 1989), 35; hereafter cited in text.
3. I use the term here according to its standard logical and grammatical meaning.
4. Among others: Noel Burch, *Theory of Film Practice*, trans. Helen R. Lane (Princeton: Princeton University Press, 1981); David Bordwell, *Narration in the Fiction Film* (Madison: University of Wisconsin Press, 1985); André Gardies, *L'Espace au cinéma* (Paris: Méridiens Klincksieck, 1993); and Stephen Heath, "Narrative Space," in *Questions of Cinema* (Bloomington: Indiana University Press, 1981), 19–75.
5. Kenneth Clark, *Landscape into Art, New Edition* (London: John Murray, 1976), 229.
6. Christopher Wood, *Albrecht Altdorfer and the Origin of Landscape* (Chicago: Chicago University Press, 1993), 9; hereafter cited in text.
7. Albrecht Dürer, *Journal de voyage aux Pays-Bas pendant les années 1520–1521* (Paris: Editions Maisonneuve et Larose, 1993), 52.
8. See Maj. J. Friedländer, *Landscape, Portrait, Still-Life: Their Origin and Development* (New York: Schocken Books, 1963), 47; Robert A. Koch, *Joachim Patinir* (Princeton: Princeton University Press, 1968), 48–49.
9. André Piron, *Joachim Le Patinir, Henri Blès: Leurs vrais visages* (Gembloux: J. Duculot, 1971), 19.

10. The most often cited defender of this position is without a doubt the art historian Ludwig von Baldass, "Die niederländische Landschaftsmalerei von Patinir bis Bruegel," *Jahrbuch der Kunsthistorischen Sammlungen in Wein* 34 (1918).

11. Malcolm Andrews, *Landscape and Western Art* (Oxford: Oxford University Press, 1999), 43–44; hereafter cited in text.

12. Reindert L. Falkenburg, *Joachim Patinir: Landscape as an Image of the Pilgrimage of Life* (Amsterdam/Philadelphia: John Benjamins, 1988), 2–3.

13. Jacques Derrida, *La vérité en peinture* (Paris: Flammarion, 1978), 69.

14. Ernst Gombrich, "The Renaissance Theory of Art and the Rise of Landscape," in *Norm and Form: Studies in the Art of the Renaissance* (London: Phaidon, 1966), 109; hereafter cited in text.

15. Wood, op. cit.

16. In 1989, the Art Gallery of Ontario presented, under the direction of the filmmaker Richard Kerr, a retrospective of experimental landscape films made by Canadian filmmakers. The works are discussed by Bart Testa in the catalogue published for the occasion, *Spirit in the Landscape* (Toronto: Art Gallery of Toronto, 1989). See also chapter 6 in this volume, Catherine Russell's "The Inhabited View: Landscape in the Films of David Rimmer."

17. It would undoubtedly be more accurate, from an historical point of view at least, to say that the cinema *first* offers a visual spectacle. It is in this regard, and not so much as a narrative artefact, that Lumière's cinematographic views were first produced. This may explain the presence of landscape at the start of cinema: in some of the "actualitiés" of the Lumière catalog, some exterior scenes from Edison, the famous "Hale's Tours," and in that popular genre of early cinema described today as "travel films." There is no doubt that early nonfiction cinema landscapes are at the source of the manifestation of landscape in later fiction films. But, as historically accurate as this formulation is, it does not completely do justice to the poetics or the reception of later narrative film, where narrativity is often emphasized over pictorial qualities. Today, of course, through the influence exerted by early cinema research, film scholars are more aware than ever of the *spectacular* aspect of the cinema. See, among others, Tom Gunning, "The Cinema of Attractions: Early Film, Its Spectator and the Avant-Garde," *Wide Angle* 8, nos. 3-4 (1986); Tom Gunning, "An Aesthetics of Astonishment: Early Film and the (In)Credulous Spectator," in *Viewing Positions: Ways of Seeing Film*, ed. Linda Williams (New Brunswick: Rutgers University Press, 1995a), hereafter cited in text; Tom Gunning, "The Whole World within Reach: Travel Images without Borders" in *Cinéma sans frontières/Images Across Borders*, eds. Roland Cosandey and François Albera (Lausanne and Québec: Editions Payot Lausanne et Nuit Blanche Editeur, 1995b), hereafter cited in text; Charles Musser, *The Emergence of Cinema. The American Screen to 1907, Vol. I: History of the American Cinema* (New York: Scribners, 1990); Charles Musser, "The Travel Genre in 1903–1904: Moving Towards Fictional Narrative," *Iris* 2, no. 1 (1984); and, in this volume, chapter 10 by Antonio Costa, "Landscape and Archive: Trips Around the World as Early Film Topic (1896–1914)" and chapter 9 by David B. Clarke and Marcus A. Doel, "From Flatland to Vernacular Relativity: The Genesis of Early English Screenscapes."

18. "The presence of woman is an indispensable element of spectacle in normal narrative film, yet her visual presence tends to work against the

story-line, to freeze the flow of action in moments of erotic contemplation." Laura Mulvey, "Visual Pleasure and Narrative Cinema," in *Visual
and Other Pleasures* (Bloomington: Indiana University Press, 1989), 19. Raymond Bellour, we recall, arrived at a similar conclusion in his analysis of a sequence from Howard Hawks's *The Big Sleep.* Raymond Bellour,
"L'évidence et le code," in *L'Analyse du film* (Paris: Albatros, 1979).

19. See Paul Ricoeur, *Temps et recit, Tome II* (Paris: Seuil, 1984). See also chapters
1 and 2 of my book *Psycho: de la figure au musée imaginaire. Théorie et pratique de
l'acte de spectature* (Montréal and Paris: L'Harmattan, 1998), 71–110.

20. It might seem pleonastic to say that spectatorial activity possesses a "spectacular mode" (*spectare*: to watch). The point is merely to emphasize that
aspect of spectatorship which consists precisely in accessing the images
(and sounds) of the cinematographic spectacle "on their own" and "for
their own sake." What I call here the "spectacular mode" knows at least
two variations: (1) shock, which may pertain to either disgust or attraction (the comments of Eisenstein in this regard are well-known; but this
was also, as Tom Gunning has rightly stressed, a spectatorial disposition
available to early film spectators, as well as viewers of avant-garde cinema in general, and of current blockbuster postmodern films); and (2)
contemplation. See Tom Gunning, 1986, 1995a, 1995b; Sergei Eisenstein,
"The Montage of Attractions" and "The Montage of Film Attractions" in
*S. M. Eisenstein. Selected Works, Volume I, Writings 1922–1934,* ed. Richard Taylor (London: BFI, 1988). Finally, it may be worthwhile to add that these
*modes* of spectatorship are distinguished from the *processes* of spectatorship
described in my book *Psycho: de la figure au musée imaginaire. Théorie et pratique de
l'acte de spectature, op. cit.,* 19–70.

21. P. Adams Sitney stresses the effect of this temporality, proper to the
medium on the filmic landscape: "The use of sublime landscapes often
coincides with spectacular meteorological displays. Cinema was the
first art that could represent the temporality and rhythm of a storm."
P. Adams Sitney, "Landscape in the Cinema: The Rhythms of the World
and the Camera," in *Landscape, Natural Beauty and the Arts,* eds. Salim Kemal
and Ivan Gaskell (Cambridge: Cambridge University Press, 1993), 112.

22. The contemplation of landscape is facilitated here by the *mise-en-scène,*
the muteness of the characters (we have to wait about 10 seconds before
Nora addresses herself to her cousin), the fixed position of the camera
(throughout the scene, the camera only makes two very slight reframings), the restrained physical action and slowness of the scene, and the
accompanying music played *largo.*

23. It belongs, in fact, to the tradition of the "outdoor conversation piece," a
very popular subgenre for British landscape paintings during the eighteenth century.

24. Among numerous other examples that we could cite, I would mention
Peter Greenaway's *The Draughtsman's Contract* (1982), where the pictorial
"intertext" (the artist's drawings) works *intratextually.* I use this term to
stress the fact that the pictorial works—the landscapes—which refer
us back and are almost identical to views shown by the camera, do not
independently preexist the film. The effect on the filmic landscape is
nevertheless identical. Indeed, the landscape drawings and corresponding film shots are juxtaposed and cite each other mutually, which
results in assisting the spectator to translate into landscape some of the
film's settings. It may be worthwhile to mention also that the drawings,

56

which are produced in the diegesis by Mr. Neville (the name, at least for a French-speaking viewer like myself, might suggest a negation of urban life and, therefore, a possible attachment to nature instead), are in reality drawn by Peter Greenaway who, as director, is also responsible for shooting the same viewpoints in the film.

25. In the case of this example, the fact that the character is shown from the back has the effect of directing the spectator's gaze toward the landscape proper.

26. Pascal Bonitzer, *Décadrages. Peintures et cinéma* (Paris: Cahiers du cinéma/ Editions de l'Etoile, 1985), 29–41. "Movement implies that a film isn't a painting, that a shot isn't a painting. And yet, it is through the notion of a shot (of the 'découpage' in time and in space that this notion supposes) that filmmakers can compare themselves to painters" (Bonitzer, 29). Despite the undeniable value of Bonitzer's essay, one can't help notice, however, that he never questions the status of the film shot nor how the spectator can relate to it in time (i.e., in relation to the shot's duration). Indeed, we can imagine cases where only a portion of a shot's duration will be deemed "painterly" by the viewer whose mode of reception can shift between the spectacle and narrative modes.

27. Van Gogh painted the Langlois Bridge in Arles in March 1888 and the fields of wheat with the crows in Auvers in July 1890.

28. The bridge we see is evidently a film set. The original was destroyed in 1926. During the 1960s, an identical replica was discovered at Fos and transported to Arles. It is found in the area south of the city.

29. The soundtrack also recalls *The Birds* by its use of electronic sounds for the crows' caws.

30. Some of these formal traits are typical stylistic characteristics of cinematic modernity such as it manifested itself especially in Europe beginning in the 1960s. I will return later to the relationship between modernity and landscape.

31. These are also called "cutaway shots." For his part, Barry Salt uses the terms "atmospheric insert," which he defines as: "A shot of a location in which actors do not appear," in *Film Style and Technology: History and Analysis*, 2nd ed. (London: Starword, 1992), 320. According to Salt, it is mostly after the 1920s that this sort of shot appears more frequently in narrative film.

32. Kenneth Clark, *Landscape into Art* (London: John Murray, 1976), 231. .

33. Denis Cosgrove, *Social Formation and Symbolic Landscape* (Madison: University of Wisconsin Press, 1998), 64; hereafter cited in text. In the introductory essay that accompanies the second edition of this work, Cosgrove offers a self-critique of the first edition that pertains somewhat to the topic at hand. More specifically, he reconsiders the little importance he had initially attached to landscape after the end of the nineteenth century: "In the book I claim that landscape as an active concern for progressive art died in the second half of the nineteenth century, after the last flourish of Romanticism, and that its ideological function of harmonising social-environmental relations through visual pleasure was appropriated by the discipline of Geography. Re-reading these claims, it seems that they derive more from theoretical imperatives associated with the book's thesis than from historical actualities" (Cosgrove, xx).

34. See John Barell, *The Dark Side of Landscape: the Rural Poor in English Painting, 1730–1840* (Cambridge: Cambridge University Press, 1980); Ann Berm-

ingham, *Landscape and Ideology: The English Rustic Tradition, 1740–1860* (Berkeley: University of California Press, 1986).

35. This is perhaps another way of binding landscape to the organizing presence of the director. As David Bordwell observes, from a narratological point of view: "Typically, the opening and closing of [a] film are the most self-conscious, omniscient and communicative passages. The credit sequence and the first few shots bear traces of an overt narration." *Narration in the Fiction Film, op. cit.*, 160.

36. *Teorema* is too well known for a synopsis here. However, it may be worth reminding the reader that this transition between diegetic and "symbolic" spaces occurs only after the father of the family and failed CEO undresses completely in the middle of the Milan train station. The fake match-cut transition shows the man's bare feet as he walks on the station's platform and then on volcanic ground. Naked and stripped of all his bourgeois pretensions, the man recognizes his alienation for the first time: his life is nothing but wandering through a lifeless and arid desert.

37. Antonioni, of course, is usually considered to be an "urban" filmmaker. Some commentators, such as Antonio Costa, even consider his "natural landscapes" to be subservient to his urban gaze: "[with Antonioni] the extra-urban, 'natural' landscape is seen, elaborated, interrogated by the same gaze that sees and interrogates the urban space. The 'natural' landscape and the urban landscape are interchangeable: the first is no different from the second." Antonio Costa, "Le regard du flâneur et le magasin culturel," in *Michelangelo Antonioni 2, 1966/1984*, ed. Lorenzo Cuccu (Rome: Ente Autonomo Gestione Cinema, 1988), 124.

38. Several critics have noted this aspect of Antonioni's cinema. Thus Seymour Chatman writes: "He [Antonioni] has virtually returned to the cinema the predominance of the visual that it lost with the advent of sound," in *Antonioni, or The Surface of the World* (Berkeley: University of California Press, 1985), 89; hereafter cited in text; and Peter Brunette: "it is true that much of Antonioni's effect does come from the visual track of his films (as opposed to dialogue, plot, character, and so on)" in *The Films of Michelangelo Antonioni* (Cambridge: Cambridge University Press, 1998), 30.

39. This will be discussed in the following section.

40. Marie-Claire Ropars, "L'espace et le temps dans la narration des anées 60," in *Michelangelo Antonioni 2, 1966/1984, op. cit.*, 214.

41. It is one of the ironies of the film that, during a lunch conversation with his editor, Thomas describes the photos of the park in the following way: "I've got something 'fab' for the end; in a park…it's very peaceful, very still…. The rest of the book will be pretty violent so I think it's best to end it like that. . . ."

42. W. J. T. Mitchell, "Imperial Landscapes," in *Landscape and Power* (Chicago: University of Chicago Press, 1994), 13.

43. I wish to thank my colleague Rosanna Maule for pointing out to me the role of photography in this allegory of the death of figuration. Indeed, it is well known that the arrival of photography during the latter part of the nineteenth century participated in the development of nonfigurative art to the extent that, for many, it "liberated" painting from the chains of figuration and naturalism. Antonioni's insight is thus revealed not only in the way he profits from the relationship between landscape and abstraction, but equally in his allusion to the historic role of the photograph in the emergence of abstract art.

44. Much has been written regarding this hypothesis. Alain Roger, the French specialist of landscape, has taken it up and conceives of the transformation of space (or land) into landscape as the task of art, what he calls *"artialisation"*: "Nature is indeterminate and only receives its various determinations from art: land only becomes a landscape under the conditions of a landscape, and that, only according to the...modalities...of *artialisation.*" In *Court traité du paysage* (Paris: Gallimard, 1997), 17–18. For a critique of the primacy of art with regards to landscape, see W. J. T. Mitchell, "Imperial Landscapes," *op. cit.*

45. In fact, the role of "impure" landscapes was recognized fairly early on by the film industry. For instance, in 1913, an article in *Variety* reported the criticisms made by European spectators and even cinema owners according to whom American films produced in California too often used the same landscapes. As a result, the author of the article anticipates an exodus of cinema production from southern California! *Variety* 30, no. 13 (1913): 8.

46. Dominique Chateau, "Paysage et décor. De la nature à l'effet de nature," in *Les paysages au cinéma*, ed. Jean Mottet (Seyssel: Champ Vallon, 1999), 97.

47. Not surprisingly, several authors in this volume (Jean Mottet, Maurizia Natali, Jacques Aumont, and Peter Rist) mention Ford and Monument Valley. See also Richard Huston, "Sermons in Stone: Monument Valley in *The Searchers,*" in *The Searchers. Essays and Reflections: John Ford's Classic Western*, ed. Arthur M. Eckstein and Peter Lehman (Detroit: Wayne State University Press, 2004), 93–108.

48. J. Mauduy and G. Henriet, *Géographies du Western* (Paris: Nathan, 1989), 69; hereafter cited in text.

49. David Bordwell and Kristin Thompson, *Film Art. An Introduction, Fourth Edition* (New York: McGraw Hill, 1993), 212.

50. Roland Barthes, "Le troisième sens," in *L'obvie et l'obtus. Essais critiques III* (Paris: Gallimard, 1982), 61.

51. Denis Cosgrove summarizes here the principal characteristics of landscape according to the American geographer J. B. Jackson.

52. Claude Raffestin, *Pour une géographie du pouvoir* (Paris: Librairie technique, 1980), 145, n. 27. Emphasis mine.

53. Edward T. Hall, *The Hidden Dimension* (Garden City, NJ: Doubleday, 1966), 1966.

54. Jay Appleton, *The Experience of Landscape* (London: John Wiley, 1975).

55. See Yves Lacoste, "A quoi sert le paysage? Qu'est-ce qu'un beau paysage," in *La théorie du paysage en France, 1974–1994*, ed. Alain Roger (Seyssel: Champ Vallon, 1995). See also the essay by Jean Mottet in this volume which alludes to Lacoste's essay with regards to the Biograph films of D. W. Griffith and the emergence of landscapes associated with the Western genre.

56. See Edward S. Casey, *Representing Place: Landscape Painting and Maps* (Minneapolis: Minnesota University Press, 2002) and *Earth-Mapping. Artists Reshaping Landscape* (Minneapolis: Minnesota University Press, 2005).

# toward a genealogy of
# the american landscape

three

notes on landscapes in

d. w. griffith (1908–1912)

jean mottet

*translated by martin lefebvre and brian crane*

Most scholars who, for some time now, have worked at renewing the study of early cinema, rightly stress how films are overdetermined by several large formations (ideologies, technologies, modes of representation, economics, etc.). As a result, we have begun to better understand the national character of some of the most important films to ever have been made, at least in the West. Yet, many of the determinants pertaining to the national character of films have not been thoroughly studied with regard to film content and film form. To be sure, narratology, for one, has devoted much attention to the various spectatorial positions specific to early cinema. However, scant attention has been paid to consideration of the formal innovations of early film images and to the sort of aesthetic experience they offer. In particular, we may ask what is the place of nature, of landscape in this aesthetic experience? To start, it is important to keep in mind that what falls under the heading of "the beautiful" for the European tradition is understood by turn of the century America to partly fall under the idea of "the inhabitable," that is, as a particular attitude toward the environment. What characterizes this attitude is the way it attends to the quotidian, the commonplace, the close at hand—especially around the homestead. To fully grasp the idea one might begin with Ralph Waldo Emerson. Here, for example, is what he wrote in 1837 in *The American Scholar*: "The literature of the poor, the feelings of the child, the philosophy of the street, the meaning of household life, are the topics of the time.... I ask not for the great, the remote, the romantic; what is doing in Italy or Arabia; what is Greek art, or Provencal minstrelsy; I embrace the common, I explore and sit at the feet of the familiar, the low."[1] And, in 1845, when Henry David Thoreau leaves the city for the wilderness, he finds refuge in a small cabin that he built on Emerson's land, near Walden Pond, from where he begins to consider new ways of appreciating the environment: the vast open spaces of America must give way to smaller and inhabitable places.

From Thomas Cole to Walt Whitman, American artists have given much importance to the homestead as the spatial and symbolic centre from which to organize the landscape. Landscape representations in early American cinema do not alter this central character, but require that we consider with as much insight as possible this new way of defining inhabitability in all of its diverse manifestations. In the American mentality, to inhabit a place consists of living in a given space for a sufficient amount of time to allow daily rituals the appropriation of a segment of territory. And when the cinema, at the start of the twentieth century, adds its own landscapes to already existing representations, it accelerated both the mobility and the multifarious forms of landscape imagery: images of the savage far west, cluttered big city streets, picturesque nature, modest suburb dwellings, and small towns, etc. In the absence of any overarching design, the constant variety of landscapes gives us the impression of a continuous transformation carried out in a fashion that is closer to ordinary processes of everyday existence than to a conscious invention of landscapes, as was the case with the European tradition. I wish therefore to put forward the hypothesis that the meeting between American landscape imagery and the cinematic apparatus led not only to the emergence of new means for rendering space, but also for thinking about it and making it visible.

## sense of place, figures of domesticity

62

By leaving the cramped Biograph studios to shoot natural exteriors for his first film, *The Adventures of Dolly* (1908), D. W. Griffith seems immediately to give great attention to shooting locations. His wife, Linda Arvidson, wrote that "David Griffith was always fastidious about 'location.' His feeling for charming landscapes and his use of them in movies was a significant factor in the success of his early pictures."[2] This opinion is confirmed by Billy Bitzer who likewise recalls the efforts made by Griffith when choosing the right river setting for *The Adventures of Dolly*: "He came to ask me where there was a river just large enough to carry a child downstream in a barrel. I suggested the Bronx River. Not entirely satisfied, he consulted others; first the Hackensack River was suggested and then Marvin advised him to use Sound Beach, Connecticut."[3]

Curiously, though, rather than exploiting such vast open spaces, Griffith instead set about to explore their immediate surroundings, exploring the close at hand, setting new spatial limits, and emphasizing specific fragments of the landscape; he forges *loci* in an otherwise vast undifferentiated *spatium*. As Martin Heidegger taught us, one does not carve spaces into specific settings, places, or pieces of landscape; instead, "it is the place that establishes progressively a finite, limited, and inhabitable space, permitting us to answer the question: Where are we?"[4] As a result, the surest way to create a sense of belonging to a place, of defining a landscape—understood as a part of nature extracted from the continuity of the natural world—is to concretely represent spatial limits such as a gate, hedge, river, or low wall, all of which are therefore the opposite of mere props or window dressing.[5]

From this point of view, *The Adventures of Dolly* (a 713-feet film consisting of 13 shots) is exemplary in that its coherence lies in good measure in the way Griffith establishes space through a series of small *loci*. Starting with the second shot, a pathway and low wall running along the river bank create a sense of depth that implies that the space will be used theatrically. But is this really the most important aspect of this space? Shouldn't we also look at the setting more closely? For example, in the background, a house barely emerges from the wooded area that skirts the river. Without entering here into a detailed discussion of the status of this background, I would say that it cannot be reduced, as in the theatre, to a mere backdrop. Once the house is perceived, a connection of a conceptual nature establishes itself between it, the river, pathway, and low wall: all these constitute as many primary forms and boundaries binding together in a stable fashion the various components of the environment, transforming the whole into an inhabited place and immobilizing time through space. Even the tall tree beside the road seems affected by this constellation of inhabitability that consumes the various elements of its surroundings: solidly rooted it also appears to participate in this overall spatial reconfiguration. In short, the setting being represented here is a place of intimacy resting squarely on the ground (notice the complete absence of the sky). Even the long and central segment where Dolly, trapped in a barrel, floats downstream in the river is not without connection to this spatial stability. In fact, Dolly's predicament only appears meaningful against it. The contrast between the free flow of the liquid element—a nondomesticated matter as underscored by the danger of the waterfalls toward which the girl is driven—and the controlled firmness and solidity of terrestrial elements tends to accentuate plasticity over theatricality and narrative. It opposes a visual figuration of domesticity to one of wandering (let us not forget that Dolly was kidnapped from her home by Bohemians).

The importance Griffith grants, in this short film, to the representation of a house surrounded by an intimate space can also be found in many other of his Biograph pictures, though they sometimes offer interesting variations in scale. For one thing, the overall represented space of many of these films tends to be more limited in scope. As a result, Griffith introduces the image of the home bordered by the famous picket fence, an emblematic image that the filmmaker will use, with slight variations, throughout the period and that will resurface in his feature films such as *The Birth of a Nation* (1915). Clearly, objective depiction of space is not as important here as the imaginary aspects such representation can accommodate, the most notable being its capacity to fold itself or withdraw into *tucked-away refuges*. Of course, many others, from John Ford to David Lynch (with his admirable *Blue Velvet*) have since made use of the emblematic picket fence image. But does this mean that the setting in question is really insignificant, only constituting mere backdrop for the actors' bodies and faces? What first strikes me, I would say, in this recurring figure of Griffith's Biograph days is the way that it points to the importance taken by the homestead, or more precisely, by some of its constitutive parts. Most often, the house is only a façade, a simple section of wall, framed with a bit of its surroundings: a small yard, shrubs, walkway, hedges, etc. In such a space, the domestic setting, even when reduced to its most simple expression, suffices to transform space into "place." Even the most destitute of characters in the Biograph shorts manage to keep some degree of privacy, an element of what constitutes a habitat. Within these defined, bordered, and delimited spaces, movements and gestures multiply themselves; entrances and exits abound. Griffith's camera allows us to see the various comings and goings as they explore the fabric of specific places; we run along the hedges, push against the barriers, cross the thresholds. These repetitive trajectories are not, however, insignificant stock gestures. In fact, I believe that, in addition to studying the more spectacular ways in which bodies may occupy space (for instance, the often studied burlesque body), it is crucial that we also take into account how actions taking place in ordinary, quotidian, routine, and otherwise banal locations are visualized and represented. Indeed, we need to consider what it is that gives them meaning, what J.-F. Lyotard has called the "comings and goings of preservation" ("*les allers et venues de la conservation*").[6] Theatrical melodrama in both Europe and the United States had already represented these small movements in and around the house[7]; but here, in Griffith, they confront a natural, outdoor setting. This changes everything. Not yet "landscapes" in the proper sense, Griffith's outdoor scenes represent nonetheless the beginning of a transition toward the external world, a first cinematic staging of the immensity of the natural world in America.

Now, such extreme attention to the details of place, to what lies close by, does not suggest withdrawal but rather is tied to a movement that leads from habitat to landscape. Unlike the paintings of Edward Hopper, for instance, where the picture frame usually defines a contested space only precariously extracted from a disquieting landscape momentarily pushed aside to the edge, Griffith's boundaries—whether it is the framing or the boundaries provided by the filmed environment (hedge, low wall, gate)—almost never open onto a disquieting space. Rather, Griffith seems to anticipate Frank Lloyd Wright's efforts to "break out from the architectural box." As we shall see later this is well evidenced by another Biograph film, *The Country Doctor* (1909), shot in Connecticut, the cradle ground for the American conception of the pastoral landscape.

Exteriors in Griffith's Biograph films are often used brilliantly. But is this sufficient to allow us to speak of them as landscapes? After all, not all exteriors constitute landscapes. Certainly Griffith's forsaking of the theatrical arch enables the view to pull back so as to embrace a broader portion of space. Yet, to be a landscape, the space must be organized into a coherent unit. "If there can be no landscape without distance," as Michel Collot writes in a study of landscape in poetry, "it is because distance allows objects to be grouped by the gaze."[8] Distance, in short, creates unity. The various natural elements being depicted in a landscape must organize into a coherent—or even autonomous—group, even if this means ruining the otherwise natural homogeneity of the *spatium*. Moreover, doesn't the procedure also require a temporal aspect? Indeed, how can we expect the "near" and the "far" to be reconciled without awakening in us a memory, say that of a myth?

### the pastoral myth

*The Adventures of Dolly* marks the first appearance of a bucolic setting in Griffith's work. It is possible that this sort of setting resulted simply from the nature of the actual exteriors where the film was shot. But this is unlikely. Indeed, the film's location is not some undifferentiated and insignificant stretch of land, subjected to the vagaries of sheer indifference. Instead, it presents itself as the disclosure of a specific form of landscape. A shooting location chosen with so much care and attention to detail must surely display more than what it offers to the sense of sight alone. Thus, on one hand, a film such as *The Adventures of Dolly* may give the viewer the impression of watching a documentary-like depiction of the sort of homestead that was becoming widespread in New York state at the beginning of the last century. But as true as this may be it misses the essential point. For, on the other hand, the pastoral charm that emanates from the film's location is such that it turns it into a quasi-symbolic imaginary setting.

But there is another prominent aspect to the places Griffith chooses to represent which concerns their role in the formation of a social environment. The first scenes of the film show the home's surroundings: far from the city, Dolly and her parents live in a country setting that reflects a distinct way of life and seeks to strike a balance between natural and human environments. As a result, the film emphasizes the transformation of nature into controlled, useful, and intimate spaces and presents the environment and the home in proprietary terms (which the surroundings frame as an image of social status). For many spectators of that period—immigrants imprisoned in urban ghettos, disoriented, detached from both their native countries and from nature, and cut off from the landscapes that had imperishably imprinted themselves upon their memories during childhood but to which most would never return—this was, without a doubt, an idyllic setting. But what exactly were they expecting? How did their need for nature interact with the unpredictability of such imaginary encounters? To which notion of landscape were these viewers gaining access?

Tom Gunning has shown that the central value awarded by turn of the century America to rural experience was tied to both a powerful political mythology and a long-standing literary tradition.[9] This phenomenon is all the more important because Americans, unlike Europeans, often contemplated turning dreams into concrete reality. Despite this fact, however, the American pastoral myth developed chiefly on fictional and imaginary grounds, and with close ties to the past. Although viscerally attached to the *idea* of a return to nature, Americans never entertained the possibility of such a return as a reality; their imagination was above all the offshoot of an urban attitude toward nature. By the time pastoral visions came to fully manifest themselves in Griffith's work, most notably in *The Message* (1909), the importance of the pastoral myth was growing in America as a result of the migration of country folk to urban centres. As Richard Hofstadter notes: "The faster the farmers' sons left for the city, the more nostalgic the culture became for its rural past."[10]

Under these circumstances, an intensification of the social role of fiction was inevitable and cinema's use of bucolic landscapes became tied up with a quest for identity. Gunning insists on the originality of Griffith's version of the pastoral myth, especially in *The Message*. He finds it "different from other American films of the period treating the pastoral theme," all the while conceding that other similar films had likely been produced at the same time (1982, 76). This being said, it seems to me that the originality of Griffith's pastoral images must also be evaluated in relation to certain components of the bucolic landscape which by that time had already been put in place in art and literature.

One of the novelties of the American tradition can be considered to be the early development of a conception of intermediate landscapes, what Leo Marx calls the *middle landscape*. Marx's views, he himself tells us, are influenced by what he believes to be implicitly stated in J. Hector St. John de Crèvecoeur's famous *Letters of an American Farmer* (1782).[11] Thus, while Crèvecoeur never mentions Arcadia or the Good Shepherd and never explicitly opposes the countryside to the city, all the themes of the pastoral are found in his writings in new forms furnished by the American experience: "Instead of Arcadia, we have the wild yet potentially bucolic terrain of the North American continent; instead of the shepherd, the independent, democratic husbandman, with his plausible 'rural scheme';…and instead of generalized allusions to the contrast between country and town, Crèvecoeur begins to explore the difference between American and European cultures."[12] Distrusting abstract ideas, Crèvecoeur considers the landscape "as an object that penetrates the mind, filling it with irresistible pictures of human possibilities…. Just to see this virgin terrain is to absorb the rudiments of a new consciousness, the American 'philosophy'" (Marx, 110).[13]

It is easy to see why the image of an idyllic agrarian community became one of the dominant symbols of seventeenth-century America. Here, the pastoral takes on a significance that far exceeds the slightly static notion of a paradise lost inherited by the literary tradition. Leaving behind the general feeling of nostalgia inherent to that tradition, Americans introduced the pastoral theme into a new set of concerns, namely of how a nation provides for itself new images, new concepts at the moment of a grand new beginning. This is a sociological and ideological phenomenon not without consequence for later representations of landscape in America.

*landscape and moral vision*

The landscape depicted in *The Message* typifies Griffith's way of describing nature for much of his Biograph period: a house (a farm in this case) perched on the side of a hill, a lake in the distance, a country road edged by a low wall, some trees and sheep in a rolling meadow: all of the signs of a countryside haven are brought together. While not comparable to the pictorial articulation of classical landscapes, the modest composition does, however, make several overlapping planes visible in the image; and in the foreground, certain details (the low stone wall, the gate) manage to hold our attention until characters enter the scene.

What makes the stone wall and the gate so compelling? Must the ideal landscape include visible confines and limits and reproduce the scope of the eyes' reach over a controlled nature? To be sure, in New England, where the film was shot, the stone wall has been a part of the natural landscape ever since colonial times. On their arrival in the region at the beginning of the seventeenth century, the early colonists found whole

67

areas covered with stones and needed to remove them before they could cultivate the land. Piling them around their plots was probably the least inconvenient solution. But whatever may be the actual origin for this practice, it was continued well into the mid-nineteenth century, and was still a characteristic element of the landscape in several northeast states (New York, Connecticut, Pennsylvania, New Jersey) at the beginning of the twentieth century.

On one hand, Griffith's landscape images stay close to their geographical referent, but on the other hand they also come under a landscape gaze, an ideal vision seeking to reveal a *genius loci*. When a shot cuts away to the landscape, the gaze is most often halted by a hillside, it drifts down, before being lifted toward the distance, all to the reassuring rhythm of gentle slopes. Moreover, Griffith often allows a certain amount of time to pass before the characters arrive or after they leave the shot. Could this be so that the spectator has time to appreciate the landscape? And though this sort of *découpage* predates Griffith, it seems obvious that landscape displays in his work a presence rarely found in pre-Griffith filmmaking. Can we therefore speak of there being a "primacy of nature" or a "natural presence that dominates human passions" in Griffith's work (Gunning, 1982, 80)?

A clear example of what appears to be a case of nature being represented for its own sake can be seen in the fourth shot of *The Message*. The shot opens onto the landscape and briefly holds the view before panning left to reveal David and Effie in an orchard. A similar effect is also achieved with the extremely beautiful camera movement that concludes *The Country Doctor*. Having examined all of its narrative intricacies and ambiguities, Gunning concludes his analysis of the shot by claiming that it "emphasizes [the film's] grim ending and the increased power Griffith invests in filmic discourse" (1991, 218). But the undeniable presence of a narrating agency does not explain away everything. Other elements must also be examined to account for an image as complex as that of the home-as-haven. For the narrative explanation, as legitimate and well grounded as it may be, is too generalizing; it erases too many of the nuances and too much of the charm of the fusion of home and landscape. In fact, the home and its nearby surroundings seem to have been there from time immemorial, and the final image of the film is also that of a quest for a pure space, one unmediated by fiction.

This feeling of immediacy, the feeling that the landscape is observed through a gaze more complicit with nature than with intimacy and forms of mediation must, however, be qualified. Indeed, though certain long shots clearly indicate a distancing of the subject in favour of the observed scene by the very nature of the framing, other shots from *The Message* create a contrary impression, that of an "ideal" landscape. The term "ideal" must be understood here in the sense usually given to it during the seventeenth century, that is to say as offering an impression of calm and balance that stems not so much from what is seen as *from a cultural context emphasizing propriety*. How then are we to describe the diffuse charm that emanates from such a picture? How are we to account for it and to what should we compare it? For it seems obvious by now that all of the elements discussed so far fail us miserably in our endeavour to describe this impression.

Above all, however, we need to stress the particular layout of the Griffithian landscape in that it is never far from being moralizing and allegorical. Hence the familiar Connecticut countryside which is made out to be attractive, peaceful, and practically idyllic. And when characters finally enter into this frame only to move among herds of animals, a truly Arcadian motif emerges from the simple rusticity.[14] David, the landlord, is first seen holding a lamb in his arms; like the shepherd of the classical tradition, he is the true inhabitant of this Arcadian landscape, living in symbiosis with everything around him. When he arrives, the intruder will be a character from the city, as in the literary and pictorial tradition. I'm thinking here of Jacopo Sannazaro's *Arcadia* published in Naples in 1504 or of Titian's famous *Concerto Campestre* (c. 1510), which according to some was directly inspired by Sannazaro.[15] Traditionally, the opposition between the shepherd and the disruptive city dweller—two figures who at the same time attract and oppose one another—resolves itself into harmony. In Griffith's work, however, the opposition is accentuated and dramatized by the montage.[16] Shot 8, for example, which shows David working in the fields, contrasts sharply with shots 7 and 9, where his wife Effie chats with the tenant on the doorstep of the house.

The discrepancy between Griffith's imagery and representations associated with the pastoral tradition manifests itself in other ways as well. For one thing, the living conditions of the countryside, which the film opposes to the various temptations offered by city life, are largely domesticated and rather comfortable. David does not live in a hostile nature world that forces him to struggle in order to survive even though he possesses only the simplest of farm equipment and relies on few of the accessories of modern life (the ability for the shepherd to live with the least material comfort is a constant component of the pastoral myth). In fact, the surrounding countryside is quite welcoming with its agriculture, pathways, and ponds. And because the scene is inspired by the actual landscape of Connecticut, it suggests an Arcadia that is almost true-to-life.[17] Not only were these hills very important locally—Griffith's images depicting a key component of the actual topography—but they also constitute a far from negligible record of a historical moment when the valleys of Connecticut were sheltered from industrialization.[18] And it is in good measure because the landscape is so pristine that it easily lends itself to an imaginary and symbolic reading: the natural order of the countryside is not to be disturbed. Griffith even seems to anticipate a certain environmental protectionism soon to emerge, with his images of rolling hills whose tranquility evokes that of a garden. It is almost as if the emotional engagement of the filmmaker with the landscape was merging with more collective aims. But is this really the case?

When, in *The Message*, Griffith juxtaposes images of the country haven with views inspired by the city, he is partaking in an age-old tradition which opposes the two ways of life and is a cornerstone of the pastoral myth. But by dramatizing the conflict by way of montage, Griffith personally involves himself in the telling of the myth. Indeed, the pastoral myth, in both literature and painting, usually makes clear that the choice to return to nature is first and foremost a poetic *topos*. Griffith, however, deviates from it by inscribing the choice in the *present* through a montage strategy that emphasizes the opposition between good and evil. Beyond its collective symbolic value, the pastoral fiction is not far here from proposing a moral view.[19] This shift does not completely eliminate the utopian dimension of the pastoral myth but it does change its meaning. In the two versions of the myth, there is the idea that our ultimate destiny will be a return to our origins; and in both cases, agrarianism furnishes the appropriate imagery. The novelty of the cinematic version, however, lies in the sort of reception these images are meant to elicit in viewers. Thus, while in the longstanding literary and pictorial traditions one is invited to merely exercise his imagination, a film such as *The Message* seems instead to encourage viewers to draw conclusions with regard to their own existence.

*ideal homestead and landscape*

By concluding *The Message* with a shot that stresses the restored family unity within a serene and benevolent natural world, Griffith evokes once more the ideological role occupied by the family in the early years of the twentieth century. Here the pastoral environment serves to underscore the return of familial bliss. The reverse apparently takes place in *The Country Doctor*, a film also shot near Greenwich, Connecticut.

The long pan shot that closes the film explores a rural setting which remains indifferent to the death of a child and a family's despair. But whether or not we consider, following Gunning, "that this movement, out to the world at large, is one of consolation for the grief *within* [my emphasis] the house, setting it in context of the rhythms of nature" or adopt, still with Gunning, an opposite reading according to which the landscape "operates in naturalistic counterpoint to the grief behind the closed door," in both cases it remains that the view of the landscape appears to be relatively independent from the on-going events inside the house (1991, 216). Gunning correctly insists on the narrative aspect of this camera movement and on its ability to reference the presence of a filmic narrator responding "to the loss portrayed as it turns from human grief back into the realm of nature" (1991, 216). But valuable as this narratological reading of the shot may be, I am not so certain as to the value of maintaining an air-tight distinction here between "inside" and "outside" or between the "house" on one hand and the "landscape" on the other. For both appear to be inextricably woven together by the English language's notion of "home" whose meaning far exceeds that of "house" in that it incorporates a much larger semantic field that includes the family life and its immediate environment. The notion of "home" is such that a familiar landscape may become a part of one's "home," as indeed Americans have a tendency to call their national landscape their "home" and even to view America as a whole as their "home" (just think of the recently named Department of Homeland Security). "Home" idealizes the national family and its environment or landscape. Such an ideal plays an important role in the formation of landscapes in Griffith, especially in the films that make use of the pastoral myth. The effect, however, is to deeply transform the Arcadian vision inherited from past tradition.

The ending of *The Country Doctor* answers back to the film's opening shot by literally inverting it. The initial shot consists of a very beautiful and long pan that moves from the empty landscape and toward the doctor's house. The sheer scope of the landscape and the great attention given to visual details make it a rare moment in films from that era. And while it may be said that in moving toward the house the shot transforms the landscape into a narrative space or diegesis (Gunning, 1991, 216), it offers much more.

Certainly, the absence of human figures, at least during the first part of the movement, accentuates the presence of the landscape; all the more so since, in America, the lack of human presence takes on a particular meaning and is more important than it would be in Europe. According to Barbara Novak: "One can first read the American landscape in terms of the presence or absence of human figures."[20] From the very first image, the dominant, relatively open view of the Stillwater valley accentuates the symbolic dimension of the place being represented (even if it is high in the frame, the horizon line is present, something that is not always the case in Griffith's work as we shall see later). The valley presents all the attributes of a place of retreat and withdrawal: the sky is visible but the valley is surrounded by hills; at its centre, a bit of water gives the site a charming atmosphere of plenitude. The river, introduced by the first title card, is the central element of the grace sweeping through the Connecticut landscape.

Various characteristics of the land come to reinforce this impression of it being a haven: the pathway leading to the river, the low stone wall, the signs of traditional farming, the tree (apparently an elm), the houses that one makes out nestled in the thick vegetation of the facing hillside. Griffith represents a symbolic setting in which all of the components of an Arcadian dream are assembled.

Of the many traits that play a part in defining the landscape, the vegetation seems to be the one in which the most precise information about the local environment is concentrated. The heavy proliferation of vegetation around the homestead suggests a nest, and characters will be seen walking across a virtual carpet of flowers in the third shot (Figure 3.1). It might be worth briefly reminding the reader of the treatment given to grassy surfaces by artists. Like most landscape motifs (water, rocks, trees, etc.), grass possesses a religious origin: in the Garden of Eden, where it stands for all phytic organisms, grass precedes the arrival of trees and man. From the flowery meadows that represent the divine in several of Fra Angelico's Annunciations to Édouard Manet's *Déjeuner sur l'herbe*, the treatment of grass surfaces vary according to the national character. England, of course, accorded it particular attention, as did the United States after it. In America there has been a growing emphasis on domesticity with regards to grass surfaces, whether it is the use Olmsted made of them in conceiving Manhattan's Central Park or their use on the lawns in suburbia. Closely associated with the house and accompanied sometimes by a few shrubs, grass quickly became a founding landscape motif for two of the three types of symbolic landscapes in America and a veritable window into the American identity.[21] And in *The Country Doctor*, even the country house's tall grass, soon destined to be reaped, fits into the familiar landscape delimited by low stone walls. But how does grass, with its connotations for the American imagination, relate to Griffith's narrative program? Of course, without first offering a full-blown investigation of the Griffithian drama it is difficult to satisfactorily account for this most important component of

Figure 3.1

The ideal homestead from *The Country Doctor* (1909), D. W. Griffith. The Library of Congress.

the landscape. Any answer provided here will therefore be succinct and provisional. To begin, however, one might consider how location shooting often entails chance encounters and discoveries, such as the particular composition, topography, and layout of a stretch of land where certain traits simply appear salient. Now, grass, especially tall grass, is apt to be associated with movement, which makes it quite suitable for cinematic representation. For instance, there is a most beautiful fixed-camera shot in *The Country Doctor* where human figures disappear from our sight as they are engulfed by tall grass blowing in the wind, only to reappear further afield a moment later. Here, the grass has ensured the mediation between the near and the far. And in the series of shots that follow, grass not only ensures continuity, it also serves to create a strong underlying sense of unity by which emerges the pastoral landscape.

Griffith's decision to film the grassland from a slight low angle with the slope inclined toward the spectator seems more readily to evoke an ideal meadow. A similar strategy is also found in other films when Griffith wants to depict moments of happiness taking place in a country setting, for instance, in *What the Daisy Said* (1910). Horizontality, on the other hand, is more frequent when the situation turns to drama, as is the case with those stunning shots in *In Old Kentucky* (1909) where a fleeing southerner travels across a field of daisies. Here, the overall effect is very different, the event (the pursuit) being no longer tied to the meadow.

The opening of *The Country Doctor*, it must be clear from what has been said so far, offers an image of the landscape as an inhabited and lived space. The home, in this case, is more than a simple refuge. In fact, contrary to Griffith's usual attempts to enclose the family dwelling, the house appears instead to open up onto nature starting with the film's very first shot. Slowly panning right to reveal the grand natural setting for the film, the camera comes to a halt as it frames the façade of a house from which we see the country doctor, his wife, and their daughter come out. The beginning of the pan creates a sense of anticipation in the viewer that finds a release with the view of the house, thus giving a sense of unity to the entire composition: the modest home perched on the hillside helping to define and even shape the landscape.

But the camera's course also gives the feeling that the movement has been planned with regard to the specific topography of this Connecticut setting. Foregrounded by the camera movement, the hilly relief connects together the various elements and articulates the overall appearance of the landscape. This visual strategy explains why Griffith refrains from showing the house in all of its architectural fullness, with its various walls and roof. This depiction of the house could be read as a symptom of the fact that, when compared to Europeans, Americans seem less preoccupied by the width of their houses' protective walls than by mastering vast spaces. These two approaches to the built environment suggest the existence of two cultural archetypes with regard to human habitat, opposing a static and closed space to a more dynamic and open space.

Griffith only shows us the lower part of the house's façade, which includes the porch. Now everyone knows that a façade may be deceptive in the cinema. Behind it there is often only some boards without a roof or any interior space. But this is not the case here. And though this is a far cry from the living architecture described by John Ruskin,[22] still we are not confronted with an inert object. Furthermore, the totality of a form need not be represented in order for it to live in our imagination. Ernst Gombrich, for example, has shown how important is the viewer's share in beholding images since it provides, among other things, an "aura of space which appears to surround any naturalistic representation."[23] Griffith's depiction of the house likewise takes its evocative power from the suggestiveness of a few carefully chosen architectural details, especially the porch which occupies the main part of the frame and gives the impression of having been built out from the interior while opening onto the surrounding exterior space. A few steps leading from the porch stress the intimacy of the location and ease the way from the house into the natural world. They do not, however, interrupt the continuity of the space by introducing a vertical hierarchy between ground and landing, but rather seem to blend with it. How should bodies move in this landscape?

As the family leaves the house, we see all three members move toward the camera which is set up in the yard. After an off-screen glance which registers the wondrous beauty of the surroundings, the three characters exit the frame in close shot. Their movement away from the house and toward its natural surroundings is also facilitated by the absence of the traditional picket fence, which, as we have seen, acts as a symbol of enclosure of the family space. Thus, contrary to most of Griffith's other Biograph shorts where the picket fence punctuates the comings and goings to and from the family dwelling, the doctor's house avoids what was quickly becoming a cliché in depicting the closed/protected space of familial intimacy. Instead, the family's happiness here is suggested by a space that immediately opens itself onto nature, as if the house was in fact a part of the yard.[24] Of course, the initial moments of the film's opening shot underscore the fact that the house does indeed benefit from a cosy security that connotes a strong sense of intimacy. By the time we see the characters leave the house and take stock in the layout that enables this outward movement, we realize that something has changed. All of a sudden we understand that there is more than simple complementarity between the house and the surrounding nature. Rather, it is as if the entire emotional load associated with the house had quite literally spilled out onto the landscape, which, as a result, organizes itself and comes to cohere around the feeling of familial bliss. By the film's third shot, it is as if the emotional unit composed of the family and their house was somehow projected outward and into the Connecticut meadow. But as for the house itself, its representation continues to stay highly elliptical.

After having shown us the façade that faces the yard, Griffith abruptly cuts to the interior of the house with the fourth shot. Inside, we now see the young daughter bedridden with her mother at her bedside. The contrast with the image of the happy family walking in the meadow could not be starker. It is moreover accentuated by the *mise-en-scène*: the mother's dress has changed to a dark tone (it was white in the previous shot) and dark rings may now be seen under the child's eyes. It is difficult, in fact, to recognize that these are the same characters we have seen before. As for the interior of the house, our view of it is restricted to this one room only which is immediately presented as the space of suffering. Limiting the interior view of the house to a single room was not unusual for the time, even though a film such as *The Lonely Villa*, made earlier that same year, shows three rooms. What is striking moreover in *The Country Doctor* is the absence of any transition space between inside and outside the house; equally striking is the absence, in the view from inside the house, of a window through which one's gaze could roam outside. The absence of matching cuts or smooth transitions between inside and outside may be explained by the fact that while the exteriors were shot on location in Connecticut, the interiors were done in a studio in New York. But the fact that Griffith avoids as much as possible describing the interior of the house suggests rather that what is at stake here is a clear aesthetic (and conceptual) bias.

Not surprisingly, therefore, the same strategy affects the interiors of a second house where another child has also taken ill. The symmetry is striking: the interior of the house is again restricted to a single room and a single camera set-up. Even the layouts of both rooms mirror each other. Again, the suffering is concentrated in a single place and the representation of the house is deliberately reduced to it. This is a place that resists being extended, that resists opening, as if the immobility to which the children are reduced by disease created a closed world. The happy symbiosis of house and landscape that had dominated the film's opening gives way to a *mise-en-scène* of suffering where grief selects and interprets the setting. But perhaps the radical opposition between these two versions of space merely expresses the two sides of a single notion of the homestead understood as *dream*, as a place always already invested with various assumptions. After all, isn't a house where one dreams of living also a place where one can die? In both scenarios, Griffith's reticence at fully disclosing the house visually can be explained by the sort of unique associations that dreams both reproduce and create.

## staging the shoreline: the dramaturgy of the ocean

The traditional pastoral framework that acts as the central reference point for *The Message* and *The Country Doctor* has been finetuned by centuries of literature and art and is bound up in moral and political discourses. As a result, the natural world it evokes is too close to man to elicit any true tragic feelings. A more untameable element is required if man is to be confronted by his own vulnerability. In Griffith's work, as in much nineteenth century literature, the sea fulfills that role.

jean mottet

Part of the appeal of the ocean is the way it occupies space: in a sense the sheer horizontality of its surface can be seen to mirror the prairie, as described for instance by Fenimore Cooper. And though Griffith never explicitly compares the ocean with the countryside, one can nonetheless find distant equivalents between them in his films. Examples might include films where the rolling countryside of Connecticut (*The Message*, *The Country Doctor*) or where the mountainous terrain of California (*The Goddess of Sagebush Gulch* [1912], *Iola's Promise* [1912]) recall the ocean either in scope or compositionally as a visual surface. Indeed, despite some formal differences, the pure infinite sweep of these various landscapes translates into a sense of eternity recovered through contact with nature. As Herman Melville has said so well, "These are the times, when in his whale-boat the rover softly feels a certain filial, confident, land-like feeling towards the sea; that he regards it as so much flowery earth; and the distant ship revealing only the tops of her masts, seems struggling forward, not through high rolling waves, but through the tall grass of a rolling prairie: as when the western emigrants' horses only show their erected ears, while their hidden bodies widely wade through the amazing verdure."[25]

Nineteenth century literature has developed a pathos-filled conception of the seaside which Griffith inherited and never forsook. In fact, he even refined it in films such as *The Unchanging Sea* (1910) and *The Sands of Dee* (1912) by foregrounding the confrontation between man and a natural world reduced to its primordial elements: water, sky, and rocks. Starting with his first films to refer to an ocean setting, *After Many Years* (1908) and *Enoch Arden* (1911), Griffith insists on portraying the vulnerabilities and emotional instability of those who live the seafaring life. From that moment onward it is as if the sea and its shore begat a fatalistic discourse. As a result one may wonder whether the dramaturgy of the sea was becoming increasingly pessimistic.

Yet, starting from around 1870 the representation of the sea and of its shoreline began to change at a rapid pace, in America and Europe alike, as the beach was increasingly a place of leisure.[26] Numerous small port towns on the east coast—Newport, Gloucester, Cape May—all but abandoned fishing activities focusing instead on the growing tourist trade. In 1896, more than 11 million visitors vacationed along the New Jersey shore, and nearly 180 miles of the Long Island coastline opened up to new tourist activities. Little by little, new representations of the beach and the sea shore began replacing the landscapes by painters of the Hudson River School.

American landscape artists at the turn of the twentieth century, most notably the impressionists, preferred the "domesticated" beaches invaded by vacationers to views accentuating natural spectacle (untamed shore-lines, infinite expanse of water). *Beach Scene*, a small painting by Samuel Carr from 1879, is particularly representative of this new mode of perception. The scene represents a group of adults and children on the beach; some watch a puppet show while others walk around or pose for a photograph. Similar paintings of the period include William Merritt Chase's *At the Seaside* (1892) and *Idle Hours* (1894).

The new sensibility toward ocean landscapes expressed by these paintings is far removed from both the contemplative melancholy of the Romantics and the highly colourful narratives depicting the drama of the seafaring life. With it an entirely new rhetoric of gestures and ways of looking is introduced into coastal scenes. The "figures of misfortune" so well analysed by Alain Corbin[27] are replaced by the search for a way to stage the new sociability that characterizes the seaside vacation. But the change in attitudes only happens gradually. In Carr's painting, *Beach Scene*, the new visitors to the coast keep their city clothes on and the children dig in the sand wearing their street shoes. The new pleasures of the beach are still very tentative, while the shadow of the French Impressionists looms large on the novel setting.

All things considered, Griffith seems to have reacted rather slowly to the changes incurred by the new sensibility toward the seaside, at least when his work is measured against that of several American painters. Indeed, Griffith's first films to be set near the ocean, *After Many Years* and *Enoch Arden*, pay little attention to the seaside landscape. Moreover, both films use the stock *topos* of the "dramatic separation" whose source lies in the tradition of travel literature. In painting, on the other hand, the ocean's shore had already become a central element for either the depiction of sociality (John Sloan, William Glackens, Carr, Chase) or, more fundamentally still, Man's confrontation with the elements (Winslow Homer). For some, the coastal landscape was even considered to incite a kind of formal experimentation where other types of landscape did not.[28] The growing interest in seascapes eventually reached Griffith, however. Around 1912 his work begins to show considerable evolution in this regard, as he shoots along the California coastline. The 1912 film *The Sands of Dee* evidences many of the changes and the new emphasis Griffith was now ready to give to the coastal landscape.

One notable shift occurring in this film is a de-dramatization of the *mise-en-scène*. This can be accounted for by the influence exerted upon the film by Charles Kingsley's poetry (one of his poems is entitled *The Sands of Dee*), but also by Griffith adopting a more introspective mood such as could be found in the work of several American artists at the end of the nineteenth century (in the paintings of Winslow Homer, for instance; Figure 3.2). The film's visual poetry is derived primarily from the natural elements of the shooting location, Santa Monica Bay, with the shoreline taking on an importance that it had never had previously.[29] After working for some time at a breakneck speed, impatiently trying to master the medium of film,[30] Griffith's pace now slows down as he develops a new awareness of his environment. In the process, he re-discovers the American seashore and transforms it into an important expressive instrument.

*The Sands of Dee* opens with a view of the entire Santa Monica Bay shot from high upon a rock promontory. This distance is immediately apparent, and from such an elevated position, contemplation of the shoreline could convey any number of things if it was not for the fact that a lone woman can also be observed, sitting on the rock. The restless sea lies distant in the background, relinquishing the centre of the composition to the beach, the cliffs surrounding it, and, most importantly, to the human figure.

The protagonist, Mary, assumes the classic position of melancholy: her head resting on her forearm, she seems detached from her surroundings. However, and this point is important, her gaze is not the bewitching one found in Lucas Cranach's work nor is it the lunatic gaze found in Albrecht Dürer's. Although her meditative immobility can easily be integrated with the landscape by the viewer,[31] her gaze never seems to come to rest on any element of her surroundings, such as the sea, for instance. Instead, her gaze remains vague, refusing to penetrate the secrets of the sea. True

Figure 3.2

Winslow Homer, *Maine Coast* (1893). The Metropolitain Museum of Art.

to tradition the melancholy individual appears to have lost any sense of correlation between inner experience and external world.

How then are we to interpret the image Griffith offers us? Can we relate the combination of melancholy and coastal landscape to the new sensibility Americans were developing toward the coastline? Here, the high angle does not express a heightened sense of drama as it often does in Romanticism, for the shot avoids setting against each other the elevated rock and the ocean, and therefore lacks any clear opposition between verticality and horizontality. Griffith's composition highlights instead the picturesque. His coastal landscape is from the beginning the setting for a love story; it is only over the course of the film that the landscape will be affirmed and that the human figures will blend into it. Griffith also shows tourists "occupying" the shore. In the first part of the film, he takes pleasure in showing the lovers running on the beach in postures that suggest that the shore, with its fresh air, is a most healthy environment.[32] The presence of a painter will however put a halt to this idyll. The new character comes from the city, which is again a well-worn *topos* of the pastoral myth. From this point on, everything changes: Mary's meetings with the artist take place in a setting that contrasts forcefully with the preceding pastoral scenes. The joyous freedom offered by the wide-open beach now gives way to dark rocks that block and close off the space.

Soon abandoned by her fiancé and driven away by her father, Mary wanders across the beach. Her silhouette is gradually integrated into her surroundings, merging with the sea and with the rocks. The solitary figure is seen in various poses, but she is no longer part of a story, and the composition seems to have abandoned all realism. Mary, in fact, looks like a dream figure who naturally brings to mind the work of American painter Winslow Homer.

Early on in his career Homer began depicting women by the sea. Paintings such as *Undertow* (1886) or *The Gale* (1883) are characterized by strong dramatization—even a fairly conventional melodramatic appearance—which he never really abandoned[33] and may even have influenced Griffith in a film like *The Unchanging Sea* (1910). Other paintings, *Four Fishwives* (1881) and *Mending the Nets* (1882), describe the lives of fishermen and prefigure another of Griffith's tendencies, this time one more akin with documentary. One is reminded here of the beginning of *Lines of White on a Sullen Sea* (1909) or even of *The Mender of Nets* (1912) in which the opening shot, a particularly lengthy one for the time, bears strange resemblances to Homer's *Mending the Nets*. In all of these representations, the way the shore and the ocean appear is through the mediation of characters (the fishermen) whose lives require a seaside setting in order to be told. The ocean coast is perceived and represented as a place of memory and the fishermen as the witnesses of the past.[34]

Another aspect of Homer's paintings concerns our discussion more directly. In effect, after his return to America in 1893, Homer gradually suppressed all anecdotal concerns from his paintings and replaced human figures with suggestive natural forms. In one of his best works, *West Point, Prout's Neck, Maine* (1900), he suggests the silhouette of a woman with a cloud of transparent ocean spray shaped to recall feminine curves. No one else in *fin-de-siècle* America expressed hopelessness on the seashore with as much power as did Homer. Beyond the spectacle of the beach, behind its diversions, loomed a most terrible solitude. One can link *The Sands of Dee*, and more particularly, the troubling images of Griffith's protagonist on the seashore just before her suicide to such solitude which expresses anxieties hidden beneath surface appearances (Figure 3.3).

To the extent that it evokes annihilation, the ocean is in fact frightening: Even when associated with the theme of love, as in *The Sands of Dee*, it carries the seeds of destruction. But it is also because the theme reflects the tension that inhabits Griffith's thoughts that the ocean takes on a hopeless character. Just as Mary, after being forced to leave the family home, frees herself from all emotional ties in order to confront the ocean, one gets the impression that, in Griffith's work, the sea encourages a rupture with ordinary experience in favor of a more spiritual quest.[35] In the second part of the film, the protagonist will continually confront the ocean, like a question unanswered.[36] The ocean *and the rocks* in fact: for in the background a massive rock formation, omnipresent and practically at the centre of the composition, counterbalances with the fragile silhouette of the woman. What is more, the striking contrast between the dark mass of rock and the waves' white spray as they beat against it produces a truly

Figure 3.3

D. W. Griffith, *The Sands of Dee* (1912). The Library of Congress.

beautiful visual effect. In that very moment, the waves possess an undeniable strength, and even if relegated to the background, they attract the eye. How are we to explain this?

While views of the shoreline are often organized by a lateral unravelling of space, here the movement of the waves over the rocks seems contained, forcing the spectator to orient his gaze toward the centre of the frame. Griffith, moreover, places the camera at the level of the waves and rocks, which helps bring the ocean and the human figure forcefully together, all the more so since the protagonist is often shot facing the open sea. Whereas the film's opening shot offered an elevated and detached perspective, the subsequent views progressively involve the protagonist (and the viewer) with the seascape by bringing them face-to-face, so to speak, with the waves crashing onto the rocky coast. Replacing whatever may have been left over from the picturesque, the waves become the dominant motif.[37] Much like Homer, Griffith concentrates on the essential, which is to say, on how Man is tragically dependent when faced with untamed nature. Confrontation with the rhythms of nature thus resolves itself in an allegory of death. As Tom Gunning observes: "This movement reaches its apogee in one of Griffith strongest 'empty' shots, in which the sea seems to sweep the screen free of characters. Shot from a somewhat high camera angle and rather close camera position, it shows a strip of beach, with lines of foam curving gently into it as the waves glide in and retreat…. This graceful and strongly pictorial image serves as a replacement for Mary's suicide" (1991, 277–278).

## the western landscape: the warrior's gaze and the aesthetic vision

Among the characteristic landscapes of the cinema, those from the American West have received much attention. All film critics, from André Bazin to Jean-Louis Leutrat, agree on the fact that the landscape is a major aspect of the Western genre.[38] John Ford liked to say that the real star of his films was the land. Could this mean that the natural landscapes of the West are somehow endowed with their own proper meaning, one that would be impervious to rhetorical constraints? This question is essentially that of the relationship between the geographic description of the landscape and its integration into preexisting models of representation. The space of the Western has so often been understood as a mythical or symbolic space that there is really no need for us to dwell on the matter any further. Suffice to say that such an approach does not explain away everything. For one thing, it tends to neglect the way in which the natural environment in itself contributes to the cinematic expression of this specific landscape. Thus although Eastern landscapes could equally be expressed through sundry visual and cultural perspectives at the turn of the twentieth century, there is no denying that Western landscapes, by virtue of the very nature of the West's topography, led to privileging the long shot, or distant view. Interestingly, this view reproduced that of explorers and migrants as well as that of soldiers and warriors.

For some time now film scholars have debated over the pertinence of the Western as a genre in discussing Griffith's Biograph days. Leutrat has convincingly shown that the category of the Western simply does not apply to Griffith's early output, even though the plot of some of the films unfold out West.[39] As he observes, for viewers of the period, a film such as *The Red Girl* (1908) was not considered as a *Western* but as a film set in the West, as a "Biograph western dramatic subject" as the *New York Mirror* called it (Leutrat, 1984, 166). Still, whether they belong to the "Western" genre or not, certain stories of the West shot by Griffith in California starting in 1910 manifest new and interesting uses of space, even if the locations chosen from the areas around Los Angeles are not exceptional. Having reminded us that the first "Westerns" were shot in the New York region, Michel Foucher notes that when the studios established themselves on the West Coast in Hollywood, "sites close to the new city were used for exterior shooting; permanent city sets were built in natural settings that varied little from other semi-arid regions: Owens Valley at the feet of the Sierra Nevada, San Fernando, the Iverson ranch near Los Angeles."[40]

Griffith chooses the same *modus operandi*: from 1910 on, his usual shooting sites are nearby the studios. Prior to the use of the extraordinary and spectacular settings that will become emblematic of the Western genre (and of the nation as well), the cinema mostly confined itself to small and unexceptional tracts of land. And yet, this dull landscape allowed the ingredients of the Western's future spectacle to be gradually established. Griffith seems to have been sensitive to these ingredients. In several of his "western dramatic subjects" title cards both evoke and stress aspects of the landscape. For instance, in *The Fight for Freedom* (1908) a title card reads "a story of the South West desert"; in *The Thread of Destiny* (1909) and *A Lodging for the Night* (1912), title cards announce that we are about to see a story from "the old South West"; *Under Burning Skies* (1912) is characterized as a story of the "American desert"; and *The White Rose of the Wild* (1911) is presented as a story set in the "mountains of the West." Despite the summary and often repetitive nature of the settings being depicted, one gets the sense that a paradigm or model is being sought out in these encounters between fragments of landscape and an evolving representational system.

82

These filmic representations of the West's natural space, while never attaining the variety and scale of western spaces in the 1920s, are linked however to several essential and primitive functions from the very beginning. Even when limited to the Hollywood Hills or Santa Monica, filming in the West wipes out familiar landscapes, calls into question accepted representations, and reveals another, more profound conception of space. The hypothesis I wish to submit to the reader is the following: while representing landscapes on the East Coast, Griffith often resorted to models of perception inherited from artistic and popular forms of representation (literature, painting, and photography); but faced with the natural spaces of the West, he instinctively turned toward other modes of perceiving and interacting with space. To systems of decoding derived from previous modes of representation, he now seemed to prefer forms of interaction relevant to anthropological categories (the relationship of the hunter or warrior to his territory, among others).

Geographer Jay Appleton has argued that landscape connects the satisfaction of basic needs by the environment with the pleasure associated with aesthetic contemplation.[41] Interestingly, the most enthralling and satisfying views in Griffith's Western landscapes are almost always linked to an ongoing battle. In *The Massacre* (1913), *Ramona* (1910), or even *The Battle of Elderbush Gulch* (1913) (to consider only well-known films) high-angle views of the landscape are those of a warring observer. The first and most beautiful long shot in *The Massacre* leaves no doubt: after showing a group of settlers led by a scout watching over the activities of an Indian village, Griffith frames the village in long shot from a very high angle corresponding to the position of the scout on the hill. The point of view is that of the invader. But who possesses this landscape? The settler who observes it or the Natives in the valley who look as threatening to the invaders as the invaders do to them? The answer is no simple matter. One could say, for instance, that no one possesses the landscape, for it is the object of the contest which is etched within it. Each party uses the space to its own advantage with regard to the confrontation.

Over the course of the surprise attack that follows, Griffith alternates between long shots taken from high up on the hill and close shots of the combat that allow the spectator to see the surviving Indians take refuge in the hills. In the long shots, the frantic flight of the Indians constitutes the dominant movement in the frame. The sequence ends with a shot showing several Indians hiding at the top of a hill (the same one previously occupied by the white aggressors), their gaze turned toward the remains of their destroyed village. Here two views of the landscape are successively compared: the first belongs to the predator's gaze for whom the land is a place for action; the second is seen through the eyes of prey in hiding and shows the well-known land reluctantly left behind.

Once they have become part of the landscape these strategic positions return later in the film where they determine how the action will be played out in space; for instance, during the Indians' revenge on the settlers who had attacked them earlier. The shots preceding this assault are particularly interesting, however. A very high-angle long shot of the convoy first shows the settlers moving onward through the land. The men are barely visible in the semi-desert and are withheld any sort of agency or mediatory power over the landscape. They are reduced to being an index of the precarious relationship that exists between explorer and hostile environment. And yet, the manner in which their movement inscribes itself in the landscape lays down, however timidly, the foundations of what will later become a characteristic trait of the "pictorial beauty" of Westerns. The point that needs emphasizing here, however, is how those panoramic views that anticipate the development of the Western's iconography serve to situate the source of the genre's typical landscape views. Indeed, their appeal lies in the connection they establish between the combatant's gaze and an emerging aesthetic sensibility toward western vistas. What is more, this connection may very well amount to more than a simple coincidence. Isn't it the case, after all, as Lacoste has pointed out, that certain landscapes come to be perceived as beautiful because they are seen, either implicitly or explicitly, to represent the conqueror's gaze (Lacoste, 64)?

The framing of Griffith's long shots in *The Massacre* takes into account both the vastness of the open range and unevenness of the terrain. But the absence of any horizon line makes it impossible to have any sense of limit and there seems to be no confines to the setting. Such limitlessness defies the gaze; it is the complete opposite of the garden's reassuring enclosure discussed earlier. The contrast with Ford who will use the mesas of Monument Valley to set clear limits to the dramatic space could not be any more striking. Hence the feeling we get from Griffith's "Westerns" that the men only have a weak understanding of the land and a vague knowledge of the territory. Not surprisingly, these films are devoid of the sort of topographical precision that will later characterize many Westerns, especially those directed by Anthony Mann. Is this to say that, for Griffith, the landscape merely serves the role of an "emblem" of the West? The term "emblem" is borrowed here from Leutrat, according to whom there exists two different uses of the landscape in silent Westerns, each corresponding to two types of films.[42] On one hand, there are films for which the landscape somehow falls outside the boundaries of the narrative; what is shown does not correspond to the entire spatial sphere of activity, or narrative field, of the film, but serves merely as an emblematic image of the West. Leutrat calls these "marvellous" or "fantastic" Westerns ("*western merveilleux*"). On the other hand, with more "realistic" Westerns, the space depicted does correspond to the film's narrative field. I believe, however, we can add a third category that brings out the symbolic aspect of experiencing the environment. The new category proves itself to be useful in describing the scene of the Indians' retaliation against the attacking settlers.

In the high-angle long shot that opens the scene—the one discussed above which shows the settlers' onward trek—latent dangers are emphasized by various elements arising from the landscape: a coyote and then a bear suddenly break into the foreground. The wild animals serve to remind us that the convoy has ventured into a lawless land. The settlers' entrance into a savage environment inverts the familiar landscape left behind, the natural surroundings evolving (or, rather, devolving) into a pure or absolute landscape.[43] There follows two shots that bring us down to a more human scale and depict the activities of the settlers: one shows the hero moving toward the wagon; the other one is a close shot of a mother and her infant sitting inside the carriage. Griffith offers here the most simple *découpage*: no intermediaries intervene to ensure the passage from the long shot of the landscape to the close shots of the characters. Nor do any of the characters look yonder into the landscape. After the intimate shot in the wagon, the high-angle shot of landscape returns: but this time around, and irrespective of the distance, our gaze has been captured by the various elements of the composition we have already identified, and in particular those in whose "closeness" we have orbited (e.g., the mother and baby inside the wagon). The bear then suddenly moves off-screen only to be replaced by an Indian dressed in animal skin. This is a demonic landscape, "a hideous and desolate wilderness, full of wild beasts and wild men," which is much how it had appeared to William Bradford from aboard the Mayflower.[44] Of course, beyond the referential meanings of the film, this journey across the untamed West must also be read as a story of man's confrontation with Wilderness.

But the mythic references activated here by the juxtaposition of the human and the animal do not eliminate the landscape; it continues to play an essential role, particularly in those long shots where characters, especially the Indians, almost seem to blend into it. "At root, the Indian [as far as the Western is concerned] belongs to Mother Nature" as Leutrat observes (Leutrat, 1985, 406). He lives, works, hunts, and defends himself in harmony with the natural landscape he inhabits. Can this sort of relation to the land be subjected to the same warring logic that we discussed earlier? Obviously, the Indians of *The Massacre* are caught up in a confrontation requiring tactical use of the terrain; thus the importance of scouts who are in control of the topography. The confrontation also further determines the use of long shots which emphasize distance and reinforce the combatant's outlook by blocking out other sentiments associated with "closeness" and the picturesque. And in case anyone misses the point, Griffith adds to the already highly evocative high-angle long shot a title card stating: "The Indians spy on their prey." In other words, the gaze should not be interpreted in times of conflict like it is in normal times. In combat, a relational entity between landscape and character is formed and the landscape cannot be understood by reference to usual pictorial rhetoric alone.[45] While in the pastoral landscape the composition aims to accommodate figures (including human figures) that accentuate the natural environment's harmony (e.g., *The Country Doctor*), in situations where the space is contested, the syntax of the landscape is affected by radical changes. The harmonious equilibrium of the pastoral landscape gives way to a space that is strained and organized with reference to various emerging dynamic *foci*. Even temporality itself is disrupted: the "now" of tranquil nature has become the "all of a sudden" of the threat of danger.

Griffith's encounter with the western territories appears to have brought him to adopt representational strategies that extend the usual frame of reference for interpreting the landscape. At times, he almost abandons a search for meanings already mediated by painting, photography, or literature in favour of a more direct, immediate, connection to the land. Yet, paradoxically, such a connection is often already pregnant with collective or anthropological knowledge that is just as meaningful as the artistic tradition. Exoticism is also a source of stereotypes. But there remains, however, an important difference: as briefly mentioned earlier, the natural attributes of the new western shooting locations compelled the cinema to privilege certain vantage points from which to capture the landscape; this of course was the case with the long shot. Few, however, could have predicted the impact of using the Western long shot in the context of stories of embattled space or how this would drastically modify the way the camera selects and organizes the various elements it gathers from the existing real space.

In this regard, the representation of the desert, an integral part of the West, poses an interesting problem. Films such as *The Last Drop of Water* (1911) or *Female of the Species* (1912) present a hostile world foreign to our usual perceptual references, and where survival itself may impose insurmountable hardships. In this world, there is no possibility of abandoning yourself to the luxury of aesthetic contemplation. In *The Last Drop of Water*, no long shots interrupt the convoy's march across "the great American desert" (as the title card describes it). The detachment which would make it possible to view the desert as a spectacle seems excluded. Likewise, the inevitable confrontation that occurs between the convoy and the Indians is very different from the one in *The Massacre*. After a title card announcing "The Indians," the Natives break into the foreground, filmed by a particularly low camera placement that accentuates the flatness of the terrain. An eerie feeling emerges of a loss of contact with time and space.

The Bible tells us that the desert is the place of thirst and death: "The paths of their way are turned aside; they go to nothing, and perish" (Job 6:18). The desert is an absolute or pure landscape, with few or no marks of human presence, which magnifies its connotations within the religious imaginary. From the moment he began shooting in California, it seems obvious that Griffith instantly understood the symbolic returns he could harvest from opposing the two terms that have traditionally divided the New World's mythical landscapes: America as Garden of Eden; and America as primitive nature and untamed land.

**notes**

1. Ralph Waldo Emerson, "The American Scholar," in *Selected Essays* (New York: Penguin Classics, 1985), 102.
2. Linda Arvidson, *When the Movies Were Young* (New York: Dutton & Co., 1925), 85.
3. Billy Bitzer, *His Story* (New York: Farrar, Straus and Giroux, 1973), 64.
4. Martin Heidegger, "Bâtir Habiter Penser," in *Essais et Conferences* (Paris: Gallimard, 1976), 183.
5. The notion of limit is not always so "unifying." Less "pleasant" limits can also signal ruptures in the landscape, most notably in urban landscapes. On this point, see Kevin Lynch, *L'image de la cité* (Paris: Dunod, 1998), 72–76.
6. J.-F. Lyotard, *L'Inhumain* (Paris: Galilée, 1988), 204.
7. On this point, see Julia Przybo's, *L'Entreprise mélodramatique* (Paris: Corti, 1987), 111–121.
8. Michel Collot, *L'Horizon fabuleux*, vol. 1 (Paris: Librairie José Corti, 1988), 19.
9. Tom Gunning, "D.W. Griffith and the Narrator-System: Narrative, Structure and Industry Organization in Biograph Films, 1908–1909" (PhD dissertation, NYU, 1982), 76; hereafter cited in text. The version I'm quoting from was handed to me by the author in 1982, before it was submitted to NYU in 1986 and before its revision for publication as *D.W. Griffith and the Origins of American Narrative Film* (Urbana: University of Illinois Press, 1991); hereafter cited in text. To the dominant literary tradition mentioned by Gunning, one should also add the considerable work done in photography and painting during the second half of the nineteenth century.
10. Richard Hofstadter, *The Age of Reform*; quoted in Gunning, op. cit., 76.
11. However, the literary origin of the notion of *middle landscape* can be found in Virgil.
12. Leo Marx, *The Machine in the Garden* (Oxford: Oxford University Press, 1970), 114.
13. Since the middle of the nineteenth century, in painting as well as in photography, one can find images of peaceful, tranquil, and domesticated nature, similar to the New England landscapes evoked by Emerson, side by side with the grandiose landscapes of the West.
14. For one, Henry James, on his return to the United States in 1904, seemed to have become acutely aware of the Arcadian connotations of the New England landscape which he saw as free from the weight of history. See Henry James, *The American Scene* (Bloomington: Indiana University Press, 1968).
15. On this subject, see Alexandra Ballarin's study in *Le siècle de Titien* (Paris: Réunion des Musées Nationaux, 1993), 392–403.
16. It is worth noticing, however, that before the conflict erupts, Griffith insists on the warmth of the relation between the stranger and the welcoming husband. As in the pastoral tradition, this can signify a moment of understanding, indeed, of actual complicity. A more elaborate version of the theme can be found in *The Ingrate* (1908), a short film likewise set in a pastoral setting.
17. It is likely that the spectators of the period did not look for hidden meanings in this sort of film, but instead appreciated them for their explicit content.

18. *The Modern Prodigal*, a film shot in 1910, offers viewers a different image of the same region. The film relates the misadventures of a young man who leaves home to try his luck in the city. Having introduced the hero in the bucolic setting surrounding the family home, Griffith, from the second shot on, shows him en route to the city. The young man faces a hilly landscape that is, as far as I know, unique in Griffith's body of work. On the opposite hill, several signs of recent industrialization can be seen: two far-away smokestacks, a building that strongly resembles a factory, and a train, partly obscured by vegetation. Together these radiate the optimism of a new energy integrated into a traditional landscape. This impression is confirmed by the response of the young hero: in the foreground, he shows renewed enthusiasm for his departure for the city.

19. In his analysis of the American version of the pastoral myth, Leo Marx clearly demonstrates how, with Thoreau, Emerson's program for pastoral retreat was put to the test: "Instead of writing about it—or merely writing about it—he tries it. By telling his tale in the first person, he endows the mode with a credibility it had seldom, if ever, possessed" (Marx, *op. cit.*, 245).

20. Barbara Novak, *Nature and Culture: American Landscape Painting, 1825–1875* (New York, Oxford University Press, 1980), 189.

21. D. W. Meinig has defined three types of symbolic landscapes in America: the New England Village, the Main Street of Middle America, and California Suburbia. Grass surfaces are an integral part of the first and third types. See D. W. Meinig, "Symbolic Landscapes," in *The Interpretation of Ordinary Landscape*, ed. D. W. Meinig (Oxford: Oxford University Press, 1979), 164–192. With regard to the stereotypical use of grassy surfaces in television series, see my *Série télévisée et espace domestique* (Paris: L'Harmattan, 2005).

22. From the first half of the nineteenth century onward, the Englishman John Ruskin travelled throughout Europe identifying buildings he believed incarnated in exemplary fashion the landscape of each region. He considered the built environment to be indivisible from the landscape. His theories on architecture are collected in *The Seven Lamps of Architecture* (London, Electric Book Co., 2001).

23. Ernst Gombrich, *Art and Illusion* (Princeton: Princeton University Press, 1960), 229.

24. One can also find in American painting—a little later, of course— images of houses radically cut off from their environment. In certain paintings by Edward Hopper, *House by the Railroad* for instance, the veranda and the front door, instead of opening on nature, are turned so that they face the railroad. But beyond these obvious differences, however, certain common traits can also be found. In Hopper's work, as in Griffith's, the gaze directed toward the landscape reveals archetypal, imaginary representations (e.g., the encounter between man and nature), by way of relatively classical figurative work. Whereas the Futurists, during the same period, dreamed of infinite potentialities (revealed through formal experimentation), Hopper seemed content to reproduce his culture's obsession with limits.

25. Herman Melville, *Moby-Dick, or, The Whale* (New York: Hendricks House, 1952), 486.

26. On this point, see Jean-Didier Urbain's fascinating book, *At the Beach* (Minneapolis, University of Minnesota Press, 2003).

27. See Alain Corbin, *Le territoire du vide* (Paris: Flammarion, 1988).

28. This is the case, for instance, of F. J. Mather who has claimed that "Maritime painting in the United States has perhaps maintained a greater inventiveness than other landscape painting." Frank Jewett Mather, Jr., *Modern Painting: A Study of Tendencies* (New York: H. Holt & Co., 1927), 174.

29. Tom Gunning paid special attention to this film (Gunning, 1991, *op.cit.,* 276–278).

30. At the beginning of the Biograph period, it is well known that Griffith shot several short films each week.

31. The speculative power of the fundamental images of melancholy, especially in Dürer (*Melancholia I* [1514]) and Cranach (*Melancholia* [1532]), comes partly from the fact that they are situated in an irrational space. Thus, notwithstanding Panofsky who seemed content to describe the space where Melancholy is situated as "not far from the sea, dimly illuminated by the light of the moon," I believe that any attempt to *fully* integrate the magnificent coastal landscape that lies in the background of Dürer's engraving into the whole of the depicted space will be met with much difficulty. Erwin Panofsky, *The Life and Arts of Albrecht Dürer* (Princeton, Princeton University Press, 1955), 156.

32. Intimations of that nature are rare in Griffith's depiction of beach scenes. Another example can be found in the 1908 film, *When the Breakers Roar,* where a group of young people in bathing suits are seen playing on the beach. The arrival of a dangerous maniac will soon put an end to the frolicking, however.

33. For an in-depth look at W. Homer's work, one can still consult Lloyd Goodrich's authoritative monograph: *Winslow Homer* (New York: The Macmillan Company, 1945); for a study of Homer with regards to turn of the century pictorial culture, see *American Art Around 1900: Studies in the History of Art*, no. 37 (National Gallery of Art, 1990); finally, Bruce Robertson's book *Reckoning with Winslow Homer* (The Cleveland Museum of Art, 1990) offers a relevant, though somewhat biased, account of the American specificity of Homer.

34. European representations of the coastline have been studied historically by Jean-Didier Urbain, in *At the Beach, op. cit.* It is worth noting, however, that it is only during his stay in England that Homer's work can be said to belong to this history and to its tradition of representation. After his return to the United States, Homer clearly manifests a desire for independence from past traditions and even from current European conventions.

35. Interestingly, in both Griffith and Homer, this change of attitude occurs after a prolonged stay at the seashore. There is a strange similarity here between the two artists. Indeed, both offer much more than mere realist depictions of the ocean: it inspires them to express their anguish. Yet, the location never becomes a pretext for stylistic exercise and the landscape preserves its strong identity.

36. The first instance in Griffith of such an encounter with the ocean takes place in *Lines of White on a Sullen Sea*. In discussing the film, Tom Gunning evokes the possible influence on it of American painting, as he underscores the importance of the visual composition, especially in those shots where the film's heroine is shown facing the sea. See Gunning, *op.cit.,* 1991, 234–235.

37. One is also reminded of Gustave Courbet who, long before Homer, tightens the framing of the ocean's view, seeking to concentrate all the

attention toward the tumultuous sea, irrespective of the immediate surroundings. See, for instance, the series of paintings Courbet produced in
1870 entitled *Vagues*.

38. The essays Bazin devoted to the Western of which most are collected
in vol. 2 of *What is Cinema?* are still very relevant today. See André Bazin,
*What Is Cinema?*, vol. 2, trans. Hugh Grey (Berkeley: University of California Press, 1967). As for Leutrat's thoughtful consideration of the Western
landscape, it can be found in Jean-Louis Leutrat and Suzanne Liandrat-
Guigues, *Les Cartes de l'Ouest* (Paris: Armand Colin, 1989).

39. On this point, see Jean-Louis Leutrat, "Le père dans ses oeuvres, ou D. W.
Griffith et le western," in *David Wark Griffith. Etudes,* ed. Jean Mottet (Paris:
Publications de la Sorbonne /L'Harmattan, 1984), 164–177; hereafter cited
in text.

40. Michel Foucher, "Du désert, paysage du western," in *La Théorie du paysage
en France (1974–1994)*, ed. Alain Roger (Seyssel: Champ Vallon, 1995), 78.

41. Jay Appleton, *The Experience of Landscape* (New York: Wiley, 1975), 70. An
interesting variant of this theory can be found in the work of a few
French geographers. Yves Lacoste, for example, claims that "Of the relatively few places from which one can see the landscape, the one from
which the view is the most beautiful is almost always the one that is the
most important for tactical, military reasoning." Yves Lacoste, "À quoi
sert le paysage? Qu'est-ce qu'un beau paysage?" in *La Théorie du paysage en
France (1974–1994)*, *op. cit.*, 61; hereafter cited in text.

42. Jean-Louis Leutrat, "Les cartes de l'Ouest: Histoire, nature et déréalisa-
tion dans les films des années 20," *Revue française d'études américaines*, no. 26
(November 1985): 404–405; hereafter cited in text.

43. In *The Massacre*, as in other "Westerns" by Griffith, the beginning of
the story usually places the characters in traditional family settings.
Though the "western" homes are somewhat different from their East
Coast counterpart which, as we have seen, emphasize the idea of a country haven, they still possess the traits of the typical family enclosure: the
picket fence, a small yard, etc.

44. Quoted in Sylvie Mathé, "Désir du désert: hommage au grand désert
américain," *Revue française d'études américaines*, no. 26 (November 1985): 421.

45. A completely different image of the Indian can be found in the films
Griffith shot on the East Coast. In response to the public's fondness for
idyllic representations of Indian life, Griffith used largely pastoral terms
to describe the relationship between the Indians and the landscape. For
instance, in *The Mended Lute* (1909), shots 3, 4, and 5 show an Indian couple
in a landscape of meadows, rivers, and waterfalls. The setting recalls the
paintings of Worthington Whittredge, Albert Bierstadt, and even the photographs of Carleton Watkins. Much like the farmers of the pastoral tradition, these Indians stand for the state of nature before its destruction.

# the course of the empire

four

sublime landscapes in the

american cinema

m a u r i z i a   n a t a l i

The overtures to sublimity in America's early history painting were readily transferred to the landscape, and lead to a study of artistic rhetoric, that style of formal declamation which is the appropriate mode for public utterance. Such a study also involves a consideration of art as spectacle. Persisting late into the nineteenth century, this art had a clear twentieth-century heir in the film, which rehearsed many of the nineteenth century's concerns.

**Barbara Novak**[1]

Theodore Roosevelt represented the extermination of American Indians as a selfless service to the cause of civilization: "The settler and pioneer have at bottom had justice on their side; this great continent could not have been kept as nothing but a game reserve for squalid savages" (1889).

Zygmunt Bauman[2]

America is saying to the world "get out of the way."

Robert Morris[3]

*The Searchers* exemplifies the power of trauma western to transform physical landscape into a mental *traumascape* for characters and spectators alike.

Janet Walker[4]

## introduction

During the nineteenth century, landscape paintings, photographs or prints, large panoramas or small postcards played a large ideological and "nation-building" role within American visual culture. They illustrated religious utopias and political projects concerning the expanding frontier and the wars against Natives, stimulated the birth of "landscape taste" in modern urban spectators, and translated in myriad images long-lasting slogans such as "the American destiny," "the American dream," or "the American way of life." At the same time, the panorama buildings, avatars of cinema, presented huge scenic views as collective and immersive entertainment, transforming icons of imperialist expansion, the "magisterial gaze," and panopticism into popular visual attractions.

A virtual panorama, or perhaps a circular wall of screens, would be the appropriate format to replay all the landscapes that American cinema has created in one century. As a spectacular "art of memory," Hollywood has repeatedly stated to the whole world that, for the American nation, Nature is a gift of God and a Frontier to reach; the Past (that is, History or Europe) is just a prologue to leave behind, and the Future is written in terms of territorial adventures and new horizons to conquer. Westerns and science fiction films have perpetuated these old iconological formulas and encrypted them within new popular clichés. Now that many film landscapes are hybrids of digital layers, studio miniatures, and photographs, we can read through them the traces of perennial political and aesthetic polarities, such as those of wild nature and spectacular technology, millenarist ecology and capitalist economy, and landscape as civilized grid or as an escape toward wilderness and unwritten blankness.

These are the philosophical questions of the sublime as grand American style, in high art or low media, in the landscape culture as well as in the landscapes of war.

This essay argues that Hollywood landscapes and cityscapes, nineteenth-century American landscape painting, and the recent 9/11 "traumatic sublime" can be investigated not only as part of the same cultural archive, but also as revealing persistent ideological and iconological scenarios. My aim is to reconnect broadly film landscapes, paintings, and TV icons within the rhetoric of a wider national "landscape art." This includes American media and real wars considered as *landscape projects and installations* for the "background" of the Empire's new world order.

In an age when images of world landscapes from art or reality reach us mainly in the screen format which serves as the general interface for TV, cinema, and the Web, we are implicitly invited to confront, or even collapse, science fiction images (allegories of landscapes to come such as *Matrix*-like dystopias or medieval sagas) with real 9/11 terrorist icons, U.S. tunes of a grand "democratic" mission scoring shots of military occupation or G.I.s's tortures, refugees in the Middle East's "landscapes of resistance," and demonstrations of antiglobal groups and pacifists in major world cities. All these dramatic iconographies speak in terms of landscape turmoil, crowds in movements and territorial catastrophes; many of them take place in countries in which the U.S. is deeply involved. Thus, if this U.S. "landscape art" produces "shock and awe" spectacles, it is because America is still acting out the sublime imperial fantasies of its bicentennial culture.

Indeed, ever since images of the atomic bomb or the Vietnam War have been deposited in the collective world memory, it has become difficult to quietly enjoy the spectacular U.S. cinema as being nothing more than the entertaining superstructure of a market-invading democratic Empire. The film theory and history of the past 30 years have largely explored Hollywood's ideological construction of fictional space and subjectivities. In such a context, my essay considers American film landscapes as ideologically and aesthetically enacting the *primary U.S. fantasy* of being (and behaving as) an Empire. My approach seeks to respond to the current political anxiety, theoretical emergency, and merging tendency in film and media studies in the post-9/11 climate so appropriate to the aggressive landscapes produced by the U.S. Media Empire.

93

I invite the reader to proceed back and forth between the "clear and present danger" of shocking landscapes he/she is offered every day on TV, and the panoramic "wall of screens" full of landscapes that American cinema has created during the last 100 years.

The essay is divided into three sections. The first two, Traumatic Landscapes and Clear and Present Danger, the Sublime Shock and Awe of 9/11, are dedicated to a theory of American landscape as *traumatic sublime*, and are inspired by nineteenth-century grand painting, particularly by Thomas Cole's *The Course of Empire*. In the third part, Landscape Film Gallery from *The Course of Empire*, I briefly revisit some significant Hollywood films and authors of landscapes. These examples illustrate and expand the visual and cultural implications of Cole's five canvases, which in my essay play the role of seminal *pathos formulae*, and visual matrix for the American traumatic sublime.

## traumatic landscapes

> The presence of the sublime in science fiction—a deeply American genre—implies that our fantasies of superiority emerge from our ambivalence regarding technological power, rather than nature's might (as Kant originally had it)...The sublime becomes a means of looking backward in order to recognize what's up ahead.[5]
>
> **Scott Bukatman**

*history as dystopia*

Hollywood is the creator of a vast archive of landscape images that for decades has haunted American and global audiences as spectacles of "shock and awe," the sublime name the Pentagon gave to the second war in Iraq. In terms of aesthetics, only an iconology of such traumatic imageries can interpret the American film's landscape politics in general as a screen-size sublime and as a flamboyant ideology of "nation building." In the folds of their landscape rhetorics lies the truth of U.S. visual culture and policy. But since the nineteenth century's grand landscape paintings, this rhetoric has been too spectacular to be considered *true as well*. As a result of this all too reasonable collective resistance to such a truth, U.S. cinema and its ideological violence speaks to viewers instead as a fascinating aesthetic experience, the multitudes that resist reading it ideologically being happy to enjoy it merely as entertainment.

Our diligent moral distinction between the Hollywood war aesthetic and the reality of U.S. wars and other political horrors is perhaps one of America's major ideological victories. When the Twin Towers were attacked, the images of airplanes slicing into them produced painful incredulity not only because Americans thought for a number of reasons that "they hate us," but because no one was prepared to believe that the language of Hollywood could be used to perform this sudden, traumatic, horribly sublime, *real* attack against the most famous cityscape of the modern world.

In U.S. history, pilgrims left behind Europe and discovered the new continent, which was either a splendidly intact Promised Land, a God-given gift, or an overwhelming wilderness inhabited by savages. This anthropologically dramatic "close encounter" and landscape trauma was followed by the bloody extermination of Natives which the whites staged in every territory of the virgin land, using ghettoized reserves as well as numerous secondary wars and expansions to push forward or protect the frontiers of the Empire. In its various morphing and ghostly forms, U.S. Manifest Destiny has always been, and still is, a mission into new territories.

Aggression, the conquest of lands, cities, and people dominated the Imperialist nineteenth century, an age when America too was becoming an Empire. In 1845 the American journalist John O'Sullivan preemptively declared the U.S.'s "manifest destiny to overspread and to possess the whole of the continent which Providence has given us for the development of the great experiment of liberty and federated self-government entrusted to us."[6] This doctrine became a justification for actions that had already happened or were still happening, but also for a vast ideological program for the future. Later, during the twentieth century, the only Americans to ever experience disastrous war landscapes were the soldiers who contributed to staging them by dropping bombs on cities and causing massive casualties. With the exception of the attack on Pearl Harbor, which took place far from national soil, the U.S. territory had been safe until September 11, 2001.

The dystopian narratives of science fiction and disaster movies have constituted a huge smoke screen of spectacular entertainment, a shield of denial made of fulfilled fantasies. They have projected worldwide the U.S.'s paranoiac nightmares of landscapes under attack, and staged the U.S.'s grand fear of a backlash from alien enemies. When the Twin Towers were attacked and the trauma of future aggression so many times evoked by science fiction was actually staged in real time on millions of TV screens, the paradoxical likeness with Hollywood stories produced guilt feelings in viewers who could instantly connect the live images of the besieged Towers to special effects disasters. In hyperrealist sci-fi terms, the U.S. Empire was indeed under attack by aliens on its own soil.

*thomas cole's* the course of empire: *between past and future sublime*

Between 1834 and 1836, Thomas Cole, the father of the Hudson River School of landscape art, painted a cycle of five allegorical landscapes entitled, *The Course of Empire.* They illustrate five phases of a cycle of civilization from *The Savage State* (Figure 4.1) to *The Arcadian or Pastoral State* (Figure 4.2), from *The Consummation of Empire* (Figure 4.3) to *Destruction* (Figure 4.4), and finally, to *Desolation* (Figure 4.5). He intended these landscapes to delineate the ideal course of any past or forthcoming Empire. Already acting in a preemptive spirit, he executed his canvases as an ominous warning aris-

Figure 4.1

Thomas Cole, *The Course of Empire, The Savage State* (1834). The New-York Historical Society.

Figure 4.2

Thomas Cole, *The Course of Empire, The Arcadian or Pastoral State* (1834). The New-York Historical Society.

ing from a past History that provides models for infinite future scenarios. With its five tableaux staging a fatal and spectacular series of romantic landscape *capricci*, *The Course of Empire* may appear to us now as a blueprint for numerous film decors. Each painting is dominated by the same rocky hill overlooking the Empire's symbolic harbor and which appears to resist any civilization or destruction. Cole's discourse and rhetoric were inspired by the painter John Martin's biblical fantasies, and thus implied historical and ideological affinities between the Roman Empire and the young American republic. Such fantasies return fully in hyperrealistic Hollywood epics, the first being D. W. Griffith's *Intolerance* (1916). Their visionary spirit continues in science fiction utopias, disasters, and decadence.

Figure 4.3

Thomas Cole, *The Course of Empire, The Consummation of Empire* (1835–1836). The New-York Historical Society.

Figure 4.4

Thomas Cole, *The Course of Empire, Destruction* (1836). The New-York Historical Society.

In 1836, when Cole successfully presented the cycle, which New York benefactor Luman Reed had funded, the American Empire was already expanding west. Thus, Cole's landscapes of power and decadence appear as a series of dreams and nightmares about things to come. They stage a prophetic "theatre of memory" with wilderness, arcadia, architectural triumph, and decay as mnemonic places. After all, isn't the inscription "What is past is prologue" cut into the facade of the National Archives Building in Washington, DC? Cole's visionary but conservative message invited the conquering people of the eastern states to contemplate his

Figure 4.5

Thomas Cole, *The Course of Empire, Desolation* (1836). The New-York
Historical Society.

mythical sequence of wilderness, followed by a pastoral "middle landscape" *à la* Thomas Jefferson, then development and expansion, and
finally, wars and degeneration. A few years afterward, the trauma of the
Civil War produced the first deep political crisis of the Republic while the
greed of a bloody "nation building" effort was expanding rapidly into the
West.

Each of Cole's canvases is separated by a temporal ellipsis from the
next; the last both ends and restarts the cycle with the ruins yielding to a
wild nature and a new course. *Destruction* is a spectacular full-screen the-
ater dominated by bloody episodes from a civil war or the invasion of a
harbor under a menacing statue of Mars overlooking a crowd of victims
and aggressors dressed in classical costumes. *Desolation*, a postcatastro-
phe vision, shows the harbor as a horizon of ruined temples and marshy
waters with an almost invisible bird nesting atop a huge column off to the
left. The solitary column stands at the place generally occupied by a tree
(dead or alive) in many landscapes of the Hudson River School, and the
ancient solid rock face is now clearly visible. The burning buildings under
a stormy sky and fighting people found in *Destruction* have been replaced by
this deserted final dawn in *Desolation*, an abrupt change for the viewer who
examines the canvases sequentially. But something is missing in the cycle:
there is no Decadence between Destruction and Desolation, only the final
twilight peace of ruins, where nature renews its dominion over historical
empires. Cole painted unknown enemies destroying the empire's harbor
(Where did they come from? Why so much hatred?), but he did not paint
the slow and complex phase of decadence, corruption, and poverty.

Later, with its infinite plots of alien attacks and universal wars directed
against glorious empires, but also with its hundreds of plots dealing with
corruption and degeneration, Hollywood restaged these seminal can-

vases, realizing the narrative possibilities of Cole's operatic cycle. In an uncanny effort to both enact and exorcize his foundational, ominous course, Hollywood remediates, enlarges, and renders hyperreal all of Cole's special effects and potential plots, while American politics works its way through these fatal scenarios of empire. Cole's *The Course* (a symbolic *curse*?) seems to allegorically anticipate and imply all the landscapes and cityscapes to come. Cole's *pathos formulae* are the origin of a true iconology of American cinema, serving as ready-made scenarios and settings for many Hollywood genres. Within its film cycles U.S. cinema uncannily refashions these landscape dreamworks, staging so much of U.S. history, ideology, and art. From *The Savage State* and *The Arcadian State* to the three scenes of the Empire's harbor, film landscapes can be traced back to these seminal *pathos formulae* which perform the terrible "natural history" of the U.S. trying to expand globally.

## contemporary landscapes, a screened "mnemosyne atlas"

Hollywood landscapes' repetitions and variations result in an "iconology of intervals," which recalls the one theorized by art historian Aby Warburg when he observed the contradictory survival and return of classic *pathos formulae* (*Pathosformel*) in European Renaissance art. Warburg used the very cinematic term of "dynamogram," the "graph of the image as symptom,"[7] to define the moving cycle of the *pathos formulae*. This term is appropriate also for the description of landscapes in American genre films in which a technologically based aesthetic continuously refashions the traumatic layers and spectacular conflicts of the U.S. landscape in sublime terms. These landscape dynamograms of America's Manifest Destiny may have their grand model in the five canvases of Cole's *The Course of Empire*, with its powerful allegorical project of future *mise-en-scène*.

Warburg's terms, "dynamogram" and "engram," define the mnemonic survival of *pathos formulae* in the collective memory of European art. He applies dynamogram to compositions originating in Greek and Roman art that resurface in later centuries of European art: a hypertextual vocabulary of infinite variations on the same formulae have lived and survived. Dynamograms form a visual vocabulary that stresses the dramatic movement through space of bodies in passionate states. *Pathos formulae* is the term for the arrangements of mythological characters in trances that are present in pagan sculpture and later transposed into Christian art. Finally, Warburg uses engram precisely to underline the mnemonic traces that such compositions have left in the metamorphic language of visual culture. As a mnemonic surface or "magic pad" similar to the one described by Sigmund Freud to explain the functioning of our memory, visual culture can store engrams, reactivate them, and yet be ready to produce new forms.

I extend such dynamic terminology to Hollywood films' landscapes and bodies, which continually transform into newly pathetic icons.

Dynamogram can be applied specifically to the language of film genres in which spaces and bodies constantly return as mnemonic recompositions in "moving" landscapes. In this iconological context, I argue that the original landscape *pathos formulae* of the U.S. Empire, and their fatal rhetoric of self and nature, savagery and civilization were first articulated by Cole in *The Course of Empire* as well as in other of his religious and sublime landscapes, including *Expulsion from the Garden of Eden* (1827–1828) and the series *The Voyage of Life* (1840–1842). Beyond apparent variations but still within its generic rules, Hollywood refashions the rhetoric of Cole's biblical and classical *pathos formulae* and penetrates into their fictional space, reinventing it through dynamic editing, compositional effects, centrality of characters, and equally sublime special effects. Like Cole, Hollywood figures deep cyclic conflicts within U.S. history and culture, restaging in landscape their *pathos formulae* and transforming them. Moreover, Westerns and science fiction films repeat Cole's gesture of blending history with fantasy, national beliefs and fears with visual entertainment, and conservative morality with an immersive and shocking aesthetic.

Iconological terms such as *pathos formulae*, dynamograms, and engrams all deal with cultural traces crystallized in pathos-filled compositions of bodies in space. In a contemporary virtual Warburg atlas, Hollywood genre icons could figure alongside classical mythological figures and specifically American iconographies. Moreover, Warburg's art history terms can be interpreted as broad political and cultural categories, for he pinned up pictures of political events together with classical or Renaissance art reproductions on his boards.

Thus, like *pathos formulae*, Hollywood's dramatic "figures in the landscape" are iconological and political compositions that display uncanny likenesses, survivals, and returns from past U.S. history and ideology. Film landscapes are never purely narrative backgrounds nor simply distracting spectacular settings. They bear the traces of political projects and ideological messages. They press onto viewers' senses, memories, and fears and become part of their memory, carrying the subliminal strength of a past, even archaic, worldview ready to come back as future progress. Like the footprints left on the surface of the moon by U.S. astronauts, Hollywood landscapes bear the footprints of the United States' recurrent Manifest Destiny.

Our screen-made memory is full of traumatic "landscapes with figures." Neosublime science fiction *pathos formulae* circulate on our screens blended with satellite images of landscapes, war, territorial scars, and scenes of ethnic violence, each of which is soon erased but quickly returns. The visible earth on our screens is produced by a panoptical "magisterial gaze"[8] and disseminated on an infinite number of walls filled with screens. In *The Matrix Reloaded* (Wachowski brothers, 2003) Neo encounters the grand architect sitting in front of a large *wall of screens* in which each video cell frames an image of somewhere in the world. We can call this electronic grid a pixilated mosaic of live dynamograms, engrams, and *pathos formulae*, a palpitating Atlas Mnemosyne of live images. As if it were a living memory interface, its suspended frames, erasures, and returns carry out Warburg's atlas minute-by-minute.

Warburg anxiously considered the growing speed of the media (electricity, telegram, telephone, film), feeling that people no longer possessed the mental distanciation (*denkraum*) necessary to sustain the rapid engrams of mass communication. His uncanny response to the media chaos was the Atlas, an unfinished and open archive of screens full of reproductions of past and present *pathos formulae*. We too confront traumatic landscapes-information on our screens, and often we do not have the time to elaborate on their shocks, nor to clearly distinguish between the various states of the Empire they present to us, nor between the digital effects in fictions and the live shocks on TV. If we could virtually pin them all on the same grid of a gigantic Atlas, they would stage the violent *pathos formulae* of the Empire. Their survivals and resurgences activate the "magisterial gaze" that projects everywhere the matrix of U.S. culture and politics.

*traumatics, mnemotechnics, and ideo-logistics of landscape*

From 1882 to 1917 Buffalo Bill Cody successfully traveled the U.S. and Europe with his *Wild West* show, a circus-like spectacle of *tableaux vivants* showing live dramatizations of recent American battles with the Natives. Since then, the American "landscape with figures" found in movies has constituted a vast ambivalent "theatre of memory," a mnemonic technology addressed to the world. As suggested by the Renaissance memory systems described by historian Frances Yates, such narrative recompositions of bodies and spaces within the Empire not only stage the mnemonic map of U.S. nation building, but also *act out* and fulfill the most aggressive fantasies of conquest of this traumatic history. Hollywood films have been the ideological interface of the Empire's art of memory, and the screen its popular grand theatre.

This powerful mnemotechnics has been centered on Western and science fiction films, the two macro-genres of territorial conflict, occupation, invasion, and national epic; the lost dreams of escape from modern U.S. identity have been staged within the vernacular settings of late modern road movies. American territory, haunted by the Western's Natives and sci-fi's aliens, becomes an uncanny, fantastic land constantly menaced and invaded, almost destroyed, but always reconstructed. The Western and science fiction films with their stories of barbaric enemies keep up with (and remind the whole world of) the continuously morphing ideologies of the empire. (Is not "morphing" the most symbolic technique of contemporary special effects?) In the global media wars, cinema's "war machine" and image-weapons perpetuate the imperial *pathos formulae* to which America the Beautiful has been faithful for a century. The Savage

101

State, Arcadia, Consummation, Destruction, and Desolation are still on-screen. As foundational American landscapes of the principal film genres, they are *grafted* onto the world imaginary and people's subconscious much like Mount Rushmore was carved into sacred Sioux territory. As tools of American ideology, they accustom people to consider Hollywood's icono-philic Empire and its traumatic geographies as continually present and everywhere expanding.

Recent media events have refashioned what I call an *ideo-logistic land-scape* as a field of aggressive political discourses with renewed frontiers in which both fictional and real landscapes and cityscapes (both images of U.S. international politics and science fiction fantasies) form the power-ful *ideo-logistic machine* of the empire. Ideological polarities such as nature vs. technology, the mission of civilization vs. ethnic rights, and historical frontiers vs. cultural conquest have always been the prologue and then the battlefield of any imperial discourse on collective destiny. After the Cold War and 9/11, has the entire world become a potentially New Frontier panoptically overlooked by the U.S.'s new manifest destiny? On the basis of these recent events it is possible to illuminate *post-emptively* the persis-tent ideo-logistic of the U.S.'s traumatic sublime. If the sublime "shock and awe" rhetoric is still one of the basic languages of so many epic, cat-astrophic, and ruinous film icons, then terms such as "sublimate" and "subliminal" allow us to understand the allegorical pleasures of the con-temporary consummation and destruction of the empire.

*landscape as repressed trauma*

The title of Sigmund Freud's essay "A Child Is Being Beaten" (1919) is the phrase his patient uses to hide the fact that the beaten child of his fantasy is himself and that the aggressor is his father.[9] At the end of the analysis, Freud reconstructs the child's impersonal and incomplete statement of the title as: "I am/was the child beaten by my father and I witness/ed my own trauma and pleasure."

In a similar way, we can find *incomplete formulae* such as "our land is men-aced and soon will be invaded (by them)" in Western and science fiction mythologies as well as in slogans of political paranoia. Such statements hide historical facts that could be better expressed as "first we invaded this/that land and its inhabitants, and now they are going to attack us." For decades mainstream movies have propagated plots based on this trau-matic, reactive, and ideologically founded belief. Hollywood cinema, a national cinema, a collective dream, is full of self-victimization and self-heroization—masochistic and sadistic fantasies that mask or erase the reality of U.S. history. In many stories, a deep desire to dominate alter-nates with a fear of being punished or attacked for such cultural hubris. In the national context, cinema feeds people spectacular ideological injunc-tions and psychotic reconstructions of history and reality. However, as an ambivalent "poison and remedy," Hollywood is also a protective screen, offering the successful *denial* of America's paranoiac empire.

In paintings from the end of the nineteenth century by Frederic Remington, such as *Rounded-up*, *Fighting for the Waterhole*, and *The Scout: Friends or Enemies?*, we see cowboys isolated in agoraphobic spaces full of invisible enemies, though the titles do not explicitly describe who these enemies are. These unnamed and uncanny aliens are obviously Natives, and these canvases display precinematic shots of suspenseful landscapes under their menace. As in the case of Freud's patient, Remington's titles are incomplete statements hiding the entire story, the real victims, and the previous acts of the threatened protagonists. Anticipating many Westerns and their incomplete versions of the West's genocidal history, these works only show the late-arriving conquerors defending territories where millions of Native tribes lived before they were "smoked out."

Reading landscapes often means interpreting collective fallacious fantasies or filling shock narratives with off-screen details in order to trace a more complete, panoramic view of the conflicts they stage. Hollywood spatializes these conflicts and cryptically transforms historical reality into theatres of memory, presenting models of manifest destiny's relationship to the land. In the most powerful ideological genres, Westerns and science fiction, landscapes are theaters for the most complex question of U.S. history: its memory of itself as empire.

Thus, if western landscapes remediate older painting's effects and science fiction films are mainly about new special effects, it is because both of these genres are deeply invested in obsolete but still traumatic land *affects*, refashioning through them centennial and national feelings on wider screens. Even when landscape special effects renew sublime landscape art as fresh technological spectacles, they still *retell* the first traumatic Course of Empire. In a century of movies, Cole's grand style of idyllic, romantic, or sublime landscapes have morphed into hybrid new categories: the Savage Alien State in Westerns; invasions and epic planetary wars in science fiction; the Arcadian Vernacular for love, sex, city and country melodramas; the suspenseful Consummation of Empire in family sagas, thrillers, and action films; the sublime Destruction of Empire in epics, war movies, and dystopian science fiction disaster films; and the vernacular Desolation of Empire in road movies, gangster films, and other conflicts of the decadent empire.

*landscape as dream ideo-logistic*

Science fiction films have translated the territorial *instinct* of American culture into landscape special effects, which often reveal Hollywood's basic alliance with the technology of weapons, surveillance, and propaganda. Landscape effects are the "manifest content" of the U.S. Empire's dreams. Freud's term "manifest content," which defines the dream as we remember it before any interpretation, appears valid also for the U.S. landscape's history and ideology, and for how cinema remembers and restages them. Thus, we can say that film landscapes trace the "manifest content" of the American Dream as traumatic sets of sublime land conflicts beyond their Arcadian ideology.

Sequences containing landscapes have elements in common with dream sequences. As dreams, these sequences are created from previous fragments of real or fictional landscapes, materials that constitute what Freud calls mnemonic traces of the previous day. The unconscious mind of the dreamer invests his or her deepest feelings into these fragments reconnecting them to past traumas and desires and staging with them a new "manifest dream." Landscape sequences are also hybrid visual remains which retrace persistent aesthetic ideas, fragments of ideological discourses, and pictorial compositions, refashioning them in combination with more recent vernacular formations.

For Freud, the manifest content presents us with a dream facade that disguises deep but contradictory messages narratively. In narrative cinema, the ordering function of generic rules treats landscapes as facades, or perhaps backgrounds, that hide deeper land conflicts. If we interpret these decors as hybrid materials, we discover the dream ideo-logistic of landscape shots and compositions. This oneiric and political logic produces spectacle and affects, and reveals the metapsychology of the empire lurking behind the manifest content of genre plots. As dreams, filmed landscapes can be interpreted to reveal surviving fragments of historical traumas and the ruins of ideological mythologies.

Freud argued that dreams protect our sleep. Comparatively, film narratives protect the spectators' ideological sleep. Like dreams, film landscapes filter, project, and partially satisfy deep desires, fears, and anxieties linked to grand questions concerning the land, about its new and previous inhabitants and about technology and nature. Through narrative facades and sensory effects, the American ideological dream tries to keep audiences "sleeping" in front of the screen. For decades Hollywood has produced fictional paranoiac attacks against the empire, which prepared, reflected, and advertised the new aggressive post-Cold War U.S. politics. For Freud, if a dream becomes an unbearable nightmare, sleepers awake, and start to deal with it. Could 9/11's real traumatic cityscape produce such an awakening? Could the uncanny *background* of the empire become a real danger?

In nineteenth-century painting many examples of world conquest provide the background for the nation. A famous case is the *The Heart of the Andes*, painted in 1859 by Church. Basing his large canvas on travel sketches from several locations, he assembled a panoramic view of a forest, a waterfall, rich vegetation, and the grand horizon of the Andes, all with great detail and luminous atmosphere. This compound view of South America became famous overnight for the peculiar way it was exhibited in New York. Church presented it with curtains and low light and made binoculars available to paying viewers. He showed the Andes in a window-like set as if seen "from our own backyard," as Robert Hughes writes, to illustrate the magisterial gaze of a nation already acting out its fatal dream to dominate the world.[10]

During the grand age of landscape painting, artists such as Cole and Church created the sublime visual language of the empire. The "dream factory" of Hollywood has reactivated this "style of formal declamation"[11] (as Barbara Novak defines it) in its thousand-fold landscape. For the U.S.'s ideo-logistic dream, the whole world is one vast background and the object of infinite "road maps." On the screen, the latter being our most popular interface for mainstream culture, the U.S. let flow their persistent fantasies of *being* the empire, of *living* the Consummation of Empire, and of ambitiously rescuing people from nightmarish scenarios of Destruction and Desolation, many of which they have either allowed or staged directly.

## clear and present danger, the sublime shock and awe of 9/11

I think we can see the cinema as reflecting…the bloody and tragic twentieth century. This may seem strange for an art-form created largely in America, where whole cities have never been leveled to the ground, but it is not so hard to understand in the rest of the world—in Europe, Africa or Asia.

### Peter Wollen[12]

Our version of the sublime valorizes neither nature nor revolution but rather that peculiarly American *status quo* of domination and blindness. A refusal of memory…a depthless phenomenological now where awe and entertainment encircle one another.

### Robert Morris (685)

Could *those two monstrous towers* have been masking out something other than the sun?

### Robert Morris (689, italics added)

This time [9/11], no compensation was necessary for the absence of cameras at the Ur-event. Nevertheless, the inevitable sense that one lacks the perfect image of such an event, an image that would be adequate to its enormity, is evident not only in the incessant replaying of the moments of collapse but in the myriads of books, magazines, and exhibitions that strove to capture the event photographically, to reduce it to an instant.

Mary Ann Doane[13]

maurizia natali

*ruins on television*

Cole's *The Course of Empire* participates in a genre known in French as *paysage avec ruines* (landscape with ruins), which is the dark, romantic side of landscape painting and the parallel, "collateral damage" of clean neoclassical or operatic works about history. This gothic imagination and melancholic historicism deals with settings of past civilizations: ruined empires or obsolete religious architectures of Italy or Greece, countries that in the eighteenth century were the attractions of the Grand Tour. Time and history created these landscapes of ruins, and the melancholic distance of their *pathos formulae* provides artists historical lessons for the present.

Our numerous televised "landscapes with ruins of wars" are variations on this traumatic category, with the important difference that it is no longer history and time which ruin landscapes and cities but the trio of "imperialist politics, war, and technology." On the post–Cold War era's global wall of screens, we glimpse landscapes of ethnic conflict, minor and devastating wars, and collateral terrorist attacks. The figures in these scenes are no longer picturesque peasants living among the ruins of the past nor visitors seeking the awe and aura of panoramic remains. They are, instead, today's victims captured in burned spots of landscape, corpses abandoned in ugly urban relics, and fugitives barely surviving in territories attacked by so-called precision weapons and smart bombs. TV steals close-ups of bloody limbs and crying faces, which are quickly shown and just as quickly erased from our screens. Women crying among the ruins of poor houses, refugees attacked in their camps by helicopters or cluster bombs, children stoned and wounded, all are people immersed in the traumatized landscapes of globalization, which others ("we are all Americans") watch on their domestic screens. These are the most popular landscapes of empire's Destruction and Desolation.

The attack on landscape is also different from old images of ruins. In his *Destruction*, Cole already offers a version of this change well before Western, war, and disaster films' natural or technological catastrophes or science fiction's "shock and awe" encounters between the U.S. (*us*) and them, the enemy, the Other. In sci-fi wars the basic plot starts from *here*, within the U.S. as metonymy of the civilized world where *we* are under siege, and

106

then implies other nations, the planet or the universe, all waiting for help, even if the price to be paid is the destruction of landscapes, cities, planets, and more. The model for this environmental price paid for the empire's victory is clear in *Independence Day* (1996) by Roland Emmerich. At the film's close, an apocalyptic horizon occupied by the huge ruin of an evil space-ship is ignored by the victorious crew who are just happy to gather there for a self-congratulatory meeting.

9/11 images appeared on the same types of screens on which people watch disaster movies. This event created an immense and *live* wall of screens, displaying in real time the two towers attacked by two planes, crowned by smoke and fire, and then crashing down to ground zero. The attacks reenacted what American people had seen many times elsewhere both in fictions or newscasts from around the world. What had always happened far away, and been unthinkable in the U.S., was happening on American soil and was visible on domestic TV. In the collective mind of Americans, a traumatic, unbearable hole had suddenly been opened, a hole in the very symbolic fabric and historical memory of an Ameri-can landscape that had never been hit in that way. Disaster fictions were instantly drawn into this hole and uncannily reactivated. Collective memory, deprived of comparable events in U.S. history, suggested fic-tional spectacles while eyes were watching televised reality. The reaction to the trauma was an unbearable and overwhelming feeling of the *sublime*, an amoral hybrid of horror and fascination.

The confusion between film simulations and the tele-present reality was aesthetically and morally intriguing. The guilt for this collapsing of aesthetic sublimity with ethical horror occurred because the collec-tive memory could not recall previous attacks and, therefore, no shield of memories was available to be placed in front of the upsetting reality. (Americans did not think spontaneously that their country could be or become like others.) Only deep cultural traces and images from the past can protect human perception during the precious interval that takes place between a perceptual shock and its mental trauma; and between a sense of horror and one of uncanny, sublime beauty. When no cultural engram—a protective filter traced in history—is able to produce a sepa-ration from a traumatic spectacle, reality and fiction blend in a way we cannot morally accept.[14]

Had Americans acknowledged as their *own* political production the "shock and awe" landscape rhetoric as well as other collateral damages, 9/11 would certainly not have been any less traumatic; it would perhaps have produced a deeper collective mourning, however. But despite its presence in so many films, the catastrophic sublime is not commonly per-ceived as the genuine ideological expression of the empire's death drive, against which someone out there in the world and in history could strike back. Despite so many landscape allegories insistently morphing themselves into special effects disasters, few Americans read catastrophic land-scapes for what they are: a political *dream style* and the national ideo-logistic of the contemporary empire. Instead, they are considered merely as enter-taining technological "testing" aimed at delivering shock and awe to the world audience. (Nuclear experiments as well have been seen by many as tests rather than as deadly spectacles of power, political projects, and real ecological disasters.)

Hal Foster writes of historical avant-gardes as a traumatic phenom-enon, producing long-lasting aesthetic effects and moral reworkings for generations of artists and audiences. The experience of avant-gardes can-not be "historically effective or fully significant in their initial moments"[15] nor can their impact be totally absorbed or quickly symbolized when they appear for the first time. As cultural trauma, they need to be reworked at intervals, with interruptions and repetitions, in a "complex relay of antici-pated futures and reconstructed pasts" (Foster, 29). Neo avant-gardes play this secondary role, "reacting out" first subversive practices with repeti-tions and disseminations of the original strength of previous traumatic scandals addressed to the future.

Jacques Derrida has defined the fear of "rogue states" in the U.S. as "the trauma that comes from the future."[16] Derrida's and Foster's definitions of trauma as interface between past and future allow us to connect Ameri-can landscape *pathos formulae* to issues of traumatic memory, reenactment, anticipation, and preemptive imaginary. Hollywood genres accustom audiences to historical landscape traumas through narrative plots and epic repetitions, but they also anticipate catastrophic futures and world-wide conflicts. Running parallel to aggressive U.S. doctrines and policies, these reconstructed or fictional disasters prepare spectators to consider wars as mainly concerning other (usually "nondemocratic") countries and savage people. (Frontier Wars, the World Wars, and the wars in Viet-nam, Afghanistan, and Iraq have all been declared against wild Natives, dictators, oppressive regimes etc. whom the U.S. fights honorably for uni-versal civilization and freedom.)

Until the terrorist attack in New York, Americans felt relatively safe because of a false *protective screen* made of ideology, economic pragmatism, and Hollywood fictions. They then discovered (did they?) the "desert of the real."[17] Through New York's ground zero, the ruins of reality suddenly and uncannily perforated this special imaginary screen. 9/11's traumatic landscape wound staged the sublime Destruction and Desolation of the empire as not far away, but at home. Cole's allegory anticipates the sym-bolic hole created by the shattered Twin Towers, the dreadful *void* of their unsustainable wound and scar.

landscape as wound and scar: the sublime cityscape of september 11

The global loop of televised images of 9/11 was perceived as inadequate with regard to the extremity of the catastrophe which, though unique in symbolic terms due to its location, was nevertheless not an isolated event in modern history. For TV viewers around the world, a cityscape wound was carved live in the most famous harbor of the Empire. The images of the attack brought together many icons of disaster, and the overwhelming spectacle was uncannily similar to several film clichés. Matching the nightmares of so many science fiction films, the blazing towers suddenly embodied one of the foundational fantasies of the empire: destruction through backlash. New York was offering to the world the spectacle of a paranoiac fantasy *rendered manifest*: an attack against U.S. soil. Across the globe people felt compelled to compare this sudden new "desert of the real" to fictional film catastrophes. But can Hollywood fictions keep up with 9/11? When compared to historical events such as atomic bombs, the World Wars, and Vietnam—all more catastrophic in terms of the ruin, the number of victims, and duration in time—9/11 pales. Yet, these catastrophes did not take place in the most famous cityscape of the world, and the Empire did not broadcast live images of them as it did with this later sublime wound.

We can argue that there are two iconographic strategies of the Empire. One is globally disseminated and deals with the U.S. under attack *in movies*. The other circulates more rarely and deals with declassified *documents* concerning atomic bombs, nuclear tests, and the bombing of enemy countries such as Vietnam. Both these strategies had made a real attack against U.S. soil *unimaginable* in the minds of most people, and both strategies were defeated on 9/11: the terrorist attacks united what before had been kept carefully separate, namely fiction and reality, narrative and documentary. Two airplanes in a few minutes carried out large-scale and costly catastrophic special effects, while millions of television screens worldwide broadcast this "alien" (i.e., non-Hollywood) live historical production for hours. From the cinders of the towers, a new sublime landscape was reborn. And since then the Empire has struck back with two new wars that have served to promptly reconfirm its centennial style.

Have the new preemptive "landscapes of war with catastrophe" staged live and abroad (though still visible on American screens) been able to heal the wound and scar made by 9/11 and to void the way it ominously confirmed Cole's *The Course of Empire*? Certainly. The burning and collapsing towers gave way to a worldwide act of mourning for the U.S. However, they also led others to compare the wounded New York cityscape with landscape and cityscape wounds in other parts of the world that have been less visible or auratic in the media scene. And yet, as a result of 9/11, these other wounded landscapes are now *seismographically* connected with "the Big One" (the name filmmaker Michael Moore has given to the

U.S.), at least in our imagination as far as the wall of screens of traumatic landscapes is concerned. There should be no obstacle, neither ethical nor aesthetic, stopping us from considering all these landscapes of ruin as resulting from a global death drive of which the empire remains the most powerful historical embodiment. Today, the most catastrophic American landscape ever produced on U.S. soil from an alien attack has become part of a vast theatre of memory on the basis of which a global spectatorship can remember and pass judgment.

*"shock and awe" aesthetics and their sublime grain of truth*

A successor to old European imperialism, U.S. foreign policy has produced landscape wounds and scars in numerous countries. American wars, always complete with nation-building policies, democratization, and torture, have led millions to become anti-American, while others have been rethinking the course of empire and its destructive dark side. And if during the media frenzy that immediately followed 9/11 some headlines around the world read: "We are all Americans," this sentiment was never truly felt worldwide. What was felt, however, by some Americans and many others is that, for at least this one time, U.S. soil had finally joined much of the rest of the world, that it had become one with the unprotected and with territories subjected to aggression over the last two catastrophic centuries.

Two hundreds years ago the "magisterial gaze" of the empire started to survey the country of the Natives, the background for the *"novus ordo seclorum"* ("new world order") proudly inscribed on the dollar bill. Now the eye atop the pyramid is contemplating the grand theatre of the world over which, like a panning camera, it overlooks other traumatic landscapes, war installations, and theatres of ruin.

It has been observed that the 9/11 terrorists won the first media war of the new century. Actually, they were simply imitating the visual culture and bicentennial sublime aesthetic of the Empire. Like the nuclear tests done during the Cold War, 9/11, the sudden installation of a catastrophic cityscape, was a perfect imitation of the sublime "shock and awe" so common in U.S. visual culture and policy. With much less technology than is used in nuclear testing or wars and with less labor used to produce special effects, the perpetrators took seriously the U.S. pop culture of war games and alien aggressions and counted on audiences' memory in their attempt to blend fiction with reality and make pure destruction out of this hybrid.

The name given to the military operation with which the second (and still ongoing) war in Iraq began—"Shock and Awe"—recalls the aesthetic of the religious sublime landscapes of Cole, Martin Johnson Heade, Frederic Edwin Church, or Albert Bierstadt. But like "Desert Storm" during the first Iraq war of 1991, "Shock and Awe" is above all an ideologically naive attempt to give an appealing name to the dirty job of war. In fact, it was meant to traumatize both unprotected victims and protected TV viewers and to show both of them the price, in destruction of landscape, that is to be paid for U.S. democracy and market freedom. The names for these military operations belong to a rhetoric of entertainment or gamesmanship that is meant to mesmerize both enemies and viewers alike, supporting actors and spectators of a live spectacle whose title could be "Preemptive Attack for Freedom, Democracy, and Free Market" and whose star is the Empire in its role as superpower. Of course, a happy ending to this spectacle is nowhere in sight. "Shock and Awe," bombs, torture, and occupation have instead incited a bloody resistance from various Iraqi groups. To borrow a term from Marc Augé, even a horrible "non-place" (*non-lieu*) such as that produced by the ravages of war may become a landscape that people want to defend as their own, until liberation comes.[18] These people are entitled to live the authentic Kantian feeling of independence that rational subjects feel in front of overwhelmingly sublime and traumatic catastrophes.

Well beyond the ruins of 9/11, Cole's *Destruction* and *Desolation* are still contemporary landscapes all around the world, where the Empire is rehearsing the old play of Manifest Destiny in those soon-to-be-wastelands filled with people who happen to be "in the way of progress."

*back(s)lash: a flash of truth*

9/11 is a *backlash* spelled out in a language that the Empire's popular art has invented. It is the moment when decades of U.S. terrorist politics finally *backfires*, the unparalleled superpower having produced, either directly or indirectly, millions of victims and countless disaster landscapes. As two giant standing letter I's, the phallic Twin Towers had dominated the New York skyline and the global landscape for 30 years. The attack carved a new landscape engram reverberating on the world's screens. Towers, airplanes, smoke, and fire traced a new hieroglyph within the cityscape decor, as a message from another culture. This alien writing created a zone of ruinous hybridity at the heart of the Empire, the wound and scar of a flaming inscription suddenly *back(s)lashing* the city's skyline.

The towers uncannily recalled the two number ones of September 11, and fell down as ruined dots of a suspended writing. Erasing them the two airplanes traced a new inscription of ruin and void. Slashing the two imperialist letters, they transformed them into media ruins within the landscape of world TV. In a few hours the towers morphed from erected double-I's to slashed stumps crowned with fire and smoke, then to grounded gothic shadows in ruins, and finally to dramatic and ruined points of suspension. The live installation was then protracted for months, allowing it to be viewed by millions of spectators.

The *back(s)lashing* of the towers has become the first sublime image of the new century, an "*œuvre d'art totale*," as the musician Stockhausen scandalously defined the event. Predictably it announced future vengeful counter-attacks from the Empire, and the new century has started as an era of landscapes enflamed by loops of terrorist attacks and imperialistic wars around the world. The wasteland at the heart of New York will soon be filled by two immaterial glass towers, spiritual ghosts of the two destroyed materialist symbols. But, will the symbolic hole ever be filled?

Thomas Cole first presented this country with his idea of cyclical history, and his allegories still haunt America. Perhaps empires cannot change their regressive cycle. For now, we can still read into the ideological folds and plots of American Cinema the traumatic *pathos formulae* of the Empire. For within all the "shock and awe" effects that either threaten or numb us, we can read flashes of historical truth showing that Hollywood landscapes have been the true theatres of the ideo-logistic American dream. Perhaps these uncanny and blinding flashes are the only "manifest dream content" the Empire's awareness can still afford, and perhaps to the traumatized world out there they appear much clearer than U.S. culture may admit.

## landscape film gallery from *the course of empire*

*between savage and pastoral state*

Among the "cells" announcing future genres from the Edison Company shorts we find only fragmented backgrounds. For instance, part of the suspense effect in Edwin S. Porter's *The Great Train Robbery* (1903) comes from a tension between fragments of projected landscape and fragments of real landscape; between the view seen from the train's window as a moving screen onto the screen and the real forest setting for the attack and the ensuing chase, shot with great depth of field. The set-up thus opposes views taken from within the "civilized" space (train/screen) with the traumatic exterior views (attack, murder, revenge) taken in the savage soon-to-be-tamed wilderness where lawless men meet their fates. Elements of the *The Course of Empire*, are also found in the feature films of D. W. Griffith. *The Birth of a Nation* (1915), for instance, stresses the natural setting for scenes of private and public violence, such as war battles, the pursuit of the White girl by the Black aggressor, and the attack by the Klu Klux Klan, and in *Intolerance* (1916), Griffith remediated the Empire's sublime pictorial and theatrical decors from nineteenth-century painter John Martin. *Broken Blossoms* (1919) highlights Griffith's subtle use of pictorialist photography both in the filming of Lillian Gish and Richard Barthelmess and of the squalid cityscape, while *Way Down East* (1920) shows the same actors living idyllic and dramatic situations in New England landscapes: at the end, for example, David rescues Anna who is adrift on an authentic frozen river.

112

But it was mostly during the Classical Hollywood era that landscape images of major genres formed complex iconographies with refined iconological details and participated in the authorial style of filmmakers, all the while remaining popular attractions. With the advent of dramatic narrative rules and genre plots, cityscapes and landscapes became essential tools for spectacular aesthetic effects, propaganda values, and psychological reverberations.

In King Vidor's *Duel in the Sun* (1946), the "lust in the dust" final sequence shows Pearl Chavez (Jennifer Jones) and McCanles (Gregory Peck) shooting at each other under the gaze of the rocky Indian Sphinx in traumatic Technicolor sublime. The arrival of the train echoes famous photographs staging the contrast between the "metallic" East culture and the West as "land, leather, and horses." The legend of the Egyptian origins of the Natives is encrypted both in the view of the rocky Sphinx after the titles when Orson Welles's voiceover evokes the story of Pearl Chavez, and in the close-up of the medal the Sinkiller, or Peacher (Walter Houston) gives her, which, for a few seconds, shows the Sphinx and the pyramids at Giza. While the reddish Sphinx is a kitsch and mysterious postcard, the Egyptian medal condenses the "film's dream-work"[19] concerning the archaeology of a multicultural America. The most profound detail and most ancient *pathos formula* of the film, the medal shows the uncanny *likeness* between the Sphinx and the Indian rock head. This amalgamates the Sublime West and the Giza Valley and translates in visual terms certain nineteenth century beliefs of philosophers and anthropologists concerning the *Egyptian* origin of the pre-Columbian settlers of America. The enigmatic medal figures these archeo-ideological questions linked to the origin of the Empire.

Howard Hawks's *Red River* (1948) deals with land occupation, cowboys, and cattle. Filmed in Texas, Arizona, and New Mexico, it is based on the history of the Chisholm Trail used for herding cattle. Dunson (John Wayne) and Matt (Montgomery Clift) epically drive the animals within these frontiers. Their oedipal conflict is stressed when Tess (Joanne Dru), a young woman, appears. As in many classic Westerns, the landscape frames the story, but several times it also dissolves into the handwritten page of a diary; the effect of this strategy is to oppose land and document by way of the centuries-old conflict between images and words, a conflict now staged in moving format. This landscape "mise en page" reminds us that as early as 1915 Vachel Lindsay had compared the new media of captioned movies to Egyptian hieroglyphs.[20] In fact, the landscape-page suggests a hybrid of figuration and writing, while the motif of the page-landscape evokes the idea of Nature as a Book where God has written his creationist message of expansion; an open volume of Manifest Destiny and of the American dream. Dunson traces on his cattle's hide two S's which, he says, recall the course of the Red River they have crossed. Tess's name also has two S's, and like the cattle and the land, she too is considered the future possession of the men. We read her feminine body in the two sinuous lines hieroglyphically positioned by the film's dream-text between the D of Dunson and the M of Matt, in other words, at the center of their traumatic homosocial conflict. The landscape becomes a graphic *pathos formula* of gender and land conflicts.

In *The Searchers* (John Ford, 1956), Ethan's neurotic wandering in Monument Valley traces a loop-like itinerary that allows Ford a spectacular use of environmental traumas. The "cinematic painter" of Monument Valley who, since *Stagecoach* (1939), renewed the Western with several films including *My Darling Clementine* (1946) and *Cheyenne Autumn* (1964), single-handedly turned this arca of Navajo territory sitting on the border of Utah and Arizona into what now stands as an emblem and a symbol of the entire Western genre; the spectacular red mesas and buttes become a solid *cliché* of a multimedia (films, television, advertising, etc.) Western style. Ford was inspired by a tradition of painters such as Charles Russell and Frederick Remington who, at the turn of the nineteenth century, contributed to the pictorialization and "ideologization" of the West. Like them, Ford arrived *late*, at a time when the West was no longer a frontier of the Empire. Indeed, by then, the West's iconology had already begun morphing itself in various media and according to each passing political era. Ford's landscapes are often filmed through doors or windows and spectacularly connect the characters' psyche to the land. In Andrew Sarris's terms, Monument Valley, a visual leitmotif that serves as an authorial signature for Ford, is a "shadowgraph,"[21] an image already filled with ghostly images.

*consummation of empire*

Victor Fleming's *Gone with the Wind* (1939) shows visual compositions of mansions and landowners with land as the materialist setting for southern traumas during the Civil War. In the 1950s, family melodramas such as *The Long Hot Summer* (Martin Ritt, 1958), *Cat on a Hot Tin Roof* (Richard Brooks, 1958), or *Giant* (George Stevens, 1956) perpetuate this iconography of the Consummation of Empire in parks and mansions. In *Giant*, Stevens shows Texas cattle, horses, and prairies not only in reality but also painted on large canvases inside the Reata mansion of the Benedicts (Rock Hudson and Elizabeth Taylor). When poor Jett Rink (James Dean) discovers his fortune and the oil business becomes central, we see Texas oil drilling towers and highways with new cars. Douglas Sirk's *Written on the Wind* (1956), another oil melodrama, and his "women-weepies" such as *Magnificent Obsession* (1954), *All that Heaven Allows* (1955), and *Imitation of Life* (1959), all offer examples of picturesque, postcard landscapes carefully contrasting with the crises of the wealthy middle-class. Consummation of Empire stages 1950s houses and gardens in ways that anticipate the clean landscapes of later TV serials.

The archaeological landscapes and settings of epic films constitute Hollywood versions of the nineteenth-century sublime archaeologies of Thomas Cole, John Martin, and Lawrence Alma-Tadema. From *Intolerance* (Griffith, 1916) to *Cleopatra* (Joseph Mankiewicz, 1963), from *Ben Hur* (William Wyler, 1959) to *Gladiator* (Ridley Scott, 2000), and to recent Egyptian fantasies, such as *Stargate* (Roland Emmerich, 1994) or *The Mummy* (Stephen Sommers, 1999), the Hollywood Empire has always remediated Rome-mania and Egypto-mania as retro gestures full of easy metaphors, allegories, and hyperrealist effects involving past empires. *Gladiator* creates an immersive environment made out of Alma-Tadema's and Cole's archaeologies and perfects them through digital effects. The film offers landscapes of the empire, from Germanic forests on fire to North African fields, and offers as well the most hyperrealist reconstruction to date of Ancient Rome and its Coliseum, all of which appear as backdrops for flashy heroism and decadent vanity. But this is the empire that the Empire dreams for itself.

*consummation and suspense*

*Niagara* (Henry Hathaway, 1953) is a thriller advertised as "Niagara and Ms. Monroe: the most electrifying sights in the world," and as "A raging torrent of emotion that even nature can't control." Since the nineteenth century Niagara Falls have been a favorite for painters and photographers alike. And though Marilyn Monroe's femme fatale character seems indifferent to this location where she meets her lover, from the beginning her unhappy husband, Joseph Cotton, can be seen standing on a rock gazing at the falls in Romantic fascination. The waterfalls offer the setting for the film's grand finale when honeymooning "good girl" Jean Peters gets a close view of them from aboard a rocking boat, along with Cotton who has kidnapped her and killed his wife. The boat's name, *Maid of the Mist*, underscores the link between sublime nature and female sexuality. *Niagara*'s noir atmosphere collapses the landscape icon with the sublime Marilyn. In a film poster, a gigantic Monroe leans over the falls as a goddess and *esprit du lieu* ("spirit of the place"). Even star-centered blockbusters have links with ancient iconographies of landscape.

Alfred Hitchcock used the ambiguous environment of the postwar empire as suspenseful *pathos formulae*. The films' settings are backgrounds to a modern traumatized psyche, the same one also found in avant-garde painting and photography. As stations of uncanny adventures, Hitchcock's common spaces produce uneasiness, fear, and violence. The mnemonic theatres of the empire's subjects, they stage traumas and flashbacks, and stick to characters as cut-outs in a modernist collage. Hitchcock's vernacular has been compared to Edward Hopper's suspenseful blank and modern metaphysic. An alien *émigré*, he saw the empire as a place of traumatic and nightmarish settings. As in symbolist, metaphysical, or surrealist art, heroes move across locations painfully reconstructing their identity through love and crime. Safe havens become existential traps that magnify ambiguous desires. Hitchcock reveals how demonic our relation to the landscapes of modern empire can be.

In *Saboteur* (1942) the final sequence brings Pat (Priscilla Lane) and Barry (Robert Cummings) to the Statue of Liberty in New York where she meets the terrorist Mr. Fry (Norman Lloyd). Using vertiginous editing Hitchcock deconstructs the neoclassical Miss Liberty controlling the arrival of immigrants in the U.S., and transforms the stiff statue into a cinematic and modernist collage. In *Rope* (1948) two male friends have killed a third and put him in a large trunk prior to a dinner party in their New York apartment. Though the film mostly takes place indoors, Hitchcock nonetheless manages to emphasize the city setting by way of a large bay window in the background that shows a miniature cityscape, complete with variations of the sky, smoking chimneys, and flickering neon lights. In *Strangers on a Train* (1951), an amusement park in Washington, DC, the Lincoln Memorial, solitary night streets, a tennis court, and a merry-go-round all become the stage of Guy (Farley Granger) and Bruno's (Robert Walker) oedipal and homosexual exchange of murders that emblematize the American Empire of the 1950s. In *Vertigo* (1958), Madeleine (Kim Novak) and Scottie (James Stewart) wander in a melancholic San Francisco. The Golden Gate Bridge, a romantic coastal view, the sequoia forest, an old hotel, and the Spanish Mission of San Juan Bautista all become traumatic emblems of the couple's adventure between life and death, love and crime. The spiral, symbol of the film, which is present in Saul Bass's titles and in Madeleine's hair, is visible also in the section of a sequoia, where the woman traces her fingers across the rings indicating the tree's lifespan. Hitchcock places in a shadowy forest this emblem of graphic ambiguity, present in avant-garde art, from Marcel Duchamp's "anemic-cinema" spirals to Francis Picabia's and Jasper Johns's targets.

In *North by Northwest* (1959), Hitchcock includes the United Nations, an empty midwestern corn field, a Frank Llyod Wright–like villa, and Mount Rushmore. Hitchcock reconstructed Gutzon Borglum's gigantic sculptures of the four American presidents gazing proudly at the sacred Sioux region, because he did not get the permission to film this patriotic shrine to the Empire. On his reproduction he staged the "personal and political" initiation to life of Roger Thornhill (Cary Grant) and his lover Eve (Eva Marie-Saint). In *Psycho* (1960), he transformed into dead ends an anonymous hotel in Phoenix, Arizona, highways, a solitary roadside motel, and a weird Victorian house. These Hopper-like places of solitude become metaphysical places of anxiety and horror, where an empire's serial killer reigns over his archaic, unconscious decor. In *The Birds* (1963), an innocent small California village, Bodega Bay, becomes the surrealist territory occupied by thousands of birds attacking humans, perhaps because of the arrival of Melanie Daniels (Tippi Hedren) and her love for a man under his mother's gaze. The final stormy sky and the birds occupying the horizon offer an icon of the end of empire.

### destruction and desolation

A figuration in Cole's *Destruction* and *Desolation* "atomic" landscapes manifests a new aesthetic of traumatic special effects. As life-sized multimedia installations, the luminous "mushroom" clouds occupy center and horizon. Light, color, heat, sound, wind, clouds, debris, and ocean waves qualify nuclear tests as a new sublime, producing "shock and awe" in viewers overwhelmed by these spectacular weapons of mass destruction. Films such as *Dr. Strangelove* (Stanley Kubrick, 1964), *The Atomic Café* (Jayne Loader, Kevin Rafferty, and Pierce Rafferty, 1982), and many others have used actual atomic explosion footage while many science fiction films have been concerned with issues raised by the nuclear sublime. In *A Movie* (Bruce Conner, 1958), found footage of the 1950s was used to illustrate the empire's death drive: fragments of newsreels and advertising and television images form a catastrophic landscape of war, disasters, nuclear testing, suicidal accidents, dangerous sports, and threatened environments—a collage of the ecological anxiety of the empire.

Kubrick's *Dr. Strangelove, or: How I Learned to Stop Worrying and Love the Bomb* sets itself squarely against nuclear politics, the U.S. military, ex-Nazi nuclear scientists, and the cyclical paranoiac loop involving U.S. presidents and the Pentagon. When General Ripper (Sterling Hayden) decides to launch a bomb and eliminate the "commies" in the Soviet Union, from within the War Room President Muffley (Peter Sellers), General Turgidson (George C. Scott), and nuclear scientist Dr. Strangelove (Peter Sellers) try to undo the attack and save the world. But it is too late. The bomber aircraft flies over enchanting landscapes, and after the blast, a chain reaction of atomic explosions looks as sublime as the uncanny song of the score, "We Will Meet Again."

*The Atomic Café* was edited with archive materials from World War II, as well as nuclear test footage and Cold War political and military propaganda materials. The filmmakers omit the voiceover and edit clips that speak for themselves, as in a dream or free association. As a counter-propaganda compilation, the film was close to the Nuclear Freeze movement of the Carter and Reagan eras. The film builds a tragic, sublime, and grotesque landscape of the atomic empire, its Cold War and surreal "shelter" culture.

*The Atomic Filmmakers* (Peter Kuran, 1999) is a documentary made from declassified footage produced by the Lookout Mountain Studios, a secret studio headed by the Pentagon with Hollywood facilities and a special crew. From 1949 to 1969 the studio filmed 300 nuclear tests in Nevada and the Bikini Atoll. The film uses clips of tests with military crews, maps and animation, a voiceover, and dramatic scores. In the interviews, four filmmakers, still unmoved by the sublime horror they filmed, narrate various technicalities and adventures.

*new pastoral state*

*Days of Heaven* (Terrence Malick, 1978) starts with a collection of old pictures as ghosts of people, city streets, and rural regions. Bill (Richard Gere) escapes from a steel factory in Chicago where he has accidentally killed a guard. In search of another life with his girlfriend Abby (Brooke Adams) and her sister Linda (Linda Manz), he arrives in Texas where they are hired at the farm of a landowner who soon marries Abby. The director carefully filmed with Nestor Almendros the seasonal changes in the prairie of the empire, as well as grain elevators, machines and coaches, workers and animals all echoing paintings by Andrew Wyeth, Edward Hopper, and Winslow Homer.

*Dances with Wolves* (Kevin Costner, 1990) presents a revisionist interpretation of the Western. Costner plays Lieutenant John Dunbar, a Civil War soldier who goes west to Sioux territory. The title comes from the name Dunbar receives from the Natives who observe him living in an abandoned cabin where he befriends a wolf. The subject of the verb "dances" is missing while Dunbar renounces being an "English subject." His journal sketches recall painters such as George Catlin and Alfred J. Miller who in the early nineteenth century depicted Natives in colorful portraits, while aware of the genocide that Manifest Destiny was preparing. Western landscape, a space of rebirth, is where Dunbar refuses the culture of war and accepts the Natives' peaceful relationship with nature. In American paintings of the nineteenth century, such as Cole's *View from Mount Holyoke, Northampton, Massachusetts, after a Thunderstorm—The Oxbow* (1836) or Asher B. Durand's *Progress (The Advance of Civilization)* (1853), the West is depicted on the left side of the frame as "Savage Past, with Natives and Wilderness," while the East is presented on the right side as "Civilization and Expansionism." In Costner's film the Sioux live in an idyllic society of ecological harmony; but in the end, Dunbar, persecuted as a deserter, leaves his tribe, while the cold snowy landscape announces the forthcoming genocide.

*new consummation and desolation*

Road movies show the Empire's nostalgia for primitive violence and lost frontiers and the vernacular meandering of contemporary misfits on the periphery of the law. They form an "escapeland" with themes borrowed from Western and gangster films. The heroes are romantic losers who suffer modern anxiety and existentialist boredom in the desolation of small towns, and who, in their desire to leave everything behind, end up finding the "last exit." Highways, the ordinary landscapes of vernacular America, or final sublime landscapes, all form a spectacular trap. The traumatic experience of traveling "on the loose" looking for a "line of escape" or a "no man's land" ends in the "paranoia" of drug experimentation, free love, crime, and death. The connection between body and machine makes characters reach the ecstasy of speed as they hurry toward "point zero." These are "landscapes with car" such as can also be found in Hopper's realist paintings of solitary roads. Here the road interrupts the unfolding of decadent stories only to mirror them much like Richard Estes's reflective and hyperrealist cityscapes offering a baroque veneer to vernacular desolation. Violent cops await somewhere and death arrives before any dreamland. Sublime national landscapes coalesce with characters' interior exaltation and offer islands of eccentric geography. John Huston's *The Misfits* (1961) and Arthur Penn's *Bonnie and Clyde* (1967) anticipated road movies, while Dennis Hopper and Peter Fonda's *Easy Rider* (1969) is the "cult" prototype for *Duel* and *The Sugarland Express* (Steven Spielberg, 1971 and 1974), *Vanishing Point* (Richard Sarafian, 1971), *Zabriskie Point* (Michelangelo Antonioni, 1970), and, more recently, *Stranger than Paradise* (Jim Jarmusch, 1982/4), *Wild at Heart* (David Lynch, 1990), *Natural Born Killers* (Oliver Stone, 1994), and many others.

*Easy Rider* refashioned the "landscape with motorcycles" of Laszlo Benedek's *The Wild One* (1953). Counterculture commonplaces, pop songs, and pop philosophy are its ingredients. During New Orleans Mardi Gras the acid trip sequence is a gothic *vanitas* of eros and death, while night camps and a prison are the passion stations of the bikers soon to be killed on the road. Western cowboys and cattle, and even Monument Valley, appear as pop ruins of Manifest Destiny. The final river meanders as a question mark in the landscape and echoes Cole's *The Oxbow* and Robert Smithson's *Spiral Jetty* (1970), an earthwork made from a swirl of stones poured into the Great Salt Lake in Utah.

In *Thelma and Louise* (Ridley Scott, 1991), two young women flee a frustrating suburban life for the commonplaces of sunny highways, motels, and sublime canyons in the first feminist version of the male-oriented road movie. They are frozen forever in a final emblematic shot of the sublime canyon, suspended as in a canvas by Mark Tansey against the macho rocks. Bars and roads are the territory of men and truck drivers; women trespass when they simply "drive, rather than working as store clerks, waitresses or prostitutes."[22] The film highlights two main genres of the American Landscape, the vernacular (homes, highways, motels, and coffeehouses) and the sublime (scenic views shot in California and Arizona). In the end, the film's landscape is arrested in time by the Grand Canyon in which the two women decide to jump, while Scott freezes the shot thus withholding from view the car's crash. Thelma and Louise will remain suspended in midair forever, reaching emblematic stillness, the only sublime experience they could afford.

In *Natural Born Killers* (1994), Oliver Stone shows an accelerated patchwork of image-ruins from the American pop dream which form the mental landscape of two young, pre-Columbine primitives for whom

Monument Valley is one fugitive icon among others. The pair come from the empty vernacular culture and "anywhere" landscape of the contemporary Consummation and Desolation phases of the cycle of empire. Vagabond, romantic, wasted, they are the victims of the "blank" produced by traumatic TV hyperrealism.

In *The Sunchaser* (Michael Cimino, 1996), Blue (Jon Seda), a young metis thug and murderer dying of cancer, kidnaps his doctor (Woody Harrelson) and forces him to leave Los Angeles for the sacred Navajo territories of Utah and Arizona, where he hopes to find the medicine man Sunchaser. Blue cherishes an illustration of a high mountain and a lake from an old book. After a number of reciprocal challenges, the men arrive at the Navajo mountains. The doctor leaves Blue to the medicine man, and offers him the ring of his dead brother. Blue disappears in the lake through a dissolve, as if taken back into Nature. From the vernacular space of Los Angeles to the sublime vistas of the West, landscape drives the quest for this New Age narrative of "spiritual healing." When Blue and the doctor encounter some Natives on horses in Monument Valley, they ride together as though they were crossing a *commonplace* of landscape painting, photography, and Western films. The final mountain and lake are inspired by Albert Bierstadt's and Thomas Moran's grand sublime paintings. Like these artists, Cimino layers shots from different places with a similar spectacular intention.

*destruction and desolation (and back again)*

Science fiction films restage all the phases and stories of the Empire in a hybrid of technological excess and primitive sublime. Past "landscapes with ethnocide" return as alien attacks; Natives come back as "red commies," body snatchers, or aliens. Historical traumas and utopias are re-created in space exploration and allegorized as frontiers, while universe-sized catastrophes restage centennial fears and guilt still alive within the empire.

In *2001: A Space Odyssey* (1968) Stanley Kubrick uses prehistorical apemen, 1960s-style spaceships, a black alien monolith, and a final rococo *salon* to figure his past and future Course of Empires. The ape-men of the Savage State recall the views of animals or primitives seen behind protective glass in dioramas of natural science museums. Soviet and U.S. scientists meet in a spaceship slowly gliding in the dark sky of Consummation of empire; and astronauts Frank and Dave travel to reach Jupiter under the control of Hal, the softly speaking "big brother" computer equipped with a single red "eye." When melancholy Hal becomes megalomaniacal and eliminates Frank and the sleep-frozen crew, Dave disconnects his "brain" and starts his final journey. The landscape strategy of the film is revealed in the two final sublime sequences. The first opens an immersive psychedelic corridor into which Dave is absorbed with his pod. His wide-open eyes see geometric and biomorphed shapes inspired by abstract and optical art, and terrestrial oceans, deserts, and mountains (even Monument Valley) filtered with electronic colors. The sequence titled "Jupiter…and beyond the Infinite" recalls an LSD drug trip but remediated using prismatic effects from da Vinci and J. M. W. Turner. Dave's journey ends in the isolation room, where he sees himself replicated at various ages of life. Reborn as a fetus and suspended in the womb of the universe in a luminous halo, Dave finally looks at us as a new alien through the sublime darkness of the empire's solitudes.

In science fiction, Hollywood invented the "Twin Tower attack aesthetics" well before the fact. One film to use this aesthetic is *Independence Day* (Roland Emmerich, 1996), an instant political blockbuster that was immediately endorsed by both Democratic Clinton and Republican Dole: after the Cold War, a story of the U.S. and the world cooperating against violent aliens was welcomed. Emmerich clouds the sky of the most important cities of the world with giant spaceships, which instantly incinerate the White House, the Empire State Building, and other landmarks. Characters include a Jewish computer wizard (Jeff Goldblum) who is the main hero; a Christian U.S. president (Bill Pullman) who leads an airplane assault against the aliens; and a Black pilot (Will Smith) who heroically mistreats a monster in the desert as if it were just a rubber puppet (which, by the way, is what it really is!).

In the film's "happy end," destroyed spaceships pollute an African tribal region, the Valley of the Pyramids, and the Great Basin Desert in Nevada, but the happy winners meet without noticing the huge alien crafts burning against the blue sky, as if dreadful global ecological consequences were just passing collateral damage. *Independence Day* refashions the old strategy of "shock and awe" linked to the American paranoia of "enemy combatants" and "crusades" against them with convincing special effects. Ever since Cole's *Destruction* and *Desolation* canvases, catastrophic landscapes have enabled the Empire's subjects to happily enjoy the sights offered by sacred battles between America and aliens over "security and freedom." These inflammable landscapes, however, betray the nightmare of a backlash, of a possible real Destruction, ever-burning at the heart of the globally victorious U.S. culture and military power. Perhaps catastrophic landscapes simply ask for a reactionary biblical decryption, but at least they honestly manifest the Empire's cyclical paranoia of confronting hateful enemies "out there."

In his most recent film, *The Day After Tomorrow* (2004), Emmerich sends five tornados into Los Angeles and submerges New York with high ocean waves and ice. He also covers the Northern hemisphere, including the U.S., with an ice blanket. Perhaps such fantasies finally offer a means for arresting the many preemptive wars of the Empire, and inaugurate a new sublime Desolation: that of "global warming" and future catastrophes of a different nature.

# notes

1. Barbara Novak, *Nature and Culture: American Landscape and Painting 1825–1875* (New York: Oxford University Press, 1980), 19.

2. Zygmunt Bauman, *Wasted Lives: Modernity and its Outcasts* (Oxford: Polity; Malden, MA. Distributed in the U.S. by Blackwell, 2004), 38.

3. Robert Morris and Noam Chomsky, "From a Chomskian Couch: The Imperialistic Unconscious," *Critical Inquiry* 29, no. 4 (Summer 2003): 692; hereafter cited in text.

4. Janet Walker, "Captive Images in the Traumatic Western," in *Westerns: Films through History*, ed. Janet Walker (New York: Routledge, 2001), 225; italics mine.

5. Scott Bukatman, "The Artificial Infinite: On Special Effects and the Sublime," in *Visual Display, Culture Beyond Appearances*, eds. Lynne Cooke and Peter Wollen (Seattle: Bay Press, 1995), 279; hereafter cited in text.

6. John O'Sullivan, "Annexation," in *United States Magazine and Democratic Review* 17, no. 1 (July-August, 1845): 5–10. O'Sullivan's editorial is reproduced in its entirety at: http://web.grinnell.edu/courses/HIS/f01/HIS202-01/Documents/OSullivan.html (accessed 03/15/2005).

7. Gorges Didi-Huberman, *L'image survivante: histoire de l'art et temps des fantômes selon Aby Warburg* (Paris: Editions de Minuit, 2002), 176; my translation.

8. See Albert Boime, *The Magisterial Gaze: Manifest Destiny and the American Landscape Painting c. 1830–1865* (Washington, DC: Smithsonian Institution Press, 1991).

9. Sigmund Freud, "A Child Is Being Beaten," in *Penguin Freud Library*, vol. 10, *On Psychopathology*, ed. Angela Richards (London: Penguin, 1993 [1919]), 159–194.

10. Robert, Hughes, *American Visions, the Epic History of Art in America* (New York: Alfred A. Knopf, 1997) 161.

11. Novak, Barbara, *Nature and Culture, American Landscape and Painting, 1825-1875*, revised edition New York: (Oxford University Press, 1995) 19.

12. Peter Wollen, *Paris Hollywood: Writings on Film* (London; New York: Verso, 2002), 2.

13. Mary Ann Doane, *The Emergence of Cinematic Time: Modernity, Contingency, the Archive* (Cambridge, MA; London: Harvard University Press, 2002), 262, note 1.

14. At the end of a century in which newspapers and TV have fed us innumerable bloody images caused in great measure by the aerial bombings of cities and landscapes, millions of American TV viewers now regularly watch *many* traumatic landscapes from wars and disasters in faraway countries. As for the cinema, serving double duty as a prophet in the desert landscapes of history and as the most popular art form dealing with sublime (or abject) traumatic landscapes, it never tried to hide these horrors.

15. Hal Foster, *The Return of the Real: The Avant-garde at the End of the Century* (Cambridge, MA: MIT Press, 1996), 29; hereafter cited in text.

16. Jacques Derrida, "Y a-t-il des états voyous? La raison du plus fort," *Le Monde Diplomatique* (January 2003): 10.

17. Slavoj Zizek, *Welcome to the Desert of the Real!: Five Essays on September 11 and Related Dates* (London; New York: Verso, 2002).

18. See Marc Augé, *Non-Places: Introduction to an Anthropology of Supermodernity*, trans. John Howe (London: Verso, 1995).

19. See Thierry Kuntzel, "Le travail du film," *Communications* 19 (1972): 25–39; and "Le travail du film, 2," *Communications* 23 (1975): 136–189.

20. See Vachel Lindsay, *The Art of the Moving Picture* (New York: Macmillan, 1915).

21. See Søren Kierkegaard's *Either/Or*, trans. W. Lowrie (Princeton: Princeton University Press, 1971).

22. Marita Sturken, *Thelma and Louise* (London: BFI, 2000).

# asphalt nomadism

## the new desert in arab

## independent cinema

l a u r a   u .   m a r k s

> When Almighty God created things He made for each
> of them a partner. Intellect said, "I am setting out for
> Syria"; and Discord said, "And I go with you." Fertility
> said, "I am setting out for Egypt"; and Disgrace said,
> "And I go with you." Hardship said, "I am setting out for
> the desert"; and Salubrity said, "And I go with you."[1]

The odes of the pre-Islamic nomads do not *begin* as such. They are just
marked with an abrupt call to fellow riders to stop at the site of ruins.
The great ode of Imru' l-Qays (500–540) begins: "Halt, friends both! Let
us weep, recalling a love[r] and a lodging."[2] The odes do not end, but are
broken off just as abruptly, the ruins exhausted for memories, and the
riders move on.

The nomadic odes, or *mu'allaqat*, establish a certain understanding of
the passage of time and hence the meaning of story. There is no teleology in the desert, they say. Blowing sand effaces markers, erasing time
and memory. A landscape that preexists us, outlives us, and, unlike other

landscapes, forgets us, the desert makes us aware of the limitations of human perception and memory. The desert is not empty, but it can only be navigated by close attention to the wind, the dunes, the oases, and plant life. The desert is not chaotic, but it is best understood locally; it asks for embodied presence, not abstract order.

As much as this writer wishes to roll down dunes both physical and conceptual, to embrace the smooth space of the desert, her thoughts are necessarily disciplined by the striating forces of settlement, industry, geopolitics—that compel her to be something more than an orientalist looking to get lost in somebody else's landscape. The seductive concept of smooth space, Gilles Deleuze and Félix Guattari reminded us, lives only in interchange with the disciplining concept of striation.[3] Smooth space seems always to be elsewhere. Once you explore it, it springs into complex life on scales micro and macro. In the desert, acacia trees and thorny shrubs spread their limbs to protect the soil from the predations of the blowing wind, so that other plants may grow there. In the desert, nomadic people are constantly enjoined, by means subtle and forceful, to submit themselves to the civilizing forces of religion and the soporific of a daily wage. The desert is never really "smooth," for that is death. The pitiless desert is an outsider's fantasy; nomads themselves work to find succor in the desert. The more we examine the relationships between the smooth and the striated in desert space, and the relations of life and death that their movement describes, the more difficult it is to distinguish them. A true cinema of the desert sees the desert in relation to the outside forces that shape it.

Deleuze and Guattari wrote with sympathetic acuity about the smooth spaces of sand, snow, and sea and the nomadic people who draw their knowledge and sustenance from them. I do not intend to fault the philosophers for romanticizing the desert. We who inherit their thinking need to stay on the ground: both in thought, moving close to the surfaces of concepts, and literally, remaining alert to signs of life in the sand and scrub of the desert. In this chapter I stay close to a third element as well, the cinema; in particular, independent cinema from the Arab world.[4] "Independent" indexes an emergent cinematic practice, relatively outside the film and media industries and close to the surface of events. The filmmakers and videomakers whose work I discuss here are themselves nomadic thinkers, in that their practice stays close to the material and conceptual reality of life in the Arab world. Even if, as we shall see, it strays away from the sand.

My invitation to contribute this chapter asked me to write about the cinema of the desert, and I chose the deserts of the Arab world: the Arabian Desert and the Rub al-Khali (empty quarter) in the southern part of the Arabian peninsula, and the Syrian, Saharan, Libyan, and Nubian deserts. My initial thesis is that the cinema of the desert would share the properties of the *mu'allaqat*: nomadic, nonteleological, self-organized, embodied, and concrete. However, the social relation of Arab peoples to the desert has evidently changed since the time of the *mu'allaqat*. Early Islam enjoined a unity that surpassed tribal unity and facilitated urbanization and migration. As Islam replaced the nomadic worldview with its promise of a justice that surpassed life and tribe, the odes had an "ontological irrelevance" for the faithful. Pan-Arabism and transcendence both carried Arabs' allegiance beyond local territory. And while the Bedouin have continued to embody Arab ideals, the social relation of Arab peoples to the desert in the past century has been increasingly one of leaving the desert behind, leaving smooth space and local organization for striated space and abstract order. Thus, films set in the desert either tell the story of a regretted but necessary departure or use the desert as a setting for historical glory or timeless fantasy. There are few Arab films about the desert itself; most films set in the deserts of the Arab world approach them from the outside, particularly from Europe.

The new cinema of the desert, as I will explain, is set on asphalt. The new self-organized, nonteleological narrative from these parts of the world is the Arab road movie. A history of practices of striating the desert, more or less continuous with the history of the cinema, pushes the nomad onto open road—and the road into ruin.

The Arab road movie is a latecomer to the road movie genre, typically a genre of existential self-seeking. The celebration of individuality is a relatively new thing in the Arab cinema. Many of the nomadic poets, the authors of odes to traces of ruins in the sand, were outcasts and misfits. Their difference from their society gave rise to art. In concluding I will ask, is there a similar process whereby the Arab filmmaker, or Arab cinema, arises from ruins? Is there a nomadic cinema that might inherit the properties of the *mu'allaqat*?

## what might a nomadic cinema look like?

A cinema modeled on the nomadic odes would surely lack teleology. It would commence and end seemingly at random. It would devote several scenes to mournful recollection of some lost beloved who can only be recognized by the traces of his or her abandoned camp; that is, it would linger at the ruins. It would devote many more scenes to attentive description of the camel or like vehicle that permitted the nomadic filmmaker to finally ride away from this scene of destruction. It would respect no organizing principle, save that of poetry or cinema.[5]

Interestingly, the nonorganic life of sand provides another model for the nonteleological character of the desert narrative. Nature is full of emergent patterns. The desert is not a chaos, but organized according to local properties of the territory, sand, and wind. For example, physics prove that in sculpted dunes, the amplitude of the wave forms is an emergent property of the amplitude of the wavelength of the wind and the size of individual grains of sand.[6] The self-organizing character of sand dunes might be only a metaphor for the self-organizing character of nomadic life. But people become like the things they spend time with; and, as Manuel De Landa observes, sometimes human history is best explained by geological principles.[7] Desert narratives, like the forms of the desert itself, emerge from local conditions rather than universals. We might say that the human storytelling drive and the desert occupy two different scales, two different wavelengths; the story, physics suggests, emerges from the interaction between the two.

### the striated desert

Nomads themselves do not live in the high desert but move through it. Jibrail S. Jabbur, in his ardently detailed catalogue of the life of the Syrian Bedouins, explains that nomad life is organized around the search for water and pasturage and a return to the fringes of settlements to wait out the summers. He attentively describes the delicate ecosystem of the desert, devoting chapters to its multitude of indigenous plants and animals. "Desertification," usually the result of settlement and overgrazing of cattle, destroys water sources and plant and animal life: thus the desert as limitless expanse of sand is a human artifact, a place of greater interest to mad dogs and Englishmen than to nomads.

Socially, the smooth space of the desert has always interacted with striating forces. Bedouin-sedentary (*badawah-hadarah*) relations once possessed a healthy hydraulics (in De Landa's term) whereby the properties of each were refined and stimulated in interaction with the other. For example, trade relations between settled people and Bedouin nomads and seminomads (i.e., herders) maintained a flow of goods and contact between desert and settlement. Similarly, the Bedouin practice of raiding forced Arab emirs to consolidate their powers in order to defend settlements and caravans from Bedouin depredations. Arab people trace many cultural values to the Bedouin, such as kinship solidarity, honor, and hospitality. Yet these values are misted with guarded nostalgia, for example, in the writing of the great Andalusian historian Ibn Khaldoun (1332–1406), who expressed a sense that the Bedouin are somehow purer than settled people (in a noble-savage paradigm) but deplored their practices of raiding and pillage and seemed to wish them firmly in the past.

Nomadic life cannot tolerate abstraction. Close attention to the senses' relay with the subtle life of the desert is necessary for the survival of one's animals, one's tribe, and oneself. This is clear. It is not difficult to argue the obverse, as Mohammed Bamyeh does: that sedentarization is concomitant with embrace of abstract system of value. The broken narratives of the *mu'allaqat* were supplanted rather abruptly by the teleological organization of the Qur'an, Bamyeh writes, and the abstract orders of language, commerce, and spirituality that made Islam possible. Though he cracks not a reference to nomad philosophers Deleuze and Guattari, Bamyeh corroborates their argument that nomadic thought embraces immanent meaning and has no truck with overarching schemes of value. Drawing on sociologist Georg Simmel, he shows that the money system, necessitated by trade and centered around Mecca, standardized the value of objects quasi-linguistically, in that their value depended on what others would pay for them (Bamyeh, 18–22). Such value systems are meaningless to people who have little to trade, like the Bedouin. But they are essential for the establishment of a greater system of abstract order, such as Islam. The Qur'an says that the return to God is more valuable than any valued thing, thereby, Bamyeh argues, actually confirming the emerging abstract system of value.

Monotheism cannot tolerate nomads. Its transcendental absolutism abhors the persistent immanence of nomadic life. And Bedouins seem to have little use for the postponed fulfillment of the Muslim afterlife. The British explorer William Gifford Palgrave, writing in 1866, recounts that he asked a Bedouin whether, after a life of raiding and pillaging, he expected to be welcomed in Paradise. The Bedouin replied, "We will go up to God and salute him, and if he proves hospitable (gives us meat and tobacco), we will stay with him; if otherwise, we will mount our horses and ride off."[8] Jabbur's survey of Muslim chronicles shows that Bedouins had no compunction about raiding pilgrimage caravans to Mecca.

Emerging governments used many enticements to settle the Bedouin. Ibn Saud, according to a biography written by his granddaughter, "realized the bedouin cannot be educated and changed unless he settles. He cannot have discipline unless he has a house. The mobile bedouin without a house becomes the enemy of stable government. The king introduced *tawtin*, sedentarization, to replace tribal custom and tradition with holy *sharia*."[9] Note how this flattering account attributes to the founder of Saudi Arabia a double act of striation, the deft linkage of sedentary life with correct Islamic practice. Confirming this association, in the early days of the Saudi state, the 1930s, Bedouins also served as religious police (Ikhwan, predecessors to present-day Islamic fundamentalists) having "'migrated' from a nomadic life and settled in the belief that settlement facilitated proper religious practice."[10]

Youssef Chahine's epic *The Emigrant* (1994) leaves no doubt as to the relative virtues of nomadism or settlement, polytheism or monotheism.[11] It is an Egyptian reworking of the biblical story of Joseph. Ram, the youngest brother in a seminomadic family, best-loved by their father and keenly aware of the ways of plant life in the desert, ardently desires to emigrate to Egypt and learn to farm. Ram's goal is attained in a roundabout way when, having survived his jealous brothers' attempt to drown him at sea, he is sold as a slave. By dint of wit and faith Ram gets himself freed and is given a plot of unarable land in the sandy desert. If he can successfully farm it, it will be his. Meanwhile he has begun to preach against the "death cult" of the Egyptians and to admonish listeners that there is only one god and that one need not be embalmed to reach the afterlife.

Water governs *The Emigrant*, as the search for water rules nomadic travels in general. Amid a general tone of Chahinian high camp, one of the film's loveliest scenes is when Ram and his small group of allies leap awake to the sound of the first rains and joyously sow barley by midnight. Later Ram discovers fresh water flowing nearby and fashions an aqueduct of reeds to divert it to the land. Meanwhile, discord reigns in Egypt between worshippers of competing deities, and in an act of revenge the evil monarch has the peasants' crops burnt. Emigrating en masse, they come upon a peaceful agricultural kingdom over which Ram rules clemently. He permits them to stay: "Let the soldiers farm." Later still, Ram's murderous brothers throw themselves onto the mercy of this wise agricultural ruler, not recognizing him as their brother. He forgives them and the film concludes with his long-awaited reunion with his father. In *The Emigrant* the patriarchal family, the monotheistic tribe, the agricultural settlement, and rational town planning triumph over the wasteful, backward practices of superstition, venality, and herding.

## the desert is seen from a distance

Since the desert has first been represented in art in the Arab world, it has been shown over the shoulder of someone leaving. Regretfully, with a sense of descent from grace, but leaving nonetheless. Imru' l-Qays composed his ode in exile, having been ostracized by his father, the king of the Kinda tribe (Bamyeh, 51, 176–177). Contemporary North African desert movies are about leaving the desert behind. The Egyptian *Arak al-balah* (*Date Wine*; Radwan El-Kashef, 1998), the Algerian *Desert Rose* (Mohamed Rachid Benhadj, 1989),[12] and the Sudanese short *Insan* (*Human Being*; Ibrahim Shaddad, 1988) all suggest that modernity means leaving the desert and the village. Men leave, emigrating to work; women and children stay behind. To do otherwise, like the bewitched settlers in Nacir Khémir's *The Wanderers of the Desert* (1986), is to plunge backward into history.

Only since European colonization has the desert been represented as a place people go *to*. Until the second half of the twentieth century, Jabbur writes, most of the writing on the desert and on Bedouin life, in any language, was the work of European explorers (Jabbur, 14). These men explored the desert and lived with nomadic people, sending their accounts back home in English, French, and German. The desert has become a place of nostalgia for and fantasy about a time when social life could be locally organized in harmony with the sand and the winds. The campy popular Bedouin films, a staple of the Egyptian film industry in the 1920s–1940s, fed urban fantasies about nomad life. They were in fact inspired by American desert movies such as *The Sheik* (1926), in which Rudolph Valentino plays the Bedouin.[13] Hady Zaccak points out that desert movies such as *Lawrence of Arabia* (1962) and *Three Kings* (1999) comprise an "eastern" genre, an orientalist adaptation of American cowboy movies with Arabs standing in for the Indians.[14] Recent foreign films, such as *The Sheltering Sky* (1990) and *The English Patient* (1996), are drawn to the desert as though to an enveloping, maternal/destructive force and to the noble, ascetic qualities of nomadic people. These movies tend not to perceive the emergent order of the desert, though they seem to be aware that Tuareg people, for example, have such knowledge. Now the desert is seen in the Arab world, in the occasional love story and video clip, with a romantic view similar to that of the European colonials. A place to be simple again, to get lost, to revert to a fantasy life, on the weekends. Travel to the desert is time travel.

For some filmmakers, the nonteleological space of the desert serves as a setting for powerful historical reimaginings that differ from fantasy because they do not confirm the present. The Tunisian filmmaker Nacir Khemir uses the desert as a time-travel device in *Wanderers of the Desert* (1984), where the space of the depopulated desert town comes to resemble the past of the Islamic golden age in Andalusia, except that it is disturbingly unlively.[15] Khemir, who lives in Paris, has said that he constructs these fantasies of the classical Arab past in order to escape from the present of poverty and global colonization: "I cultivate my absence from home by advancing further into a fantasy world" (quoted in Shafik, 53). In an Africanization of the Bible similar to Chahine's *The Emigrant*, the Malian Cheick Oumar Sissoko sets the book of Genesis in the arid plateaus of northeastern Mali, the harsh landscape explaining the self-organization of the earliest tribes into sedentary and nomadic. Oumar Sissoko's *Genesis* (1997) is a history of striation that emerges from local organization, a pointed parallel to contemporary African civil wars.

Aside from fantasy and historical films, the desert itself is rarely a subject of Arab cinema. Fewer people live in the desert now, and those who do, do not have time to make movies about it. The cinema of the desert is really a cinema of abandoning the desert. The movement toward sedentary life, encouraged by trade and Islam, accelerated under the pressures of erosion, urbanization, nationalization, and industrialization. Talking about the desert, even in these contexts internal to the Arab world, forces a focus on issues that are already past. For the desert has been striated for good by pressures from outside the Arab world. These include Islam, colonialism, capitalism, and the search for an essential ingredient of modern social organization that you can surely guess. Any work of cinema that seeks respite in the desert from the complexity of modern life—well, it has its head stuck in the sand.

One of a few recent Arab films that presents seductive images of the desert and Bedouin life is *Alamein—A Moment of Life* (2002) by the Egyptian Ezz El-Din Said. This short, made-for-TV film begins with an erotic exchange of glances between a doe-eyed woman tending her goats in the desert and a man who eagerly climbs the dunes to approach her. He nears the lovely woman, she looks toward him expectantly, and the man blows up. In this film the desert is poisoned. Land mines planted during Egypt's hostilities with Israel have never been defused. Here the Bedouin are as glamorized as in any Hollywood fantasy, but the wars of other people's nations haunt nomadic life. The global military economy literally occupies the sand.

## asphalt nomadism

A survey of contemporary Arab cinema reveals few deserts and a lot of driving. Driving, and getting nowhere. The goal is not reached; the map becomes useless. Smooth space prevails, as in the desert of sand, but something is deeply different in these new works of asphalt nomadism. The new desert is the Arab highway. The new self-organizing, nonteleological narrative is the Arab road movie.

Emblematic of the Arab failed road movie is *Baalbeck* (2001), a triptych by the Lebanese videomakers Ghassan Salhab, Akram Zaatari, and Mohamad Soueid. Each 20-minute sections re-tells the same story, about a writer and photographer who set off from Beirut to Baalbeck, the ancient Phoenician/Roman ruin converted to an amphitheater, to cover a concert by the Syrian singer Sabah Fakhri. Each of the three trips gets hijacked by something "trivial."

Salhab's section is an Antonioniesque *dérive*. At one point, inspired by something, the writer says, "Stop a minute," and they park by a field. There he composes a poem, "As far as we can go / the days carry us / As far as we can go." Dissatisfied, he crosses out the last line. It is funny that writing a poem about the voyage is more seductive than the voyage itself. There is an implicit dread that the journey will prove no more than a string of clichés, especially as, to the photographer's annoyance, the writer appears never to have heard of Fakri. They take a detour in search of one Abu Elias, who supposedly makes the best *labneh* sandwiches in Lebanon. Later the writer becomes fascinated by a mountain spring. But when he fetches the photographer to come see it, it has disappeared. These momentary diversions take their toll on the 20-minute time allotment, and our explorers never get to Baalbeck.

In Zaatari's section, writer and photographer take up pursuit of a beautiful and mysterious youth. Abandoning their assigned route, they follow the car that picks him up hitchhiking. Following from a distance as he travels into increasingly inhospitable territory, they carefully obtain all the things he discards a used tissue, lip balm, a Kinderegg chocolate wrapper. Finally, when the youth strips to go for a swim, they take advantage to go through all his things. They carefully note the size of his underwear but not the name written on his driver's license. Nomad-style, they ignore the standard forms of evidence and search for other artifacts that might be more immediately meaningful, especially the things that touched the youth's body. Homoeroticism becomes a self-organizing principle in a country, Lebanon, where homosexuality is illegal. For same-sex desire, teleology is impossible. Desire can only be a perpetual motor, terminally creative. They never get to Baalbeck.

Soueid's section, the most evidently political critique, is harshly absurdist. As the writer drives to pick up his companion, the radio announces, "The director-general of Syrian Radio and Television said that peace with Israel is possible if Lebanon agrees to fully withdraw from the Golan Heights [the Syrian territory occupied by Israel]." The announcer adds that the pop star Céline Dion will be performing with Sabah Fakhri to celebrate the liberation of the South (referring to Israel's withdrawal from most of Southern Lebanon in May 2000). The concert, their journalistic prospect and sign of a healthy pan-Arab cultural life, has become just a pawn in a crazy game of politics and global pop culture. "Fairouz [the diva whose name is synonymous with Lebanon] was here and we're going to cover a concert by the vulgar Céline Dion." Soueid's section concludes with the journalist pissing in a river, and his voice saying, over a melancholy shot of water bugs skating on the golden pool: "I wanted to be a filmmaker, now I'm only a journalist." They never get to Baalbeck.

The road traveled also becomes a crazy dérive in *Baghdad On/Off* (2002) by the Iraqi filmmaker Saad Salman. At first it appears to be a conventional documentary by an Iraqi filmmaker, Salman, exiled for 25 years and attempting to return to Baghdad to visit his ailing mother. He hires a driver who skirts every route toward the Iraqi border from Iraqi Kurdistan. The journey is potholed with delays and wrong turns: one road is blocked, another infested with Iraqi soldiers shooting at smugglers, another, along the seemingly endless concrete wall of a military installation, seems too dangerous to continue along. On the map Salman keeps pulling out to consult, the roads to Baghdad become so many dead ends. His mysterious driver, who refuses to be photographed, intones, "You can count on me, tomorrow we'll be in Baghdad, inshallah"; yet his schemes to get to Baghdad become increasingly complicated. In the immiserated, droughtridden refugee camps, Salman is met with warm hospitality and also unremitting anger and contempt toward Saddam Hussein's regime, no less than toward the UN embargo. We hear the horrifying stories of Kurdish and other displaced people, former prisoners, a women whose son was shot in front of her, the 500 people who died when a cigarette factory was bombed. Salman learns a new verb for genocide, to Anfal, a derivation of the name of the Kurdish city where the regime killed thousands of people.

A scholar shows the flattened hole where his ear used to be, admitting that he is lucky because many people mutilated this way died of gangrene. "It's depressing. I need glasses, but how can they stay on my head?"

The film also witnesses the ingenuity and survival skills of the Iraqi people, such as the recyclers who use spent grenades to weigh vegetables, and their propulsion toward freedom even at the highest cost. A refugee woman who has lost her children still says, "Being free is better than having a house, better than life." A man who was imprisoned in Kasr el-Nahayr takes the filmmaker on a tour of the deathly jail, now empty, and points out a high, narrow window where once the prisoners piled up 40 blankets so they could put their hands and faces in the sun. "Tomorrow we'll be in Baghdad, inshallah," becomes the refrain of this circuitous, dead-end trip. Finally, as every route to the capital becomes exhausted, the tattered map becomes a useless lie. They never make it to Baghdad.

As a documentary *Baghdad On/Off* is stunning: beautiful cinematography and exquisite image and sound editing honor the people who are its subject. As a meta-documentary it is also powerful, for, as we realize that the invisible driver spouting wise aphorisms is an invention, recorded in the editing suite, we recognize that truth sometimes only arises from fiction. But needless to say, the film has been very controversial in the Arab world. In the year it was made, it was refused at every Arab film festival except Beirut Cinema Days, and rejected by the Institut du Monde Arabe in Paris.[16] When *Baghdad On/Off* screened in Beirut, the audience ignored its artistry and focused their anger on its anti-Saddam, pro-American message. Yet the film is a work of nomad epistemology. Unable to pursue official routes, it makes use of the material immediately at hand—as the Iraqi people do themselves. Salman's exquisite sense for audiovisual montage gives rise to such emergent meaning, for example, in a scene that begins with the loud buzzing of bees. A shot of bees crawling in and around some oddly shaped canisters gradually makes sense when we meet the beekeeper, who explains that spent rocket shells make good beehives.

*why did the desert give way to the highway?*

This question is complicated to answer. It has in part to do with the urbanizing and homogenizing tendency of Islam since the late sixth century. But the reader can surely guess that in recent times the first answer is Oil. The sedentary-Bedouin dialectic, though increasingly challenged by consolidations of power in the Arab world, was sustainable until oil was discovered in the desert. This new and decisive striation of the desert is not entirely a result of colonialism nor of the depredations of foreign capital, though these are involved. The final destruction of the nomadic way of life, and the source of the new asphalt nomadism, lay in a series of transactions that irreversibly translated the local into the generic.[17]

What one thing do nomads refuse to sell? Their camels, their "ships in the desert." In the *mu'allaqat*, loved ones and prized possessions may perish, but the camel, "the highest and most stable form of value is conceived of not as a means of exchange but, rather, as an enabler of life, itself often being on the verge of perishing. It is the means by which the wanderer moves perpetually away from the possibilities of discerning values in abstract themes" (Bamyeh, 24). The camel is what grounds nomadic life and the last thing a Bedouin will sell. Abdelrahman Munif's novel *Cities of Salt* chronicles the lives of Saudi Bedouins who go to work for the American company come to extract the oil from under their sand, ARAMCO. It is a gripping scene in which the workers receive their first salary payment. They are strongly enjoined to sell their camels why will they need them now that they are oil workers? The decision is wrenching.[18] Selling the camels means relinquishing their nomadic identity and becoming beholden to an abstract value system represented by the oil company. The Bedouins translate their nomadic subsistence into the liquid capital that will guarantee their dependence.

With the discovery of oil in the desert, the Arab world was incorporated into the global economy at the expense of place. We know well enough the history of wars fought to establish striating lines, national boundaries and pipelines, across countries some of whose borders were colonial fabrications. Geopolitics moved into the desert. Ibn Khaldoun had already remarked the contrast between the self-sufficiency of the nomad and the pampered sedentary life, 600 years before the Saudi-style welfare state. But oil exacerbated this contrast. Some Bedouins got air-conditioned cars and become sedentary and fat; others simply became immiserated.[19] ARAMCO's oil extraction drained water from the lands, and the resulting drought destroyed the lands where Bedouin grazed their animals (Cole, 243). A new desert came into being: the rootlessness, not of the citified Bedouin, but of the Arab in a global oil economy with its attendant neo-imperialism.

*adieu salubrity*

Now, given the economic decline in the oil-producing countries, the richest Arab people suddenly find themselves living on reduced means. There is precious little cinema produced in the Gulf countries, but I was surprised to come across some works recently that deal with this very topic. Beirut Cinema Days festival in the fall 2003 showed a program of student videos from the United Arab Emirates. These were not excellent works, but sociologically they were fascinating, as two themes kept recurring: the ruinous cost of maintaining status, and the seduction of driving on the smooth highways. A video by Shereela Abdullah, *Crazy (Women) Drivers* (2002) is about women who like to drive fast. *The Car or the Wife* (2000) by Rehab Omar Ateeq dramatizes a man's struggle to choose between, well, his car and his wife. *All That Glitters Is Not Gold* (2000), a documentary on snobbism by Zainab Al Ashoor, interviews young people on the importance of maintaining new cars, new mobile phones, and the bank loans to cover them. Also from the Emirates, Hani el Shibani's *A Warm Winter Night* (2002) is a short drama about an unhappy married couple taking an evening drive on the endless smooth roads. He confesses that he's broke and can no longer support her expensive lifestyle; they rediscover their love.

Desert suicide is a startling recent phenomenon in the Gulf countries. People who cannot face their debts drive as far as they can into the desert, then abandon their cars and walk, until they die of exhaustion and dehydration.[20] *When?* (2001), a beautiful short video by Abdallah al Junaibi made for the Sharjah satellite channel in the Emirates, eulogizes these people. In the desert, the camera circles around a man digging a hole as though for his own grave. His harried voiceover reveals that he is desperate about the bills he cannot pay and the punishing cost of status. "My neighbors have a Land Cruiser and I only have a Maxima." By some magic the video saves the would-be suicide. He sings a wistful song ("What happened to you, my pigeon?") and somehow, regaining the will to live, he fills the grave with sand again.

In Lebanon, driving is a passionate topic in Beirut during wartime, luck, *élan*, and driving as fast as possible to cross roadblocks and avoid being killed. Driving was great during the war, admits the driver (Rabih Mroué) of *Rounds* (2001) by Joana Hadjithomas and Khalil Joriege. "During the war, the bombings, the streets were deserted. I took advantage of the situation to drive. It was incredible. I flew, I was like a phantom." Driving in the war was like traveling in the desert: one had to rely on one's own knowledge of the landmarks, one's own instinct for danger. Now, the driver recounts as he deftly weaves through traffic, since the (highly selective) postwar reconstruction, Beirut is crossed with new highways and marked with traffic lights people are unaccustomed to obeying. Shot entirely inside the car Mroué is driving, *Rounds* is overexposed to make the world outside the car fade away, preserving a little island of nomadic freedom in the increasingly striated city. This little film is an inquiry into the relations of smoothing and striation. "A highway was built on the sea after the war. They packed the ruins and debris [in landfills] and pushed back the sea for two kilometers." Under the highways lie mass graves and cindered remains of swathes of the city. Highways forget, they turn space into time, particular place into distance to be traversed. "Don't be too moved! There are seven civilizations buried under Beirut."

Beirutis are not so quickly willing to give up the smooth space of wartime driving. They still drive as fast as they can.

Asphalt nomadism has a powerful subgenre of films in which travel is impossible, and not only because of third-world highway maintenance. As well as *Baghdad On/Off*, where roads are blocked for specifically political reasons, these include, as you would expect, a majority of Palestinian films. The important progenitor of the roadblock movies is *The Duped* (1972) by Egyptian director Taufik Salih, based on the novel by the Palestinian Ghassan Khanafani. Three Palestinians, desperate to find work in Kuwait to support their refugee families, travel as far as they can until the desert, glimmering with heat, rises up against them. They pay a Palestinian driver to smuggle them across the border from Iraq, hidden in a water tank. At the border, bored Kuwaiti officials detain the driver with flippant gossip. Outside, under the blazing sun, the temperature inside the tank becomes unbearable. The men's cries go unheard and they suffocate to death. Geographically they were minutes from freedom, but geopolitically, the fact of a checkpoint was murderous. This film, a Syrian production, was emblematic of pan-Arab concern about the Palestinian people (Shafik, 155); yet its conclusion is also emblematic of the paralysis of the Arab world vis-à-vis the Palestinians' struggle.

Two intifadas later, the checkpoints have multiplied and frustration and death escalated. On December 12, 2000, Israel passed a law forbidding Palestinians to drive cars between cities. Elia Suleiman's *Divine Intervention* (2002) is a document of Palestinian immobility in the grip of the Israeli occupation. Two lovers, he from Jerusalem, she from Ramallah, can only meet in a parking lot adjacent to an Israeli roadblock. The scenes where, sitting in a parked car, they tenderly caress each other's hands might be slightly erotic, but they also express the intense sexual frustration that is just one of the blocked energies resulting from the occupation. This frustration also manifests in the casual hostility of Palestinian neighbors toward each other. In *Divine Intervention* free movement exists only in fantasy, when the woman transforms into a *kefiya*ed ninja who can kill half a dozen Israeli soldiers with no more than quick reflexes and a well-aimed dart or two.

Roadblock love has more success in *Rana's Wedding* (2002), a fiction film by the Palestinian Hany Abu Assad. The movie's slapstick premise—Rana has 12 hours to get married if she is not to be shipped off to Cairo by her father—fades in the dusty drudgery of the protagonist's struggle. Her labyrinthine journey around Ramallah and East Jerusalem in search of her betrothed is absolutely deromanticized, and it is a cruel irony that the marriage must take place at a roadblock, because the judge was not able to cross. This film, like *Divine Intervention*, suggests, perhaps despite itself, how the constant trouble at checkpoints and roadblocks drains away life energy, including sexual energy. *Rana's Wedding* suggests that for a Palestinian in the occupied territories, accomplishing a marriage is like managing to get one's tomatoes across the border to market. Each is a triumph, but daily life is such a demoralizing struggle that it is hard to distinguish a major and minor life event. Rana loves Khalil, but her purpose in marrying him is short term. Who has the optimism to imagine his or her life over the course of decades?

Abu Assad was so impressed with the abilities of the driver for this film, Rajai Khatib, that he devoted a documentary to his daily grind. The result, *Ford Transit* (2002), brings on claustrophobia in the viewer. The majority of the film takes place in the confined space of the minivan of the title as it carries passengers on the tortuous daily journey, ridden with roadblocks, between Ramallah and Jerusalem. "I long to drive for an hour without stopping," says Rajai, "but there's always a roadblock." At checkpoints the Transit waits in interminable lines of identical minivans, which the Americans had given to the Israeli police, who handed them down to Palestinians.

At first the film gives a sense of the patience and good humor of the passengers, just trying to get home from work, attend a wedding, or smuggle a few cucumbers. Jokes, flirtation, and advice pass between the seats and the charismatic Rajai lets flow a stream of opinions. The lively sound track is like a love song to the passengers: Egyptian pop music playfully eroticizes the close space of the minivan, a soulful rap song indexes the similarity between Palestinians and "we niggers," a lonely cowboy tune reminds us that this *is* the desert after all, the new desert of broken roads. But the pressure of the confined space begins to be felt. The triumph of this seemingly artless film is that it makes palpable, through the confined space of the minivan, the escalating feelings of frustration, helplessness, and rage among the Palestinians in the tightening vice grip of the Israeli occupation. Learning that a fellow passenger is a lawyer, a man from Ramallah asks how much the paperwork would cost to reunite him with his wife, who lives in Jerusalem. He learns that it would be cheaper to divorce and remarry. Tired passengers vent their frustration on each other—"You're so fat you'd fill three roadblocks." Rajai solicits passengers for the pathetic short journey with fantasy destinations: "Kandahar! Tora Bora!"

Even before the advent of the apartheid wall, the Israeli roadblock system has caused untold hardship for the Palestinian workers and farmers who cannot travel to work or to sell their produce and lose their livelihood; the divided families living in different cities; the patients whose ambulances wait in vain for permission to cross to hospitals. Thus the film's secondary subject, Palestinian suicide attacks on Israelis, unfolds naturally from the sense of confinement that it so effectively communicates. The roadblocks exacerbate resentment so directly that they are "a factory for suicide bombings," Rajai asserts. Many people are interviewed in the back of the Ford Transit on the subject of the suicide bombings:

138

from famous people like Hanan Ashrawi to a woman whose daughter became a martyr. "Our fear for death is dead. It doesn't matter," Rajai says, changing a punctured tire on the dusty road.

The affect of a road movie usually moves forward, with the direction of the vehicle on the highway. In the roadblock movies that affect spirals inward, concentrates, and becomes explosive. As in *Baalbeck* and *Baghdad On/Off*, the only alternative seems to be fiction; the film's most optimistic sign is the driver's creativity when the usual routes do not function. He detours onto dirt roads (a driver passing the other way warns, "Be careful going down. They tried to shoot"); he speeds on the wrong side of the road, cheerfully paying the fine. These limited practices restore the desert to the highway and reward fast, nomadic thinking. But moments of liberty are seized only temporarily in the face of the implacable roadblock system. The film ends abruptly when Rajai, unable to repair the punctured tire, disappears up the dusty road, leaving behind his small clutch of silent, patient, immobilized travelers.

*"halt, friends both, and let us weep..."*

Beirut is a city that profoundly lives its ruin despite the glittering postwar reconstructions. In Ghassan Salhab's *Terra Incognita* (2002), the city becomes a *paysage quelconque*,[21] peopled with asphalt nomads. The characters seem to spend half their time driving the city streets, the traveling shots following their wan gazes through the windshield.

*Terra Incognita* is structured somewhat like the *mu'allaqat*, an arbitrary-seeming extract from the endless series of unrolling events. Both the film and its principal character are characterized by mournfulness and sharply focused desire. Soraya (Carole Abboud) appears to have no psychology, no "depth," no soul or morality to be tortured. It is her wanderings that define her. A tour guide to the remains of those seven civilizations that sprinkle the surface of Lebanon, Soraya is a professional halter at ruins. In carnal matters too she is nomadic, taking on lovers with indiscriminate hunger. Then if she sees the man after the encounter, she ignores him utterly.

The discarded lovers do not understand. Soraya orients herself by landmarks that are constantly changing, by differences that arise from no law but from local conditions (Deleuze and Guattari, 493). She lives Beirut as smooth space. The lovers are sedentary types. In the film's troubling conclusion, one of them assaults Soraya brutally, in an attempt "to remind her of the law of men"[22] as settled people attempt to impose their laws and religion on the nomads. He fails, and the film's final shot witnesses Soraya, with one eye blackened, again roaming her city with her wild dignity.

Soraya moves among a group of people each of whom also carries a burden of grief, but none so lightly as she. One, Tarek, emigrated during the war and has returned to woo Soraya. It turns out that she holds several visas and could easily emigrate, as so many Lebanese young people do in the bleak postwar economy. She stays because she has the energy to live on the trajectory of her own desire and depthless (i.e., without depth) grief.

The film's perception moves on the surface of Beirut as on a shifting sand, observing details of the audiovisual environment with singular devotion. It is a story without a narrative, where meaning arises from minutely local events. In one scene, after a late night at the club, the friends step out of their cars onto the seaside Corniche to eat *manaeesh*, the big flat bread, hot from the oven, seasoned with thyme and sesame. "Lebanese food is the best in the world," somebody exclaims through a mouthful, taunting Tarek, the émigré, "How could you leave such pleasure behind?" "Food can't give you a job," he retorts. But *Terra Incognita* chooses the *manaeesh* over the job.

"There my companions halted their beasts awhile over me / saying, 'Don't perish of weeping; restrain yourself decently!'"[23] So Imru' l-Qays concluded his bout of mourning. Get over it already! Collective life, together with the necessity to keep moving, protected the Bedouin. In the ruin of Beirut, its people lack the *esprit de corps* that for Ibn Khaldoun defined the nomads.[24] Beirut's ruins are less to be found in the bullet-ridden buildings that remain from the civil war than in the glassy towers and Potemkin townlets that intimate that the war never happened. Most of all, Beirut's ruins are internal. Beirut does not know how to invent its future, but it has no choice but to try. The exhausted city needs energy; not the striating power of foreign investors, but the vector of the nomad.

*the double ruin*

Recall that a couple of these Arab road movies, *Baalbeck* and *Baghdad On/Off*, are falsified documentaries. This form, a favorite way to tell stories that diverge from official histories, is especially popular among Lebanese filmmakers. The falsified documentary, deeply suspicious of the truth-telling function, allows something deeper than mere facts to come into existence.[25] The prevalence of this form begins to describe a double ruin: externally, in the dreams of modern Arab self-determination, and internally, in the cinematic enterprise itself.

140

*The Lost Film* (2003) by Joana Hadjithomas and Khalil Joriege, another failed road movie, becomes a document of the status of cinema in the Arab world. The two Lebanese filmmakers set off to Yemen in search of a print of their feature, *Around the Pink House*, that disappeared after a screening commemorating the tenth anniversary of Yemen's reunification. Their quest is met with almost total indifference. Movie houses are few in Yemen these days, and movie-going frowned on. Still, they decide to retrace the bus journey north, from Aden to Sana'a, that their precious

35 mm is thought to have taken. You can guess the ending: they never retrieve the film. What Hadjithomas and Joriege do find on this desolate journey is a particular cultural attitude toward the image.

The filmmakers pay a visit the Yemen Film Archive, where film canisters lie seemingly haphazardly on shelves, yet the small staff is terribly proud of its efforts to maintain the collection. They solemnly unfold posters of Egyptian thrillers and Jackie Chan and hold them up to the camera. The archive's director, Hussein Chaibane, explains that all he hopes to do is maintain these films, as production has halted since the Islamist north gained influence after reunification. He treats the filmmakers to a trailer for a Lebanese film, *The Beauty and the Giants* (*Samir el Ghoussayneh*, 1980). Faded to pink, the trailer still boasts a hero resplendent in mustachios and aviator sunglasses to the sound of Gloria Gaynor's "I Will Survive." The disco anthem unfolds surreally in the dusty cavern of the Archive.

Although the filmmakers insist that they wish to retrace exactly the route of their precious film, their driver makes a detour to a wedding party, where men shoot celebratory volleys with guns and cameras. A photographer named Al-Sima shows them his matte technique that allows his subjects to appear to be in Istanbul or New York, or double exposed. When Hadjithomas and Joriege learn that he gives away the negatives with the photographs, something clicks into place: Yemen is not a country where people cherish images. When the photographer reminds his father, now blind, of the contents of a photograph and the elder al-Sima recalls in a flash, this view is modified: Yemen is a country where images are not externalized. This is confirmed in the very next scene, which consists of Joreige's voice over black leader describing a graveyard they saw that had no tombstones, no plaques, only large stones to mark the body, small stones to mark the head.

The climax of this modest film takes place in the scrap metal market of the Sana'a souk. Hadjithomas sees film canisters among the ghee tins and other reusable metal. The conclusion finally comes home: it was not their film that interested the thieves of Yemen, it was its container.

These two ruins, that of modern politics and of the valued image, are complexly implicated in each other in the Arab world. In this writing I have relied on Jibrail Jabbur's wonderfully detailed account of Bedouin life in the Syrian desert. His book, richly illustrated with his own photographs, attests that the nomadic life remains at the heart of Arab identity, disavowed and disappearing though it may be. This book captured the attention of Akram Zaatari and forms the center of Zaatari's video *This Day* (2003). The video begins with the voice of Jibrail Jabbur's granddaughter, Norma, describing one of his 1950s vintage photographs, while we see a digital pan of the same photograph. It's a rather ironic image of an Arab man lying under a Jeep to repair it, out in the desert, while two men in

Western dress look on. Camels stand around. The photographer's shadow is visible in the lower edge.

As the digital editor pans geometrically around Jabbur's photograph, we begin to sense the staginess of the photograph. This is a major theme of *This Day*. Zaatari, retracing Jabbur's travels to photograph nomadic life in the Syrian desert, 50 years later, reveals and exploits the degree to which these photographs were staged, shots of Bedouins playing themselves. The reliability of Jabbur's archive comes into question. "Taking photographs of the desert and of the camels is looking at an eastern object with a western optic, a camera," Norma Jabbur says. "The spirit to document such a thing is a western idea"—a notion that corroborates the Yemenis' disdain for the Lost Film. The archive is something that matters terribly to Zaatari, as does the indexical evidence so intently pursued in *Baalbeck*. He is a founder of the Arab Image Foundation, one of whose aims is to collect amateur photographs of the Lebanese and Arab past. This archive is assembled in the knowledge that official histories tend to rewrite the past, and also that photography is a witness to experiences that otherwise submerge completely.

Zaatari and his small crew travel "further toward the East," as an intertitle says, to see the camels so beloved by Jabbur and so foundational to nomadic identity. The camels are real, but the shot is digitally edited, two frames forward, one frame back, so the beautiful animals shimmer like an object of desire just out of reach. The effect is disturbing and enchanting.

*This Day* begins to be a video in search of the real. Or rather, in nomadic fashion, in search of the ruin. What becomes apparent is that the photograph is a ruin, at which we mourn at the traces of our beloved's campsite. The ruin is in the camera, the apparatus (of capture). Norma Jabbur's statement that it's Western even to take photographs is an exaggeration; but there is something imperial about staking down nomadic life with the vertical axis of significance, of representation. Representation is striation, as it strips the appearance off an event in order to mobilize it for another purpose. It's not nomadic to photograph nomads.

It *is* nomadic to alter photographs of nomads. In the editing suite, Zaatari exploits the photographic wish-fulfillment that Jabbur initiated in his sincere journey of documentation. An epic digital composite brings together all Jabbur's lovingly photographed Bedouins, camels, Jeep-repairing Arabs, family members in Bedouin costume, and all the rest in an impossible group portrait. Without attempting to disguise the artifice of the composite, the editor creates a rough animation where identical camels float through the uncertain space.

As *Terra Incognita* incorporated nomadism into cinema's way of perceiving the world, so *This Day* incorporates nomadism into the digital apparatus itself. A certain virtual nomadism is required to survey the ruin of the cinematic enterprise.

There is another ruin to which *This Day* travels to mourn, embodied in the activist, pro-Palestine e-mails Zaatari receives every day. Photographs of Palestinians being beaten by Israeli soldiers, of Palestinian children menaced by tanks, accompany accounts of ongoing Israeli violence and, sometimes, requests for donations. Some of these seem legitimate, some do not. This volley of pleas from small organizations reflects Arabs' frustration and rage at their own governments' lip service to the Palestinians, yet bad faith when it comes to concrete action: this is the external ruin. Uncaptioned, recombined, and re-sent again and again, like pornography, these e-mails do violence to the idea of documentary witness. They come to represent nothing. This is the internal ruin.

*This Day* visits another archive of militant photographs. To the rousing strains of a resistance anthem, we see a photographic parade of the rebels who posed in the studio of photographer Hathem Al Madani in 1970 in Saida, southern Lebanon. Young men and boys stand confidently, wielding semi-automatic weapons and whiskers as luxuriant as they can muster. Precursors to the pre-martyrdom portrait or video common now among expectant suicide bombers, these portraits do not make us doubt the existence of these young rebels, but they tie their existence to their representation. Documentary stakes down the meaning of an event, so that its image can serve other functions. A photograph is a surface, a document insists on depth. The CD playing the militant song begins to skip.

In the face of all these uncertainly indexical photographs, Zaatari's wartime diary is perhaps the most reliable document of all. The history of the Lebanese civil war is impossible to write, at least as long as its protagonists are still alive and holding political office. Zaatari's diary skims the surface of wartime actuality. Its pages, filled with neat writing and glued-in pictures, recount matter-of-factly the day's mix of military, political, meteorological, and personal events. "February 2nd, 1984. This afternoon we heard the sound of violent explosions. It turned out later that they had come from the southern suburbs. The film that I had been planning to watch was cancelled for security reasons. It was *La Bête Humaine*." This modest written document is only a trace of past events, like ashes of a fire. It too shifts and shimmers delicately in the digital ether; it seems to breathe.

*whither wander?*

The asphalt nomads retain some qualities of their sand-based forebears: To continue to move, in attention to the immediate and the surface. To avoid depth, hierarchy, roots, causality. To invent according to local needs. To respect ruins and leave them behind.

The asphalt nomads are lacking in one quality of their sandy forebears: the energy necessary for decisive motion. The nomads of contemporary Arab cinema have not yet gathered up enough potential energy. The many frustrations have been borne for so long—since the 1947 occupation of Palestine, the Six Days War, the first war on Iraq, the second war on Iraq. . .—that the energy keeps running out.

Can this intensity be rediscovered on an inward journey? The Western road movie is motored by individualism, an inward turn in the face of social alienation. Its heyday was arguably in the 1960s and 1970s, around the time of the relapse of the Hollywood system, when individuality was a newly hot commodity. Independent cinema arrived later in the Arab world, and it might be that, in the Arab cinema in 2000, a newly discovered individuality will provide the motor of a cinema that has outgrown its creaky, inadequate institutions. This is the argument of Tunisian film historian Khémais Khayati. He holds that Arab cinema can only mature when the voices of individual *auteurs* are heard. Further, this can only occur against the grain of official culture; in exile, whether physical or psychic, from the overbearing weight of Arab social institutions. "En libérant son Ego, le cinéaste a libéré son héros, a libéré le langage, a libéré ses propres representations du monde proche et du monde éloigné."[26] As the nomadic poet comes into being in exile, this argument would have it, so does the Arab independent filmmaker.

But this argument makes me uneasy, for it casts the Arab world, yet again, as a belated version of Western modernity. Arab filmmakers are emerging as *auteurs*; this is a short-term good insofar as they destabilize the dead weight of social institutions (moribund descendants of the nomadic tribe) of family and religion. But it is no good if they inherit the disenchanted, empty individualism of the West. Individuality is a trap; it carves us all into the same dull grid. A nomadic cinema has to invent its own trajectory. The greatest strength of independent cinema in the Arab world is that it does not follow Western models.

What the asphalt nomads accomplish, and what Arab cinema is presently in a position to offer, is another strategy. An activist or pedagogical cinema engages with striating forces, for example the discourse of nongovernmental organizations; and this too is part of how change comes about. But the nomadic strategy in cinema is to draw energy from the space it inhabits, and this requires disengagement from institutions. "The nomad distributes himself in smooth space; he occupies, inhabits, holds that space; that is his territorial principle. It is therefore false to define the nomad by movement."[27] We glimpse this strategy when Salhab, Zaatari, and Soueid abandon the failed project of Lebanese nation building in favor of a labneh sandwich, a beautiful boy, a good piss. When Salman witnesses the devastation of the Iraqi people yet lingers at an ingeniously constructed beehive. When Soraya, living lightly among the ruins, follows the trajectory of her desire. When Abou Assad hears, from the humanity in the back seats of the Ford Transit, the articulation of despair into the lethal energy of the suicide bomber. When Zaatari in the quiet space of the editing suite traces an index of potential, virtual life, among the dead and dying images. Blocked movement intensifies energy.

Historically the nomadic way of life was made obsolete by Islam, a social order that transcends tribe and nation and organizes the faithful in cities. But Arabs needed the Bedouin to persist to uphold an ideal of noble independence. The nomads' hearty loyalty to the local and suspicion of abstraction seemed to offer an implicit critique of modern ideals, both Arab and imported, of technological advancement, large-scale social organization, and sweeping intercultural exchange. No less did Orientalists of the West, the philosophers of nomadology among them, draw inspiration from the people who navigated close to the shifting lands with no more possessions than their camels could carry. Yet meanwhile the desert itself has been translated into capital, and the lofty structures that nomadism opposed have broken on the shifting sand. Now the nomadic way of life returns not as an ideal but as the only viable option.

Thus, it is not triumphantly but with regret that I reiterate the maxims proclaimed in the ancient nomadic odes. Identify the ruins, weep, and ride on. If it is not possible to ride on, cultivate your trajectory. Above all, stay close to the surface.[28]

## notes

1. A tale related by Ka'b al-Ahbar to 'Umar ibn al-Khattab, in *al-Mawai'iz wa-l-i'tibar bi-dhikr al-khitat wa-l-athar*, al-Maqrizi (Cairo, 1324), quoted in Jibrail S. Jabbur, *The Bedouins and the Desert: Aspects of Nomadic Life in the Arab East*, trans. Lawrence I. Conrad (Albany, NY: SUNY Press, 1995), 48; hereafter cited in text as *Jabbur*.

2. Mohammed A. Bamyeh, *The Social Origins of Islam: Mind, Economy, Discourse* (Minneapolis: University of Minnesota Press, 1999), 7; cited hereafter in text.

3. Gilles Deleuze and Félix Guattari, "1440: The Smooth and the Striated," in *A Thousand Plateaus: Capitalism and Schizophrenia*, trans. Brian Massumi (Minneapolis: University of Minnesota Press, 1987), 500; hereafter cited in text.

4. Arab cinema, for the purposes of this essay, is cinema in Arabic. The linguistic commonality helps to bypass more complicated issues of ethnicity (not all Arab filmmakers think of themselves as "Arabs") and religion (though Islam is the dominant religion in the Arab world and Arab culture is inextricable from it, not all Arab filmmakers are Muslim) and to establish a common body of practice. It also distinguishes this body of work from Iranian cinema.

5. This typical desert cinema is modeled on the discussion of the nomadic odes in Bamyeh, *The Social Origins of Islam, op. cit.*

6. Stephen Morris, "Structure from Instability," talk at the Subtle Technologies: Blurring the Boundaries between Art and Science conference, May 11, 2002. See also Philip Ball, *The Self-Made Tapestry: Pattern Formation in Nature* (Oxford: Oxford University Press, 2001).

7. Manuel De Landa, "Geological History: 1000–1700 A.D.," in *A Thousand Years of Nonlinear History* (New York: Zone, 1997), 55 and *passim*.

8. William Gifford Palgrave, *Narrative of a Year's Journey through Central and Eastern Arabia, 1862–1863*, quoted in Jabbur, The Bedouins and the *Desert, op. cit.*, 377.

9. M. 'Abd el-'Aziz, 1993, quoted in Madawi al-Rasheed, *A History of Saudi Arabia* (Cambridge: Cambridge University Press, 2002), 154; hereafter quoted in text as *al-Rasheed*.

10. Daryl Champion, *The Paradoxical Kingdom: Saudi Arabia and the Momentum of Reform* (New York: Columbia University Press, 2003), 49.

11. I thank Haidar Sadek for pointing out the double striation at work in this film.

12. Mouny Berrah, "Algerian Cinema and National Identity," in *Screens of Life: Critical Film Writing from the Arab World*, ed. Alia Arasoughly (Québec: World Heritage Press, 1996), 74–75.

13. Ali Abu Shadi, "Genres in Egyptian Cinema," in *Screens of Life: Critical Film Writing from the Arab World, op. cit.*, 103.

14. Hady Zaccak, "Les Arabes dans 'le western'," *Regards*, annual publication of the Institut des Études Scéniques, Audiovisuelles et Cinématographiques (IESAV), Université St. Joseph, Beirut, 5 (January 2003): 53–58.

15. Viola Shafik, *Arab Cinema: History and Cultural Identity* (Cairo: The American University in Cairo Press, 1998), 53, 197; hereafter cited in text.

16. Unpublished interview of Saad Salman with the author; October 9, 2002.

17. Donald P. Cole argues that "Bedouin" now designates less a way of life than a cultural identity, as a result of the intertwining forces of colonization, commercialization of pasturage, new occupations, and sedentarization. "Where Have the Bedouin Gone?," *Anthropological Quarterly* 76, no. 2 (2003): 235–267; hereafter cited in text.

18. Abdelrahman Munif, *Cities of Salt*, trans. Peter Theroux (New York: Vintage International, 1987), 185–186.

19. The disenfranchised people of Saudi Arabia, for example, are the most recently sedentarized Bedouins; the oasis peasantry, primarily Shi'a Muslims who face extreme discrimination in Saudi Arabia, and the people who lack connections to powerful families. (Many of these are also the people who turned to religious fundamentalism.) (al-Rasheed, 154).

20. I am indebted to Mohamad Soueid for this information.

21. Deleuze's term for a place that has been stripped of its specificity, in *Cinema 2: The Time-Image*, trans. Hugh Tomlinson and Robert Galeta (Minneapolis: University of Minnesota Press, 1989), xi.

22. E. C., "Beyrouth au crible," *L'Humanité*, 12 February 2003.

23. Quoted in Bamyeh, *The Social Origins of Islam, op. cit.*, 147.

24. Deleuze and Guattari write, "Ibn Khaldoun defines the war machine by: families or lineages PLUS esprit de corps." "1227: Treatise on Nomadology: The War Machine," in *A Thousand Plateaus, op. cit.*, 366.

25. See my essay "Signs of the Time: Deleuze, Peirce and the Documentary Image," in *The Brain Is the Screen: Gilles Deleuze's Cinematic Philosophy*, ed. Gregory Flaxman (Minneapolis: Minnesota University Press, 2000), 193–214. Films from Beirut, including works by Walid Ra'ad, Jalal Toufic, and the Lebanese-Canadian Jayce Salloum, provide my central examples of the falsified documentary.

26. "In liberating his ego, the filmmaker has liberated his hero, has liberated language, has liberated his own representations from the world both

near and distant." Khémais Khayati, *Cinémas arabes: topographie d'une image éclatée* (Paris and Montréal: L'Harmattan, 1996), 207. My translation.

27. Deleuze and Guattari, "1227: Treatise on Nomadology: The War Machine," in *A Thousand Plateaus, op. cit.*, 381.

28. Warm thanks to Haidar Sadek, Akram Zaatari, and Mohamad Soueid for fruitful conversations in the course of this writing. This research was supported by Carleton University and by the Center for Behavioral Research at the American University of Beirut.

*Distributors (where known):*

*Baalbeck* (Ghassan Salhab, Akram Zaatari, and Mohamad Soueid, Lebanon, 2001), V Tape, http://www.vtape.org

*Baghdad On/Off* (Saad Salman, France, 2002), Vents du sud productions, 9-17, rue Henri-Poincaré, Paris 75020 France. Tel: (33-1) 43618161, Fax: (33-1) 43618161, E-mail: vdsprod@noos.fr

*Date Wine* (Radwan El-Kashef, Egypt, 1998), Arab Film Distribution, http://www.arabfilm.com

*Divine Intervention* (Elia Suleiman, Palestine, 2002), Arab Film Distribution, http://www.arabfilm.com

*The Duped* (Taufik Salih, Syria, 1972), Arab Film Distribution, http://www.arabfilm.com

*The Emigrant* (Youssef Chahine, Egypt, 1994), Arab Film Distribution, http://www.arabfilm.com

*Ford Transit* (Hany Abu Assad, Palestine, 2002)

*Insan (Human Being)* (Ibrahim Shaddad, Sudan, 1988), Arab Film Distribution, http://www.arabfilm.com

*The Lost Film* (Joana Hadjithomas and Khalil Joriege, Lebanon, 2003), Idéale Audience, http://www.ideale-audience.fr

*Rana's Wedding* (Hany Abu Assad, Palestine, 2002), Arab Film Distribution, http://www.arabfilm.com

*Rounds* (Joana Hadjithomas and Khalil Joriege, Lebanon, 2001), Idéale Audience, http://www.ideale-audience.fr

Student videos from the United Arab Emirates:

*Terra Incognita* (Ghassan Salhab, Lebanon, 2002), Ad Vitam, Paris, advitam@cineinde.com

*This Day* (Akram Zaatari, Lebanon, 2003), V Tape, http://www.vtape.org

*The Wanderers of the Desert* (Nacir Khémir, Tunisia, 1986), Médiathèque des Trois Mondes, Paris

*When?* (Abdallah al Junaibi, United Arab Emirates, 2001), Sharjah Television, P.O. Box 111, Sharjah, Emirates, Tel: 971-506339191, Fax: 971-26210205

# the inhabited view

landscape in the films

of david rimmer

six

catherine russell

The whole history of art is no more than a massive footnote to the history of film.

**Hollis Frampton**[1]

Landscape in David Rimmer's films and videos is always already an image. It is not "nature" but an allegory of nature, referring to the image of nature rather than to nature itself. Landscape is thoroughly penetrated by the apparatus of vision—the camera, the gaze, the frame—and the technologies of visual culture. In this chapter I will argue that this allegorisation, or quoting, of the image of landscape constitutes a form of inhabitation, a means of bringing the landscape closer. Once the landscape is an artefact, we are better able to recognize ourselves—the human—in its construction, and the image might be said to become ecological. Nature is not "out there," existing independently of humans and technologies, but is intimately bound up with them at their mercy and as their support.

In Rimmer's "structural" films of the 1970s, landscape constitutes a pure form of "image" in which nature itself is an endangered species. Although his use of landscape imagery evokes some paradigms of Canadian aesthetics, it also challenges such a notion of nationalist art practice. I will argue that the "inhabited" landscape is a more localized representation of place than the abstract spaces implied in the discourse on Canadian art.

The vital connections between Canadian experimental filmmaking and the Canadian landscape were aptly demonstrated at a film series at the Art Gallery of Ontario in 1989. Programmed by Bart Testa, the series featured five themes that Testa further explored in the accompanying catalogue as "Presence," "Movement," "Allegory," "Philosophy," and the final "Machine in the Garden," which featured the single 180-minute film *La region centrale* (1971) by Michael Snow. In keeping with the predominant themes in Canadian art and literature, Testa situated the 13 films within a discussion of the encounter with a threatening wilderness. Following on the work of Northrop Frye and Margaret Atwood, he notes that, while cinema "allows the journey through the landscape to be made in ways that seem remarkably free of the constraints the static art of painting imposes," the films tend to return to the "compositional devices, the iconography, and motifs of Canadian art."[2] Experimental filmmakers are said to have taken over where the painters have left off, expressively countering the indifference of a vacant land with a cinema that in various ways represents consciousness through technology.

Testa's program and accompanying catalogue provide a valuable entry-point to a discussion of landscape in Canadian experimental film, and his analyses of individual films often go well beyond the paradigms of "anxiety" and "garrison mentality" that he borrows from Frye and Atwood. However, the preoccupation with landscape in David Rimmer's cinema lends itself to a very different interpretation. While evoking some of the formal paradigms of Canadian landscape painting and experimental film practice, Rimmer manages to articulate a much more "inhabited view," one in which the landscape is not a threat but a production. As the Inuit-produced feature film *Atanarjuat* (Zachrarius Kunuk, 2001) demonstrates, the Canadian landscape can be integrated into the visual culture of everyday life, even in its vastness and apparent emptiness. Rimmer's work of the late 1960s and early 1970s indicates how experimental visual culture is implicated in new and changed relationships to the Canadian landscape.

How long can the myth of the threatening wilderness be sustained? This is not only a question of interpretation, but also a question about the intersections between experimental film, aesthetics, and cultural nationalism. In the latter half of the twentieth century the industrialization and development of the landscape brought on a new set of concerns, turning the tables so to speak, so that it is arguably the landscape that is threatened by Canadians. Ecology may be a term more familiar to the social sciences than to aesthetics, but through a discussion of Rimmer's film practice, I hope to show how an ecological view of landscape can be interpreted within the formal conventions of structural film. Pat Brereton (one of the few critics to consider the relation between film and ecology) defines ecology as an ideological system in which "harmony with nature" is conjoined with the recognition of "finite resources." It is at once a philosophy, a social vision, and a political strategy.[3] Working primarily within the parameters of "structural film," Rimmer's non-narrative approach is by no means dramatic, and his ecological aesthetics are anything but didactic. It is important to note that, unlike his contemporary Joyce Wieland, Rimmer is not an activist filmmaker, and the ecological effects that I would like to focus on are articulated on the level of the everyday.

For Andrew Ross, the power of ecology lies in the links between the shape of everyday actions and a quantitative world-picture of physical causes and effects.[4] In the politicization of nature, the sensory realm of everyday life becomes contested space. By picturing landscape as an effect of technology, as an extension or production of the gaze, it is not denaturalized, but becomes "artifactual." In Donna Haraway's notion of "natureculture," nature and culture are recognized as contiguous rather than opposed as universal categories.[5] For Haraway, "a relationship to nature besides reification and possession" means that nature "is not the 'other' who offers origin replenishment and service." She writes: "Neither mother, nurse, nor slave, nature is not matrix, resource, or tool for the reproductive man. Nature is, however, a topos, a place, in the sense of a rhetorician's place or topic for consideration of common themes; nature is, strictly, a commonplace."[6] The "commonplace" or the banal temporalities and spaces of everyday life are precisely the terrain of the structural filmmaker, for whom "content" is more or less the means by which the technology of image production is foregrounded. According to P. Adams Sitney, who introduced the term, structural film had four characteristics, not all of which needed to be present for a film to be considered a member of the group. These were: "fixed camera position (fixed from the viewer's perspective), the flicker effect, loop printing and rephotography off the screen."[7]

Structural film is about looking, and in many cases, about looking at landscape.[8] Produced within the context of the art world, its tendency toward documentation is anti-documentary, but not non-documentary. Many structural films operate as experiments in seeing. Sometimes "nothing" is seen (in flicker films, for example); but sometimes the scene is inhabited, and in these instances the film looks at itself looking at others. Because "content" is not insignificant in many structural films, they enable an analysis of the cinematic gaze as an embodied technology. On the margins of the structural film canon, David Rimmer's films test the definition and push the limits of the form as it was originally theorized.

It is the fixed frame which is perhaps most distinctive of this filmmaking practice because it registers the imposition of a form onto reality. A frame which has its own autonomy acquires the integrity of a picture frame limiting the view to a strict economy of inside and outside. Inside, there is composition and detail; outside, there is an unknown space that is never filled in. The fixed frame represents the intentionality of phenomenological consciousness, but it equally determines the limits of the visible and the knowable. The fixed frame points to the subject of perception, and also to the four sides of the frame, beyond which is the continuity of the real as defined by the discontinuity of the frame.

The theorization of structural film as a radical mode of film practice was taken up by the British filmmaker and theoreticians Peter Gidal and Malcolm Le Grice in their *Structural Film Anthology* (1976) and *Abstract Film and Beyond* (1977), respectively.[9] Drawing on a Brechtian rhetoric of anti-illusionism and Althusserian Marxism, Gidal and Le Grice cast structural film as both "materialist" and "minimalist." They privileged the real-time aesthetic, in which the time of viewing would be equal to the time of shooting, as a means of subverting illusionist codes of montage. Duration, and the reflexive attention to the materiality of the medium, were understood as anti-idealist techniques, and outside the meaning-production mechanisms of dominant ideology. In foregrounding the technology and the process of film, this mode of practice was essentially a mode of knowledge. For Gidal, the proximity of theory and practice was so close that structural film could be considered "theory" (Gidal, 15).

Structural film developed in the avant-garde as a kind of parallel practice to the structuralism that informed apparatus theory in the 1970s. Most commentators deny any relation between the two, and yet both structuralisms entailed a theorization of cinema as an instrument of bourgeois ideology. Sitney, whose discursive frame remained that of Romantic American poetics, understood structural film as an unmediated representation of consciousness, "a cinema actively engaged in generating metaphors for the viewing, or rather the perceiving, experience."[10] Both American and British theorists, such as apparatus theorists, assumed an analogy between camera and consciousness. The transcendental ego of philosophical phenomenology became the "I" of the viewer/camera/ideological subject. In structural-materialist film, however, the look was supposedly unsutured by narrative, and was therefore outside ideology.

Only one writer has taken the Gidal-Le Grice theorization of structural film to task for its idealist critique of idealism. In 1977 Constance Penley pointed to the parallels between apparatus theory and structural-materialist film, arguing that the latter fetishised the viewing process and effectively re-centred the subject as the "pure" subject of vision.[11] Far from freeing the spectator from the technology of the gaze, structural-materialist film, according to Penley, secured an identification of the viewer as transcendental subject. Narrativity and illusionism may be negated, but the desire invested in looking is not.

However, insofar as the gaze is linked to a specifically aesthetic practice, the desiring subject is not necessarily abstract. The metaphoric inscription of a window in many structural films (as frames within the frame, or as the surface plane of the image) marks a divide between two spaces, situating the seeing subject in a material relation to the profilmic. Penley's critique may be pertinent to those structural-materialist films that reduced the visual field to the rhythmic flicker of light—which, as she points out, enacts an oscillating presence/absence of the film itself. But when the image attains the status of content, when it "signifies," the seeing subject may be more appropriately described as an observer. As Paul Arthur has argued, structural film denotes a "trajectory in the American [sic] avant-garde canon since the late fifties [that] has been the promotion of a dialogue between optical engagement and redefinition of the viewing experience in terms of object and spectator."[12]

The images that provide the support for structural filmmaking are often "documentary" images (which is not to say that they are not "fictional").[13] Because the temporality of structural film tends to refer back to itself, as form, it eliminates any sense of narrative space,[14] and frequently entails a temporality determined by the profilmic. In its durational aesthetic, "nothing happens" in structural films because "nothing happens" in the quotidian realm of the referent. Canonical examples of structural film practice are Andy Warhol's *Sleep* (1963) and *Empire* (1964), the latter arguably a form of cityscape.

In theory, most structural filmmakers were in search of "pure cinema" and attributed a specificity to the cinematic gaze that failed to account for that which was gazed at, the profilmic, which lies outside the system. Neither apparatus theory nor structural filmmakers were prepared to account for documentary representation, despite the clear parallels between the viewing apparatus of the cinema and the phenomenology of scientific observation.[15] And yet, signification is not easily repressed. In practice, structural filmmaking varied quite widely, even during its heyday in the early 1970s.[16] David Rimmer is one filmmaker who allows "content" to return, to leak into the field of vision, and in many instances this is through the use of landscape as his visual field.

## david rimmer and the canadian landscape

Active from 1967 through to the 1990s, Rimmer's work provides something of an index of the expansion and transformation of the avant-garde in postmodern film culture. As early as 1975 Rimmer began working with video, and with *As Seen on TV* in 1986 and *Local Knowledge* in 1992, he began incorporating video effects into his film practice. Despite his "structuralism," he departed at an early stage from the medium-specificity aesthetics of structural film that, for many critics and practitioners, constituted the high modernist cinematic equivalent to Greenbergian minimalism. Paul Arthur notes that, as an aesthetic theory, structural film set up "an oscillating field which bracketed connections between materiality and narrative, between the formal and the social" (1986, 81). It may be because Rimmer's work insists on these kind of connections that it has received so little critical attention. Because Rimmer's version of structural film does not evacuate "content" or "signifieds" in the interest of formal experiments, his work has fallen through the cracks of avant-garde theory and criticism.

Rimmer is able to transform the structural mode by bringing it to bear on a wide range of images of people, places, objects, and activities, a process which begins with and remains premised on his use of landscape. To the extent that we can recognize landscape as "nature," Rimmer's aesthetics enable us to view landscape as a "particular production" of nature. As Haraway notes, nature is not in itself ideological (1992, 298), but is a discursive construction, and through the aesthetics of structural film, it becomes an effect of the camera, which is in turn not simply a "machine" but a cyborg hybrid of man and machine. When he turns the camera onto people they are likewise viewed as products of the interaction of camera and subject.

*Landscape* (Rimmer, 1969) is the pure form, in the best structural tradition, of a theme that informs many of Rimmer's films. A continuous fixed shot of an ocean inlet, it was intended to be rear-projected onto a plexiglass screen in a suspended wooden picture frame. Through time-lapse photography, a complete day from sunrise to sundown is condensed into seven and a half minutes. *Landscape* takes the great Canadian picture-postcard and re-animates it with the rapid passage of clouds and shadows across the screen and progressive changes in coloration that take place over the course of the "day." The composition in depth, from foreground grasses to two levels of mountains dipping into the centre of the frame, is enhanced by the play of light on the middle-ground water surface which seems to move toward the viewer, while clouds travel rapidly above the horizon line. A critic in 1969 commented: "The film asks for relaxation, for thought, for dreams, for drifting, for humanity."[17] One does indeed become drawn into the scene, addressed more as a participant than a witness.

Bart Testa has argued that Rimmer's landscape films are exemplary of Gaile McGregor's "Wacousta syndrome." For McGregor, the representation of landscape in Canadian painting and literature exhibits a "garrison mentality," as opposed to the American mythology of the frontier. A characteristic "anxiety about the horizon" is contained in an emphasis on framing and enclosure; a wilderness perceived as threatening and monstrous is held at bay through pictorial compositions in which "the viewer is protected from imaginative participation."[18] Of Rimmer's film *Canadian*

*Pacific* (1974), Testa writes: "the enclosing frame and the obstruction of the view by the boxcars in *Canadian Pacific* doubly articulate a Canadian mentality of perception and representation, namely what McGregor terms a 'boxed experience, a distinction between inside and outside'" (11).

Rimmer made two *Canadian Pacific* films, the second (*Canadian Pacific II* [1975]) shot from a window slightly higher than the first, in a building overlooking Burnard Inlet. Both are composed, like *Landscape*, in depth. Railway cars in the foreground, ships in the middle ground, and snow-covered mountains in the distance create a landscape that is thoroughly industrialized, as the title, which appears on several box cars, suggests (Canadian Pacific, aka C.P. Rail, is a well-known and historically important Canadian company). Both films include weather stripping around the window frame, as a frame-within-the frame, and both films end with the camera capturing its own reflection on the darkened window of nightfall. Losing the light, losing the image, the cinematic apparatus is redundant, having nothing left but itself to film. The strict separation of inside and outside in the two *Canadian Pacific* films may indeed suggest a "garrison mentality," and yet both the formal composition and the narrativisation of daylight also refer to the structure of the gaze within the landscape.

Landscape in these three films, *Canadian Pacific I* and *II* and *Landscape*, completes the look, and is an extension of a gaze that in turn domesticates the scene of nature. The natural world does not thereby become a "garden" (with its connotations of being tamed and controlled), but becomes a patterned, textured environmental space that changes according to the viewpoint from which it is framed. Far from being "monstrous," it becomes a home for the eye, a restful and welcoming sight that reaches forward to the vanishing points of perspective, completing a structure of representation that includes and is predicated on the viewing subject-position. In splitting the vantage point over two films in *Canadian Pacific I* and *II*, and in contextualizing both scene and seer as industrialized and technologised, the construction of subjectivity is materialist rather than idealist.[19] Neither the "eye" of the camera nor the "nature" of landscape become symbolic properties, but find themselves bound into an apparatus of perception.

Despite the framing and inhabited foreground, two characteristics of McGregor's "Wacousta syndrome,"[20] it is difficult to see any evidence of a "garrison mentality" in Rimmer's landscape films. McGregor's highly reductive and ahistorical formalism not only misses the aesthetic point of Rimmer's treatment of landscape, but it also belittles the regional specificity of his West Coast reference points. In the interests of a "Canadian identity" McGregor's theory mimics the worst features of the American mythology it aims to counter. It ignores the vital differences within Canadian culture, and between Canadian regions, and it belittles the vast differences within the Canadian landscape, not to mention the way it might be altered through translation into different media.

A more appropriate context for the representation of landscape in Rimmer's films might be found in the local art history of Vancouver. An instructor at the Emily Carr College of Art, Rimmer has been closely involved with the Vancouver artistic community since the mid-1960s. Similar treatments of landscape can be found in the work of some of his contemporaries in the visual arts, e.g., Tom Burrows' *Untitled* (1971)[21] and Don Ellis's *Grounds* (1974).[22] A history of landscape painting in Vancouver would also necessarily include the painters F. H. Varley, Lawren Harris, and Emily Carr, and the abstract expressionist landscapes of Jack Shadbolt, Takao Tanabe, and Gordon Smith. As a remote outpost of a colonial culture, British Columbian artists who originated "somewhere else" have looked to their dramatic landscape for a sense of place and identity.[23]

One can no doubt find traces of McGregor's "themes" in Carr's dense forests and Varley's *Open Window*, but what McGregor reads in the Manichean terms of hostile nature/safe enclosure, can often also be read as a domestication of the wilderness; domestication, not as a "taming" but as a being-at-home-within, an inhabitation. Scott Watson says of the Vancouver painting of the 1950s:

> It is ironic that the heroic, individualistic myth informing the New Yorkers often resorted to a nineteenth century image of man in the frontier while on the actual frontier, a place like Vancouver, the image is in the urban present tense.... [T]he painting of this period, although it has been characterized as landscape—by Shadbolt, Reid and others—is best understood as part of the desire to "become cosmopolitan".... The "landscape" element of the Vancouver fifties painters was a compositional device, used to make images that refer to interior emotions as much as, if not more than, exterior places.[24]

Rimmer's structural film technique, refined in New York from 1970 to 1972, was brought home to bear on the local scene in a very literal way. Like the modernist painters associated with the Group of Seven (including Carr, Varley, and Harris) and the abstract expressionism of the 1950s in British Columbia, it has the effect of familiarizing a landscape which is distinctively West Coast and making a place within it, transforming a "vista" into an environment.

The perspectival compositions of *Canadian Pacific* and *Landscape* are complicated somewhat in *Narrows Inlet* (1980), a film in which the camera pans back and forth, completing at least one 360-degree movement around an unidentified centre. Unlike Michael Snow's *La région centrale*, these camera movements are random and swinging, as if the camera were mounted on a boat. Wooden pilings in the middle ground are evidence again of an inhabited natural environment, and the first half of the film is so drenched with mist and fog that the shore and rising mountains of the background are entirely hidden. When the lushly coloured pine forests emerge from the blue-grey fog, a landscape appears to emerge from the grain of the image; an abstract expressionist surface composition of line and texture materializes to gradually clarify as a photographic image. The horizontal pans inscribe a centralized but unstable point of vision, constructing a shifting, apparently "floating" subjectivity within this painterly landscape. Like the *Canadian Pacific* films and *Landscape*, *Narrows Inlet* represents landscape as a phenomenological production of an invisible but determining seeing camera/subject/viewer. Landscape depends on point of view, and at the same time extends and embodies that point of view as part of its nature.

## the weathered image

Landscape in Rimmer's films is clearly much more than framing and horizon lines. It is a dynamic space of movement and light, often captured by time-lapse cinematography. The patterns and rhythms of cloud movement and the play of light and shadow over water surfaces articulate and formalize the domestication of the natural environment. A certain familiarity with landscape is evoked by the cycles of weather patterns and daylight that structure many of the films. Landscape in some of his later works, such as *Along the Road to Altamira* (1986), *Black Cat White Cat* (1989), and *Local Knowledge* (1986), tends to be lit with sunsets and sunrises, and comes to function as a powerful index of change, transformation, and travel. In *Black Cat White Cat*, the Chinese landscape is repeatedly shot from a moving train, often as the sun sinks behind a silhouetted forest. This fiery imagery is fundamental to the film's sense of social and historical movement. Toward the end, a huge industrial landscape is similarly silhouetted by a horizontal camera movement at sunset.

The title graphics in all three of these late films crawl across the screen horizontally, announcing the filmic practice as a trajectory taking place in the time of travel and the space of landscape. In *Altamira*, the titles travel below an image of the sun rising over a desert horizon, to a light Spanish guitar soundtrack. Using various structural filmic techniques, this film represents the tourist experience as a fragmentary and decentred quest for an impossible knowledge of time and space. A rapid montage of postcards of Mont Saint-Michel collapses a multitude of perspectives into a single image. In seeking an alternative to this commodification of landscape, the filmic trajectory is toward the cave paintings of Altamira. The barely discernable drawings are a surface form of representation, and the rephotographed Super 8 film of the cave tends to conflate the screen surface with the cave wall. The tourist's quest for authentic spectacle ends, finally, with a very literal inscription on the inverted landscape of the pre-historic rock face.

*Local Knowledge* is organized around Rimmer's most complex representation of landscape, extending the surface/depth dialectic, as well as the patterns and metaphors of weather and sunlight, into an epic form. The title refers to the familiarity with landscape necessary to uncharted navigation in coastal waters. An image of a West Coast inlet surrounded by mountains dipping into the middle distance recurs throughout this densely textured film. In fact, this is the same scene as the one in *Landscape*, Skookumchuck Rapids, leading out of Storm Bay to the ocean beyond. The scene is shot from the water, above the prow of a motorboat speeding into the centre where the horizon seems to part and reveal an opening. It evokes a strong sense of security and home, especially when the image recurs after sequences of mysterious and slightly threatening imagery. The composition in depth, framed from a fixed vantage point that appears to be entering into and received by the landscape, breaks down mythic dualities of insides and outsides, nature and technology.

This coastal landscape is also shot from other, less stable, less secure perspectives in *Local Knowledge*, radically transformed by fog, by clouds swirling in time-lapse movements, and by sunsets. The sun keeps going down in this film, making the broad daylight shots from the boat all the more comforting. An ominous soundtrack of Asian and electronic instrumentation increases the sense of foreboding as the landscape is lost again and again to darkness. Another key image of the film is a stand of trees behind which sunsets are reflected in rapid overhead cloud movements. This image has been digitalized in video, and as a frame within the frame, revolves on a central axis at the beginning and end of the film. As it does to so much of the imagery, video flattens the scene onto a two-dimensional surface, highlighted in this case by special effects.

Breaking down images in video and rephotographing them in film makes them literally "weathered." The grain of the image, which since *Canadian Pacific* has been somewhat analogous to the effect of weather on landscape (fog, rain, and mist), becomes a sign of transformation. The meeting of videography and landscape in *Local Knowledge* goes beyond formal mediation to evoke social and historical change of revolutionary and apocalyptic dimensions. In one shot, distinctively marked by video tracking signals, trees can be seen bending in violent winds (the footage is U.S. Army documentation of an atomic blast). Combined with further threatening representations of violence and technology—a weather station surrounded by barbed wire, and a military weather report—the weather in this film becomes an iconography of danger and inevitability. The codes of TV news embedded in its videographed representation seem to turn the weather in *Local Knowledge* into an ominous ecological disaster.

In stark contrast to the landscape shots of *Local Knowledge*, a repeated image of fish fills the frame in a mass of writhing bodies. The flatness of the image is enhanced by superimposed geometric graphics, dialectically related to the depth of the mass. Intercut with shots of water surfaces, the fish suggest both the "repressed" content of the ocean and the erotics of the unconscious. Disorienting and vaguely disturbing, the image points to the industrial exploitation of the coastal waters and also to another depth besides that of depth-of-field. As another videographed image, it pushes the structural film's preoccupation with screen surface to a certain paradoxical extreme, radically obliterating horizontal space.

One of Rimmer's early films, *Blue Movie* (1970), is a study of ocean waves and clouds, completely without framing devices, perspectival markers, or anything except water; not even a horizon. It is a study of the kind of image that Snow's long zoom dissolves into at the end of *Wavelength* (1967): an image of no dimensions, no perspective, no subjectivity. The high angle flattens the surface as the waves become patterns of movement, colour, and light. While this level of abstraction returns for brief moments in later films, it tends to be contextualized in order to refer back to the subject of vision. *Local Knowledge* contains a quick upside down shot of water rushing under (or over, as the case may be) a boat-mounted camera with the sky on the bottom of the frame. The disorientation it produces is echoed in another shot from the stern of a boat travelling away from the shore; the reverse-action photography depicts a certain stasis, a rapid movement that goes nowhere. Landscape, along with its various inversions, becomes a vital substance of vision for an iconography of emplacement, familiarity, and transformation.

*Surfacing on the Thames* (1970) is Rimmer's most exacting experiment with movement in landscape, which in this case is the remote and foreign London skyline. The passage of a boat across the fixed frame, broken down into constitutive frames that are then dissolved into each other, is a retarded and almost mystical motion. Surface and depth take on historical significance as we look through the scratches and flaws of the rephotographed film to the found footage below. Critics have pointed out the resemblance of the slightly unfocussed scene to J. M. W. Turner's painting, and to the Pointillists, and it is indeed an ironically romantic effect which is created through an analysis of the materiality of the film medium.[25] Rimmer's films often aspire to the condition of painting by way of imagery composed around a horizon, but even in *Surfacing*, that horizon refers to a subject of vision: the zoom out of the centre of the image at the beginning of the film, and in again at the end, penetrate the illusion of depth to reveal its dependency on structures of perception and composition. The use of dissolves in *Surfacing* is a device which few of Rimmer's contemporary structural filmmakers used, and one which he favours in many of the later films, especially *Local*

*Knowledge*. Dissolving images into each other is a means of merging film and landscape in this early prototype of cinematic "weathering."

Nature and technology tend to be thoroughly combined in Rimmer's films. Their dualism is transcended in the deconstruction of perspectival vision implicit in his structural film form, and the phenomenology of camera-vision is turned back on itself. In her discussion of *Wavelength*, Annette Michelson refers to the "horizon characteristic of every subjective process and fundamental as a trait of intentionality" to explain the constitution of the viewer in time.[26] When "horizon" is literalized in landscape, as it is in Rimmer's experimental films, spatial determinants take priority over temporal ones and the viewer is located spatially within the perspective and the film. In the very limited freedom of the fixed-camera position, the phenomenological "transcendental subject" is referenced, but not mobilized. The view of nature unsettles the instrumentalised gaze, rendering it dependent on the scene itself, which, through darkness and weather, also limits the field of vision. Landscape is a vehicle of and for movement, the movement of history and industry, and it is a receptacle for the eye, a home for vision, until it is transferred to video. With the loss of depth, the technologised landscape takes on a threatening demeanour, a vaguely discomforting two-dimensionality. Even in *Local Knowledge*, though, this apocalyptic postmodernism is counterbalanced by recurring images of the security of a West Coast inlet.

Landscape is the first order of image-content to be admitted to the purist structural project (Arthur 1979, 127). Mute and empty, it answers and rewards the "address of the eye." Although it is often an empty stage, landscape also frames the entry of the human figure into the visual field of structural film. Examples of this tendency would include Chantal Ackerman's experimental documentaries *News from Home* (1977) and *D'Est* (1993) as well as some of Bill Viola's video works from the 1980s.[27] In Rimmer's *Real Italian Pizza* (1971), shot in New York City from September 1970 to May 1971, the structural aesthetic is turned onto a street scene. This is not only Rimmer's most overtly ethnographic film, but because of the setting, it serves as a foil or counterpoint to Snow's *Wavelength*. Outside the loft window he finds the life of the street which Snow so radically excludes. Turning the camera onto the patrons of an Italian pizza and sandwich shop, their rhythms of coming and going and just hanging out on the sidewalk, Rimmer assumes the position of the spy. From his elevated angle across the street, the New Yorkers, many of them African American, look like ants on a hill or bees revolving around a buzzing hive. The pizza makers/shop owners remain invisible inside the shop. They come out to shovel snow off the sidewalk, but for the most part, their invisibility and centrality on the other side of the scenario mirrors and compliments that of the camera.[28]

Each of the three overlapping camera positions in *Real Italian Pizza* has the effect of framing the scene like a stage onto which people exit and enter. Collapsing nine months into 13 minutes, Rimmer's editing exaggerates the rhythms and patterns of the routines of daily life, lingering on those who loiter outside the shop during the summer months, pixilating rapid activity, and when the police drag someone out of the shop, he dramatically cuts into the scene to see the apprehended man stuffed into a patrol car. This brief shot is the proverbial exception which proves the rule of the otherwise statically framed film. In comparison to many of Rimmer's films, the "real" documentary image is more or less sustained in its integrity.

The example of *Real Italian Pizza*, a key text in Rimmer's body of work, serves to underline his construction of what I am calling an "inhabited view." To return to his works based on the Canadian landscape, it is evident that his "structural film" project cannot be accounted for by formalist aesthetics alone. The profilmic event, whether it be the New York street scene or the British Columbian weather, is always a structural component of the film. Before it is a landscape or a cityscape it is a place, a location and a site, one which is traversed by technology and reinvented as an artifactual "thing" by virtue of being filmed. If we can describe Rimmer's ethnography as passive and unobtrusive, we can likewise describe the landscape in his films as being endowed with subjectivity. It looks back, it is in constant movement, it has presence.

## nation, landscape, territory

In films such as *Real Italian Pizza*, *On the Road to Altamira*, and *Black Cat White Cat*, it is evident that Rimmer's landscape films exceed the Canadian territory. We might say that when he turns to the cityscape it is always outside Canada, and that his depiction of Canada tends to be in terms of landscape, but I do not think that implies that his treatment of the Canadian landscape is necessarily bound up with his identity as a Canadian filmmaker. The critical agenda of Bart Testa, Gaile McGregor, Margaret Atwood, and Northrop Frye should be recognized as belonging to a particular moment in the Canadian culture wars when an aesthetic vocabulary needed to be forged in order to understand the nation-state as having a recognizable personality.

Stan Brakhage has taken up the arguments presented by Testa in an essay entitled, "Space as Menace in Canadian Aesthetics: Film and Painting" (1989) to argue for a distinctive Canadian aesthetic "which is essentially defensive."[29] Brakhage's argument is based on the parallels between Canadian experimental films and the paintings of the Group of Seven, a loose-knit group of painters whose work—mostly landscapes—from the 1910s through to the 1950s has been canonized as emblematic of Canadian art. Brakhage points out that in their stylized Art Deco strategies of "taming space," the Group of Seven managed to bring nature under control. They did so by privileging surface over depth, a practice that enabled them to keep the nothingness of the emptiness of the land at bay. Brakhage writes, "It is my contention that this tactic of skeining a landscape, as it were—of blocking a view with a veritable net across the surface of the canvas—was so influential in Canadian aesthetics because of a deepseated cultural aversion to any concept of Space as would allow a being-nothing-there" (88).

When Brakhage turns to Canadian filmmakers such as Rimmer, Bruce Elder, and Michael Snow, he discusses their various ways of making tolerable the blankness "out there." Their specifically Canadian aesthetic, in his view, is a strategy of "picturing space" in such a way that it "points inward" (101). Rimmer's systematic articulation of the surface of the image—through his use of horizontals and image grain—is singled out by Brakhage as exemplary of the displacement of the vastness of depth by the tangibility of surface (95). While Brakhage's version of the Canadian landscape aesthetic is perhaps more existential than the survivalist rhetoric of McGregor and Atwood, he nevertheless shares their assumption that national identity can be mapped on to the Canadian territory through the mediations of landscape art and filmmaking.

This view of cultural nationalism has been challenged most forcefully by Erin Manning, for whom the Group of Seven and the nationalist rhetoric that is spawned by their work constitutes a "language of territory and identity that is borrowed from the ideological assumptions of imperial Britain for which the colonial landscape existed to be consumed, identified, and ruled."[30] Manning proposes a "deterritorialized" approach to Canadian landscape art as a means of moving beyond the colonialist precepts of the Group of Seven and the homogeneous idealism of the cultural nationalism that their paintings have come to stand for. To consider landscape as a chronotope, for example, in which geography and history intersect, we may be able to move out of the formalist aesthetics espoused by structural film critical practice and the nationalist aesthetics proposed by Brakhage et al. In a dialogical approach to landscape, says Manning, "we begin to notice the biases, ethnocentricities, and exclusions inherent in the notion of territoriality" (14).

Rimmer's particular deployment of structural film aesthetics is "dialogical" in the sense that time and space are configured jointly; his is not an eternal landscape but a temporal one. In fact, I would argue that the binary opposites of inward/outward, surface and depth are less appropriate to this work than a consideration of these films as depictions of place. Brakhage's use of the term "space" implies abstraction, whereas if we consider these landscapes as "places" rather than "spaces" they may not be as threatening or empty as the conventional analysis implies. The space/place distinction derived from de Certeau is more often applied to the depiction of urban space, in which "space" refers to the voyeuristic, panopticonic view of the city from above, like a map, and "place" refers to the perspective of the flaneur, walking the city streets.[31] A film like *Real Italian Pizza* might be said to blur this distinction, as the structural film aesthetic is by definition panopticonic, but Rimmer works within and against it precisely by betraying his own subjectivity as a participant flaneur. In the landscape films, the surface of the image, the frame of the image, and the special effects tend to enact the filmmaker's signature and presence in and at the place of the filming.

The sense of inhabitation implied in Rimmer's "artifactual" landscape can also be found in the work of Inuit filmmaker Zacharius Kunuk, whose films and videos set in the Canadian arctic also render the landscape as an inhabited space.[32] Kunuk may deploy conventions of ethnographic film and melodramatic storytelling, which produce very different effects from Rimmer's structural film practice, and yet he indicates the direction in which Rimmer's films of the 1970s point. In Kunuk's films, the video image is an effect of technology in which the frame and the lighting are frequently deployed in a reflexive manner. For his community, which is both the star and the first audience of his films, the landscape is a kind of home. Despite the extremely harsh weather conditions, and the unmarked expanse of white-on-white landscape, he finds that there are stories there to be told, as most of his work consists of people performing rituals and practices and acting out stories that are recalled by the elders.[33]

If Kunuk is able to use the aesthetics of visual culture to create a home for the eye out of the arctic expanse, it is precisely by overcoming the nature/culture divide and looking at the landscape in an "artifactual" manner, which is to say, as a cultural production. Kunuk's "ecology" is clearly grounded in a social program that has more urgency than Rimmer's project, as his films are made under the threat of cultural loss and social amnesia. However, taken together, the landscape in the work of these two very different filmmakers suggests that new critical methods are required to appreciate their projects. As the debate over the national character of the landscape demonstrates, it is as much a question of interpretation as aesthetics that is at issue.

In Canadian art and film criticism, the landscape has been harnessed to a particular ideological construction of the nation, one which is clearly outdated. A more ecological consideration of the landscape would enable us to understand a filmmaker such as Rimmer within the specificity of his chosen medium and his specific geo-historical setting. Rather than fitting his experimental practice into a formula derived from another time and another medium (pre-war painting), we would do well to recognize his articulation of place. Structural film aesthetics are, by definition, highly disciplined, in the sense of the fixed frame, which tends to "quote" its own picture-making practice. But this disciplined restriction of movement and editing has the effect of creating and even foregrounding off-screen space—the space around the frame, and the space occupied by the filmmaker.

In conjunction with the documentary image at the heart of the structural film project, Rimmer's work suggests the Canadian landscape—as image—can be apprehended as an endangered "place." If this can be said to constitute a "deterritorialization" as Manning suggests, it does so only to underscore the enculturation, occupation, and penetration of landscape by technology. Through the experimental practices of filmmakers such as Rimmer and Kunuk, we may be better able to understand the Canadian landscape as a production of visual culture, and as "natureculture" rather than an "other" space of threatening emptiness. The technology of vision, allegorized in David Rimmer's structural film practice, is a strategy of inhabitation in which aesthetics and ecology are tentatively aligned.

## notes

1. Hollis Frampton, *Circles of Confusion* (Rochester, NY: Visual Studies Workshop Press, 1983), 123.
2. Bart Testa, *Spirit in the Landscape* (Toronto: Art Gallery of Ontario, 1989), 5; hereafter cited in text.
3. Pat Brereton, *Hollywood Utopia: Ecology in Contemporary American Cinema* (Portland, OR: Intellect Books, 2005), 16, 21.
4. Andrew Ross, Strange Weather: *Culture, Science and Technology in the Age of Limits* (London: Verso, 1991), 194.
5. Donna Haraway, *The Companion Species Manifesto: Dogs, People, and Significant Otherness* (Chicago: Prickly Paradigm Press, 2003), 8. Haraway credits the ethnographer Marilyn Strathern for the term.
6. Donna Haraway, "The Promises of Monsters: A Regenerative Politics for Inappropriate/d Others," in *Cultural Studies*, eds. Lawrence Grossberg, Cary Nelson, and Paula Trichler (New York: Routledge, 1992), 296; hereafter cited in text.
7. P. Adams Sitney, "Structural Film," *Film Culture* 47 (Summer 1969): 1–10. P. Adams Sitney, *Visionary Film: The American Avant-garde 1943–1978*, 2nd ed. (New York: Oxford University Press, 1979), 370.
8. Other key structural films about landscape include Joyce Wieland's *Sailboat* (1967), Michael Snow's *La région centrale* (1971), and George Landow's *Remedial Reading Comprehension* (1971). Landscape often functions as a concluding section for structural films, such as Hollis Frampton's *Zorn's Lemma* (1970), Michael Snow's *Wavelength* (1967), and Wieland's *Pierre Vallieres* (1972). Cityscapes also feature prominently, as in *New York Eye and Ear Control* (Snow, 1964) and *One Second in Montreal* (Snow, 1969).
9. Peter Gidal, ed., *Structural Film Anthology* (London: British Film Institute, 1976); hereafter cited in text. Malcolm Le Grice, *Abstract Film and Beyond* (Cambridge, MA: MIT Press, 1977). Le Grice put a subsequent Derridean twist on his theory of structural film in *Materialist Film* (London: Routledge, 1989).
10. David James notes that Sitney endowed structural film "with a quasi-spiritual motivation that enables him to situate it as the logical culmination of the visionary tradition through its capacity, not simply to record, but to induce extraordinary states of consciousness." David E. James,

*Allegories of Cinema: American Film in the Sixties* (Princeton: Princeton University Press, 1989), 242n.

11. Constance Penley, "The Avant-Garde and Its Imaginary," *Camera Obscura* 2 (Fall 1977): 3–33. See also Constance Penley and Janet Bergstrom, "The Avant-Garde: History and Theories," *Screen* 19, no. 3 (Autumn 1978), 113–127.

12. Paul Arthur, "Structural Film: Revisions, New Versions, and the Artifact," *Millennium Film Journal* 1-2 (Spring 1978): 12.

13. The limitations of these terms "documentary" and "fiction" are most particularly related to the false opposition that they presuppose. Structural filmmakers frequently worked with "found fictions" from early cinema.

14. Paul Arthur has pointed out that Sitney's description of Structural Film varied quite a bit from 1969 to 1977, and that his definition of "shape" was never adequately pinned down. "Structural Film: Revisions, New versions and the Artifact. Part Two," *Millennium Film Journal* 4-5 (Summer, Fall 1979), 123; hereafter cited in text.

15. Annette Michelson's essay on Michael Snow suggested that experimental film might in fact make a contribution to the philosophy of consciousness: "Epistemological inquiry and cinematic experience converge, as it were, in reciprocal mimesis." Annette Michelson, "Toward Snow," in *The Avant-Garde Film: A Reader of Theory and Criticism*, ed. P. Adams Sitney (New York: New York University Press, 1978), 173.

16. In fact, as Paul Arthur has pointed out, "the unalloyed investigation of film's material substrate exists as a tiny chapter in the history of the American avant-garde and a not much larger episode in Structural Film's moment." "The Last of the Last Machine?: Avant-Garde Film Since 1966," *Millennium Film Journal* 16/17/18 (Fall/Winter 1986–1987), 81; hereafter cited in text. In addition to the films and filmmakers discussed below, one could add Standish Lawder's *Necrology* (1970) and many of Hollis Frampton's films, which consistently investigate the construction of meaning in photographic images, as instances of experimental ethnography.

17. Kirk Tougas, quoted in "David Rimmer: A Critical Collage," *Canadian Film Reader*, compiled by Joyce Nelson, eds. Seth Feldman and Joyce Nelson (Toronto: Peter Martin Associated Limited, 1977), 340.

18. Gaile McGregor, *The Wacousta Syndrome: Explorations in the Canadian Landscape* (Toronto: University of Toronto Press, 1985), 99; hereafter cited in text.

19. See Stephen Heath, "Repetition Time: Notes Around 'Structural/Materialist Film'" in *Questions of Cinema* (Bloomington: Indiana University Press, 1981). On the idealist construction of this film practice, he writes: "The disunity, the disjunction of 'structural/materialist film' is, exactly, the spectator" (167).

20. The name Wacousta derives from a 1923 novel by Major John Richardson in which "a profound fear of nature often seems to override any other response" (McGregor, 7).

21. Reproduced in *Vancouver: Art and Artists 1931–1983* (Exhibition Catalogue, Vancouver Art Gallery, 1983), 228; hereafter cited in text as *Vancouver Art and Artists*.

22. Reproduced in *Vancouver Art and Artists, op. cit.*, 230.

23. Scott Watson, "Terminal City: Place, Culture and the Regional Inflection," in *Vancouver Art and Artists, op. cit.*, 226–255. Many visual artists also turned to the styles and iconography of the Northwest coast native

cultures, which are by and large absent from Rimmer's filmmaking, perhaps because they don't lend themselves to cinematic appropriation. It may not be stretching the landscape theme too far to see it reappear in *Media Wall*, an installation by Rimmer, Bill Fix, and Tom Shandel, which is also somewhat totemistic in concept. The ruins of television sets are banked in "mountains" and "pillars" against a gallery wall, as part of the 1969 Electrical Connection exhibition at Vancouver Art Gallery (*Vancouver Art and Artists, op. cit.*, 186).

24. Scott Watson, "Art in the Fifties: Design, Leisure, and Painting in the Age of Anxiety," in *Vancouver Art and Artists, op. cit.*, 97–98.

25. Blaine Allan, "David Rimmer's Surfacing on the Thames," *Cinetracts* (Winter 1980): 58.

26. Annette Michelson, "Towards Snow," in *The Avant-Garde Film, op. cit.*, 175. She goes on to cite Husserl as the philosophical source for her notion of horizons of perception.

27. See my *Experimental Ethnography: The Work of Film in the Age of Video* (Durham, NC: Duke University Press, 1999), 157–192, for a discussion of the ethnographic aspects of structural film.

28. The tightly structured scenario of the empowered gaze which is reproduced in *Real Italian Pizza* is a variation on that described by Foucault in "Las Meninas." Michel Foucault, *The Order of Things: the Archaeology of the Human Sciences* (New York: Vintage Books, 1973).

29. Stan Brakhage, *Telling Time: Essays of a Visionary Filmmaker* (New York: Documentext, 2003), 87; hereafter cited in text.

30. Erin Manning, *Ephemeral Territories: Representing Nation, Home and Identity in Canada* (Minneapolis: Minnesota University Press, 2003), 7; hereafter cited in text.

31. Michel de Certeau, "Walking in the City," in *The Cultural Studies Reader*, ed. Simon During (London: Routledge, 1993).

32. Kunuk's films include *Atanarjuat* (*The Fast Runner*, 2001); *From Inuk Point of View* (1985); *Alert Bay* (1989); *Qaggiq* (*Gathering Place*, 1989); *Nunaqpa* (Going Inland, 1991); *Saputi* (Fish Traps, 1993); *Nunavut* (*Our Land*, 1994-1995); *Nipi* (*Voice*, 1999). Before the success of *Atanarjuat*, Kunuk's videos were distributed in the "south" of Canada mainly in galleries as video art.

33. See biography of Zacharius Kunuk, *Current Biography, International Yearbook 2002* (New York: H.W. Wilson Company); available at http://www.hwwilson.com/print/cbintl_skunuk_biography.htm (accessed May 1, 2005); and Kimberly Chun, "Storytelling in the Arctic Circle: An Interview with Zacharius Kunuk," *Cineaste* 28, no. 1 (Winter 2002): 21–23.

# sites of meaning

gallipoli and other mediterranean

landscapes in amateur

films (c. 1928–1960)

heather nicholson [1]

Semi-close up:…. He raises his hand to point and another member of the party joins him from behind to follow his gaze.
Long shot: What they see: The view…. The inexperienced will succumb to the temptation to make a panorama. Don't do it…. (D)on't spray the camera over the landscape as if it were a hose.[2]

Suzy, the guide points out the best view of Florence. It's just the sort of picture postcard view I'm anxious to avoid…. Suzy sits on a low wall waiting for me and eases her shoes off each with the other foot. That's a close up I *can* make use of among the museums and art galleries of the excursion sequence.[3]

**Heather Nicholson**

From the early 1920s, the rapid adoption of cine cameras as a lightweight travel accessory enabled hobby filmmakers unprecedented freedom to picture landscapes in moving imagery. Pitfalls soon confronted the new enthusiasts as their footage disclosed the unsuitability of rapid panning shots, insufficient depth of field, blurred detail, and other technical limitations. Just as camera technologies seemed to bring the capacity to emulate big screen effects within reach of nonprofessional cinephiles, the medium itself demonstrated its visual limitations over still photography.

Landscape imagery, nonetheless, was a popular subject matter among both amateur filmmakers and their viewers. Scenes of familiar and more distant localities remained established elements within the repertoire of British home moviemakers for the next 40 years, and indeed, thereafter when video technologies began to grow in popularity and replace cine cameras during the 1970s. Tips on tackling landscape representation soon contributed to the mushrooming specialist literature that arose to encourage better amateur filmmaking. For over four decades, advice on what, where, how, and who to film abounded throughout the publications published for and by nonprofessional enthusiasts. Gale and Pessels (1939), among many other American and (slightly later) European authors, offered their readers suggestions for story boards, shooting scripts, and forthright opinions on every conceivable aspect of making and showing amateur footage.[4] Specialist magazines, including *Amateur Cine World* and *Amateur Films,* soon featured insights based on personal experience. Hill's (1956) suggested close-up of Suzy's ankles in preference for filming Filippo Brunelleschi's early Renaissance dome-topped cathedral in Florence not only uses an unexpected holiday shot for audience amusement, it also points to the assumed readership for what was still largely—although not exclusively—a male, middle-class leisure activity even in the mid-1950s. While neither the tone nor the message of the opening quotations are particularly unique, they encapsulate some of the central issues for this discussion of amateur visual practice and landscape representation in nonprofessional travel footage in the years circa 1920 to 1960.

How did amateur enthusiasts reconcile the contradictions of their hobby? The visual freedom offered by their new equipment seemed to contrast with the recommendations by specialists to show restraint and concentrate on close- and medium-range subjects. This may be seen as being part of a more general questioning, after World War I, about "what photography could and could not do" that was informed by growing realisation about objectivity's deceptive gaze and the camera's capacity to shape landscape meanings.[5] Advertising, in contrast, promised hobby filmmakers the wonder and excitement of professional cinematic picture making. Their audiences, by now, were also increasingly accustomed more to newsreels and commercial cinema than magic lantern slides and similarly enjoyed the novelty of watching landscapes in movement.

Poised between these opposing influences, amateurs tried to find effective ways to capture spatial aesthetics and portray experiences of landscape. As with any attempts, not all were successful and inevitably, the blurred and shakily held results of some experiments have become responsible for the frequent dismissal and often pejorative labelling of nonprofessional footage in wider studies of film and film history.

In a collection that brings together cinematic representations of landscape crossing the entire span of cinema's first century, it seems fitting for this chapter to turn attention to landscape subjectivities in amateur productions. As early advocates of the amateur film movement were swift to point out, even the professionals began as amateurs: indeed, it is a point taken up by Rachel Low in her study of Britain's documentary film movement in the 1930s.[6] Moreover, hobbyists, like their professional counterparts in different countries, made and showed their films in contexts not totally unconnected to the wider circulation of ideas about the value, aesthetics, and meaning of landscape. It is appropriate therefore to explore why and how amateurs included landscape imagery in their holiday and travel movies and how the making and showing of their footage contributed to the formation and circulation of specific landscape meanings in the middle years of the last century.

These opening remarks define a context for this chapter's focus on landscape in amateur film. I have written elsewhere on the rise of the amateur film movement in Britain, and considered its contribution to an understanding of identity formation, place representation, and ideological meanings at home and abroad during the mid-twentieth century.[7] My present focus on a particular landscape of commemoration inevitably connects with aspects of earlier writings on landscape history, travel, and memory, although this discussion weaves a hitherto uncharted route. Attention focuses on recently located film footage made by a British amateur filmmaker and war veteran when revisiting the contested landscapes associated with the Gallipoli campaign of 1915–1916. Accordingly, two closely related ideas are explored, namely landscapes as sites of meaning in nonprofessional footage and, secondly, the practical attempts to photograph landscape in moving imagery for subsequent viewing.

This discussion forms part of an ongoing publication from a two-year analysis of Mediterranean-related travel footage held by the North West Film Archives at Manchester Metropolitan University and the British Film Institute in London, funded by the Kraszna-Kraus Foundation and the British Academy. Qualitative in nature, the research has involved the identification, selection, and shot listing (i.e., detailed listing on a shot-by-shot basis) of relevant footage deposited at both archives. Wherever possible, contact with surviving family and friends as well as the study of any associated paperwork, correspondence, or other documents pertaining to the footage have also informed the interpretation of film imagery.

Given the overall time frame and the range of issues raised by the material, broadly based reading contributes to the analysis as outlined below. Attention turns next to identify those background areas and writings that have helped to shape various historical and theoretical perspectives that inform my empirical findings. With these ideas in mind, I then look closely at the Gallipoli footage as one particular example of landscape representation in amateur film.

## amateur film, landscape, and memory

During the early 1920s, new photographic opportunities became possible in Britain when Kodak introduced a portable cine camera and associated accessories for the home screening of moving imagery. Motion brought a novel dimension to the tradition of "picturing place" well established by the photographic surveys of governments, scientific organisations, transportation companies, missionaries, travellers, and others during the nineteenth century.[8] The cine camera could stretch single poses into sequences and isolated views into moving panoramas. Cine technology's capacity to enable spectators to see beyond an individual frame redefined forms of visualisation available to amateur photographers and their audiences.

Cine cameras captured the speed, mobility, and light that had so attracted earlier photographers and others to evolving transport technologies of the late nineteenth and early twentieth century.[9] Literally, cine cameras mobilized and broadened the photographic gaze. And yet, as the opening quotations indicate, early amateur practitioners were routinely instructed to avoid movement within shots or certain kinds of shots, and to look for more novel angles and forms of composition.[10] Moreover, since many early cine camera users started with still photography, much activity was rooted in the conventions of existing visual practice. Like their audiences, amateurs had been weaned on a diet of pictorial representation, ethnographic attention to detail of people and places, and the seemingly insatiable desire for vicarious consumption of views.[11] Both amateurs and audiences clearly had preconceived ways of seeing.

For all their apparent transparency and precision as visual documents, of course, still and moving imagery also manipulated time and space; yet many early amateurs, such as Britain's emerging documentary makers, often espoused realist approaches. Despite much continuing acceptance of the camera's objectivity, at popular and public levels, there was also growing awareness that photographic technologies could yield highly selective versions of reality (Schwartz and Ryan, 2003). As Edwards suggests, photographs were both a medium and a product of specific sociopolitical relations and situations could seem to be naturalized and neutralized by their appearance of reality.[12] Contemporary fiction was often more overt in its disclosure of visual trickery and persuasive power than those whose authority, ideologies, and ambitions were furthered by use of photography. In Conrad's discussion of how technology alters experience in *A la recherche du temps perdu*, he contrasts one character's attraction to the alchemy of "fixing the past on paper" with the "subtler, stealthier purpose" of moving imagery, the "conspiratorial twilight of the cinema," and the dreamlike flickering of the magic lantern.[13] Early amateur moving imagery, watched in darkened private and public spaces, practiced its own visual deceits too: its seemingly long, inclusive, flickering gaze masked its even greater capacity for selective representation. In fact, the cine camera's panoramic vision held out deceptive promises of actuality, as their imaginative landscapes, perhaps even more than single captured views, were the complex products of decisions at different stages of production about what to include and omit from any sequence.

Whatever the actual subject matter, home movies were often as much about the person behind as the scenes or individual(s) framed in the camera lens. Accordingly, the interpretation of overseas landscape encounters found in amateur footage is assisted by insights gleaned from writings on the "picturing impulse" (Schwartz and Ryan, 2003) in various colonial contexts. Studies of photography and memory, particularly family photographic memories that may help us to understand how families mediate, negotiate, and circulate specific identities in public spaces[14] also inform the analysis of some footage. Similarly, help also comes from various sociohistorical, autobiographical, and other perspectives on memory making and film.[15]

The making of amateur films, like the social uses of other camera technologies, was often a deliberate memorializing act.[16] Typically, when enthusiasts used their cameras to record such specific domestic events as birthdays, family gatherings, or anniversaries and local civic or special occasions, they also included situational details including landscape. Sometimes the wider setting barely features but frequently being in a particular place—on the beach at Brighton, Blackpool, or Biarritz, for instance—is central to the stories people liked to tell about themselves at home and elsewhere. Places and localities contextualize family activities and are imbued with particular subjectivities according to specific experiences. Once framed on film for successive reviewing, they connote distinctive associations that, as with most visual forms, trigger to recollection and tend to become the dominant memories for those involved at the time. Indeed, as discussed later, the objectification of memories in material form may contribute to their own eventual displacement and erasure.[17] Furthermore, the cinematic processes that cut, splice, edit, and discard both reorder holiday time and reconfigure travel space. The resultant visual narratives of reconnected time and space[18] become filmic topologies of travel memories in which different localities acquire significance as sites of personalized significance.

Travel footage is both a response to and consequence of being somewhere else and, as with written travel narratives, it represents personal engagement and self-expression (Norris Nicholson, 2004a). However clichéd the sequences and sentiments may now appear, these filmic recollections of sites, encounters, and visually striking moments may approximate the diaries, notebooks, and image making of earlier commentators. Equally, one person's travel tales may be played out in settings that may, for others, hold more widespread meaning. Clearly the fascination with capturing on film sites of antiquity or, as discussed in this chapter, a landscape of commemoration, has its forerunners in nineteenth-century interests in photographing monuments at home and abroad.[19] It also invites comparison with studies that explore the politics of remembrance, contested meanings and identities associated with symbolic structures, statuary and other surviving landscapes, and material cultural remains from different times and places.[20]

The recent upsurge of interest in varied kinds of travel texts contributes helpful insights to the analysis of travel-related film footage too.[21] As discussed elsewhere, written travel narratives and amateur travel footage often share certain characteristics (Norris Nicholson, 2003a; 2003c; 2004a). Most obviously, they offer an outsider's perspective and are intended for distant, nonlocal audiences. Second, the basic experience of travel as catalyst for self-expression in verbal or visual form is common to both. Sometimes they seek validation by reference to previous or other travel-related texts and reiterate earlier patterns of response and encounter. Lastly, although much harder to identify in visual than in written texts, there may be important interplay between inner and outer worlds of meaning prompted by the experience of being somewhere else. Although it would be misleading to over-emphasize their similarities, useful guidance on the reading of travel texts has also come from the ideas of Pemble, Pratt, Duncan and Gregory, and Carr.[22]

Amateur cinematography—the preferred term by many early enthusiasts who defined their hobby in relation to professional activity—associated closely with tourism. Early cinephiles tended to travel and thus combine two costly hobbies. As cine photography's relative costs decreased, it gradually became more widely accessible as a leisure time activity that became closely linked to changing holiday patterns and an increase in overseas travel. As considered elsewhere (Nicholson 2002b; 2003a; 2004b), the analysis of the social contexts within which footage was made and shown links readily to developments within tourism history and leisure-related patterns of consuming places.[23] Travel-related footage made in Mediterranean contexts may be seen as a variant within a long representational tradition by those Northern Europeans who underwent the *rite de passage* of the Grand Tour or alternatively journeyed south to selected destinations for diverse other personal, political, and intellectual reasons.[24]

172

Let us now consider one particular type of camera-touting vacationer and consider the various meanings that may be disclosed by filmic visualizations of landscape.

## filmic acts of commemoration

During the interwar years, cine enthusiasts were a tiny minority among the steadily growing numbers of visitors to the battlefields and commemorative sites associated with World War I. Thomas Cook's Tours and other companies facilitated visits for bereaved families, war veterans, as well as younger generations to locations where relatives or former comrades had fought and, in many cases, lost their lives.[25] Battlefield tourism long predates the First World War, and the public demand for witnessing sites associated with the Western Front was already so intense in March 1915 that objections by the French authorities prompted Thomas Cook to advertise suspension of its tours until the cessation of hostilities.[26] Postwar, artistic, media, and other responses[27] maintained public interest and visits. As the war's social, economic, political consequences, and, above all, its devastating loss of life underwent continuing reassessment, the publication of guide books and tours to war graves and memorial parks in France, Belgium, and further afield became more widespread.

Saunders suggests, with reference to the Western Front, that as the war had been represented to the British public through official drawings, paintings, photographs, films, and maps, those early battlefield visitors who "sought to correlate photographic images with reality"[28] soon encountered discrepancies as well as "disappointment, fulfillment and irony in varying parts" (44–45). In contrast, constraints of distance and cost meant that fewer visitors went to the Eastern Front battlegrounds and as discussed later, other imagery was less available. Only two instances of visits with cine cameras to battlefields associated with the ill-fated Dardanelles expedition have been identified in connection with writing this chapter. Given the catastrophic level of fatalities and injuries incurred by Lancashire regiments in the ill-fated Gallipoli campaign, it is not surprising that both known examples of Gallipoli footage derive from Lancashire filmmakers. Discussion here focuses on the imagery of one filmmaker about whom more biographical details are known as well as information of his other filmmaking activities. Interestingly, both men record cruises for veterans and their families arranged by the Royal Navy Division and share a broadly similar itinerary across the Mediterranean and at Gallipoli.

*Gallipoli Revisited, 1934. A Pilgrimage Cruise* documents on 16-mm, black and white, silent film stock with intertitles a commemorative tour of different battlefield sites and war memorials associated with the Gallipoli campaign. The title employs terms used by contemporary, battle tour organizers and points perhaps to "the redemptive and quasi-religious"

(Pollard, 28) experiential quality associated with the planned and progressive journeys of modern pilgrims. For the filmmaker, if not for at least some of his subsequent audience members, Lt. Colonel James Fitzwilliam O'Grady's return visit to the Dardanelles seems to have been more than simply a cine variant on nineteenth-century war zone sightseeing: "a fascination in wandering over the battlegrounds…a spell that spreads over all and charms the imagination of all."[29] Rather, O'Grady's filmic framing of landscape features convey a poignancy associated with his own acts of remembrance. Perhaps, as discussed later, his cinematic testimony had other more public meaning too. Did these images of overgrown trenches, twisted fragments of gun carriages, and semi-submerged rusting hulls and decking in offshore waters help those at home to also bear witness belatedly to Gallipoli's infamous landings and evacuation points and to commemorate a tragic episode in regimental history?

On August 22, 1914, only weeks after the start of World War I, James Fitzwilliam O'Grady interrupted his medical studies at Manchester University and was commissioned into the Seventh Battalion of the Royal Lancashire Fusiliers. Two weeks later, the Battalion travelled by train to Southampton and embarked for Alexandria aboard the *SS Saturnia*.[30] O'Grady's company saw action in Egypt before receiving the order to sail to Gallipoli where their landing on May 5, 1915, thrust them into the horror of trying to beach through submerged tripwires, barbed wire, and landmines under heavy machine gunfire and shrapnel.[31] For the next month, O'Grady took part in successive attempts to capture and recapture Turkish trenches amid the confusion of skirmishes, advances, and retreats associated with the efforts to reach and defend different positions across the gullied terrain of the Gallipoli peninsula. On June 10, O'Grady was one of many casualties sustained in the assault known as the Battle of Krithia that attempted to secure a position amidst trenches straddling the major communication road through the peninsula.

O'Grady was invalided home to Lancashire where he subsequently completed his medical training and volunteered to serve as a doctor with the Manchester Brigade Royal Army Medical Corps. There is no mention of him as a serving officer during World War I after September 1916. O'Grady acquired a cine camera in the early 1930s and throughout the decade, he made films of his young family and a range of short documentary-style records of army training camps, manoeuvres, parades, and other regimental events. His filmmaking continued sporadically into the 1950s particularly on holidays at home and abroad. Although he films the rugged mountain terrain as setting for training events in Snowdonia and carefully portrays holiday locations in Britain and overseas, nowhere else does his handling of landscape imagery attain such visual intensity as at Gallipoli.

For many people, family home movies were idealised supplements to memory, or as Sutton has called them, "epic celebrations" and "dreams (projected) onto film emulsion."[32] O'Grady's Turkish landscape footage documents an act of commemoration but also offers a reorientation of memories: his filmic record combines his sense of place, time, and action based on previous experience with new architectural structures of monumental (and epic?) scale. Architecture offers alternative material sites of "preserved" meaning that, for O'Grady, also confer new visual identities to the landscape.

Remembering the victims of war through filming memorials to fallen comrades thus offers not only the possibility of emotional re-exhumation and closure but also, as Yilmaz (2003) suggests, displacement and erasure. It combines O'Grady's private visual narrative with his public sense of duty implicit in making a film for future screening. In a pertinent discussion of identity and recent violence, Wood also examines "the kind of symbiotic relationship between self-identity and different localities, including 'bleak inhospitable places.'"[33] He suggests that such sites of "both public and private memory" are "another way of talking about past and future, about opportunities for action and inaction" (35). O'Grady's interweaving of private actions (personal memory, paying tribute, taking pictures) and quasi-public arenas (commemorative places, later film showings) also illustrates the complexities of space-action relations as discussed by Staeheli and Mitchell.[34]

O'Grady returned to Gallipoli after an absence of 19 years. His initial encounter was brief but its effects on his subsequent life were profound: injury, convalescence, and professional commitment to medical service within the army. His continuing regimental involvement maintained strong regional and personal bonds with families and individuals whose lives had been irrevocably altered by the loss of life and injuries that had occurred at Gallipoli. On his return visit, his handling of the camera hints at various landscape subjectivities, albeit framed through an informed military gaze. A slow, broad panoramic sweep across the scrubby inland landscape, headlands, and sandy foreshore provide the first impressions of Gallipoli's battle zone. From deck height aboard the *SS Duchess of Richmond,* O'Grady's gaze encompasses the bleak and seemingly empty vastness of low hills, ridges, and heathland across the peninsula. Camera movements within a succession of establishing shots are slow, steady, and in focus. The gaze is that of a trained military eye and conveys an understanding of the overall terrain. It approximates to O'Grady's initial offshore impression of the site on his first visit, although it now encodes specific meanings rather than the complex emotions of anticipation associated with his previous disembarkation in May 1915.

The sandy foreshores between steep headlands backed by the predominantly low undulating relief of the hinterland are recognizably part of a

Mediterranean coastal view. During the 1930s, O'Grady's monotone footage probably also evoked a generalized Mediterranean setting that was becoming familiar to audiences through the imagery of films, advertising, and, for some people, personal experience of a rapidly emerging sunshine-orientated tourism. Yet, at another level, O'Grady's landscapes also seem placeless in their apparent lack of recognizable features and landforms. The difficulties of capturing a sense of place were not unique to cinema. The poet John Masefield implies a similar problem in *Gallipoli* (1916), an account based on observations from the relative safety of an offshore motorboat whilst helping to evacuate wounded personnel. "Those who wish to imagine the scene must think of twenty miles of any rough and steep sea coast known to them, picturing it as roadless, waterless, much broken with gullies, covered with scrub, sandy, loose, and difficult to walk on and without more than two miles of accessible landing throughout its length."[35] O'Grady's later visual record conveys more direct engagement with the terrain. Retrospection and solemnity also contrast with the earlier rhetoric of triumphalism. Long close-ups direct attention to significant details transformed but still recognisable over time; rusting gun mountings, riveted plating twisted in sharp relief against the sky, Anzac Cove and other place names stencilled onto surviving shoreline masonry pockmarked with bullet marks, howitzer, and shell damage. Once reorientated, he still knows where to look and point the camera.

Yet O'Grady's footage denotes moments of visual uncertainty too as invasive vegetation had already begun to transform the landscape. While some inland localities remain recognisable, others have now less discernible features. For instance, O'Grady depicts the Eski Lines as sharply defined dark diagonal shadows made by the gash through the earth of the stone-lined trenches. Elsewhere, his steady and well-composed shots give way to rapid panning movements that suggest a search for more elusive visual clues. Was this ridge, ravine, or watercourse the location of digging saps, a communication or support trench, or where a soldier had been killed or injured? Where had the enemy fire come from? The roving shots seem to imply a continuing quest for explanations. Medium-length shots, as at Vineyard Trench, very slowly trace the route of a shallow overgrown depression and the irregularities of disturbed soil. It is as if the occasional inserted, place name intertitle confers a visual authority that the physical remains of the once battle-scarred landscape now only yields grudgingly.

Camera work and identified locations hint at other subjectivities too: short stabbing pans take us through the dunes at such named points as De Totts Battery and Monto Bay. Was this a retracing of his own or a comrade's route ashore or chaotic line of retreat? Given the scattered nature of the soldiers across the terrain and without detailed knowledge of O'Grady's personal manoeuvres ashore, any attempt to attribute meaning to his long, identified sweep of Sulva Bay—the site of another chaotic landing and subsequent battles that left hundreds dead from Lancashire, Manchester, and West Yorkshire—or his lingering images of the low depression of the Salt Lake is mere speculation. The camera moves across the shell-cratered summit of Achi Baba and then across shallow standing water, rocks, and scrubby banks at Krithia Nullah where the filmmaker was injured. Military records and written historical accounts add other names that are absent from O'Grady's visual memories and detail their significance. Fir Tree Spur, for instance, is now part of Gallipoli's known landscape narrative but is just one among several focused shots of trees in the film that suggest a military rather than aesthetic association. Such details provide landscape features that contrast with the dominant dry and dusty views. They survived O'Grady's careful editing process so their inclusion seems intentional.

This footage also testifies to better known aspects of the human toil exacted upon the Lancashire regiments. O'Grady records the location of West Beach landing and the long track winding up from the long, open cove. Here, interlocking fields of fire had once rained down from Turkish redoubts on combatants who managed to cross the mines, wire, and trenches of the shoreline. From his vantage point, O'Grady now captures different forms of cultural negotiation that juxtapose with the beach's earlier contested meanings. Slow moving, horse-drawn carriages, donkeys, and groups of lightly dressed visitors brought ashore by small launches with Turkish ensigns indicate the nascent enterprise of overseas battlefield tourism in action. It is also one of the few sequences with people: most frames exclude all evidence of the other tour members. Generally, O'Grady's landscapes of Gallipoli may be full of memories but now empty of people. Even the occasional passing donkey with smoking rider is waved on and the camera's focus is elsewhere. Ethnographic details, usually a stock ingredient of amateur travel footage, play little part in this particular act of pilgrimage.

As suggested at the beginning of this chapter, there are practical difficulties involved in trying to portray landscape through moving image. Over time, film has also become a persuasive determinant of landscape meanings. Many readers, even if they have not visited Gallipoli National Park (Gelibou Yanmadasi), will be familiar with the cinematography of Peter Weir's *Gallipoli* (1981). His strong sense of place, response to the actual battleground, and evocation of vastness makes the Turkish landscape a driving force in the mood and narrative of this rather neglected antiwar film.[36] Unencumbered by such representational associations, for the most part, other more practical concerns affect O'Grady's landscape depiction. His own search for meaning through the ill-defined and overgrown battlefield manages to avoid the visual pitfalls of successive sweeping panoramic shots. His focus on details adds an aesthetic unattainable in wider views. Arguably, the camera's visual detective-work as O'Grady seeks to retrieve earlier knowledge of different locations results in more effective footage. Pointing the camera downward to film earth-works also helps to avoid the glare of unfamiliar sunlight on bare rock and other eroded surfaces.

Perhaps, the close focus helps O'Grady to personalise an alien and alienating environment too. A foreign war zone linked to catastrophic defeat fits uneasily into national symbolism and iconography. This territory is associated with national loss, yet outside the associative values of being colonial space. Where does a survivor fit in a setting so dominated by the missing? Perhaps most comfortably among the tributes erected by the living? Not surprisingly, O'Grady devotes over a third of his Gallipoli footage to the depiction of different war graves and cemeteries that were, and remain, key components of organised battlefield itineraries. Memorialisation, like cinematography, reconfigures spatial and psychological realities: commemorative spaces become "selected tourist stops" or "landscapes within landscapes" (Saunders, 45) that help to offer emotional and psychological orientation.

War memorials are part of the code of remembrance for the defeated dead. They bear witness to the lives or life sacrificed for a specific set of values. Their erection by official sponsorship symbolizes particular ideologies. In the words of Sturken, memorials "embody grief, loss and tribute. Whatever triumph a memorial may refer to, its depiction of victory is always tempered by a fore grounding of the lives lost" (165). Whether at home or in foreign territory, such structures and their well-cared-for precincts (that usually contrast greatly with their surroundings) acquire for many visitors, the characteristics of "national shrines" (Jäger, 120). Such assemblages and their associations often distant in time and place offer dignified, public acknowledgement of loss, a tangible focus for individual and collective commemoration and, according to Griswold, they also "instruct posterity about the past."[37]

O'Grady depicts visitors with heads bowed among the well-tended lawns and cypress-treed enclave of Lone Pine cemetery (commemorating loss of Australian and New Zealand troops) quite briefly and includes short shots of Chunuk Bair and a French cemetery. He concentrates on the Helles Memorial, a massive obelisk on the tip of the Helles Peninsula that is visible from considerable distance over land and water. Designed by Sir John Burnett and completed in 1924, its listing of over 21,000 names, texts, and overall form are representative of a specific period of commemorative Western public art. The largest number of names are from the Lancashire Fusiliers (1,357 commemorations) and the Manchester Regiment (1,215 commemorations). The Helles Memorial serves the dual function of commemorating the deaths of all service personnel from the British Empire and colonies. It is also serves as a memorial for those who have no known grave.

O'Grady's filmic intentions seem twofold: to pay personal tribute and to allow others at home to make their own cinematic pilgrimage to locations beyond their reach. His camera work is straightforward in its use of wide views and close-ups. He records the memorial's phallic form in conventional ways, positioning it centrally in the frame. He documents the not yet weathered masonry and traditional use of light stone that contrast with his other close-ups of dark cypress trees and contorted metal shapes. He includes the successive approaches to the central plinth as part of the visual journey and details the darkened evergreens and poppy heads of circular wreaths, seen earlier in a service held on deck before coming ashore. The privacy of setting individual wreaths in position is respected in his cut away shots. Visitors, filmed from behind, stand alone facing the inscriptions. The whole sequence respects anonymity, although it features more people in view than most of the onshore footage and has a static quality that contrasts with the mix of long and roving shots discussed earlier.

O'Grady's visual aesthetics, at this and other memorials (Chunuk Bair, Lone Pine, and Anzac), conform entirely with traditional commemorative codes and established conventions of representation. Indeed, they do not evoke any overt antiwar message, merely the human emptiness of a former battle zone, a message that surely resonates for his viewers back home. All the more striking therefore are two other details that hint at other subjectivities. First, during the memorial service on ship, O'Grady films in close-up a wreath and the wording of its attached card: "In respectful memory of our foes." Second, his final lingering image of Gallipoli is a close-up of an old and solitary Turkish headstone engraved in Arabic. It stands erect amidst the rubble-strewn surface of a barely recognisable burial ground. Among the anonymity of such contested territory, it confers identity and claims personal space.[38] It also evokes other facets of the peninsula's history: a landscape in which people had worked and lived as well as fought and died for centuries. The gravestone's surroundings contrast with the order of the commemorative sites. The calligraphy is also O'Grady's only inscription filmed in close-up. Despite being so close, the unfamiliar script, for both filmmaker and his subsequent audiences, seems to evoke the ultimate inexplicability of death. Implicitly, O'Grady also seems to acknowledge that making sense of past conflict involves remembering both sides.

O'Grady's images prompt questions about who and why were people watching amateur imagery of landscapes associated with past conflicts during the earlier 1930s? Militarism, jingoism, and imperial "dreams of military glory"[39] had long lost much of their allure, except perhaps among more conservative and right wing circles in the aftermath of the bloody slaughter of World War I, and given way to greater tolerance of pacifism and antiwar stances. Moreover, early British official propaganda films, for instance, the Topical Committee's *Battle of the Somme* (1916), had prompted contradictory commendation by people both opposed to and in support of the war effort.[40] There was also much enduring scepticism over the authenticity of wartime film footage.[41] Changes in official policy and public mood meant that filmgoers' appetite for wartime subject matter lessened as detailed memories of the conflict faded through the 1920s and other topics gained popular attention and commercial support. The dominance of conservative cultural consensus helped to maintain an appetite for Empire and rural nostalgia until Alexander Korda's *The Lion Has Wings* (1939) heralded another generation of war imagery on screen (Aldgate and Richards, 57; 68–69). So where, how, and why did O'Grady's landscapes of commemoration gain an appeal?

One possible reason for audience interest and prompt for O'Grady was the release of *Tell England* (*The Battle of Gallipoli*) by British Instructional Films in 1931. Directed by Anthony Asquith and George Barkas, the narrative followed the relationship of two friends who, like O'Grady, enlisted at the outbreak of war and were sent to Gallipoli. Made only three years after the death of his father, Hubert Herbert Asquith, whose successive cabinets had presided over the disastrous Gallipoli campaign, *Tell England* gained Asquith a reputation as Hitchcock's equal[42] and included an innovative soundtrack. In the absence of further evidence, it would be misleading to push the connection too far, but renewed public filmic interest in Gallipoli certainly did occur within a few years of O'Grady's own film.

Clearly, amateur footage rarely reached large audiences. Exceptions exist as exemplified by the making, screening, and extensive touring nationwide of films by Charles Chislett, a bank manager and amateur enthusiast from Rotherham, south Yorkshire, who from his own self-reflexive engagement with his hobby was professional in all but how he earned his living (Norris Nicholson, 1997a; 1997b; 2001a). For the most part, local advertising attracted local people for whom the subject matter, the filmmaker, or even the venue exerted some influence. The predominantly military content of O'Grady's surviving film footage suggests that his material was intended for audiences that had local regimental connections. Moreover, he inserted place names and hand-drawn maps to assist his viewers' understanding of the different named and unnamed locations at Gallipoli. Annotations on his outline maps include specific shoreline and hinterland positions associated with the Lancashire landings and subsequent attempts to move troops, equipment, and supplies inland. Their purpose seems obvious: to inform and clarify viewers' understanding of significant localities across the conflict zone. The instructive style recurs within much early amateur travel-related footage (Norris Nicholson, 2002b) and is a reminder that part of the pre-television appeal of watching home movies lay in its combination of palatable information and amusement. Contrived human interest was unnecessary for those who had compelling reasons to see places associated with deaths of people known or in some way related to them.

Moving imagery of Gallipoli's contested landscapes were, moreover, unusual as few pieces of newsreel or other sources can be convincingly dated to before the middle of 1915 and very little footage covers British armed forces during the first 18 months of the war.[43] Ellis Ashmead-Bartlett, a war correspondent sent initially by the Newspapers Proprietors' Association, made the only known footage of the actual Gallipoli campaign. He returned with a cine camera to begin filming with the help of Ernest Brooks, the Royal Navy still photographer, in July 1915, three months after hostilities began.[44] Archival sources suggest that after a showing in London, the original film disappeared although the Australian War Records Section obtained a copy in 1919. Thus, apart from those who might have seen *Tell England*, scenes of Gallipoli on film may only have reached Lancashire and Manchester audiences with O'Grady's pilgrimage material in 1934. No wonder another veteran, Major G. B. Horridge (who fought with the Fifth Battalion, Lancashire Fusiliers) returned with his own cine camera the following year. In the past century, visual information about tragedy has travelled with increasing but very unequal speeds in different contexts. O'Grady's 1930s audiences are a reminder of how historically, when conflict and death occurred beyond the local level, visualisation has not been typically part of the closure after bereavement.

*Gallipoli Revisited* was not just about landscapes of commemoration. Although Gallipoli was the ultimate destination, O'Grady's pilgrimage also involved a cruise through the Mediterranean. His filmic record of the ship's route via Gibraltar, Pompeii, Istanbul, and Athens shares many similarities with other cruise-related footage made by amateur enthusiasts in the same period. Admittedly, many of the shipboard scenes differ quite significantly from those in more typical forms of cruise footage. Here, the crew and passengers have an affinity created through aspects of shared and more profound experience that extend beyond the social bonds that derive from being on board together for a three-week cruise. Many scenes hint at bonds of wartime camaraderie and friendship that withstand the passage of time. As former comrades socialize or assemble for group poses, spontaneous individual tributes occur deliberately to the camera as gestures and expressions and in the raising of an occasional real or imaginary tankard. The informal dress codes, swapping of hats, queuing for rum rations, laughing faces, and general physicality contrast with the solemnity and restraint of other shipboard scenes, including the memorial service and display of wreaths as well as the footage ashore.

In between such scenes, however, are sequences reminiscent of other Mediterranean holidays, recorded on amateur film. O'Grady includes a long, detailed, cinematic exploration of ruins at Pompeii; a lengthy climb up through the current excavations and various remains on the Acropolis during a visit to Athens on the way home; and scenes of passing through the Straits of Gibraltar. Such sequences include much more conventional holiday cinematography, as shown by his detailed focus on Greek passersby in decorative local costumes—women in full skirts, embroidered bodices, veiled heads and men in long wrap overgowns and flat skullcaps. Such attention to detail, seemingly halted only when one woman shields her face with her hands, typifies the holidaymaker's cinematic gaze and photographic consumption of visual difference and distinctiveness. The frequency of such imagery in holiday footage is a reminder of how power relations shaped by gender, race, and status determine the authoritative gaze by outsiders (Norris Nicholson, 2003a).

## conclusion

Arguably, amateur productions help us toward a more precise understanding of how filmic landscape meanings may be determined and circulated in particular social arenas. Cine photography and film showings clearly flourished in Britain during the middle decades of the twentieth century and extended beyond their predominantly upper and middle class appeal as the relative cost of cine equipment decreased after the Second World War. The hobby's popularity began to decline during the mid- to late 1970s as a result of wide-ranging changes in home-based recreation and other leisure pursuits, television ownership, family life, and, of course, innovations in early home videorecording. Although cinema attendance fell as television watching increased, audiences were already familiar with sophisticated means of portraying landscape imagery through zoom, filter, and controlled camera movement. Within this context, the survival of interest in making and watching home movies remains an intriguing component within the history of moving images and enables us to question the significance of amateur landscape imagery.

Throughout the last century, the portrayal of different landscapes in the commercial cinema increasingly contributed to the valorising and exoticising of specific landscapes at the cost of others. Home movies, by contrast, often provided cinematic testimony of landscapes other than those with spectacular scenery in localities deemed accessible to major film production centres. For hobbyists and their viewers, amateur footage offered ways of seeing and being seen on big screens. Such visual encounters were also ways of remembering and giving meaning to particular places. Many such filmed localities were often familiar to both filmmakers and their audiences as places to visit locally or on excursions or even perhaps on holiday. Cine photography's close association with tourism and recreational travel, discussed elsewhere and strongly resembling the relationship between tourism and still photography, inevitably seems to have reinforced notions of place and the visual identity of specific visitor destinations.

Just as much footage from overseas holidays tended to replicate views and vantage points, local beauty spots and favoured landscape settings also gained new emphasis through being shown on the amateur screen. As with any mimetic process, the framed view for future recollection endowed places with meaning. In the decades prior to and at the start of regionally broadcast television in Britain, amateur material offered important visual alternatives to many localities shown in mainstream cinema. Sequences set in local places contrasted with those overseas landscape settings associated with American productions and the still popular, although increasingly controversial, films of Empire. Yet, perhaps, judging by the documentary character of much amateur material, British documentaries and some commercial material also attracted some hobbyists to specific topics and localities. Ongoing research has yet to assess how far similarities in choice of themes and landscapes might be more than mere coincidence among professional filmmakers and their amateur counterparts. Certainly, many resemblances in how and where urban lives and industrial landscapes were portrayed on amateur and professional film do occur as shown by footage made in Salford, Sheffield, west Yorkshire, and elsewhere over a 30-year period (Norris Nicholson, 1997a; 1997b; 2001a; 2001b; 2004c).

As mentioned earlier, amateur filmmakers did not work in a visual vacuum. From as early as the mid-1920s, contemporary literature and advertising, particularly from the United States, point to various ways in which home enthusiasts were prompted to emulate professional cinematography (Zimmerman, 1995). Gradually, specialist publications by British authors offered tips on how to film particular types of landscape. Their guidance often became as formulaic as in other aspects of the extensive output on practical advice. Articles in *Amateur Cine World* and other contemporary magazines illustrate how seaside, mountains, foreign cities as well as their inhabitants, and other overseas cruise or travel destinations prompted suggestions on how and how not to frame particular views (Norris Nicholson, 2004b). Some amateurs, nonetheless, remained imaginative in how and what they filmed at home and elsewhere. They chose to ignore or were unaware of the increasingly available hobby literature. Such practitioners were often independent of the cine clubs and networks that had developed to support amateur activity. Their choice and handling of landscape footage is more subjective even if at times less technically sophisticated. Sometimes, competence and a compelling level of personal engagement combine to produce, despite the experts' warnings, memorable landscapes. O'Grady's footage of Gallipoli is one such example.

Landscape setting in amateur film footage, no less than its professionally made equivalent, holds diverse meanings. Their production and subsequent consumption by family, friends, and wider audiences constitutes an important source of visual imagery, in particular sociocultural milieus for approximately four decades. In many ways, much amateur moving imagery maintained preeminently pictorial representational styles that are traceable to nineteenth-century photographic traditions. Early on, their framing of subject matter in urban and rural localities not infrequently evokes both conservative artistic convention and popular nostalgia. Mid-century scenes of barefoot children in urban settings that span from Leeds to Ibiza denote the outsider's capacity to aestheticise poverty. Diverse photo opportunities, such as gutting fish on a quayside in the Hebrides, a bread seller in the medina at Tangiers, or street traders in different parts of southern Europe, record more than local people involved in daily activities that may now have disappeared (Norris Nicholson, 2002a; 2003a). Unwittingly, the contextual details of setting reveal landscape details and character that may also have been erased by technological, sociocultural, economic, or even environmental change. Despite the mobile gaze, cine landscapes remain extended snapshots captured at a particular moment in time. As with other forms of visualisation, these landscape portraits were also framed by prevailing ways of seeing.

Finally, it is appropriate to return to the amateur film movement's position within Britain's domestic leisure trends in the postwar period. Interest in watching home movies continued alongside the flourishing of other local amenity interest groups. Evidence of evening programs at amateur cine clubs and other venues, together with instances of collaboration between film enthusiasts and members of other local societies, attest to the prevailing level of locally organised social evening and weekend hobby-oriented activity. Group produced films on local environmental issues and campaigns also indicate that elements of social engagement associated with some early amateur filmmaking found new foci in the changing conditions of postwar Britain and the wider world. Significantly, as rural and urban areas were experiencing redevelopment, modernization, and technological transformation at home and abroad, cine film enthusiasts continued to write about, film, and find audiences for their own cinematic landscapes at home and abroad.

Did the sharing of valued and remembered views reinforce their significance and even at times the desire for their survival? Did these moving sites of meaning offer symbolic as well as real landmarks and pointers in a fast changing socio-political and increasingly visible diverse world? Could the filmic claiming of other places offer reassurance even as Britain's imperial identity and territorial grasp on the world was weakening? As visual *aide-memoire*, did they help both their makers and their audiences to negotiate memories and also the unequal patterns of change at local and more distant levels? Such speculative closing remarks signal the potential scope for further analysis of amateur materials on and beyond themes of landscape value and visualisation. This chapter's focus on how nonprofessional footage both celebrates and commemorates facets of landscape encounter is one more step toward placing home movies within a more inclusive sociocultural history of film interpretation.

## notes

1. I wish to thank the British Academy and Krazsna-Krausz Foundation for supporting this research. Special thanks are also due to the staffs at the North West Film Archives, Manchester Metropolitan University and the British Film Institute, London. Comments on a earlier draft of this manuscript have also been much appreciated.
2. A. L. Gale and K. Pessels, *Make Your Own Movies for Fun and Profit* (New York: Coward-McCann, 1939), 26; hereafter cited in text.
3. D. Hill, "Pages from Two Diaries. A Six Week Series on Making Holiday Film," *Amateur Cine World* (1956): 819; hereafter cited in text.
4. See also R. Odin, *Le film de famille: usage privé, usage public* (Paris: Méridiens Klincksieck, 1995); *Le cinéma en amateur* (Paris: Seuil, 1999); and P. Zimmerman, *Reel Families* (Bloomington: Indiana University Press, 1995); hereafter cited in text.
5. J. Foster, "Capturing and Losing the 'Lie of the Land': Railway Photography and Colonial Nationalism in Early Twentieth Century South Africa," in *Picturing Place. Photography and the Geographical Imagination*, eds. J. M. Schwartz and J. R. Ryan (London: I. B. Tauris, 2003), 150.
6. Rachel Low, *Film Making in 1930s Britain* (London: George Allen and Unwin, 1985).
7. H. Norris Nicholson, "In Amateur Hands: Framing Time and Space in Home Movies," *History Workshop Journal* 43 (1997a): 198–212, hereafter cited in text; "Moving Memories: Image and Identity in Home Movies," in *The Jubilee Book. Essays on Amateur Film*, ed. N. Kapstein (Charleroi: Association Européene des Inédits, 1997b), 35–44, hereafter cited in text; "Seeing How It Was?: Childhood Geographies and Memories in Home Movies," *Area* 33, no. 2 (2001a): 128–140, hereafter cited in text; "Two Tales of a City: Salford in Regional Filmmaking, 1957–1973," *Manchester Regional History Review* 15 (2001b): 41–53, hereafter cited in text; "Picturing the past: Archival film and historical landscape change," *Landscapes* 3, no. 1 (2002a): 81–100, hereafter cited in text; "Telling Travellers' Tales: The World through Home Movies, 1935–1967," in *Engaging Film: Travel, Mobility and Identity*, eds. T. Cresswell and D. Dixon (Lanham, MD: Rowman & Littlefield, 2002b), 47–66, hereafter cited in text; "British Home Movies of the Mediterranean, c. 1925–1936," *Film History* 15, no. 2 (2003a): 152–165, hereafter cited in text; Nicholson, ed., *Screening Culture: Constructing Image and Identity* (Lanham, MD: Lexington Books, 2003b); "Journey through the Balkans: Early Amateur Filmmaking and Travel Writing in the 1930s," *Tourism and Histories*, ed. J. Walton (U.K.: Conference proceedings, University of Central Lancashire, June 19–21, 2003) forthcoming in *Tourism Studies* (2006/7) Special issue edited by J. Walton and E. Mazierska, hereafter cited in text; "At Home and Abroad with Cine Enthusiasts: Regional Amateur Filmmaking and Visualizing the Mediterranean, c.1928–1962," *GeoJournal* Volume 59, no. 4, pp. 323–333, December 2004, hereafter cited in text; "'As if by Magic': Authority, Aesthetics and Visions of the Work Place in Home Movies," in *Mining the Home Movie: Excavations into Historical and Cultural Memories*, eds. K. Ishizuka

and P. Zimmerman (Los Angeles: University of California Press, 2004c), hereafter cited in text; "Shooting in Paradise: Conflict, Compassion and Amateur Film Making and the Mediterranean, 1923–1939," *Journal of Intercultural Studies* 26, no. 5 (2006, forthcoming).

8. J. R. Ryan, *Picturing Empire. Photography and the Visualization of the British Empire* (Chicago: University of Chicago Press, 1997); J. M. Schwartz and J. R. Ryan, "Photography and the Geographical Imagination," in *Picturing Place. Photography and the Geographical Imagination, op. cit.*, 1–18, hereafter cited in text; see also Norris Nicholson (2003a; 2003b).

9. See for instance the seminal discussions by W. Schivelbusch, *The Railway Journey: The Industrialization of Time and Space in the 19th Century* (New York: Berg, 1986); and N. J. Thrift, "Inhuman Geographies: Landscapes of Speed, Light and Power," in *Writing the Rural: Five Cultural; Geographies*, eds. P. Cloke, M. Doel, D. Matless, M. Phillips, and N. Thrift (London: Paul Chapman Publishing, 1994), 191–248; and "On the Determination of Social Action in Space and Time," *Environment and Planning D: Society and Space* 1, no. 1 (1983): 23–57. See as well recent studies by J. Foster, *op. cit.*, 141–161; and B. Osborne, "Constructing the State. Managing the Corporation, Transforming the Individual: Photography, Immigration and Canadian National Railways, 1925–30," in *Picturing Place. Photography and the Geographical Imagination, op. cit.*, 162–191.

10. J. P. Lawrie, *The Home Cinema* (London: Chapman and Hall, 1933); G. H. Sewell, *Amateur Film Making* (London and Glasgow: Blackie, 1938); A. Strasser, *Amateur Films. Planning, Directing, Cutting*, trans. P.C. Smethurst (London: Link House Publications, 1936).

11. J. Urry, *Consuming Places* (London: Routledge, 1995); *The Tourist Gaze*, 2nd ed. (London: Sage, 2002).

12. E. Edwards, "Photographs as Objects of Memory," in *Material Memories. Design and Evocation*, eds. M. Kwint, C. Breward, and J. Aynsley (Oxford: Berg, 1999), 221–236.

13. P. Conrad, *Modern Times, Modern Places. Life and Art in the 20th Century* (London: Thames and Hudson, 1999), 73.

14. D. Chambers, "Family as Place: Family Photograph Albums and the Domestication of Public and Private Space," in *Picturing Place. Photography and the Geographical Imagination, op. cit.*

15. R. Chalfren, *Snapshot Versions of Life* (Bowling Green, OH: Bowling Green State University Popular Press, 1987); M. Citrone, *Home Movies and Other Necessary Fictions* (Minneapolis: University of Minnesota Press, 1999); A. Schneider, "Home Movie Making and Swiss Expatriate Identities in the 1920s and 1930s," *Film History* 15, no. 2 (2003): 166–176.

16. P. Bourdieu, *Photography: A Middle Brow Art*, trans. S. Whiteside (Stanford, CA: Stanford University Press, 1990).

17. A. Yilmaz, "Architectural Memorialisation of the Past: The French, British, Anzac and Turkish Dead in Gallipoli," Unpublished paper presented at *CongressCATH 2004, Architecture of Philosophy, Philosophy of Architecture* (Bradford: University of Leeds/ National Museum of Photography, Film, Television and Video, July 8–11, 2003), available at http://www.leeds.ac.uk/cath/congress/2004/programme/paper_index.shtml (accessed August 11, 2005); hereafter cited in text.

18. M. Crang and P. S. Travlou, "The City and Topologies of Memory," *Environment and Planning D: Society and Space* 19 (2001): 161.

19. J. Jäger, "Picturing Nations: Landscape Photography and National Identity in Britain and Germany in the Mid-19th Century," *Picturing Place. Photography and the Geographical Imagination, op. cit.*, 117; hereafter cited in text.

20. M. Heffernan, "Forever England: The Western Front and the Politics of Remembrance," *Britain, Ecumene* 2 (1995): 293–324; M. Sturken, "The Wall, the Screen and the Image," in The Visual Culture Reader, ed. N. Mirzoeff (Routledge, London, 1998), 163–178; hereafter cited in text.

21. See J. P. Sharp, "Writing Travel/travelling writing: Roland Barthes detours the Orient," *Environment and Planning D: Society and Space* 20 (2002): 155–166.

22. J. Pemble, *The Mediterranean Passion: Victorians and Edwardians in the South* (Oxford: Oxford University Press, 1987); G. Pratt, *Imperial Eyes. Travel Writing and Transculturation* (London, New York: Routledge, 1992); J. Duncan and D. Gregory, "Writes of Passage: Reading Travel Writing," in *Writes of Passage*, eds. J. Duncan and D. Gregory (London, New York: Routledge, 1999), 1–13; H. Carr, "Modernism and Travel (1880–1940)," in *The Cambridge Companion to Travel Writing*, eds. P. Hulme and T. Young (Cambridge: Cambridge University Press, 2002), 70–86.

23. J. Urry, *Consuming Places, op. cit.; The Tourist Gaze, op. cit.*; D. MacCannell, *The Tourist* (New York: Schocken, 1999); J. Walton, *The British Seaside* (Manchester: Manchester University Press, 2000).

24. J. Buzard, *The Beaten Track. European Tourism, Literature and the Ways to Culture, 1800–1918* (Oxford: Clarendon Press, 1993); C. Chard, *Pleasure and Guilt on the Grand Tour. Travel Writing and Imaginative Geographies, 1600–1830* (Manchester: Manchester University Press, 1999); J. Pemble, *The Mediterranean Passion: Victorians and Edwardians in the South, op. cit.*; R. Aldrich, *The Seduction of the Mediterranean: Writing, Art and Homosexual Fantasy* (London: Routledge, 1993); M. Crang and P. S. Travlou, "The City and Topologies of Memory," *op. cit.*; H. Carr, "Modernism and Travel (1880-1940)," *op. cit.*

25. T. Pollard, "The Value of Enmity: Remaking and Revisiting Historic Battlefields in the United States and Britain," *Landscapes* 4, no. 2 (2003): 25–34; hereafter cited in text.

26. D. W. Lloyd, *Battlefield Tourism: Pilgrimage and the Commemoration of the Great War in Britain, Australia and Canada, 1919–1939* (Oxford: Berg, 1998), 23.

27. A. D. Harvey, *A Muse of Fire. Literature, Art and War* (London, Rio Grande: The Hambledon Press, 1998).

28. N. J. Saunders, "Matter and Meaning in the Landscapes of Conflict: The Western Front, 1914–1999," in *Contested Landscapes. Movement, Exile and Place*, eds. B. Bender and M. Winer (Oxford: Berg, 2001), 40; hereafter cited in text.

29. W. Grainge, *The Battles and Battlefields of Yorkshire* (Ripon, UK: Harrison, nd, c.1880s).

30. *Lancashire Fusiliers Annual, 1914/1915: The (First) Seventh Battalion*, Lancashire Fusiliers Annual, 202–203.

31. Ibid., 203–225; L. A. Carlyon, *Gallipoli* (London, Sydney: Bantam Books, 2003).

32. Quoted in V. Williams, *Who's Looking at the Family?* (London: Barbican Art Gallery, 1994), 41.

33. D. Wood, "Identity and Violence," in *Cultural Readings of Imperialism. Edward Said and the Gravity of History*, eds. Ansell K. Pearson, B. Parry, and J. Squires (London: Lawrence and Wishart, 1997), 198.

34. L. Staeheli, "Publicity, Privacy and Women's Political Action," *Environment and Planning D: Society and Space* 14 (1996): 601–619; D. Mitchell, *Cultural Geography* (Oxford: Blackwell, 2000), 211.

35. J. Masefield, *Gallipoli, 1916,* quoted in *A Muse of Fire. Literature, Art and War,* ed. A.D. Harvey (London and Rio Grande: The Hambledon Press, 1998), 78.

36. P. Weir, *Gallipoli* (1981, Australia), DVD (Paramount Pictures, 2001).

37. C. Griswold, "The Vietnam Veterans Memorial and the Washington Mall," in *Critical Inquiry* 12, no. 14 (Summer 1986): 689.

38. D. Storey, *Territory: The Claiming of Space* (Edinburgh: Pearson Educational, 2001).

39. A. Aldgate and J. Richards, *Best of British. Cinema and Society from 1930 to the Present* (London, New York: I.B. Tauris, 1999), 19; hereafter cited in text.

40. N. Reeves, "The Power of Film Propaganda—Myth or Reality," *Historical Journal of Film, Radio and Television* 13, no. 2 (2003): 181–201.

41. N. Hiley, "Hilton DeWitt Girdwood and the Origins of British Official Filming," *Historical Journal of Film, Radio and Television* 13, no. 2 (1993): 129–148.

42. E. Katz, The Macmillan International Film Encyclopedia, 4th ed. (London: Macmillan, 2001), 57.

43. S. Badsey, "The IMW Series. A Guide to the Imperial War Museum Collection of Archive Material of the First World War," *Historical Journal of Film, Radio and Television* 13, no. 2 (1993): 203.

44. G. Imashev, "Gallipoli on Film, Wartime 2002," cited in *Heroes of Gallipoli.* IWM Collections Online. 2002. Available at http://www.iwmcollections. org.uk (accessed October 10, 2003).

eight

# the presence (and absence) of landscape in silent east asian films

peter rist

To note that the tradition of landscape painting in China is "ancient" is a huge understatement. Although not as old as figure painting and although only copies, and no originals, survive from the period, landscape painting became highly developed at the end of the seventh century and the beginning of the eighth, during the T'ang dynasty, especially in the "green and blue" work of Li Ssu-hsü and his son, Li Chao-tao.[1] Paintings by masters of both Southern and Northern schools have survived from the eleventh century, including Kuo Hsi's (Guo Xi) *Early Spring* (1072), the complexity of which is found in the "curving lines of mountains, trees, and rocks" as well as the atmospheric "naturalism" and "life" created by "using blank areas of silk to suggest the penetrating clouds and mists."[2] Other surviving masterpieces of the Northern Sung dynasty period housed at Taiwan's National Palace Museum include Kuan T'ung's *Awaiting a Crossing* (c. 900), Fan K'uan's *Travelling Among Mountains and Streams* (c. 1000), and *Soughing Wind Among Mountain Pines* painted by a follower of Kuo Hsi's, Li T'ang in 1124. All are dominated by the verticality of a craggy mountain peak, coursed by streams, dissected by mist and clouds, and dotted with trees; and, if human or other figures are present, they are rendered minuscule in the vast natural environment.[3] All these works are hanging scrolls, a format which encourages a vertical scanning of the image, from land and water to sky, or vice versa. There is no single focal point or eye level in these paintings and the remoteness and eternality of the "master mountains," coupled with "an overpowering sense of scale when they are related to human beings" can be considered as being "Taoist."[4]

The tendency toward a "narrative," time-based viewing of landscape found its ideal expression in the horizontal scroll, which would be gradually unravelled and "read" from right to left to reveal a theme or progression of some kind, and which was also developed in the late tenth and eleventh centuries.[5] Northern Sung dynasty landscape paintings then travelled to Korea and Japan where they influenced the art of these countries, profoundly. Michael Dunn argues that, in particular, it was the meditative aspect of Ch'an Buddhist philosophy—which became "Zen" Buddhism in Japan—behind the work that drove the influence in both countries.[6] It is important to note that the technical mastery involved in "copying" great works of Chinese art has always been revered in East Asia. As Laurence Sickman notes, "Over and over we read that a certain artist studied one or more old masters, based his style on theirs and then, as he reached maturity, developed a style quite his own" (Sickman and Soper, 227).[7] In China, Japan, and Korea, the ability to copy from memory was a tradition of long standing, and in the first Korean film to win a prize at the Cannes International Film Festival, Im Kwon Taek's *Chiwaeson* (2002), based on the life of a nineteenth-century Korean painter, Jang Seung-ub, the artist is shown to make the transition from brilliant copyist of Chinese landscapes to rebellious, highly original stylist.

The Southern Sung dynasty court style in the thirteenth century developed the use of ink on paper, rather than silk, and moved away from monumentality and harsh "realism" toward a simplified, more "poetic" approach, where empty space and depth became prominent features (Hesemann, 156). A good example of these tendencies is found in Ma Yüan's (fl. 1190–1225) *On a Mountain Path in Spring*, where the mountain itself is barely sketched, and where the left bottom corner of the frame is filled with detail and one of the two male figures (larger than normal), standing in the foreground, gazes up and right past delicate hanging willow branches to a distant bird, alone in the top right quadrant, except for lines of verse: "wild blossoms dance when brushed by his sleeves, the secluded birds cut short their song to avoid him."[8] This painting exemplifies the bringing together of the different art forms of the "Three Perfections"—poetry, calligraphy, and painting—in Southern Sung court art.[9]

Whereas most of the original landscape masterpieces have been lost, and whereas, with collectors putting their seals and inscriptions on works, sometimes obscuring the artist's own seal, it is difficult to correctly attribute the paintings that have survived, some important written texts of history, theory, and criticism have been passed down to us.[10] The oldest surviving written reference to painting, by Confucius, dates from the sixth century B.C.E., and some *Notes for a Landscape* were written by Ku K'ai-chih in the fourth century ce, while, arguably the most significant critical text, *The Six Techniques of Painting*, was written in the fifth century C.E. by Hsieh Ho.[11] The first two of these are judged to be the most important, "creating a life-like tone and atmosphere (ch'i-yün sheng-tung)" and "building structure through brush-work." Dr. Lin Yutang devotes a long discussion to the problems of translating Chinese characters and writes of Hsieh Ho's first technique: "As the Chinese use it *ch'i-yün* is a bisyllabic word, a noun meaning *tone and atmosphere*; *sheng-tung* is another bisyllabic word, an adjective, meaning *fully alive, moving, lifelike*. The whole phrase means a 'vital tone and atmosphere.' It suggests a successful creation of tone and atmosphere that is moving and alive, and by all Chinese criteria this tone and atmosphere, rather than verisimilitude, is the goal of a painting" (Lin, 36). According to Lin's translation, the other "techniques of painting" are "third, depicting the forms of things as they are; fourth, appropriate colouring; fifth, composition; and sixth, transcribing and copying" (Lin, 34). Alexander Soper takes a slightly different approach, translating the first "condition" of "(good) painting" as "animation through spirit consonance," where "first importance" is "given to some quality that is never obtainable by technique alone," and thus separating artistry from craftsmanship (Sickman and Soper, 133). According to Sickman (aided by Soper's translation), the "remaining five Principles are all concerned with the making of a picture and involve technical procedures."[12] Clearly, the seeds of a kind of "realism" in the first, third, fourth, and fifth principles, a creative "impressionism" in the first, second, and fifth principles, and, even, a "modernist" regard for the medium itself—the properties of brush and ink—are evident in the second principle. Along these lines, one could understand that the Northern Sung dynasty featured a period of "realist" landscape painting, followed by an "impressionist" tendency in the Southern Sung dynasty, while a "modernist" concern with the play of brush and ink on the silk surface together with the texture of this medium and its scroll format pervaded all.

While a growing interest in the history and aesthetics of East Asian art is continuing to develop in the West, it is apparent that not nearly enough recognition has yet been accorded the brilliance of Chinese, Korean, and Japanese landscape painting. For example, although H. W. Janson (with Dora Jane Janson) recognizes that they have omitted the "major area" of Chinese and Japanese art, in a standard text in North American university art history curricula, *History of Art*, their rationale for doing so is that these "indigenous artistic traditions are no longer alive today, and because these styles did not, generally speaking, have a significant influence on the West"; questionable claims, both.[13] They admit that "even if they [the arts of Indian Asia, Pre-Colombian America, as well as China and Japan] are not essential for our account, they are nevertheless important in their own right," but their recognition that Chinese landscape paintings influenced Islamic art (for which they find room in their book) and their question, "Did such landscapes reach medieval Europe?" are ominous signs that, indeed, the teaching of these art traditions should be regular, perhaps mandatory (Janson, 244, 722).[14] I suspect that giving full recognition to Chinese/Japanese/Korean art theory and practice before the Renaissance could throw the entire discipline of European/North American art history out of kilter, and could even create a crisis for the art market. In any event, the art of landscape painting did not fully emerge in Europe until the seventeenth century with the work of Peter Paul Rubens and other Dutch artists, Nicolas Poussin and Claude Lorrain in France, and Annibale Carracci in Italy, having first appeared in the backgrounds of some German and Netherlandish religious paintings of the fifteenth century. By this time, landscape painting was not only well established as a complex and vital art form throughout East Asia, but had gone through numerous transformations.

In looking at East Asian landscape paintings with Western eyes it is easy to notice the differences from European and North American works. Thus we notice multiple perspectives and vantage points (and the absence of a single vanishing point), flatness rather than depth, the smallness of figures and objects, and vast areas of space containing emptiness. As valid as these perceptions of difference might be, it seems to me that the tendencies for East Asian artists to be "exotically" different from Western norms (and hence "oriental") and to depart from reality are emphasized too much. Clearly the Chinese, Japanese, and Korean people alike have a tremendous affinity with nature, which has always been reflected in their art. Of Chinese landscape art, William Watson wrote in "Realism as Landscape" that "[h]owever philosophized the meaning of landscape painting became, its style never parted company completely with reality."[15] Arthur de Carle Sowerby went even further, in his book on nature in Chinese art, where he illustrates his chapter entitled "Rocks, Mountain, and Water" (from the "Chinese name for a landscape, *shan shui*, literally 'Mountains and Water'") with contemporaneous black and white photographs of Hua Shan (in southeastern Shenshi) and the Huang Shan or Yellow Mountains (in southern Ahnwei), in comparison with monochrome reproductions of classic landscape paintings, in order to demonstrate how "realist" these paintings of tree-speckled, craggy, mist-laden peaks were.[16] With this penchant for the natural world together with the temporal dimension enabled by the art of scroll painting, one would think that the invention of cinema would be embraced in East Asia, especially for its ability to reveal the landscape, alive with movement.

During the silent film era, which lasted until 1936 in China and Japan, and even later in Korea, there was very little aesthetic use made of the landscape and even less in the way of allusion to landscape painting. Of course, with such a disastrous survival rate for East Asian silent films, it is impossible to make such a claim with any real certainty. Only 70 Japanese films or fragments of films made before 1930 have survived, less than 1 percent of the total estimated production for this early period: complete statistics are not available, but for the four years 1924, 1927–1929 alone, 3,171 Japanese feature films were made! The number of surviving Chinese films made before 1930 is smaller, but as a percentage of the total Chinese production (less than 600) it is much higher. Only one Korean silent film has survived and this was made in the 1950s! Most of the extant Chinese features of the 1920s are popular martial arts/adventure films, often crudely made with sets built to show off the jumping skills of the acrobatic performers. They are notable for the centrality of *xia nü*, female swordfighting heroines, who saw more action than their male counterparts. But, when exterior locations were used on these films, they served only as stages for the action and, sometimes, sky-dominated backgrounds for special effects. In the first part of the serial, *Swordswoman of Huangjian* (1929), a "wonderful bird" which kidnaps a boy is animated over the mountains and sky, and the star of *Red Heroine* (1930) is enabled to fly across the sky through wire-work and superimposition. The swordplay genre was more developed in the Japanese than the Chinese cinema, and was similarly dominant on domestic screens. Much more grounded in realism, the *chambara* (or *ken-geki*) swordplay films often made good use of exteriors, allowing for dynamic, free-flowing action followed by a moving camera. With few restrictions—natural rather than studio lighting, no cumbersome sound recording equipment—the camera operators were free to move around at will and often the hand-held camera became a component in the action-drama.[17]

Teinosuke Kinugasa, best known as the director of the experimental feature film *Kurutta Ippeiji* (*A Page of Madness*, aka *Crazy Page*, 1926), also headed up an independent studio, Kinugasa Eiga Renmei, for which he produced a number of sophisticated *jidai geki* (period) films, very few of which have survived.[18] A condensed 20-minute version of *Tempei Jidai-Kaito Samimaro* (*The Time of the Tempei Shamimaro*, 1928) survives on a French inter-titled, sound compilation, *Nippon*, enough to show remarkably directed action sequences by Eichi Koishi, complete with apparent zooms and stylized black-background interiors, similar to those of Kinugasa-directed films. *Fuun Joshi* (*Castle of Wind and Clouds*), directed by Toko Yamasaki, begins and ends with an almost identical series of landscape shots: a young samurai (Chojiro Hayashi) arrives on his horse at the castle in the beginning, and goes wandering at the end, now a *ronin*. Throughout the film there are striking compositions of interiors and exteriors alike, including low-angle shots of a building which appears at the very bottom of the frame, the rest dominated by trees and sky. Many Japanese films from earlier years, which were set in the countryside, deliberately included location shots for effects: the climactic scene of *Hototogisu* (*The Cuckoo*, 1922), a *Shinpa* film directed by Yoshinobu Ikeda for Shochiku, was set on a beach, where crashing waves echo the tumultuous fate of Namiko, dying of tuberculosis, who meets her estranged husband for the last time.[19] The Western-influenced *Kohitsuji* (*The Lamb*, 1923, Shochiku)—it begins and ends with biblical quotations—continually returns to a sheep pasture where a farmer's daughter had rescued a wandering student. Kenji Mizoguchi's oldest surviving film, *Furusato No Uta* (*The Song of Home*, 1925, Nikkatsu) is an "educational" film which champions farming over city life. But, none of these films contain the kind of landscape shots in *Fuun Joshi*, which seem to be placed there just to be contemplated for their own intrinsic sake and understood in poetic or pictorial contexts rather than narrative ones. It is suggested that Kinugasa, although he was always known himself to be somewhat "westernized" in style, could well have been the first Japanese filmmaker to consciously transpose the Japanese tradition of landscape painting to film.

Only one extant Chinese film from the 1920s is comparable in its "classicism," *Xixiang Ji* (*Romance of the West Chamber*, 1927), directed and written by Hou Yao for the Minxin (China Sun) Motion Picture Company, of which some 50 minutes (about half) has survived. Perhaps it was too difficult for the Shanghai-based film companies to travel to regions of China which sported spectacular mountain landscapes, but a great deal of effort was expended on making *Xixiang Ji* worthy of its literary source. At the film's opening, a student's journey to the capital to sit his exams is accompanied by images of beautiful settings. We see goldfish swimming in a pond while girls feed them, followed by a wide shot of a pagoda by a lake, and then by shots of a temple with a spectacular entrance. But, it is not until the founding of the Lianhua (United Photoplay) Company by theatre owner Luo Mingyou and Li Minwei, the manager of Minxin, in March 1930 that truly elegant filmmaking became the norm in Shanghai. Sun Yu became one of the principal directors at Lianhua. His films were characterized by cheerful young protagonists, male and female, who work together to make good lives for themselves and struggle against the forces of nature and feudal society. Often a bucolic rural life is contrasted with the corrupt, mechanized, fast-paced world of the city, and a strong influence of late 1920s Hollywood can be felt, especially through F. W. Murnau's *Sunrise* and Frank Borzage's melodramas, all made by Fox and starring Janet Gaynor. Sun Yu borrowed Murnau's tracking camera and gave it "Chinese characteristics." Often his films open in the countryside, on or near a river. In *Tianming* (*Daybreak*, 1933), a strong distinction is drawn between the naive and relatively happy times the heroine (Li Lili as Ling Ling) had experienced in the country, with tracking shots along the riverbank in the beginning of the film showing the openness of the landscape and emphasizing the playfulness of youth and, later, with flashbacks to an idyllic tryst on a small boat where the camera tracks the young couple through giant lily pads. In other films directed by Sun Yu, for example, *Loving Blood of the Volcano* (1932) and *Xiao Wanyi* (*Small Toys*, 1933), the tracking camera seems to affirm life in a rural setting and is used to open up interior sets, not unlike *Sunrise*. But, it also goes further in linking people together in their environment, looking forward to Jean Renoir's "realist" style of the latter part of the decade (what critic André Bazin terms "lateral depth of field"), while injecting a stronger emotional force to a scene, not unlike Alfred Hitchcock's mature, Hollywood use of the tracking camera in the 1950s.[20] For example, in the opening, silhouette shot of *Small Toys,* we view two small boats on a lake as the screen brightens at dawn. In the second shot, the camera tracks with a boat, viewing the river's tree-lined bank and other small crafts. This is immediately followed by a closer shot on the boat arriving in a fishing village. The action of the film, proper, begins with one of the fishermen selling a fish to the father of a household. Indoors, the man and his daughter are found getting ready for their working day, trying not to wake the family breadwinner, the woman of the house, mother and toy maker (played by Ruan Lingyu). Here, movement, as a life-affirmative motif, is continued, with the camera simply following the actions of the characters and their dog (comically equipped with booties on its paws) around their house, through panning and tracking.

*Daybreak, Loving Blood of the Volcan,* and *Small Toys* were all shot by "ace cameraman" (in Derek Elley's words) Zhou Ke, who may have had considerable input into decisions of camera style.[21] Zhou was also the cinematographer for director Cai Chusheng's *Nanquo Zhi Chun* (*Spring in the South*, 1932) which features a less interesting narrative and characterization than the other films, but which is remarkably good to look at, while (inadvertently, perhaps) accentuating the art deco beauty of bourgeois life. The film begins in the spring with a pan from blossoms across water; and, in a later scene of young love, the camera tracks out through overhanging vegetation and tracks again with the couple as they ride horses. Although none of these examples are found in extremely long takes and although none of the shots cover a large range of narrative incident, the elegant camera movements in these films, directed by Sun Yu and shot by Zhou Ke, can certainly be compared to the effect of unravelling a Chinese, horizontal scroll, landscape painting.

We are a long way from declaring that a distinctly "Chinese montage" exists in the Lianhua films of the 1930s, and yet editing patterns akin to Catherine Yi-Yu Cho Woo's 1985 scheme of the "technique of a lyrical montage of simple images filmed with a static camera," linking the Chinese cinema with "the soul of Chinese painting and poetry" in offering "the

195

vision of the unity of the human and natural worlds" that she found in *Yijiang chunshui xiang dong liu* (*A Spring River Flows East*, 1947), can be detected.[22] This film was co-directed by Cai Chusheng (and Lianhua actor/star Zheng Junli) who was variously known as one of the more "leftist" directors at Lianhua and as "an artist influenced by the *yingxi* [shadowplay] tradition, who emphasizes dramatic tension and intriguing plot lines."[23] Given that Cai's 1930s films rarely dwell on harmonious situations, it would be surprising to find a great deal of life-affirmative "lyrical montages" in them. Yet, at the beginning of *Spring in the South*, flowers are in almost every shot, where Miss Li Xiaohung (Chen Yanyan) and a male student, Hong Yu (Gao Zhanfei), gaze at one another (and the moon) from their balconies. He is seen with one of his college chums in an Ozu-like two-shot, where they adopt identical poses.

In *Yu guang qu* (*Song of the Fisherman*, 1934), when a grandmother dies, the shot of this occurring is preceded by a low-angle view of birds in a tree nest, and is followed by a shot of waves breaking on the seashore, bracketing death with life. More typical of Cai's cross-cutting in these films, though, is where narrative connections between people who have been separated, even driven apart, are made more profound through editing. Near the beginning of *Spring in the South*, when Xiaohung reads a letter from Hong, a dissolve connects the two of them. After a series of idyllic countryside episodes involving them fishing, riding horses, and picking flowers together, Hong learns that his father is sick. He goes home and his dying father tells him he must marry the daughter of Mr. Biao, because it is he who has paid for his studies. After writing a letter to his beloved Xiaohung on how the "old ethical code of conduct has won," a tracking camera emphasizes the distance between the lovers through a series of super-impositions and cuts between the newly married couple and the lonely Xiaohung. At the end of the film, after a cross-cut from Hong Yu, now living in Paris, to a sick Li Xiaohung, reading his letter, a boat arrives in Hong Kong harbour, and a montage of train wheels, car wheels, and Hong Yu travelling in an open convertible cross-cuts to a long shot of a dying Xiaohung together with her doctor and family. The pathos and energy of the parallel editing found in *Spring in the South* is clearly derived from the American work of D. W. Griffith.[24] But, interestingly, by 1932, "cross-cutting," where simultaneous action is always implied, was no longer a central narrative device in Classical Hollywood cinema (although it had not disappeared altogether), while "parallel editing" between disparate spaces, where no determinate temporal connection may exist, has never become conventional in Hollywood.[25]

It seems to me that Cai Chusheng's consistent use of parallel editing is closer to what David Bordwell found in Carl Dreyer's films, a "stylistic procedure" of foregrounding "narrative parallels" which he calls "alternation."[26] Also, it has been noted that *Song of the Fisherman*, in particular, contains specifically Chinese, poetic elements in its narrative structure, including "the technique of using scenes to express emotions, the technique of comparison, the technique of echoing," all of which can be emphasized through montage.[27] Li Suyuan and Hu Jobin also discuss this film in terms of its "narrative method of multi-layered comparisons," arguing that in Cai's work, "there was a series of deeply rooted contradictions and internal conflicts, including both the antithesis between the poor fishermen and the rich fishermen, and the striking contrast between the prosperous metropolis and the completely bankrupt rural area."[28]

In *Song of the Fisherman*, a young woman, Xiao Mao nicknamed "Kitten" (Wang Renmei), and her weak brother, Xiao Hou "Little Monkey" (Han Lang'en), have grown up in the countryside with the child of a rich family, He Ziying "Young Master" (Luo Peng). The siblings' father was a fisherman who died at sea, while Ziying's father owned a fishing company. Throughout the film, the domains of rich and poor, exploiter and exploited are intercut. A key example of this is where The Whayang Fishing Co. is introduced through the person of its General Manager, Mr. He, seen on the deck of a large fishing vessel. A cut is made to a very small craft occupied by Kitten and Little Monkey. In this one, highly "emotional," parallel edit we can find "comparison" (and contrast), "echoing," and a very strong sociopolitical message. A city/country dichotomy is also set up when the Xiaos look for work in Shanghai, and a kind of balance between the classes is restored when the He family is beset by financial disaster and Mr. He shoots himself. Meanwhile the Xiaos lose their mother and uncle, and, at the very end of the film, Little Monkey dies following a fishing accident. Thus, although the incidence of landscape shots comparable to classical paintings appearing in the Lianhua films is low, we can still find in their use of cinematic devices such as camera movement and editing some resonant visual and emotional correspondences.

With the popularity of *chambara* waning in early 1930s Japan, along with the emergent popularity of urban-set contemporary dramas (*gendai-geki*), it is understandable that landscape cinematography rarely appeared. Shigeyoshi Suzuki's *Eikan Namida Ari* (*Tears Behind Victory*, 1931), which focuses on the camaraderie of a college rowing team, features many lyrical shots on or alongside a river, showing poplar trees, reeds, road and railway bridges. The tracking camera, following a group in its jogging exercises, is matched with running trucks to follow the progress of its boat. Remarkably, some of these shots are overlaid with written lines of poems and songs, a style of presentation that Noël Burch terms *super-inscription* and which he regards as being a characteristically Japanese "acknowledgement of the surface" technique.[29] On the other hand, the film's director, Suzuki, was known to be a great admirer of European and American films, and he even contributed articles to the British-Swiss film journal, *Close-Up*.[30] As with Chinese films of the period, where contemplative, long take, landscape shots are rarely found, "nature" is often incorporated expressively in brief montages used as interludes or to bridge sequences in early 1930s Japanese films.

In Suzuki's *Kuma No deru Kaikonchi* (*The Reclaimed Land Where Bears Live*, 1932), which was the second production of the independent Fuji Eiga company (*Tears* was the first), the Hokkaido countryside provides more than just a backdrop. This film focuses on the revenge of two generations of farmers against a despicable landowner. The very first Japanese attempts at agriculture were made in Hokkaido and the film mirrors that activity. In one edit there is a pan across a winter scape dotted with tree stumps to the same view; but in springtime, with the land being cultivated, the theme of reclamation is dramatically rendered. A number of high- and low-angle shots of field work follows. In *Beni Komori* (1931, Nikkatsu), directed by Tsuruhiko Tanaka, in between the title samurai character, the Crimson Bat (Ryuzauro Mitsuoka), taking a bath and going about his business, we observe trees blowing in the wind/cut to a shot of rain in a pipe/cut to a low-angle shot of the sky, with the sun emerging from the clouds.

We also find two directors who are later to be acclaimed as original stylists, Yasujiro Ozu and Kenji Mizoguchi, beginning to suggest allusions to landscape painting in their work. Noël Burch regards *Tokyo no Gasso* (*Woman of Tokyo*, 1933) as the first of Ozu's films to systematically employ *pillow shots*, which most often consist of what he calls "cutaway still-lifes" but which can also be landscape shots (160). Indeed there are almost as many "still-life" shots in this film of objects (e.g., clocks, lamps, pots, kimonos) as there are of shots containing people, and they do not all function as "cutaways"; but Burch's later description of *pillow shots* (a term which he derives from *makkurakotoba* or *pillow* words of *haiku* poetry) is apt: "People are perhaps known to be near, but for the moment they are not visible, and a rooftop, a street-light, laundry drying on a line, a lampshade or a tea-kettle is offered as *center of attention*" (161). Further, Burch notes that "[u]nmoving, often lasting a long time (seldom less than five seconds which we at least experience as long for an 'unpeopled' shot), fully articulated from the graphic point of view, they demand to be *scanned* like paintings, not like *inhabited* shots which, even in Ozu, are relatively more centred around characters" (162). David Bordwell, in his rich and detailed study of the Japanese director, develops a complex analysis of these transitions of "intermediate shots" as being mostly "contiguous" in spatial terms and argues that the duration of each shot is carefully planned for clarity: "Ozu gives us time to see everything."[31] This is an interesting approach because on the one hand we learn from Bordwell that the director's system was very much a "pictorial" one in keeping with Japanese and Chinese traditions—we observe the film frames and shots as carefully composed images—but, on the other hand, in the Hollywood tradition, these images are clear and can be understood efficiently. Most of Ozu's landscape shots, if not minimalist, are not overly complex. Invariably we will only see a single mountain in the background, or, at most, two.[32]

All of Ozu's surviving films are *gendai-geki* with contemporary settings, and most feature middle-class, urban characters and situations in the *shoshimin-geki* genre.[33] Thus, it is not surprising that there are very few urban exterior shots in many of the films, apart from transitional shots. Only 11 of the 26 films that Ozu made before *Woman of Tokyo* have survived, but some of these contain more exterior scenes than usual. In *Wakaki hi* (*Days of Youth*, 1929), his oldest surviving film, a long sequence takes place on ski slopes. It is comic rather than picturesque, but much of the filming was done in long and extreme-long shot. Ozu's eccentricity is also on display here, where one of the students sits down in the snow and the camera views him from a very low, seated position. As Bordwell notes, the most original and distinctive aspect of Ozu's "poetics" is his framing, where the camera is consistently positioned closer to the ground than in the films of any other director in history, Japanese or otherwise. Bordwell notes: "Ozu's rule is to set the lens axis between halfway and two-thirds of the way down the object to be filmed. When shooting a human figure, this position puts the head quite high in the shot" (Bordwell, 1988, 14). If the actor is standing, she or he will be filmed waist high, or lower. What is most surprising to me, though, is how often Ozu's characters are seated, not just inside homes, restaurants, and other dwellings, but outside. How often do skiers sit themselves down in the snow, deliberately (rather than accidentally)? Never, would be a likely answer. And yet, Ozu thought of filming such a scene in *Days of Youth*. Perhaps his preference for such strangely low camera positioning had to do with his own predilection for sitting on the ground, or perhaps it is a reflection of his feeling of closeness to the earth. In any event he was very much aware of the originality of such a stylistic choice. Bordwell quotes a conversation which allegedly took place in Japanese film director Daisuke Ito's garden where Ozu set a sake bottle on a rock and discussed the low position of the bottle as a camera position which was his, alone: "This is exactly it. Absolutely mine. I'd never let anyone sit in this position, the position I've created" (1988, 78).[34]

Much of the 14 minute fragment, all that survives of Ozu's next extant feature, *Wasei kenka tomadachi* (*Fighting Friends*, 1929), takes place outdoors. It was possibly an early road movie, focusing on the comic antics of a truck driver and his assistant, and the fragment includes travelling shots on trucks and a train as well as a trademark Ozu shot of two factory chimneys viewed in low angle against the sky. Although one would hardly relate to any of the shots in *Umarete wa mita keredo* (*I Was Born, But . . .*, 1932) as real "landscapes," the most memorable sections of the film involve boys making their way to school. With the continually moving camera combined with the regularly returning image of a single car train passing in the background, and the comic, broad gestures of the boys, a tremendous sense of rhythm is created. And, although one doesn't necessarily think of paintings while watching it, the film feels far more "musical" or "poetic" and "painterly" than "narrative" through the force of its lyrical, leisurely, but youthful rhythms, which seem both natural and communal (but driven by the boys' perspective, not the adults).

Ukigusa Monogatari (*The Story of Floating Weeds*, 1934), unusually, for Ozu, takes place entirely in the countryside. A touring Kabuki theatre group, down on its luck, is performing in a small town. Befitting the nocturnal work of actors, much of the film takes place at night, but there are a number of key daytime scenes set against simple mountainous backdrops, including one of father and son fishing in unison, and another of an actress seducing the son nearby a symbolically religious tree. Regardless of where the camera is positioned, the far background is not going to change appreciably in perspective, but a low-camera position always tends to emphasize whatever can be seen in the foreground, and Ozu consistently takes advantage of this. Nevertheless, even early in his career, the city, specifically, Tokyo, was Ozu's principal setting, and his last silent film, *Tokyo no yado* (*An Inn in Tokyo*, 1935), one of the finest examples of social realism in film history, made magnificent use of it.[35] There are some suggestions of urban decay in *Hogaraka ni ayume* (*Walk Cheerfully*, 1930) where a confrontation between small-time crooks takes place in a patch of wasteland, and in *I Was Born, But*, where the boys walk to school past background rubble and foreground weeds. But, in *An Inn in Tokyo*, a depression-era tale of a father of two sons looking for work, such settings dominate. Factory chimneys, electricity pylons, cranes, and other industrial landscapes provide backgrounds for the job search, while a particular gasworks is returned to regularly to designate the beginning of each day. This "morning" view is always accompanied by the foreground presence of two large, disused cable drums, which eventually become occupied by the two brothers who sit atop one of them, majestically. Because of the repeated low-camera position we see very little of the ground, but we are always made aware of it by the drums, the walking of characters across it and by the concomitant appearance of weeds and other natural growth in the immediate foreground. Along with the rhythm of the editing and the cycle of day and night in *An Inn in Tokyo*, the human characters who often sit on the ground or on logs and hang their clothes on the cable drums, and the glimpses of foliage and grass, are Ozu's subtle, beautiful markers of the "natural" world in a predominantly industrial landscape.

According to David Bordwell's statistical analysis, the average shot length of *An Inn in Tokyo* is 4.5 seconds (at the standard sound film transport rate of 24 frames per second) and the average for all of Ozu's extant silent features is just under 4.9 seconds.[36] This is a much faster cutting rate than for silent films in general, but is probably closer to the average Japanese rate.[37] In any event, the audience did not have time to dwell over the compositions of Ozu's shots, or those of other East Asian films of the period, as one is supposed to do when one confronts a landscape painting, except for the films directed by Kenji Mizoguchi.[38]

Mizoguchi's status as a long-take director is legendary. David Bordwell writes of his work being exemplary of the "pictorialist" approach, where emphasis is placed on "the individual shot as a rich visual design," Darrell Davis recognizes the director's *Genroku chushingura* (*The Loyal Ronin of the Genroku Era*, aka *The Forty-Seven Ronin*, 1941–1942) as exemplifying the "monumental style" of the late 1930s and early World War II period, while Tadao Sato and Noel Burch have both stressed an affinity of Mizoguchi's long-take aesthetic with the *e-makimono*, Japanese scroll-painting (Bordwell, 1995, 22). David Bordwell has observed, "From 1935 to the end of his career, the average shot lengths of Mizoguchi's films range from fifteen seconds to ninety seconds, with most ranging between twenty-five and forty seconds."[39] Whereas *The Forty-Seven Ronin* is the film most often cited in relation to the *e-maki* painting style (comprising high-angle views of roofless dwellings as well as linear, narrative scrolling) and whereas his 1950s films are most often written about in terms of their pictorial beauty, we can find the roots of Mizoguchi's mature style in some of his silent films.[40] There are a number of impressive camera moves in *Orizuri Ozen* (*The Downfall of Ozen*, 1935), especially in the beginning, when the heroine Ozen is involved in a chase, and, in *Taki no shiraito* (*Taki the Water Magician*, aka *White Threads of the Waterfall*, 1933), beautiful markers of the natural world are incorporated into the sets of performing venues and other, mostly urban, locales. Tree branches hang into the foreground of frames, leaves fall to the ground, and in a springtime scene we see blossoms and the reflection of water on clothes.

There are probably many reasons why the great historical tradition of landscape painting is not prominently reflected in East Asian films during the silent era, including David Bordwell's comment that "[w]e are not in the habit of explaining contemporary Hollywood style by reference to Northern European Renaissance painting, so why should ancient aesthetic traditions be relevant to twentieth-century Japanese film?" (2005, 98). Indeed, the most likely explanation is that of "modernity." Cinema was regarded everywhere as *the* modern ("seventh") art form of the twentieth century, and as a commercial medium of entertainment. The technology of cinema was invented in France, Britain, and the United States and was brought into East Asia by entrepreneurs from these countries.[41] Zhang Zheng provides a very interesting account of the situation in Shanghai where the "time lag between early Euro-American cinema and early Chinese cinema speaks certainly to the semicolonial nature of Chinese modernity, especially with regard to 'belated' technological transfer and implementation. This temporal disparity, ironically, also supplies testimonies to the persistence of early cinema not so much as a rigidly defined aesthetic or period category, but as an emblem of modernity, or rather multiple modernities."[42]

In her doctoral dissertation, "The Production of Modernity in Japanese Cinema: Shochiku Kamata Style [SKS] in the 1920s and 1930s," Mitsuyo Wada-Mariano argues that the "construction of Japanese modernity can be located in the Japanese search for a modern subjectivity, based on Japan's resigned acknowledgement towards a dominant Western model and the assertion of its own national identity."[43] Hollywood narrative films and, to some extent, those from Europe had a tremendous effect on Chinese cinema made in Shanghai in the 1920s and 1930s and (perhaps to a lesser degree) on the Japanese and Korean film industries of the same period.[44] Throughout the world it was understood that films had to "move" and to move audiences, so that there was very little room for meditative reflection on the glories of landscape. Surprisingly, perhaps, there was no equivalent in Japanese and Chinese films to the consistently expressive use of the natural landscape in Swedish films of the 1910s, especially those directed by Victor Sjöström and Mauritz Stiller or the highly popular American genre of the Western, within which John Ford had begun to include panoramic shots of the vast open range as early as 1917 with *Bucking Broadway*. Again, it is important to reiterate that, because of the tragic loss of the vast majority of silent films made in Korea, Japan, and China, we cannot be sure what was there. In fact, one Japanese director, Hiroshi Shimizu, may have fit the bill.

Only nine of Shimizu's silent films appear to have survived, and I've only been able to see one of them, *Minato no nihon musume* (*Japanese Girls at the Harbor*, 1933), and a very small part of another, *Mori no kajiya* (*Forest Blacksmith*, 1929), with English translation. The other extant films are *Fue no shiratama* (*Eternal Love*, 1929), *Nanatsu no umi* (*The Seven Seas*) released in two parts in 1931 ("Virginity Chapter") and 1932 ("Frigidity Chapter"), *Naki nureta haru no onna yo* (1933), *Daigaku no waka-danna* (*The Boss's Son at College*, 1933), *Kinkanshoku* (*Eclipse*, 1934), and *Tokyo no eiyu* (*A Hero of Tokyo*, 1935).

The opening shot of *The Seven Seas* shows a young "flapper" standing on the observational platform at the back of a train, gazing at the receding tracks, with the camera mounted inside the carriage. It is a travelling shot, seemingly associating the young woman with the freedom of movement. During the first "virginity" part of the film there are many lateral tracking camera movements to follow walking characters, mostly women, but whereas approximately a quarter of the shots in this part contain camera movements, only 24 of the 390 shots in the "frigidity" second half contain any camera movement at all, and most of these are associated with the heroine, Yumie Sone, who has married, and subsequently rejected the higher class Takehiko Yagibashi, a playboy who stole her virginity. *Japanese Girls at the Harbor* begins on a long, slow pan left across Yokohama harbour, leading to a large ocean liner (later revealed to be one of the Canadian

Pacific Empresses). Immediately, we are in the realm of scroll landscape painting, and this connection is continued with a laterally tracking camera following the movements of two school girls, Sunako (Oikawa Michiko) and Dora (Inoue Yukiko), who watch the ships go by as they walk, and long to escape their dull lives. The road to and from school runs along a hill fronting the bay so that Shimizu's camera can view his subjects and the object of their gaze, simultaneously. The camera also tracks the girls' journey, walking past trees, up and above the city, and their meetings with a very modern young man, Henry (played by the Eurasian actor Egawara Ureo) who wears shorts and rides a motorcycle. Wada-Marciano recognizes that "realism" and "subjectivity" are key components of Japanese modernity which come together in moving landscape shots in the SKS films.[45] Indeed, throughout *Japanese Girls at the Harbor* we are drawn into experiencing the world along with the female subjects, while only rarely seeing things perceptually through their eyes (in point-of-view shots). I believe that, whereas we can understand these long-shot compositions as "modernist" in this Japanese sense of the term, we can also understand them in a "classical" sense, where the human characters are considered to be potentially in harmony with the natural world, in all its "realism."

In *Eclipse*, a film which contains very little camera movement, there are numerous landscape shots in the first half where living in the countryside is depicted somewhat idyllically (in contrast to life in Tokyo). In particular, one very long take (interrupted only by dialogue titles) shows three male friends in the foreground looking out into a picturesque background of fields and mountains. Although one can interpret this shot in the context of Wada-Marciano's Japanese modernity, I am persuaded to see it in a much more "classical" context. Even more strikingly, in the first part of *The Seven Seas*, where a sympathetic male character, Ichiro, the owner of a sporting goods store, visits his female friend, Ayako, in the country. She is trying to recover from the shock of an Englishman committing suicide because she would not marry him.[46] The camera which had panned left with the movements of the two of them, now takes off on its own, panning left into the wilderness. The shot fades out and in on another "still life" shot, lacking human subjects, also panning left past a copse of trees. This second shot also fades out and into a high-angled shot of trees reflected in water as the couple move back into and across the frame from left to right, also in reflection. There is a dissolve to a fourth shot, dominated in high angle of a lily pond as stones which Ichiro have thrown cause the water to splash and ripple. This poetic sequence, where movement in nature is key, seems to transport the film spectator away from a scene of mourning to one of contemplation and back, again, wherein the fades and dissolve are suggestive of transcendence. Again, the placement of the human characters in the natural landscape may indicate a kind of modernist subjectivity at work, but here, allusions to classical painting and poetry are far more compelling.

The only instance in a Shimizu silent film I can recall of a landscape shot being edited into a scene to indicate perceptual subjectivity is, like this scene of mourning, somewhat enigmatic. It occurs in the opening scene of *The Seven Seas*, on a train, where Yagibashi Takehiko, a young, unsympathetic, spoilt young man is talking to another man and sarcastically referring to the "flapper" seen in the first shot. A cut is made from a frontal shot of his figure to a moving shot of Mount Fuji, viewed through a train window, and marked as his point-of-view. So early in the film, it is not possible for us to know that he will be its villain, but, retrospectively we ponder Shimizu's decision to relate this particular character to the deeply symbolic image of traditional Japanese culture. Could he have been criticizing it? In all of the extant silent films, the moving camera is not just confined to exteriors. In *Japanese Girls at the Harbor*, it tracks past rows of pews in a church, it tracks along a bar in a drinking establishment and it tracks laterally inside houses, apparently just for decorative purposes. In *Eclipse*, the two best friends, Shuichi and Shinji, have met again in a Tokyo theatre. The camera tracks a long way left with them in the lobby and then moves in the reverse direction to follow the woman they both love, Kinue, and a male suitor. She has travelled to the metropolis to find Shuichi. In its double movement the camera expresses the longing the characters feel for one another and the tragedy of their misconnection. Thus we can find in these early surviving films that Shimizu insisted on moving his camera in a very obvious way, very much in the manner of the *e-maki* narrative scroll.

Until the major retrospective mounted at the 2004 Berlin International Film Festival, and followed by a similar tribute at the Hong Kong Film Archive (with an accompanying monograph published by the Hong Kong International Film Festival Society), Shimizu's work was not well known outside of Japan.[47] Noël Burch devoted most of one chapter of his groundbreaking 1979 book to the director, but this did not have the effect of making the films more available. Burch called Shimizu the "most 'spontaneously Japanese' director of his generation, unscientific though this judgement may be" (247). He likened Shimizu's "agglutinative" narratives to the *haikai* verses of the seventeenth-century writer Ihara Saikaku, which consist of "a succession of related digressions," and analyzed *Hanagata senshu* (*A Star Athlete*, 1937) as exemplifying this kind of "cameo" structure (Burch, 247–255). Burch also noted the musicality of the "play of the camera up and down the road," whereas Bordwell in his 1995 article was struck by Shimizu's "incessant tracking shots, moving only forward or backward" (Burch, 247; Bordwell, 1995, 24). Indeed, in *Arigato-san* (*Mr. Thank You*, 1936), named after the bus driver who continually thanks people (and animals) for getting out of the way of his vehicle, we only see views inside and outside of the bus filmed along the axis in which the bus is travelling. This film is a definitive "travelogue," and is extremely "modernist" (in a Western sense) in its insistent formal aspects. In addition to deep tracking on the road, Shimizu also employed dissolves on a fixed frame to elide the movement of a character either out of or into the scene or to a position farther away, not unlike the last shot of Dimitri Kirsanov's *Menilmontant* (France, 1926), where two sisters are walking down a poplar-lined avenue. The effect in the Shimizu films, as in Kirsanov's, is very poignant. The fact that the frame of the camera is fixed receives emphasis while we see different stages in the characters' movement. The device is used a few times in *Japanese Girls at the Harbor* and most of the other films in the cycle, and is particularly effective near the conclusion of *Anma to onna* (*The Masseurs and a Woman*, 1938), where the "woman," carrying a parasol, with her back to the camera, walks into the background across a bridge, as she has on previous occasions, but now there is no one with her. The dissolves freeze her movement, while making her placement in the landscape much more obvious.

Sharon H. Hayashi devoted two chapters of her doctoral dissertation, "Travelling Film History: Language and Landscape in the Japanese Cinema, 1931–1945," to Shimizu's work. She finds, contra-Burch, that the "formalism" and symmetrical comic play of *Aragato-san* are "more productively analyzed in relation to the literary milieu of the times."[48] She asserts that Shimizu "set out to create a pure film based on Akutagawa [Ryunosuke]'s notion of the pure novel," involving a rejection of plot and "*dessin*" (204). While noting that the "road itself" could be called the "real protagonist of many of Shimizu's films," Hayashi interestingly claims that the director's portrayal of the human "subject as part of the landscape rather than as a distinct entity from it" (205–206) is not unlike Heidegger's notion of the "phenomenological subject" where "subjectivity is not divisible into the subject and the space surrounding the subject."[49] Hayashi recognizes that Shimizu's characters are invariably outsiders and misfits, and discusses the "mysterious woman" of *Anma to onna* who is running away from an adulterous affair as one who "remains outside of the norms prescribed for women by their familial roles" (220-221). For Hayashi, the dissolves on the woman at the end of *Anma to onna* effectively project her "melancholy" onto the landscape (222).

Based on the evidence provided by the 10 films made by Shimizu from 1933 to 1948 that were shown in Hong Kong, I can safely state that, in this era, he was virtually the equal of Mizoguchi and Ozu as an original stylist and may have gone further than either in forging his own personal style, at least in the films where he was allowed by Shochiku to take a crew out on the road.[50] Even before the coming of sound, he started to develop his travelogue narrative structuring; he experimented with a lateral tracking camera, at times in ways analogous to narrative scroll painting and he played with placing and moving characters in natural landscapes. He was almost certainly the first important director of road movies in world cinema history, he was also one of the first "experimental" narrative filmmakers outside France and the Soviet Union, and, in all probability, he was East Asia's first truly original "landscape" filmmaker.

## notes

1. See Jean Buhot, *Chinese and Japanese Landscape Art; with Sections on Korea and Vietnam*, ed. Charles McCurdy, trans. Rémy Inglis Hall (New York: Anchor Books, 1967, 120. Michael Sullivan is somewhat sceptical about the importance of Li father and son, but traces the development back much further and provides numerous examples of surviving seventh century Sui dynasty cave paintings including landscapes, at Tunhuang; Michael Sullivan, *Chinese Landscape Paintings in the Sui and T'ang Dynasties* (Berkeley, Los Angeles: University of California Press, 1980), especially 111–112. The oldest surviving hanging scroll painting on silk dates from the Western Han dynasty, about 180 B.C.E.; Michael Sullivan, *Chinese Art: Recent Discoveries* (London: Thames & Hudson, 1973), 45–46.

2. In Ch'en Yun-ru, *The Art and Aesthetics of Form: Selections from the History of Chinese Paintings*, ed. Wang Yao-t'ing, trans. Donald E. Bix (Taipei: National Palace Museum, 2003), 25; hereafter cited in text. See also Hsü Kuo-huang, *The Landscape Painting Tradition of Li Ch'eng and Kuo Hsi* (Taipei: National Palace Museum, 1999).

3. See Ch'en Yun-ru, *op. cit.*, 24–29; and Lawrence Sickman and Alexander Soper, "The Masters of Landscape," in *The Pelican History of Art: The Art and Architecture of China* (Harmondsworth, Middlesex: Penguin Books, 1st int. ed., 1961), 203–214; hereafter cited in text.

4. Mary Treagar, "Space and Monumentality," in *Chinese Art*, rev. ed. (London: Thames & Hudson, 1997 [1980]), 107–108.

5. Sabine Hesemann discusses the horizontal scroll as it was developed in the Southern style, exemplified by the work of Dong Yuan (e.g., *The Xiao and the Xiang*), who worked for the court of Nanjing (937–962), where the land was relatively flat. According to Hesemann, he was "a man of the south [and], created an effect of great scope in his landscape compositions"; Hesemann, "China: The Song Period and the Aesthetics of Simplicity" in *The Art of East Asia*, ed. Gabriele Fahr-Becker, ed. of English edition Chris Murray (Cologne: Könemann, 1999), 145; hereafter cited in text. A much later work measures 24.8 x 528.7 cm, which is illustrated on pages 156–159 (to be "read" in reverse), is *Life Along the River on the Eve of the Qingming Spring Festival*, in ink and color on silk, and attributed to Zhang Zeduan (early twelfth century).

6. On Korea, Dunn notes that "With the new interest in Ch'an Buddhism and its emphasis on meditation came a taste for monochrome ink paintings that were inspired by those of the Song dynasty in China" (*The Art of East Asia, op. cit.*, 689), and he provides the example of an Yi dynasty (sixteenth–seventeenth century) ink on silk landscape to illustrate the "heavy flavor of Zen ideals…, even though Buddhism had been suppressed during the early Yi dynasty [1392–1910] in favor of Confucian ethics and ancestor worship" (*The Art of East Asia, op. cit.*, 687). On Japan, he writes: "Towards the end of the 12th century, another sect of Buddhism

was introduced into Japan by priests who had visited China and studied there" which "espoused the practice of meditation in order to directly achieve the enlightened awareness of truth"(*The Art of East Asia, op. cit.,* 507). He discusses Zen aesthetics at length and relates the Song dynasty influence in the Muromachi period (1392–1573) with its "haunting misty landscapes" (*The Art of East Asia, op. cit.,* 508–510). See M. Dunn, "Korea," in *The Art of East Asia, op. cit.*

7. Sickman continues, "The Chinese attain their particular kind of technical perfection in calligraphy and painting by the same kind of application that a Western student of music would employ in mastering the violin or piano. Armed with a perfectly controlled technique and drawing upon his imagination and visual memory, rather than what he saw directly before him, the Chinese artist's painting of a picture was not unlike the performance of a skilled musician."

8. In Ch'en Yun-ru, "Lyricism Revisited," *op. cit.,* 34–35. See also Treager, "Court and Chan Buddhist Arts," *op. cit.,* 124; and Rhonda Cooper and Jeffrey Cooper, *Masterpieces of Chinese Art* (New York: Todtri Productions Ltd., 1997), where they discuss the "more intimate, lyrical style of landscape painting" called the "Ma-Xia style" (from "Ma Yuan" and "Xia Gui") of "asymmetrical compositions [used] to create the misty, atmospheric effects that conveyed the feeling of the southern landscape." Here they name the same painting as *Walking on a Path in Spring* (83).

9. See Treager, *op cit.,* p. 124; Cooper and Cooper, *op cit.,* p. 83; and Ch'en Yun-ru, *op cit.,* 35.

10. See Ch'en Yun-ru's discussion and illustration of the history of a particular handscroll, Chao Kan's *Early Snow on the River* (early tenth century, Five Dynasties period), which was subsequently owned by the Southern T'ang ruler, Li Hou-chu (937–997), the Sung court Emperor Hui-tsung (reigned 1101–1125), and so on, changing hands (imperial and otherwise) and receiving different seals and inscriptions until the eighteenth century (Ch'en Yun-ru, *op cit.,* 5–9).

11. Yutang Lin, *The Chinese Theory of Art: Translations from the Masters of Chinese Art* (New York: Putnam Sons, 1967); hereafter cited in text.

12. Soper's translation of the other five principles is as follows: The second is "structural method in use of the brush." The third is "fidelity to the object in portraying forms." The fourth is "conformity to kind in applying colors." The fifth is "proper planning in placing (of elements)." The sixth is "transmission (of the experience of the past) in making copies" (Sickman and Soper, *op. cit.,* 133).

13. In, Horst Woldemar Janson, *History of Art: A Survey of the Major Visual Arts from the Dawn of History to the Present Day,* 2nd ed. (Englewood Cliffs, NJ: Prentice-Hall, 1977), 722; hereafter cited in text.

14. In another Prentice-Hall/Abrams publication used extensively as a university textbook, *Varieties of Visual Experience* by Edmund Burke Feldman, there are only two references to Japanese art and one to Chinese: a comparison of a Maoist poster with an example of contemporary European artwork! Edmund Burke Feldman, *Varieties of Visual Experience* (New York: Harry H. Abrams, Inc., 2nd ed., 1981), 44. In Catherine King ed., *Views of Difference: Different Views of Art* (New Haven, London: Yale University Press in association with The Open University, 1999), the problem of neglect is addressed in a chapter entitled, "What about Chinese art?" (case study 5) by Craig Clunas: "Many of the standard works of art history for the

English-speaking world either ignore China altogether, or else restrict their coverage to a very limited series of generalizations. For example, *The Story of Art* by E. H. Gombrich includes a few pages on China in a chapter entitled "Looking Eastward," which makes it clear that in the (singular) story of art the people doing the looking stand very firmly in something called 'the West.' It is as if 'art history' and 'Chinese art history' are two very different things" (119).

15. William Watson, *Style in the Arts of China* (Harmondsworth, Middlesex: Penguin Books, 1974), 83.

16. Arthur De Carle Sowerby, *Nature in Chinese Art* (New York: The John Day Company, 1940), 153, 161–168.

17. See my article, "Camera Movement in Japanese Silent Films (and the Twentieth Giornate del Cinema Muto, in Sacile, Italy, October 2001)," *Asian Cinema* 14, no. 2 (Fall/Winter 2003), 197–205.

18. See Mariann Lewinsky Farinelli's program notes for *Le Giornate del Cinema Muto, 2001 Catalogo/20th Pordenone Silent Film Festival Catalogue*, where she writes that "The first two film extracts [of *Nippon*] along with *Fuun Joshi* (being shown elsewhere in this [silent Japanese film] series), enable an appraisal of the output of the company Kinugasa Eiga Renmei (Shochiko Kyoto), revealing its films to be sophisticated, formally inventive *jidai geki* featuring a love interest in the form of the star couple Chojiro Hayashi and Akiko Chihaya, and a team of good character actors" (34).

19. The *Shinpa* tradition of stage play began in the late 1880s as a reaction or at least alternative to the stylized *Kabuki* and *Nô* forms. These plays tended to focus on the lives of young people in a contemporary setting. *Shinpa* films began to be made after 1907.

20. See, especially, André Bazin, "The French Renoir," in *Jean Renoir*, ed. François Truffaut, trans. W. W. Halsey II and William H. Simon (New York: Dell Publishing Co., Inc., 1974), 74–91.

21. See Derek Elley's notes for Nanguo zhi chun (Spring in the South, 1932) in the 1997 Pordenone Silent Film Festival Programme, *op. cit.*, 58.

22. In Catherine Yi-Yu Cho Woo, "The Chinese Montage: From Poetry and Painting to the Silver Screen," *Perspectives on Chinese Cinema*, ed. Chris Berry (London: British Film Institute, 1991), 22 [first published as no. 39 in the Cornell East Asia Papers series]. The first example she offers of film montage from *A Spring River Flows East* is as follows: "The camera first focuses on the wedding picture of a young couple. . . , on a dresser, cuts to two embroidered pillows at the top of the double bed, and then to the side of the bed where two pairs of shoes rest neatly side by side. The next image is of a leafless branch of spring blossom, followed by a leafy branch laded with fruit. The final shot is of a hand embroidering 'Precious Little Baby' (*xiao baobao*) on a bib."

23. Yingjin Zhang characterizes Cai in these different ways through a review of Chinese film literature. Yingjin Zhang, ed., Introduction to *Cinema and Urban Culture in Republican Shanghai, 1922–1943* (Stanford: Stanford University Press, 1999), 9–10. Zhang refers to Taiwanese, anti-Communist Du Yunzhi's two volume, *Zhonghuaminguo dianyingshi* [A history of film in the Republic of China] (1988) for Cai's leftism; and to Zhong Dafeng and Shu Xiiaoming's text written for the Beijing Film Academy, *Zhongguo dianying shi* [History of Chinese cinema] (1995) for the *yingxi* influence. For Cai's leftist tendency, see also Yingjin Zhang and Zhiwei Xiao, *Encyclopedia*

*of Chinese Film* (London, New York: Routledge, 1998), especially "Leftist Film," 13–15, and the entry on Cai, 105–106.

24. I am thinking here especially of the chase-to-the-rescue, cross-cutting structure that Griffith began to develop with *A Lonely Villa*, and the unusual contrast of social classes through parallel editing in *A Corner in Wheat* (both 1909, Biograph).

25. There is an excellent introduction to "parallel editing" and "cross-cutting" written by David Bordwell in David Bordwell, Janet Staiger, and Kristin Thompson, *The Classical Hollywood Cinema: Film Style and Mode of Production* (New York: Columbia University Press, 1985), 48–49. In the same book, Thompson writes: "The crosscut scene had become a staple of the silent cinema by the late teens and twenties. More often than not, cross-cutting provided a simple way of constructing an exciting story without the script writer's having to sustain a single line of action. It seems to have reached its most frequent usage for this purpose in the few years after 1915. By the twenties, script writers had gained more experience at creating situations which could sustain themselves for whole sequences. Crosscutting did not disappear, but became a more localized device, occurring mainly in scenes where the narration demanded the juxtaposition of multiple lines of action" (212).

26. David Bordwell, *The Films of Carl Theodor Dreyer* (Berkeley: University of California Press, 1981). See especially 30–32, where Bordwell argues that Dreyer's narrative system of parallel editing was derived from Griffith, but that "[i]mpersonal causal systems and pervasive Narrative parallels change the status of the protagonist." He continues, "The goal-orientation of the Hollywood hero springs from a desire to remake circumstances, and the development of this desire, the move toward the goal, constitutes the primary line of action. But since Dreyer's characters are enclosed within larger causal systems, the protagonists become more passive. Things happen to them; they register effects more than they create causes" (32).

27. Li Yiming, "*Song of the Fisherman*: A Chinese Melodrama and Latent Political Illusion," in Cheng Jing Liang, ed., *A Collection of Papers Presented at the Symposium on Film Collections in Asia* (October 1996), Beijing: China Film Archive, 1997, p. 319.

28. Li Suyuan and Hu Jobin, *Chinese Silent Film History*, English edition edited by Wang Rui, revised by Wang Rui and Tabetha Miller, translated by Wang Rui, Huang Wei, Hu Jubin, Wang Jingjing, Zheng Zhong, Shan Wanli, and Li Xun, from Zhongguo Wusheng Dianying Shi, Beijing: China Film Press, 1997, p. 344

29. Noël Burch, *To the Distant Observer: Form and Meaning in the Japanese Cinema*, ed. Annette Michelson (London: Scolar Press, 1979), 120; hereafter cited in text. Burch concludes the chapter, "Surface and Depth," by writing that "[t]he procedure of super-inscription, which has many precedents in Sino-Japanese culture, from the sutra-inscribed mirrors of the Fujiwara period to the 'painting-poems' of later eras, provides us with a remarkably enduring example of the manner in which the notions of *surface* and *writing* reveal essential affinities within the text-which-is-Japan" (121–122).

30. I cannot find references to three articles contributed by "Yasuchi Ogino" on sound (1930), "Before Daybreak" (1931), and, "1932, Japanese Film

Problems," and, I assume that Suzuki gave himself this pen name for his English-language writing.

31. David Bordwell, *Ozu and the Poetics of Cinema* (London: British Film Institute, 1988), 76; hereafter cited in text. On transitions, Bordwell argues that Ozu was expanding Hollywood's practices of "placing" shots—"one or a few shots that lead in to the locale that will be shown in establishing shots"—and cutaways—"inserted shots that interrupt the main action by enlarging detail not present in the prior shot." He writes: "What attracted Ozu about these devices, I think, was exactly their degree of narrational overtness. They offered a way for transitions to become as self-conscious as the non-anthropocentric camera position or the 360-degree space. He thus expanded the 'placing' shot and the cutaway, making them the basis of his transitional sequences. The underlying premise was his recognition that both devices relied upon a loose notion of *contiguity*" (105–106).

32. The single mountain landscape, which appears increasingly in Ozu's work, can, of course, be compared to the image of Mount Fuji, which is symbolic of Japan itself and which is adopted by Shochiku as their title card emblem.

33. Bordwell defines this genre specifically as being "films about lower-middle-class life," and that it was the Shochiku company's "speciality" (Bordwell, 1988, 14). (Ozu worked for Shochiku for virtually his entire career.) Most others use a shortened version of the Japanese term, *shomin-geki*, which Burch defines as the genre of films about "townspeople" (Burch, *op. cit.*, 152). According to Rüdiger Tomchak, the Berlin-based editor of the German-language film magazine, entitled *Shomingeki*, he chose this title, obviously inspired by Ozu's work, but also, because he believes the term refers to "films about the lives of ordinary people," an expanded notion of its meaning, apparently derived from Tadao Sato. Telephone conversation, January 25, 2004.

34. Bordwell is quoting from "Ito Daisuke on Ozu," in ed. and trans. Leonard Schrader, *The Masters of Japanese Film*, unpublished manuscript (Berkeley, CA: Pacific Film Archive, n.d.), p. 311.

35. Bordwell notes that "[o]f Ozu's fifty-four films, forty-nine take place in Tokyo, and five of those mention the city in their title. His work is saturated with references to the teeming mass culture of the metropolis. The films celebrate the city's streets, alleys, cafés, bars and wharves" (Bordwell, 1988, 39).

36. The figure for *Inn in Tokyo* is taken directly from the table of "Some Quantitative Aspects of Ozu's Films" in Bordwell's Appendix, whereas the 4.9 sec. average is my own calculation from all the 14 silent film "Average shot lengths" in the same table (Bordwell, 1988, 377).

37. For his article, "Visual Style in Japanese Cinema, 1925–1945," David Bordwell analyzed a sample of 163 films. Of those that were made between 1925 and 1933, he claims that all had an average shot length of less than 12 seconds, and 86 percent of them had average shot lengths of less than six seconds. David Bordwell, "Visual Style in Japanese Cinema, 1925–1945," *Film History* 7, no. 1 (Spring 1995): 23n1, 29n37, 31; hereafter cited in text.

38. The only other director who may well have been similarly leisurely in the pacing of his editing and action (and as distanced in viewing human characters) was Hiroshi Shimizu. See my concluding discussion of this director's remarkable work.

39. David Bordwell, *Figures Traced in Light* (Berkeley: University of California Press, 2005), 94; hereafter cited in text.

40. See, for example, Tadao Sato, "Japanese Cinema and the Traditional Arts: Imagery, Technique, and Cultural Context," in *Cinematic Landscapes: Observations on the Visual Arts and Cinema of China and Japan*, eds. Linda C. Ehrlich and David Desser, trans. Ann Sherif (Austin: University of Texas Press, 1994), where he writes of Mizoguchi being the "one Japanese director familiar with the *emaki* tradition" (170). In the same book, Donald Richie likens one of the scenes in *The Forty-Seven Ronin* to a scroll illustrating the *Tale of Genjii* and notes that "this scene is taken from such an angle that one is reminded of the unroofed chambers in the scrolls." Donald Richie, "The Influence of Traditional Aesthetics on the Japanese Film," in *Cinematic Landscapes, op. cit.*, 161.

41. The Lumière brothers introduced the cinema to China in 1896 and Japan in 1897, while an Anglo-American company first showed films in Korea in 1900. See *The Guiness Book of Movie Facts and Feats*, 4th ed., ed. Patrick Robertson (Enfield, Middlesex: Guiness Publishing Ltd., 1991), 3.

42. Zhang Zheng, "An Amorous History of the Silver Screen: The Actress as Vernacular Embodiment in Early Chinese Film Culture," *Camera Obscura* 48 (2001): 235–236.

43. Mitsuyo Wada-Mariano, "The Production of Modernity in Japanese Cinema: Shochiku Kamata Style [SKS] in the 1920s and 1930s" (PhD dissertation, The University of Iowa, 2000), 8; hereafter cited in text.

44. David Bordwell has written most extensively about the Western influence on Japanese films: "European and American films were influential from the moment that the moving picture was introduced. Around 1910, French chase films and serials were the predominant influence" (Bordwell, 1995, 6). On the other hand, Mitsuyo Wada-Marciano is critical of Bordwell's "approach that is heavily weighted toward comparisons with Hollywood norms" (Wada-Marciano, *op. cit.*, 17). She argues that Bordwell's "attempt to historicize the study of Japanese cinema tells us little about the Japanese historical and cultural contexts and his approach rests on the conceit of Hollywood cinema as the centre of a linear history" (Wada-Marciano, *op. cit.,* 18). For the Hollywood influence on Shanghai cinema see my own "Visual Style in the Shanghai Films Made by the Lianhua Film Company (United Photoplay Service): 1931–1937," *The Moving Image* 1, no. 1 (Spring 2001), 212. For the development of early Korean cinema against the grain of Japanese colonialism, see my article on *Jayu Manse* ("Hurrah! for Freedom, 1946") in *The Cinema of Japan and Korea*, ed. Justin Bowyer (London: Wallflower Press, 2004), 33–48 (24 Frames series).

45. In discussing travelling shots of storefronts in Shimazu Yasujiro's *Tonari no Yae-chan* (*Our Neighbor, Miss Yae*, 1934), she writes, "The characters gaze at the commodities, but they cannot fix on the same goods for any length of time; the present is always lost, as the horizontally moving images disappear into the dark, outside of the screen. The film viewing experience itself becomes blurred, merging with that of the gaze through the window of the moving car. The characters' experience of the scenery indicators that a 'new' subjectivity has been formed and the film renders the subjectivity as the audiences' own" (Mitsuyo Wada-Marciano, *op. cit.*, 28–29).

46. I am grateful that William M. Drew has provided extensive reviews of most of the extant silent films directed by Shimizu, so that I have been able to reconstruct synopses of the unsubtitled films before and after watching them. William M. Drew, "Hiroshi Shimizu: Silent Master of the Japanese Ethos," *Midnight Eye* (2001); available at http://www.midnighteye.com/features/hiroshi_shimizu.shtml (accessed April 15, 2004).

47. A major retrospective was mounted at the National Film Theatre in London in 1988, and 10 of his films comprised the first ever U.S. Retrospective mounted in New York by the Japan Society in 1991–1992. Manohla Dargis wrote a brief, but favourable review for the *Village Voice* on the latter; Manohla Dargis, "Lost and Found," *Village Voice* Vol. 36, no. 50, (December 10, 1991); 68. Alan Stanbrook wrote a much longer piece on the occasion of the former, noting strangely that Shimizu was a "director marginally better known in the West than in his native Japan." Alan Stanbrook, "On the Track of Hiroshi Shimizu," *Sight and Sound* 57, no. 3 (Summer 1988): 122–125. The 96-page, bilingual (Chinese and English) book, *Shimizu Hiroshi: 101st Anniversary*, edited by Kinnie Yau and Li Cheuk-to (Hong Kong: Hong Kong International Film Festival Society, 2004), contains essays by the filmmaker and interviews with people who worked with him, as well as four critical essays written by Wong Ain-ling, Yamane Sadao, Sharon Hyashi, and Tanaka Masazumi, notes on 13 films, and a partial filmography.

48. Sharon H. Hayashi, "Travelling Film History: Language and Landscape in the Japanese Cinema, 1931–1945" (PhD dissertation, The University of Chicago, 2003), 203; hereafter cited in text.

49. Martin Heidegger, "Building, Dwelling, Thinking," in *Basic Writings* (New York: Harper & Row Publishers, 1977), 334–335, quoted in Hayashi, *op. cit.*

50. The other films are *Koi mo wasurete* (*Forget Love for Now*, 1937), *Kaze no naka no kodomo* (*Children in the Wind*, 1937), *Uta-jo oboegaki* (*Notes of an Itinerant Performer*, 1941), *Kanzashi* (*Ornamental Hairpin*, 1941), *Sayon no kane* (*Sayon's Bell*, 1943), and the truly amazing, independently made, postwar travelogue, where the director used a "troop" of orphaned child actors, all of whom were living in his house, *Hachinosu no kodomotachi* (*Children of the Beehive*, 1948). According to the film notes to *Sayon's Bell*, translated by Sharon Hayashi from the Japanese catalogue, *Shimizu Hiroshi Eiga Dokuhon* (Tokyo: Film Art Sha, 2000), "Although the film was planned by the Shochiku Ofuna studios it was completed in their Kyoto (Shimokamo) studios. Jealousy and strong resentment from other directors against the perceived insolence of first rung director Shimizu led studio head Kido Shirou, Shimizu's long time protector, to finally decide to relegate Shimizu to the Kyoto studios. Shimizu lost the base which had made possible his expensive productions and his freedom. He never returned to the mainstream of Japanese cinema afterwards" (82).

# from flatland to vernacular relativity

## the genesis of early english screenscapes

d a v i d   b .   c l a r k e
a n d   m a r c u s   a .   d o e l [1]

> The real voyage of discovery lies not in seeking new
> landscapes but in having new eyes.

**Marcel Proust**

## introduction

> A landscape also has the seductive power of all
> *pictures....*[2]

**Henri Lefebvre**

Although landscape and film are often seen as having been made for one
another, their affinity is far from straightforward. For example, early films

(c. 1895–1906) present something of a paradox in relation to landscape. Thus, whilst Tom Gunning has elucidated the significance of landscape with respect to the travel genre[3]—"one of the most popular and developed" forms of early cinema[4]—it is instructive to note that the prevailing conceptions of landscape and film could also be regarded as profoundly antinomical in the early years of filmmaking. In 1897, for instance, "The Showman" found no difficulty in asserting that "there is a want of beauty in animated photographs from the fact that they depend on the reproduction of street scenes and others in which moving objects predominate simple landscape subjects, which are perhaps the most beautiful of all, being quite out of the question."[5] The apparent tension between the movement inherent to animated photography and the historically and geographically specific picturesque notion of landscape is central to our present concerns. For Gunning, "The unique aspect of motion pictures, the representation of movement," not only "supplied a new way the world could be transformed into pictures," it also "transformed the nature of the picture" itself (1998, 30). By extension, therefore, it equally transformed the picturesque notion of landscape.

It has become something of a cliché to note that the very earliest animated photographs, taken in the late nineteenth century, typically sought "to capture the maximum intensity of urban life and its actions."[6] What moving pictures required, above all else, was *movement*. It is therefore no mere coincidence that what are frequently regarded as the first ever filmed images—Louis Le Prince's experimental shots of Leeds Bridge, taken in the autumn of 1888—featured the hustle and bustle of the city at "the busiest moment of the day." Accordingly, Stephen Barber suggests that Le Prince "selected that moment and site in order to saturate the image with the greatest possible accumulation of human movement" (2002, 18). However, that the view of Leeds Bridge was also the view from Le Prince's workshop, and that he had reputedly already filmed family scenes in his mother-in-law's garden in Roundhay, might suggest that the connection between film and movement was rather less a matter of active selection and more a fortuitous opportunity than Barber seeks to imply. Nevertheless, it is undoubtedly the case that the "disadjusted" rhythms of the modern city were particularly well suited to the requirements of motion photography.[7] This was especially evident at the outset of motion photography, when the camera itself remained immobile and editing techniques were yet to be developed.[8] In the absence of panning, tracking, stop-motion, continuity editing, and so on, motion photography merely produced a "living picture" or "animated photograph." Despite the force of "*the* founding myth of cinema,"[9] that an awe-struck audience saw a train *dart out of the screen* during the first public exhibition of the Lumière cinématographe in Paris in 1895,[10] the very earliest films quite simply failed to break out of the frame which continued to hold them securely as a picture.[11]

By situating the camera amidst "the greatest possible accumulation of human movement," early filmmakers often found the apparatus itself became a centre of attraction for the hustle and bustle of modern life. The appearance of sometimes sizeable crowds of onlookers in front of the camera quickly became a problem for many filmmakers, as the gathering multitudes finding their way into any number of early English films attest.[12] The problem was already well known in still photography:

> Gustave Doré was once in Vienna with his friend Dalloz, who intended to do photographic work in some of the picturesque streets. Of course, a great crowd of inquisitive idlers soon congregated, in spite of Doré's efforts to keep them off. The more he shouted and gesticulated the larger grew the crowd. At last he had a happy idea. He took off his coat and threw it on the ground, then with his cap in his hand and a piteous expression on his face, he began to beg a collection from the onlookers. The effect was marvellous; in the shortest possible time the crowd had disappeared, and Dalloz could photograph at his leisure in the deserted street.[13]

The simple problem of controlling what or who appeared in front of the lens might seem entirely separate from any tension between movement and landscape, especially when it is acknowledged that the same problem plagued *still* photography. Yet such a literal interpretation would be misleading. To illustrate as much, we have elected to focus not only on the question of movement in relation to film and other visual technologies,[14] but also on the virtual depth of the cinema screen.[15] The latter relates to the former more closely than is apparent at first sight, particularly because movement is a function not so much of passage, but of dimensionality, as the Cubists and Futurists knew so well.

Ruoff has recently remarked that "cinema remains a machine for constructing relations of space and time," and cinema's "vernacular relativity," to borrow an apposite phrase from Ian Christie (1994), turns out to be crucial to containing—though never quite resolving—the tensions between movement, depth, and landscape that have haunted film since its inception.[16] However, as we have begun to intimate, film did not emerge as a ready-made "space-and-time machine," nor was it a self-evidently suitable medium for engaging with the new forms of "vernacular relativity" ushered in by the late nineteenth-century advent of a strongly urbanized machine age. Starting out as little more than a device for securing "animated photographs," anima-photographers, as the contemporary English trade journals were wont to call them, had to grope their way toward the construction of the kind of cinematography that came to fruition in the first decade or so of the twentieth century. As improbable as it may seem, landscape played a central role in this transition from "animated photographs" to "film."

## vision in motion

> Displacement in place … has always been the "still-frame" for film as far as the landscape through which we walk is concerned.[17]

Paul Virilio

Don Mitchell's proposition that we need to consider "not just what landscape 'is' or 'means' but what it does, how it works as a cultural practice,"[18] has become central to a wealth of literature on landscape.[19] Drawing on insights derived from the tradition of landscape painting founded on the Quattrocento space of Renaissance art—particularly its deployment of linear perspective to produce "the effect of the real"[20]—a remarkably broad consensus of opinion has converged on the idea that landscape amounts to a representation of space that affords the subject a position of apparent mastery by aligning vision and truth; an alignment established by Brunelleschi's famous experiment of 1425. Thus, for Lefebvre, "The power of a landscape does not derive from the fact that it offers itself as a spectacle, but rather from the fact that, as mirror and mirage, it presents any susceptible viewer with an image, at once true and false, of a creative capacity which the subject (or Ego) is able, during a moment of marvellous self-deception, to claim as his own" (189).[21]

The significance of a certain configuration of landscape, in other words, resides in its capacity to effect a "practical appropriation of space"[22] by authorizing a sovereign view of the world as a world within reach: not merely "a picture of the world but the world conceived and grasped as picture."[23] As Anthony Easthope remarks, "This is Renaissance space, bourgeois space, undiscovered by the ancient world. It is a dimension in which the masculine ego can move as fast as thought, mastering nature as far as the eye can see."[24] Yet remaking the world as picture evolved gradually, in tandem with the advent of walking for pleasure and the acquired taste for Nature, particularly over the course of the eighteenth century.[25] The connection between the picturesque conception of landscape and the history of walking is important because the former was always configured for the appreciation of a *mobile* spectator. Whilst formal gardens were typically structured on the basis of a single axial view, picturesque gardens and landscapes were "more cinematic than pictorial; [they were] designed to be experienced in motion as a series of compositions dissolving into each other rather than as a static picture" (Solnit, 90). This constitutive motility has been frequently overlooked in static conceptions of the picturesque landscape, which often led to the misconception that animated photography was inevitably ill-suited to landscape subjects. Once one acknowledges the centrality of movement to the picturesque conception of landscape, one can appreciate why films taken from trains rapidly became a staple of early filmmaking. Accordingly, in Charles Urban's February 1905 film catalogue, descriptions of the "The Rocky Mountains, Canada" series of films make great play of their movement: not only of the passing landscape, but also of the speeding train itself. For example:

1098 ...PANORAMA OF THE KICKING HORSE CANYON

> A wonderful picture of majestic scenery as the train (from the front of which these photos were secured), speeds over the rails, around curves, over bridges and ledges cut into the rocky sides of the mountain, with the torrent below and the towering mountain peaks above, ever in view, and of constant changing aspect.

1218 ...WITH THE IMPERIAL EXPRESS ALONG THE COLUMBIA RIVER—ROCKY MOUNTAINS IN WINTER

> A raging mountain torrent runs parallel with the railway, and as at each curve another aspect of the panorama opens to view, the picture is one of the most interesting ever taken....[26]

For Heidegger, only when the world is grasped as a picture "is there any such thing as a 'position' of man." From that point on, "Man himself expressly takes up this position as one constituted by himself" (132). Yet it is precisely this positioning of the subject that is at stake in relation to a wide variety of visual media that came to fruition in the nineteenth century, particularly with respect to moving images, especially with regard to film. In every case, it is true to say that the positioning of the subject is redefined, and not at all undermined, by the various changes in visual technology.

Given that, as Gunning (1998, 31) observes, the otherwise heterogeneous visual technologies in question share the characteristic that "the view [they construct] cannot be exhausted from one viewpoint at a single moment," it is worth recounting Schivelbusch's classic thesis that such technologies actively foreshadowed the transformation of space and time soon to be wrought by revolutionary new transport technologies, such as the railway. "[W]hat the opening of major railroads provided in reality—the easy accessibility of distant places—was attempted in illusion, in the decades immediately preceding that opening, by the 'panoramic' and 'dioramic' shows and gadgets."[27] Compared to earlier, slower modes of transport, such as walking and riding, which maintained an intimate link between the physicality of the landscape through which the traveller passed and the bodily sensation of the traveller, rail travel promoted a form of seemingly disembodied movement that had more in common with waterway than land-based travel. With the railway, it is paradoxically the body at rest that moves, such that for all intents and purposes it could appear to be the landscape itself that travelled, rather than the passenger. Indeed, anxiety about the wholesale "annihilation of space" and the transmutation of sensuous travellers into disembodied parcels was a popular theme in Victorian England. For example, an article in an 1839 issue of the *Quarterly Review* feared that if railroads "were to be suddenly established all over England, the whole population of the country would…at once advance *en masse*…nearer to…their metropolis [i.e., London] by two-thirds of the time which now separates them from it" (quoted in Schivelbusch, 34).

The strange experience of travelling upon seemingly empty space without the sensation of travelling through a physical landscape enabled the world through the rail-carriage window to be seen as never before. It was seen not only as a *picturesque* landscape set back into the distance, but as a *panoramic* landscape that continuously unfolded before one's very eyes. The link between rail travel and the panorama is explicitly made in the 1865 observations of the Parisian journalist Jules Clarétie. "In a few hours, [the railroad] shows you all of France, and before your eyes it unrolls its infinite panorama, a vast succession of charming tableaux, of novel surprises. Of a landscape it shows you only the great outlines, being an artist versed in the ways of the masters. Don't ask it for details, but for the living whole. Then, after having charmed you thus with its painterly skills, it suddenly stops and quite simply lets you get off where you wanted to go."[28] So-called panoramic perception was characterized by "the tendency to see the discrete indiscriminately" (Schivelbusch, 61). For example, the original incarnation of the panorama in the late eighteenth century, which positioned the spectator at the centre of a 360° circular painting of a landscape, created "an image without borders" (Gunning, 1998, 31), anticipating the kind of "annihilation of space" soon to be routinely attributed to the railway.[29] Indeed, one of the chief novelties of the panorama was its apparent ability to disrupt erstwhile geographical and temporal certainties. It seemed to be capable of revealing sites and sights distant in time (such as historic battlefield scenes) as well as in space (exotic, far-flung corners of the earth), producing the sense of dislocation relayed, not without a certain knowing irony, in this report inspired by Barker and Burford's 1824 *Panorama of Pompeii.*

Panoramas are among the happiest contrivances for saving time and expense in this age of contrivances. What cost a couple of hundred pounds and half a year a century ago, now costs a shilling and a quarter of an hour.... The mountain or the sea, the classic vale or the ancient city, is transported to us on the wings of the wind.... We have seen Vesuvius in full roar and torrent, within a few hundred yards of a hackney-coach stand.... Constantinople, with its bearded and turbanned multitudes, quietly pitched beside a Christian thoroughfare.... Switzerland, with its lakes covered in sunsets, and mountains capped and robed in storms... stuck in a corner of a corner of London...and now Pompeii, reposing in its slumber of two thousand years, in the very buzz of the Strand.[30]

As well as ushering in the possibility of such temporal and spatial displacements (and reflexively engendering a blasé attitude to such unseemly disruptions in space and time), the panorama, despite comprising of a static image, also revolutionized the mobility of the observer. Oettermann proposes that the panorama was "the pictorial expression or 'symbolic form' of a specifically modern, bourgeois view of nature and the world" (6). Crary adds that the panorama, as a quintessentially urban attraction, grasped Nature for the metropolis: "The city dweller, whose political supremacy over the provinces is demonstrated many times in the course of the century, attempts to bring the countryside into town. In panoramas, the city opens out to landscape as it will do later, in subtler fashion, for the flâneurs."[31]

For Mitchell, the "sovereign eye" (or "sovereign I") produced by traditional landscape painting "is itself highly mobile."[32] This is a questionable point, despite the motility of the picturesque conception of landscape. It is true that, as Virilio notes, "The *veracity* of the work [of art]...depends, in part, on this solicitation of eye (and possibly body) movement in the witness who, in order to *sense* an object with maximum clarity, must accomplish an enormous number of tiny, rapid eye movements from one part of the object to another."[33] Yet at the same time, the position of the viewer of conventional landscape painting is, in accordance with the dictates of linear perspective, fixed and stabilized in relation to the vanishing point. Hence Mitchell is forced to conclude that viewers of landscape paintings "are themselves mobilized around the edge of the canvas, always outside, to be sure, but always controlling, in part through their legitimated mobility" (2000, 117). This overlooks the extent to which the look of the viewer presupposes the gaze of the Other; the way in which the linear perspective of Quattrocento space involved "a certain *dompte-regard*, a taming of the gaze."[34] By contrast, the role of the frame and the vanishing point in preserving the fixity, as opposed to the mobility, of the observer becomes particularly evident with the advent of the panorama, where the spectator becomes fully immersed in the represented scene.

Visitors to the panorama were situated on a central platform that offered the same vantage point as the one from which the circular painting was sketched. The viewing platform was accessed from below and fenced off, with three-dimensional "false terrain" situated between the platform and the two-dimensional landscape that was painted onto the circular wall of the rotunda. The viewer's angle of vision was truncated from above by a velum (an interior, umbrella-shaped roof), and there are reports of visitors feeling seasick because of "the relatively small diameter of the rotundas; observers adjusted their eyes to the illusion of distant vistas, and then when they walked around on the platform, it seemed as if they were wearing seven-league boots and covering vast distances with each step" (Oettermann, 59). The 360° curvature of the panorama clearly departed from the tenets of centred linear perspective, offering an infinite number of viewing positions. This democratization of perspective "broke with the localized point of view of perspective painting or the camera obscura, allowing the spectator an ambulatory ubiquity. One was compelled at the least to turn one's head (and eyes) to see the entire work" (Crary, 113). Although elements of continuity with earlier forms of representation and spectacle are sometimes mooted—in claims, for instance, that the panorama was comparable with Baroque stage design—its discontinuity with all earlier instances of *trompe l'oeil* is paramount. Its democratization of spectatorship and the new kind of mobile vision it entailed legitimized a thoroughly bourgeois worldview—thereby accomplishing only the modification, and hence the preservation, of the positioning of the subject. In this regard, it is unsurprising that Michel Foucault should reflect on whether Jeremy Bentham, in proposing his ill-fated design for the Panopticon ("all-seeing") prison, was "aware of the Panoramas that Barker was constructing at exactly the same period."[35] The panorama could offer an unprecedented illusion of reality only by fully enclosing the spectator within the apparatus itself.[36]

The panorama's unleashing of a mobile form of vision is especially evident in its principal offshoot: the extended, linear, or moving panorama. This highly popular attraction invariably involved a simulated journey, positioning the spectator in a stationary location and producing the sensation of movement by the use of moving canvases fitted between rollers to re-create "a stretch of landscape as it might appear to a traveller from a moving post coach, railroad carriage, or river steamboat" (Oettermann, 63). One of the most celebrated examples was John Banvard's *Mississippi from the Mouth of the Missouri to New Orleans*, launched in Louisville, Kentucky, in 1848. The panorama originally comprised 29 scenes and measured around 400 metres (1,312 feet). It was later extended to no fewer than 67 scenes. As well as reversing the relative movements of traveller and landscape found in actual travel, the moving panorama also reversed the effect achieved by the circular panorama. For whilst restricting the ambulatory autonomy of the spectator might at first sight appear to be a retrograde step, the moving panorama nevertheless succeeded in dramatizing the mobility of vision already presupposed by the circular panorama, simultaneously constraining *and* accentuating it. The two forms might be seen as polar opposites, positioned at either end of the same scale, were it not for the fact that the moving panorama effectively relinquished the novel perspective of the circular panorama. Their similarity is pointed up by the fact that the moving panorama provided a moving image in the most limited of senses: it achieved a movement *of* the image, not a movement *in* the image. This contrasts markedly with the mutability of the image in the various devices dedicated to the production of "transforming views"—most notably Louis-Jacques-Mandé Daguerre's diorama but also the magic-lantern slide projector, the phantasmagoria, paper animation, and so on. Time-lapse was the diorama's *raison d'être*, in contrast to what one might call the "space-lapse" of the panorama. In the case of the diorama, "The illusion of reality was forcefully conveyed through the actual presence of contrasts, change, movement—techniques which...drew on the codes of landscape art training."[37] Such was the accomplishment of the diorama that an English girl reputedly remarked to Daguerre: "Here is an extraordinary mixture of art and nature producing the most astonishing effect, so that one cannot decide where nature ceases and art begins"; to which he replied: "My only aim was to provide the most complete illusion: I wanted to rob nature, and therefore had to become a thief" (quoted in Green, 97).

The diorama earned particular renown from its ability to simulate the passage between night and day by applying ever-changing lighting effects to a landscape rendered in two different forms on either side of a translucent canvas. In his *Description of the Techniques of Diorama Painting and Lighting*, Daguerre writes: "Only two effects were actually painted on—day on the front of the canvas, night on the back, and one could only shift from one to the other by means of a series of complicated combinations of media the light had to pass through. But these produced an infinite number of additional effects similar to those Nature offers in its course from morning to night and vice versa" (Virilio, 1994, 41). If this "double effect" diorama did much to ensure the longevity of this spectacle, its sheer scale was the principal attraction when its initially simpler form was first unveiled by Daguerre in the early 1820s. Indeed, its scale allowed Daguerre to borrow shrewdly from the nomenclature of the panorama, although the attractions had little else in common. "In the word *panorama*, 'pan' is the constituent that creates the idea of totality, the total vision of given reality dependent on a circular horizon. Yet the diorama, because it was flat and like a painting...did not contain either the same logic or, more importantly, the same aim. Its concern was to incorporate the passage of time and movement into a representation."[38]

As a stage spectacle, the diorama's accomplishment of the illusion of movement *within* the image came at the cost of a return to centred perspective—implying a single ideal viewing position, with all other vantage points being subject to varying degrees of distortion. Like the moving panorama, moreover, it relied on "the incorporation of an *immobile* observer into a mechanical apparatus and a subjection to a predesigned temporal unfolding of optical experience" (Crary, 112–113). In fact, the passage from night to day rendered *within* a given landscape by the diorama, and the journey *along* a stretch of landscape presented in the moving panorama, both accord to the same logic. Both are primitive "movement-images."[39] In the moving panorama, the simulation of movement across space is marked by the passage of time; in the diorama, the simulated passage of time produces the illusion of movement.

The nature of this illusory movement becomes most apparent in relation to its "reconstitution" via a series of still images in such optical devices as the Thaumatrope, Phenakistiscope, Zoëtrope, Praxinoscope—and, of course, film. Yet Bergson's convenient labelling of this problem as the "cinematographic illusion" risks hiding its presence in earlier, seemingly quite separate and disparate, visual technologies.[40] Indeed, Deleuze's distillation of Bergson's "first thesis" on movement—"movement is distinct from the space covered"—directly lends itself to an appreciation of the illusory movement enacted in a variety of kinaesthetic attractions (simulated journeys, phantom rides, etc.) from the moving panorama onwards (Deleuze, 1). In fact, it is no surprise to find the imaginary journey a much-favoured narrative device of the lanternist, particularly given the centrality of the time-honoured tradition of storytelling to the lanternists' art. The weaving of stories by conjuring images held audiences in thrall, and the centrality of the journey to storytelling since time immemorial gave it an obvious place within the lanternists' repertoire.[41] In the most obvious context of the illustrated travel lecture, following an itinerary became a well-established means of effecting a coordination of space and time. Slides of elsewhere represented "a source of wonderment to nineteenth-century audiences," particularly with the advent of photographic slides in the 1840s: "audiences new to photographic slide-shows found it thrilling to move quickly from country to country," sometimes journeying around the world in the course of a single evening.[42]

The narrative tradition of the lantern did not, however, make it inevitable that film would conform to the same purpose when it eventually arrived on the scene, or even that it would find a role at all. In fact, the aesthetic, commercial, technical, and even the moral character of animated photography was widely regarded as questionable, especially when compared to the established quality and solid tradition of still photography and lanternism.[43] Nevertheless, the longstanding association of the magic lantern with moving images—from the metamorphosing spectres of the phantasmagoria in the 1780s, to the ingenious use of dissolves and specialist slides that made complex moving images an established fact by the 1860s—meant that animated photography was gradually introduced into preexisting formats.[44] This is well illustrated in relation to the origins of travel cinema (Musser, 1984). However, rather than suggesting its own potential as a narrative medium, the moving images of film were initially regarded as interchangeable with slides, even where they explicitly contained a narrative element of their own. Short film sequences were invariably subordinated to the narrative concerns of the travel lecturer—a pattern that repeats itself in a variety of other contexts. Nevertheless, if numerous other narrative devices pioneered by the lanternists would later be taken up by filmmakers—the staging of scenes, the sequencing of images for dramatic effect, and techniques such as close-ups, point-of-view shots, and even reaction shots—the particular conceit of the simulated journey did offer one of the most suggestive initial uses for film.[45]

## depth of vision

> The most difficult problem [for art] was perfect relief, deep perspectives carried to the most complete illusion.

### Antoine Wiertz, 1870 (quoted in Benjamin, 530)

In 2003, Rodney Graham exhibited what might best be termed a "retrospective invention" at the University of British Columbia. Christening his creation the *Millennial Time Machine*, the artist commented: "A moving, camera obscura image in the interior of a darkened, itinerant, 19th century horse-drawn carriage would have constituted a pre-figuration of the cinema, had such a thing existed. To realize this 'philosophical toy' in a post-cinema age is to fabricate a kind of time machine in which the spectators, looking forward, may see backwards and upside-down, that which is forever receding behind them."[46]

Curiously enough, one of the first suggested uses of animated photography occurred in a preliminary patent application for a "*Time Machine*" lodged by Robert W. Paul in London in 1895.[47] The popular success of H. G. Wells's "weird romance [*The Time Machine*] had suggested an entertainment to [Paul], of which animated photographs formed an essential part."[48] He intended to mount a "novel form of exhibition whereby the spectators have presented to their view scenes which are supposed to occur in the future or past, while they are given the sensation of voyaging upon a machine through time" (Patent Number 19984, lodged 24 October 1895).[49]

The plan was to project moving photographic images—a technological feat yet to be accomplished—onto a screen that would serve as the "window" of the Time Machine. Despite numerous elaborate trappings, the projection of moving photographs lay at the heart of this conception, as its abandonment in the wake of the public début of the Lumière Cinématographe clearly reveals. However, Paul's seemingly prescient conception of film as an operation on time is ultimately deceptive. Anticipating the way in which short sequences of animated photography would initially be regarded as interchangeable with lantern slides, Paul intended to treat his projected animated photographs not as a complete sequence of real-time living pictures, and still less as a space-time unto itself, but as a succession of animated photographs and slides. Paul's Time Machine apparently proposed a hybridization of the moving panorama with animated photography, making it a precursor to subsequent simulated rides employing film to impart a sensation of motion—most notably "Hale's Tours of the World," which became extremely popular in the United States in the mid-1900s. However, this appearance is somewhat deceptive.

According to his patent application, Paul intended to achieve the effect of time travel by seating the audience on a rocking platform whilst rapid "alternations of darkness and dim light" would feign the swift passage of night and day (a contrivance borrowed from Wells's novel). The duration of this lighting effect would signify the elapse of "a certain number of centuries," whereupon "the mechanism [i.e., the moving platform] may be slowed and a pause made at a given epoch," such that the spectators might "have presented to their view scenes which are supposed to occur in the future or past." Clearly, the sensation of time *travel* was to be achieved through media *other than film*: moving platforms, gusts of air, and flickering lights. Animated photographs of scenes and views would only be shown once the passengers were at rest. Specifically, there would be "a number of powerful lanterns, throwing the respective portions of the picture, which may be composed of, (1) A hypothetical landscape, containing also a representation of the inanimate objects in the scene. (2) A slide, or slides,...of objects such as a navigable balloon etc., which is required to traverse the scene. (3) Slides or films, representing in successive instantaneous photographs...the living persons or creatures in their natural motions" (i.e., "made up characters performing on a stage, with or without a suitable background blending with the main landscape"). Paul's vision of a cinematic time machine was firmly rooted in the tradition of the magic lantern with its superimposition of multiple images and animated slides. Like a living tableau, movement is restricted to persons and creatures within an essentially immobile scene. As if to underscore this essential stasis, the patent states that Paul prefers "to arrange the film to travel intermittently instead of continuously and to cut off the light only during the rapid displacement of the film as one picture succeeds another, as by this means less light is wasted than in the case when the light is cut off the greater portion of the time, as in the ordinary kinetoscope mechanism."

Just as Paul's Time Machine grinds to a halt, however, the patent proposes to heighten the effect of time travel by allowing the spectators to alight from the platform at certain locations and—borrowing from the tradition of the panorama or waxworks—"be conducted through grounds or buildings arranged to represent exactly one of the epochs through which the traveller is supposed to be travelling." By implication, Paul considers the scenes and views to be both temporally and spatially retarded: one cannot go into them; one can only scan their surface. With regard to the slides that represent those vehicles required to traverse the scene (2 above), the patent notes that they may only be "traversed horizontally or vertically," in the fashion of panoramic and dioramic magic-lantern slides. So, although animated (a portion of the image moves) and dated ("the future," "the past"), one can only infer that Paul's films would be both depthless and timeless. Its innovative technological basis notwithstanding, Paul's proposal was considerably less novel than appearances first suggest. Paul's Time Machine was not, in fact, a *time* machine at all.

A less literal but ultimately more apt appreciation of film's potential in this regard is captured by another film pioneer, Wordsworth Donisthorpe. In the context of his travel book, *Down the Stream of Civilization*, Donisthorpe wrote: "Shall we never be able to glide back *up* the stream of Time, and peep into the old home, and gaze on the old faces? Perhaps when the phonograph and the kinesigraph [Donisthorpe's own patented movie-machine] are perfected, and some future worker has solved the problem of colour-photography, our descendants will be able to deceive themselves with something very like it: but it will be but a barren husk, a soulless phantasm and nothing more. 'O for the touch of a vanished hand, and the sound of a voice that is still!'"[50] If, as Herbert (with Heard) suggests, this "melancholy reflection on the fact that recorded image and sound are no substitute for lost realities" is simultaneously "an anticipation of home movies," at a more basic level it signals the significance of the *indexical* aspect of mechanical forms of reproduction (Herbert, 90). That the photographic effect of the real carried over from still to animated photography is evident in the comparability of their respective initial receptions. However, there are also significant differences between the two, which we shall eventually track down in relation to the persistence of the journey motif.

Schivelbusch proposes that photography recovered what the railroad had seemingly destroyed in abstracting from the detail to give, like the panorama, a picture of the whole: "the intensive experience of the sensuous world, terminated by the industrial revolution, underwent a resurrection in the new institution of photography. Since immediacy, close-ups and foreground had been lost in reality, they appeared particularly attractive in the new medium" (63). According to Buddemeier, fascination with photography was aroused "not by the taking of any specific object, but by the way in which any random object could be made to appear on the photographic plate. This was something of such unheard-of novelty that the photographer was delighted by each and every shot he took, and it awakened unknown and overwhelming emotions in him. Tiny, until then unnoticed details are stressed continuously: paving stones, scattered leaves, the shape of a branch, the traces of rain on a wall."[51]

Likewise, the reception of film was marked not by astonishment at seeing a moving image, which was already commonplace across a variety of media, but by the way in which movement could be seen to inhabit the *detail* of the image: waves, leaves, grass, dust. As late as 1905, for instance, *The Optical Lantern and Cinematograph Journal* could casually note, "Sea pictures have always been the most popular of animated subjects."[52] But if the realism of subjects such as seascapes continued to exert a fascination in some circles, the move to hyperrealism suggested by Paul's proleptic Time Machine project was already underway. The rush to add animated photography to established attractions can be read as either an expression of faith in the new technology or simply a way of exploiting its potential while it lasted—since it was seen as "a sensation of the moment" by many.[53] Whilst animated photography found a role as an occasional substitute for slides in lantern shows or a music hall turn amongst others, its possibilities as an attraction akin to the panorama was actively embraced. The advent of still photography witnessed numerous attempts to construct photographic panoramas, which were invariably dogged by technical problems. The fact that photographic plates and prints "could not be altered or retouched to adjust their perspective" typically resulted in "jarring dissonances of perspective at the seams" (Oettermann, 83).

The panoramic projection of photographic lantern slides, introduced in 1894 by Charles A. Chase's Stereopticon-Cyclorama and the Lumières' Photorama, seemed to offer a more promising alternative. However, the fact that neither took off as a commercial entertainment points to a profound tension in late nineteenth-century visual culture. If the panorama and animated photography appear complementary with respect to the cultivation of a total simulation, they nevertheless pull in opposite directions. Although both turn away from the Ideal toward the vernacular, panoramic perception tends toward totalisation, whilst photography returns to the particular. Nonetheless, these early attempts to fuse animated photography and panoramic perception are precursors of one of the most successful early uses of film: the simulated railway journeys of Hale's Tours.

A direct link between the panorama and photography is found in Raoul Grimoin-Sanson's 1897 patent for the Cosmorama, which did little more than replicate Chase's Stereopticon-Cyclorama and the Lumières' Photorama, except that it simulated a hot-air balloon ride. By the time of the

Paris Exposition of 1900, however, Grimoin-Sanson had ambitiously sub-stituted film for slide projection, renaming his attraction the Cinéorama or Cinécosmorama. Unsurprisingly, it was dogged by operational prob-lems, although the myth persists that it was closed down by the authori-ties who judged it a fire risk.[54] The spectacular failure of this cinematic variant of the moving panorama at the Paris Exposition, directly alongside such accomplished moving panoramas as the sea voyage enacted by the Marèorama and the Trans-Siberian [Railway] Panorama,[55] marked the end of an era. As Comment remarks, "the panorama's resurgence in 1900 can be likened to the last gasp of a dying man. The cinema was already begin-ning to work its magic" (75). If this risks overstating the case, implying that animated photography found a place already staked out in advance, it nonetheless draws attention to the aspect of film that was exploited most successfully in Hale's Tours: its hyperrealism.

Although the attraction is generally attributed to George C. Hale, a retired Kansas City fire chief, it actually originated with William J. Keefe. After providing financial backing, Hale and Judge Fred W. Gifford bought the rights to the system before its commercial launch at the 1904 Loui-siana Purchase Exposition in St. Louis.[56] Hale's Tours were, in Fielding's estimation, "the first permanent, ultrarealistic cinema attraction"[57]—though given the status of both photography and film as forms of "secular magic,"[58] the attraction might be better regarded as *hyperrealistic.*[59] Whilst there are evident similarities between Paul's Time Machine and Hale's Tours, their differences also deserve underscoring (Doel and Clarke, 2002). Most notable in this regard is the production of a sensation of move-ment whilst at rest accomplished by the latter, which is conspicuous by its absence in Paul's conception. Whilst Hale's Tours can hardly lay claim to the discovery of this effect—which Virilio (1989, 110) aptly describes as the invention of "the first static vehicle"—the attraction managed to harness it to considerable acclaim over a relatively short period, c. 1905–1907. Life-size moving images were projected onto a screen at the front of a mocked-up train, using rear-projection to hide the projector from view. Mechanisms swayed the carriage and provided sounds of a mov-ing train.[60] The theatre was often done up as a railway station, staffed by guards, and conductors lectured on points of scenic interest (Figure 9.1). Although the attraction sometimes included discontinuous or incongru-ous elements—abrupt changes of location; comic or romantic interludes (e.g., the difficulty of dressing on a moving train or a kiss in the tunnel); cityscapes or natural features filmed from a static point of view—its cen-tral feature was undoubtedly the simulation of a real train ride, using a continuous take filmed from the front (or occasionally from the back) of a moving train.

At its peak, there were around 500 Hale's Tours operatives in the United States alone, although by 1906 their popularity was on the wane,

Figure 9.1

Hale's Tours.

with many operators discarding the railway trappings and transforming themselves into nickelodeons. The export of Hale's Tours to Europe prolonged their success, and a 1906 report from England notably echoes the sense of astoundment previously recorded for the panorama: "In 'Hale's Tours' we have one of the cleverest optical illusions of modern times, and the scheme of taking a company by apparent travel through all the countries of the world, has taken the public fancy and brought to the promoters a phenomenal success.... The sensation of the actual travel is made intensely realistic by the various means provided.... Indeed, as we step out of the car, with our auditory and visual faculties still vibrating, it seems a contradiction of nature to find ourselves still in Oxford Street, London."[61] The heightened realism of the "stationary trip," granted by mounting the ciné camera on the moving platform of the train (Figure 9.2), was unlike anything provided by such apparent antecedents as the moving panorama. The particular novelty of Hale's Tours lay in their capacity to be experienced as a *sensation* and to discombobulate the spectators' faculties. To this extent, though, Hale's Tours merely heightened an effect *auto-*

**Figure 9.2**

Cameraman Billy Bitzer taking a shot from the front of a train.

*matically* ensuing from the mounting of the film camera onto a moving platform. What Charles Musser terms the "spectator as passenger convention" thus assured such phantom rides a significant degree of popularity, quite independently of the trappings offered by Hale's Tours.[62]

It was not, in fact, a railway engine but the perennially unlikely moving platform provided by a gondola from which the mobile camera was first reputedly deployed. Its potential was first spotted in 1896, by the Lumière cameraman, Eugène Promio, whom—in conversation with Coissac some 25 years later[63]—recalled his reasoning at the time: "If the immobile camera allowed the reproduction of moving objects, then perhaps one could reverse the proposition and film immobile objects with a moving camera."[64] The mobile camera, in other words, offered an ideal means of ensuring that animated photography captured a suitably animated world. Hence the fact that panoramic films burgeoned once the technique had proved successful. As Gunning notes, it was the *speed* of movement that most frequently received emphasis: "The terms which early film catalogues use to make these panoramic travel films attractive to exhibitors contrast sharply with the experience of absorption in the contemplation of nature associated with a traditional landscape painting (although they may be related to the romantic sublime landscape which pictures nature as an overwhelming force). Again and again descriptions of panoramic travel films emphasize that the camera is not only moving, but moving at a high rate of speed" (Gunning, 1998, 32).

Whilst the *content* of such films was undeniably important—tapping into the well-established picturesque conception of landscape and the lure of the exotic, soon to be captured by amateur as well as professional filmmakers[65]—the particularity of their *form* grants them an additional, and arguably far greater, significance. The movement of the mobile camera gave one of the first suggestions of the virtual depth of film. It is, by now, well established that the very earliest films were typically treated as tightly framed animated pictures (Burch, 1990), as wholly enclosed living tableaux, which aimed "to present the totality of an action unfolding in an homogeneous space."[66] This is primarily true of nonactuality films, where the technical requirements of filming outdoor stage sets and the reliance on conventions from histrionic acting and still photography typically encouraged the use of frontal presentation to an immobile camera adopting a centred viewing position: "The shift from a cinema of frontal presentation to a cinema of articulated depth" and "the installation of perspective in the cinema—the fulfilment of its 'three-dimensional vocation'—was not immediate and obvious…but was striven for and awkward, producing discontinuity in the spatial worlds early cinema offered spectators" (Lant, 53, 69). The stark discontinuity between the flat, frontal presentation of most early fiction films, and the way in which the mobile camera subsequently came "to recreate the actual penetration of space that travelling involves," is especially significant: not least because "the moving camera creates a sort of stereoscopic illusion as the varied rates of apparent movement of objects at different distances within the visual field provide another depth cue" (Gunning, 1998, 32).

The significance of the depth cues provided by the parallax effect of the moving camera demands explicit consideration in the light of Crary's (1990) thesis that vision underwent a profound transformation in the early decades of the nineteenth century. This transformation involved the undermining of the traditional organization of vision, rooted in geometrical optics and founded on the alignment of truth and vision for a detached Cartesian subject,[67] by a process of modernization that mobilized physiological optics and in so doing reconfigured the observer as "a bundle of neurological responses."[68] According to Crary,

> What takes place from around 1810 to 1840 is an uprooting of vision from the stable and fixed relations incarnated in the camera obscura…. In a sense, what occurs is a new valuation of visual experience: it is given an unprecedented mobility and exchangeability; abstracted from any founding site or referent…. Thus certain forms of visual experience usually uncritically categorized as 'realism' are in fact bound up in *non-veridical* theories of vision that effectively annihilate a real world. Visual experience in the nineteenth century, despite all the attempts to authenticate and naturalize it, no longer has anything like the apodictic claims of the camera obscura to establish its truth. (14)

Much of this transformation was underpinned by research on perception which aimed to "unpacked the visual at the level of nervous response," and was associated with new technologies that "also destabilized the viewing subject by introducing spatial and temporal complexity into the process of producing images" (Crang, 19). Indeed, "A crucial feature of these optical devices of the 1830s and 1840s is the undisguised nature of their operational structure and the form of subjection they entail. Even though they produce access to 'the real,' they make no claim that the real is anything other than a mechanical reproduction" (Crary, 132). For instance, optical devices capable of generating an impression of movement from the rapid succession of still images—such as the Thaumatrope, Phenakistiscope, Zoëtrope, and Praxinoscope—came into vogue on the back of a flurry of research activity, dating from the 1830s, into certain puzzling aspects of perception: optical illusions, retinal afterimages, and the so-called persistence of vision. It is not difficult to see such devices as exemplary precursors to film: not merely because their capacity to project moving images was rapidly developed and soon accomplished (by Emile Reynaud in the 1880s) but also because of their amenability, in principle at least, to the projection of moving *photographic* images.[69] Nonetheless, it was the stereoscope—originating from research into binocular vision in the 1820s and 1830s, and commercialized as a popular pastime in the 1850s—that did most to usher in a truly modern mode of observation. The absolute novelty of the stereoscope lay in its ability to render an impression of solidity. No previous visual technique or apparatus was able to represent faithfully a proximate solid (stereo) object. The stereoscope "aimed to simulate the actual presence of a physical object or scene, not to discover another way to exhibit a print or drawing" (Crary, 122). Its significance is obliquely signalled in the popularity of phantom rides: "Early film catalogues frequently stressed the stereoscopic nature of their moving panorama films" (Gunning, 1998, 32).

Sir Charles Wheatstone's reflecting stereoscope of 1838, and its adaptation into the more familiar lenticular stereoscope by Sir David Brewster (which achieved popularity after gaining the patronage of Queen Victoria at the Great Exhibition of 1851), served to make vision *tactile*: "[T]he desired effect of the stereoscope was not simply likeness, but immediate, apparent *tangibility*.... No other form of representation in the nineteenth century had so conflated the real with the optical" (Crary, 123–124). Hence the fascination that it exerted. Fascination ensues when "what you see, even though from a distance, seems to touch you with a grasping contact, when the matter of seeing is a sort of touch, when seeing is a *contact* at a distance."[70] Thus, the stereoscope's production of an intense "reality effect" dispensed entirely with linear perspective. For the "fundamental organization of the stereoscopic image is *planar*. We perceive individual elements as flat, cutout forms arrayed either nearer or further from us. But the experience of space between these objects (planes) is not one of gradual and predictable recession; rather, there is a vertiginous uncertainty about the distance separating forms" (Crary, 125). In short, the stereoscope was "inherently *obscene*, in the most literal sense. It shattered the *scenic* relationship between viewer and object that was intrinsic to the fundamentally theatrical setup of the camera obscura" (127) and the picturesque conception of landscape. If the stereoscope was dedicated to the problem of depth, this problem was intimately related to the problem of time. Their relationship was at the source of a strong cultural current, which gathered its full force with the publication of Darwin's *Origin of Species* in 1859. It is no accident that Wells's novel should have adopted the narrative device it did. "Since evolutionary processes proceed in deep time," as Williams puts it, "the narrator of *The Time Machine* must find a way to move across millions of years."[71] Edwin A. Abbot's *Flatland*,[72] published in 1884—at once a moral satire and an introduction to the notion of the fourth dimension—had already raised similar issues, which were later given a mystical spin in the "noumenal psychology" of P. D. Ouspensky (in works such as the *Tertium Organum*, first published in Russian in 1911, and *The Psychology of Man's Possible Evolution*, published posthumously in 1950).[73] Freud's discovery of the unconscious, which explicitly leaned on Darwin, entertained the suggestion that the time of the ego is distinct from unconscious time, the latter of which equates to the time of the species.[74] The stereoscope, with its reliance on two nonidentical images captured *simultaneously*, dramatized this relationship between time and depth. It introduces to the eye the possibility of following any number of trajectories over an indeterminate time period. "Our eyes follow a choppy and erratic path into its depth:...an assemblage of local zones of three-dimensionality, zones imbued with a hallucinatory clarity, but which when taken together never coalesce into a homogeneous field" (Crary, 126). More precisely, the trajectories taken and the time periods involved are determined *by the observer*, anticipating Boltzmann's identification of "*the present* with the presence of a *living* observer at a certain place and time...as if, apart from 'mortals,' time had no specific duration, no 'quantity' and 'quality' distinguishing Before from After."[75] In destroying the spatial and temporal integrity of the point of view of a detached Cartesian observer, therefore, the stereoscope prefigures one of the most important aspects of film: its vernacular relativity.

## landscape into screenscape

> With the cinema, it is the world which becomes its own
> image, and not an image which becomes world.
>
> **Deleuze (57)**

In an 1859 article on "The Stereoscope and the Stereograph," Oliver Wendell Holmes begins with the following reflection: "Democritus of Abdera, commonly known as the Laughing Philosopher,...believed and taught that all bodies were continually throwing off certain images like themselves, which subtle emanations, striking on our bodily organs, gave rise to our sensations. Epicurus borrowed the idea from him, and incorporated it into the famous system, of which Lucretius has given us the most popular version.... Forms, effigies, membranes, or *films* are the nearest representatives of the terms applied to these effluences."[76] On this account, light itself cannot be seen, but the "evanescent films" cast off by objects bathed in light "may be seen...by the consciousness behind the eye in the ordinary act of vision." Accordingly, "Under the action of light...a body makes its superficial aspect potentially present at a distance." Or, as Lacan puts it, "That which is light looks at me."[77] Hence his invagination of panoramic perception: "I see only from one point, but in my existence I am looked at from all sides."[78] Vision entails not only that I can see, but that I can be seen, from innumerable points of view from which I can never see and which belong to the Other. "[I]n the scopic field, the gaze is outside, I am looked at" (1977a, 106). Thus, as Easthope clarifies: "To 'see the world' comes within the dominion of the conscious I, the imaginary;

to 'be the object of the gaze' represents the operation of the unconscious, the domain of the symbolic on which I depend but which I can never lay claim to."[79] Lacan's account of vision and subjectivity is developed with particular reference to Quattrocento space, and centres on the way in which the apparent veracity of perspectival representation maximizes the look of the sovereign individual whilst minimizing the effect of the gaze of the Other. In this regard, the subject's attempt to tame the gaze of the Other occasions a desire in the subject: "*The* objet a *in the field of the visible is the gaze*" (1977a, 105). In other words, vision institutes a lack between the look of the subject and the gaze of the Other that cannot be made good. "The subject is presented as other than he is, and what one shows him is not what he wishes to see" (1977b, 104).

As we have already seen, however, the introduction of moving pictures and mobile spectators renders this particular configuration of subjectivity infinitely more complex, ultimately threatening to destabilize if. We have also dwelt at length on the way in which a coordination of space and time is effected by the notion of the journey and by narrative, which generalizes and preserves the same basic coordination. This, as Heath's classic account of the "narrative space" of cinema suggests, also amounted to one of the solutions to the problem of coordinating space and time posed by film, and quickly coalesced into the dominant regime of spatio-temporal exposition.[80] Although early filmmakers experimented with and adopted a variety of contradictory ways of handling film, the so-called cinema of attractions slowly gave way to classic realist cinema.[81] The tension between the perspectival tradition of Quattrocento space enshrined in the individual photographic frame (which achieves a central, fixed, apparently all-embracing point of view), and the movement inherent to the medium of film (which constantly threatens to undermine that fixity), could be contained by the advent of continuity editing and the unfolding of a narrative plot. Heath refers to the various practices devised to convert *seen* into *scene*, in a manner which "contains the mobility that could threaten the clarity of vision" by constantly recentring the observer's point of view (36). Despite the incompatibility of their respective derivations, Heath's narrative space clearly resonates with Deleuze's movement-image, where "the identification of movement with action assures the continuous unfolding of adjacent spaces."[82] The introduction of such techniques as point-of-view shots and continuity editing were, however, initially an uncomfortable, seemingly unnatural, experience; at least according to the response of the Sheffield-based filmmaker, Cecil Hepworth, to his own seminal 1905 film, *Rescued by Rover*.

*Rescued by Rover* follows a dog as it pursues a kidnapper to her hide-out, returns home to summon help, and then makes its way back to the hide-out to precipitate a rescue (Figure 9.3). It served as a precursor to many subsequent chase-and-rescue films featuring animals. Barr characterizes

Figure 9.3

Cecil Hepworth, *Rescued by Rover* (1905). Cinémathèque québécoise collection.

it as "a precocious model of the cinematic system," and it undoubtedly made a significant contribution to the creation of a coherent filmic space-time through continuity editing.[83] Its systematic sense of visual organization anticipates many of the later hallmarks of narrative cinema, although there is no parallel action, and the camera remains almost totally immobile for the duration of each shot. Yet although *Rescued by Rover* quickly became a classic, Hepworth unequivocally turned his back on the techniques it pioneered: "Smoothness in a film is important and should be preserved except when for some special effect a 'snap' is preferred. The 'unities' and 'verities' should always be observed, to which I should add the 'orienties.' Only the direst need will form an excuse for lifting an audience up by the scruff of the neck and carrying it round to the other side, just because you suddenly want to photograph something from the south when the previous scene has been taken from the north."[84] It has been a constant source of disbelief amongst film historians that Hepworth should have produced a film so advanced so early, only to reject it in favour of what Barry regarded as a singularly exasperating directorial failing: "the one, common in England, of using the screen as though it were a stage with exits left and right, the actors free to move only across a circumscribed oblong area, with a low skyline and the movements all parallel to the plane of the screen, not, as they should be, for the sake of depth illusion, at angles to it."[85] Yet Hepworth's retreat from continuity editing might be interpreted not as an affront to what should be, but as a peculiarly English attempt at the restitution of the inviolability of the audience's point of view. If the techniques pioneered (only to be rejected) by Hepworth are seen as according to the kind of vernacular relativity already apparent in the modernization of vision effected by other visual technologies, it is tempting to speculate that an intrinsic abhorrence at the mutilation of space and time might have been heightened by the centrality of landscape painting to English national identity (Daniels, 1993).[86]

It is well known that although English filmmaking initially figured amongst the most technically accomplished in the world, the thriving incunabula of a national film industry spectacularly failed to flourish. As Barr puts it, "all the obvious rival countries to Britain managed to produce at least one set or strain of films whose national character was distinctive and attractive enough to make a strong, lasting impact, abroad as well as at home. When America came to dominate the world market, it continued to import films from Europe and to learn lessons from European countries, and often to sign up their directors, like Lubitsch and Murnau from Germany and Sjöström from Sweden. No British film of this time made any significant impact, nor was any British film-maker head-hunted by Hollywood" (5). Many reasons lie behind the fact that Britain, a leading producer and exporter of films in the period 1896 to 1907, was not part of the massive world-wide growth in production in the early 1910s. The ambivalence, and often distaste, of cultural intermediaries such as journalists and scholars undoubtedly played a significant role. The ambiguity of film in relation to the solid English tradition of empiricism partly explains this cultural ambivalence,[87] whilst the rigidity of the English class system also ensured a struggle over film—as the interminable debates in the trade journals over the need to promote its edifying potential as against its slap-stick reality attest.[88] In conclusion, then, one might venture the hypothesis that the significance of the landscape tradition in England, and its centrality to national identity, served as a particularly important backdrop to the decline of the English film industry. It heightened an underlying fear that, with the advent of screenscapes at the dawn of the twentieth century, the picturesque conception of landscape would be left on the world's cutting-room floor.

### notes

1. We acknowledge the support of the Arts and Humanities Research Board (Award No. B/SG/AN2054/APN10258), which enabled archival work at the British Film Institute/National Film and Television Archive; and thank Andrew M. Butler, Stephen Herbert, and James Kneale for helpful suggestions.

2. H. Lefebvre, *The Production of Space* (Oxford: Blackwell, 1991), 189; hereafter cited in text.

3. T. Gunning, "'The World within Reach': Travel Images without Borders," in *Travel Culture: Essays on What Makes Us Go*, ed. C. T. Williams (Westport, CT: Praeger, 1998), 24–37; hereafter cited in text.

4. C. Musser, "The Travel Genre in 1903–1904: Moving Towards Fictional Narrative," *Iris* 2, no. 1 (1984): 47–60; hereafter cited in text.

5. *The Optical Magic Lantern Journal and Photographic Enlarger* 8, no. 97 (June 1897): 105.

6. S. Barber, *Projected Cities* (London: Reaktion Books, 2002), 17; hereafter cited in text.

7. L. Charney and V. Schwartz, eds., *Cinema and the Invention of Modern Life* (Berkeley: University of California Press, 1995); N. Verhoeff and E. Warth, "Rhetoric of Space: Cityscape/Landscape," *Historical Journal of Film, Radio and Television* 22, no. 3 (2002): 245–251.

8. M. A. Doel and D. B. Clarke, "An Invention without a Future, a Solution without a Problem: Motor Pirates, Time Machines, and Drunkenness on the Screen," in *Lost in Space: Geographies of Science Fiction*, eds. R. M. Kitchin and J. Kneale (London: Continuum, 2002), 136–155; hereafter cited in text.

9. I. Christie, *The Last Machine: Early Cinema and the Birth of the Modern World* (London: British Film Institute, 1994), 15; hereafter cited in text.

10. The viewing public did not have to wait until the 1895 arrival of the Lumière train to experience an object darting out of a two-dimensional screen. This was already a long-accomplished fact in nineteenth-century landscape painting (e.g., J. W. M. Turner's 1844 *Rain, Steam and Speed: The Great Western Railway*).

11. N. Burch, *Life to Those Shadows* (London: British Film Institute, 1990); hereafter cited in text.

12. Gunning interprets this phenomenon in the context of the colonialist treatment of "inhabitants of other lands…as curious sights," theorizing the flight of the onlookers in the 1903 Edison film, *Native Woman Washing a Negro Baby in Nassau, B. I.*, in terms of Bruno's (*Streetwalking on a Ruined Map: Cultural Theory and the City Films of Elvira Notari* [Princeton: Princeton University Press, 1993]) notion of "transito"—a polysemic term eluding translation but referring to all forms of circulation, flux, and flight capable of resisting containment and capture (Gunning, 1998, 34). In the context of the industrialized world, flight is rarely a reaction. Jung notes that, when Charles Moisson filmed people exiting Cologne cathedral in 1896, he "had at least two assistants at hand, standing right behind the camera, just outside of the frame, urging people not to stand and gaze at the recording device but rather to move on." U. Jung, "Local Views: A Blind Spot in the Historiography of Early German Cinema," *Historical Journal of Film, Radio and Television* 22, no. 3 (2002): 253. Such films would shortly become a popular means of encouraging cinema-going. "The showman who has not tried a 'local' does not really know what success means," claimed the *Kinematograph and Lantern Weekly* 2, no. 44 (12 March 1908): 315.

13. *The Photographic Review of Reviews: A Synopsis of Photographic Literature of the World* 1, no. 6 (15 June 1892): 212.

14. D. B. Clarke and M. A. Doel, "Engineering Space and Time: Moving Pictures and Motionless Trips," *Journal of Historical Geography* 31, no. 1 January 2005, 41–60; hereafter cited in text.

15. A. Lant, "Haptical Cinema," *October* 74 (1995): 45–73; hereafter cited in text.

16. J. Ruoff, "'To Travel Is to Possess the World,'" *Visual Anthropology* 15, no. 1 (2001): 1–2.

17. P. Virilio, "The Last Vehicle," in *Looking Back on the End of the World*, eds. D. Kamper and C. Wulf (New York: Semiotext(e), 1989), 108; hereafter cited in text.

18. D. Mitchell, *The Lie of the Land: Migrant Workers and the California Landscape* (Minneapolis: University of Minnesota Press, 1996), 1.

19. J. Barrell, *The Dark Side of the Landscape: The Rural Poor in English Painting: 1730–1840* (Cambridge: Cambridge University Press, 1980); B. Bender, ed. *Landscape: Politics and Perspectives* (Oxford: Berg, 1993); A. Bermingham, *Landscape and Ideology: The English Rustic Tradition, 1740–1840* (London: Thames & Hudson, 1987); D. Cosgrove, *Social Formation and Symbolic Landscape* (London: Croom Helm, 1984); D. Cosgrove, *The Palladian Landscape: Geographical Change and Its Cultural Representation in Sixteenth-century Italy* (Leicester: Leicester University Press, 1993); D. Cosgrove and S. Daniels, eds., *The Iconography of Landscape: Essays on the Symbolic Representation, Design and Use of Past Landscapes* (Cambridge: Cambridge University Press, 1988); S. Daniels, *Fields of Vision: Landscape Imagery and National Identity in England and the United States* (Cambridge: Polity, 1993); hereafter cited in text; E. Hirsch and L.M. O'Hanlon, eds., *The Anthropology of Landscape: Perspectives on Place and Space* (Oxford: Oxford University Press, 1995); D. Mitchell, *The Lie of the Land: Migrant Workers and the California Landscape, op. cit.*; S. Schama, *Landscape and Memory* (London: Fontana, 1995).

20. N. Bryson, *Vision and Painting: The Logic of the Gaze* (London: Macmillan, 1983).

21. Lefebvre scrupulously avoids Freud's suggestion that landscapes in dreams are "invariably the genitals of the dreamer's mother" (since "emphasis is laid in the dream itself on a convinced feeling of having been there once before," and "there is no other place about which one can assert [this] with such conviction"). S. Freud, *The Interpretation of Dreams*, ed. and trans. J. Strachey (London: Allen and Unwin, 1954), 399. Yet Lefebvre's account is not at odds with the psychoanalytic account, despite his antipathy towards Lacan. V. Blum and H. Nast, "Jacques Lacan's Two-dimensional Subjectivity," in *Thinking Space*, eds. M. Crang and N. Thrift (London: Routledge, 2000), 183–204.

22. D. Cosgrove, "Prospect, Perspective and the Evolution of the Landscape Idea," *Transactions of the Institute of British Geographers* 10, no.1 (1985): 46; hereafter cited in text.

23. M. Heidegger, "The Age of the World Picture," in *The Question Concerning Technology and Other Essays*, trans. W. Lovitt (London: Harper & Row, 1977), 129. The notion of landscape, as Cosgrove details, was connected with "the surveying and mapping of newly acquired, consolidated, and 'improved' commercial estates in the hands of the bourgeoisie; with the calculation of distance and trajectory for cannon fire and of defensive fortifications against the new weaponry; and with the projection of the globe and its regions onto map graticules by cosmographers and chorographers, those essential set designers for Europe's entry Centre-stage on the world's theatre. In painting and garden design landscape achieved visually what survey, map-making and ordnance charting achieved practically: the control and domination over space as an absolute, objective entity, its transformation into the property of individual or state" (Cosgrove, 1985, 46).

24. A. Easthope, *What a Man's Gotta Do: The Masculine Myth in Popular Culture* (London: Paladin, 1986), 48; hereafter cited in text.

25. R. Solnit, *Wanderlust: A History of Walking* (New York: Penguin, 2000); hereafter cited in text.

26. The February 1905 edition of the Charles Urban Trading Co. film catalogue is reproduced in *A History of Early Film: Volume 1*, ed. S. Herbert (London: Routledge, 2000), 78–414.

27. W. Schivelbusch, *The Railway Journey: The Industrialization of Time and Space in the Nineteenth Century* (Oxford: Berg, 1986), 62; hereafter cited in text.

28. J. Clarétie, *Voyages d'un Parisien* (Paris, 1865), quoted in Schivelbusch.

29. The phrase that became synonymous with the railways was later applied to film: "It has annihilated space." M. A. Pyke, *Focusing the Universe,* in *A History of Early Film, Volume 3*, ed. S. Herbert, (London: Routledge, 2000), 26. *Focusing the Universe* is a pamphlet publication which is reproduced in full in the third volume of Herbert's *History.* The pamphlet is actually not dated but is known to be c. 1910. For detailed consideration of the parallels between the railway and film, see L. Kirby, *Parallel Tracks: The Railroad and Silent Cinema* (Exeter: Exeter University Press, 1997).

30. Blackwood's Magazine, quoted in S. Oettermann, *The Panorama: History of a Mass Medium* (New York: Zone Books, 1997), 113–114; hereafter cited in text.

31. J. Crary, *Techniques of the Observer: On Vision and Modernity in the Nineteenth Century* (Cambridge, MA: MIT Press, 1990), 6; hereafter cited in text. Of the Parisian dioramas and panoramas, Benjamin writes: "It was, in the first moment, as though you had entered an aquarium.... But what came to light here were open-air, atmospheric wonders." W. Benjamin, *The Arcades Project* (Cambridge, MA: Bellknap Press, 1999), 533; hereafter cited in text.

32. D. Mitchell, *Cultural Geography: A Critical Introduction* (Oxford: Blackwell, 2000), 117; hereafter cited in text.

33. P. Virilio, *The Vision Machine* (London: British Film Institute, 1994), 2; hereafter cited in text.

34. J. Lacan, "What Is a Picture?" In *The Four Fundamental Concepts of Psycho-analysis*, trans. A. Sheridan (Harmondsworth: Penguin, 1977a), 109; hereafter cited in text. As the English translator notes, Lacan's *"dompte-regard"* is to the gaze what *"trompe-l'oeil"* is to the look (q.v.).

35. M. Foucault, *Discipline and Punish: The Birth of the Prison*, trans. by A. Sheridan (London: Allen Lane, 1977), 317.

36. The tension between the mobility of the eye and the fixity of the subject in conventional landscape painting—and revolutionized, if not resolved, in the panorama—might be considered in the light of Alpers' characterization of the innovations accomplished by Dutch art, where "The eye of the viewer ...and the single central vanishing point to which it is related in distance and position, have their counterpart...within the picture." S. Alpers, *The Art of Describing: Dutch Art in the Seventeenth Century* (Harmondsworth: Penguin, 1989), 53. Here is a neglected presumptive forerunner of the panorama.

37. N. Green, *The Spectacle of Nature: Landscape and Bourgeois Culture in Nineteenth-century France* (Manchester: Manchester University Press, 1990), 97; hereafter cited in text.

38. B. Comment, *The Panorama* (London: Reaktion Books, 1999); hereafter cited in text.

39. G. Deleuze, *Cinema 1: The Movement-Image*, trans. H. Tomlinson and B. Habberjam (London: Althlone, 1986); hereafter cited in text.

40. H. Bergson, *Creative Evolution* (Lanham, MD: University Press of America, 1984).

41. Horton's contention that visual technologies were not marshalled straightforwardly on one side or the other in the conflict between Romantic and empirical conceptions of vision, but were used to derive a subjective spectacle from scientific technique, is well illustrated by the magic lantern. The cultivation of enchantment went hand in hand with ever-increasing technological sophistication. S. Horton, "Were They Having Fun Yet? Victorian Optical Gadgetry, Modernist Selves," in *Victorian Literature and the Victorian Visual Imagination*, eds. C. T. Christ and J. O. Jordan (Berkeley: University of California Press, 1995), 1–26.

42. X. T. Barber, "The Roots of Travel Cinema: John L. Stoddard, E. Burton Holmes and the Nineteenth-century Illustrated Travel Lecture," *Film History* 5, no. 1 (1993): 68.

43. R. Fabian and H.-C. Adam, *Masters of Early Travel Photography* (New York: Vendome Press, 1983).

44. O. Cook, *Movement in Two Dimensions: A Study of the Animated and Projected Pictures Which Preceded the Invention of Cinematography* (London: Hutchinson, 1963); D. Robinson, S. Herbert, and R. Crangle, eds., *Encyclopaedia of the Magic Lantern* (London: Magic Lantern Society, 2001).

45. J. Ruoff, "Around the World in Eighty Minutes: The Travel Lecture Film," *Visual Anthropology* 15, no. 1 (2001): 91–114.

46. See http://www.belkin-gallery.ubc.ca/webpage/online/millennial.html (accessed 12/08/03).

47. Paul, as Rossell notes, "became known as 'Daddy Paul,' the founder of the British film industry." D. Rossell, *Living Pictures: The Origins of the Movies* (New York: SUNY Press, 1998), 92. He was celebrated "for his technical and mechanical excellence, film quality and originality, and 'up-to-dateness'," as the Who's Who of the English film industry published by the *Kinematograph and Lantern Weekly* 1 (16 May 1907) put it.

48. *The Era* (25 April 1896).

49. Quoted in J. Barnes, *The Beginnings of the Cinema in England* (London: David and Charles, 1976), 37.

50. W. Donisthorpe, *Down the Stream of Civilization* (London: George Newnes, 1898), 32. The quotation is from Alfred Lord Tennyson's poem, *Break, Break, Break* (S. Herbert with M. Heard, *Industry, Liberty, and a Vision: Wordsworth Donisthorpe's Kinesigraph* [Hastings: Projection Box, 1998], 118; hereafter cited in text as *Herbet*). Cf. Georges Demenÿ, "The future will see the replacement of motionless photographs, frozen in their frames, with animated portraits that can be brought back to life with the turn of a handle" (quoted in Burch, 26).

51. H. Buddemeier, *Panorama, Diorama, Photographie: Entstehung und Werkung neuer Medien im 19. Jahrhundert* (Munich: W. Fink, 1970), 78.

52. *The Optical Lantern and Cinematograph Journal* 1 (February 1905): 73.

53. S. Bottomore, "'Nine days' Wonder': Early Cinema and Its Sceptics," in *Cinema. The Beginnings and the Future: Essays Marking the Centenary of the First Film Show Projected to a Paying Audience in Britain*, ed. C. Williams (London: Routledge, 1996), 146.

54. R. Abel, *The Ciné Goes to Town: French Cinema, 1896–1917* (Berkeley: University of California Press, 1994).

55. E. Toulet, "Cinema at the Universal Exposition, Paris, 1900," *Persistence of Vision* 9 (1991): 10–37.

david b. clarke and marcus a. doel

56. T. Gunning, "The World as Object Lesson: Cinema Audiences, Visual Culture and the St. Louis World Fair," *Film History* 6, no. 4 (1994): 422–444.

57. R. Fielding, "Hale's Tours: Ultrarealism in the pre-1910 Motion Picture," in *Film Before Griffith*, ed. J. Fell (Berkeley: University of California Press, 1984), 117.

58. S. During, *Modern Enchantments: The Cultural and Secular Power of Magic* (Cambridge, MA: Harvard University Press, 2002); R. O. Moore, *Savage Theory: Cinema as Modern Magic* (Durham, NC: Duke University Press, 2000).

59. B. Landon, "Diegetic or Digital? The Convergence of Science-fiction Literature and Science-fiction Film in Hypermedia," in *Alien Zone II: The Spaces of Science Fiction Cinema*, ed. A. Kuhn (London: Verso, 1999), 31–49; L. Rabinovitz, "From *Hale's Tours* to *Star Tours*: Virtual Voyages and the Delirium of the Hyperreal," *Iris* 25 (1998): 133–152.

60. For an enthusiastic description of "mechanical surroundings" to support the realism of train, balloon, and car films, see "Mechanical Effects and Moving Pictures: A Profitable Innovation," *The Optical Lantern and Kinematograph Journal* 2 (June 1906): 146–147.

61. *The Kinematograph and Lantern Weekly* 1, no. 3 (30 May 1907): 44.

62. C. Musser, *The Emergence of Cinema: The American Screen to 1907, Vol. I: History of the American Cinema* (New York: Scribners, 1990), 429.

63. G. M. Coissac, *Histoire du cinématographe de ses origines a nos jours* (Paris: Librairie Gauthier-Villars, 1925), 196.

64. Translation from Gunning, 1998; Virilio, 1989, provides a slightly different rendition.

65. H. Norris Nicholson, "Telling Travellers' Tales: The World through Home Movies," in *Engaging Film: Geographies of Mobility and Identity*, eds. T. Cresswell and D. Dixon (Lanham, MD: Rowman & Littlefield, 2002), 47–66.

66. A. Gaudreault, "Temporality and Narrative in Early Cinema, 1895–1908," in *Film Before Griffith*, ed. J. Fell (Berkeley: University of California Press, 1984), 322.

67. L. Bailey, "Skull's darkroom: the *camera obscura* and subjectivity," in *Philosophy and Technology: Practical, Historical and Other Dimensions* (Volume 6), ed. P. T. Durbin (London, 1989), 63–79.

68. M. Crang, "Rethinking the Observer: Film, Mobility, and the Construction of the Subject," in *Engaging Film: Geographies of Mobility and Identity*, eds. T. Cresswell and D. Dixon (Lanham, MD: Rowman & Littlefield, 2002), 19; hereafter cited in text.

69. Eadweard Muybridge's high-speed still photographic sequences of human and animal locomotion, dating from the 1870s and initially published as contact prints, readily lent themselves to animation in such devices. Nonetheless, practical difficulties meant that, when Muybridge began projecting moving images using his Zoöpraxiscope from 1879 onward, he resorted to painted silhouettes. It was not until 1894, when Ottomar Anschütz succeeded in projecting repeat-sequences of photographs, that such devices realized their potential. Animated photography was, then, not only widely anticipated, but virtually accomplished by the end of the 1880s. The remaining problem was the emancipation of the movement-image from the small loops within which it had been ensnared.

70. M. Blanchot, *The Gaze of Orpheus*, ed. P. Adams Sitney, trans. L. Davis (Barrytown, NY: Station Hill Press, 1981), 75.

71. R. Williams, *Notes on the Underground: An Essay on Technology, Society, and the Imagination* (Cambridge, MA: MIT Press, 1992), 124. *The Time Machine* appeared in 1895, the same year as the Lumière Cinématographe. An earlier version was serialized as "The Chronic Argonauts" in 1888, coinciding with Le Prince's development of moving photography. Le Prince then mysteriously disappeared in France (Rawlence, 1990). The serialization of *The Time Machine*, in the *New Review* of 1895, opened with the line: "The man who made the Time Machine...was well known in scientific circles a few years since, and the fact of his disappearance is also well known." Quoted in M. Moorcock, Introduction to *The Time Machine*, by H. G. Wells (London: Everyman, 1993), xxix.

72. E. A. Abbott, *Flatland: A Romance of Many Dimensions* (Harmondsworth: Penguin, 1987).

73. P. D. Ouspensky, *Tertium Organum: The Third Canon of Thought; A Key to the Enigmas of the World* (Rochester, NY: Manas Press, 1920); *The Psychology of Man's Possible Evolution* (London: Hodder & Stoughton, 1951).

74. Darwin claimed not only that the survival of a species depended on the instinct for survival (*The Origin of Species*, 1859), but also on the instinct for reproduction (*The Descent of Man and Selection in Relation to Sex*, 1871). Freud supplemented Darwin's instincts with corresponding species-specific drives: narcissism and sexual desire.

75. P. Virilio, "Kinematic Optics," in *Polar Inertia* (London: Sage, 2000), 51.

76. O. W. Holmes, "The Stereoscope and the Stereograph," *The Atlantic Monthly* (June 1859): 738–748. See http://www.looking-glass.co.uk/stereograph/holmes.htm (accessed 13/09/03).

77. J. Lacan, "The Line and Light," in *The Four Fundamental Concepts of Psychoanalysis, op. cit.*, 96; hereafter cited in text as *Lacan 1977b*.

78. J. Lacan, "The Split between the Eye and the Gaze," in *The Four Fundamental Concepts of Psycho-analysis, op. cit.*, 72

79. A. Easthope, *Privileging Difference* (Basingstoke: Palgrave, 2002), 10.

80. S. Heath, "Narrative Space," in *Questions of Cinema*, (Bloomington: Indiana University Press, 1981), 19–75.

81. A. Kuhn, "The History of Narrative Codes," in *The Cinema Book*, ed. P. Cook (London: British Film Institute, 1985), 207–220.

82. D. N. Rodowick, *Gilles Deleuze's Time Machine* (Durham, NC: Duke University Press, 1997), 3.

83. C. Barr, "Before *Blackmail*: Silent British Cinema," in *The British Cinema Book*, ed. R. Murphy (London: British Film Institute, 1997), 15; hereafter cited in text.

84. C. M. Hepworth, *Came the Dawn* (London: Phoenix House, 1951), 139.

85. I. Barry, *Let's Go to the Movies* (New York: Arno Press, 1972), 233.

86. For an account of the numerous tensions between modernity and the English conception of landscape, see D. Matless, *Landscape and Englishness* (London: Reaktion Books, 1998).

87. A. Easthope, *Englishness and National Culture* (London: Routledge, 1999).

88. A great many English nonactuality films in the 1890s and 1900s played out this class conflict in comedic form by endlessly rehearsing the calamitous encounter of different social types—tramps and aristocrats, villains and policemen, cyclists and pedestrians, gypsies and stolen babies, would-be lovers and their chaperones, soldiers and natives, chil-

dren and adults, curates and convicts—which typically resulted in escalating chases, and invariably involved beatings, especially by policemen. Yet it is typical that the first issue of the *Cinematography and Bioscope Magazine*, published in April 1906 by the St. Albans-based Warwick Trading Company, should give pride of place to an article on "The Educational Value of the Cinematograph."

# landscape and archive

trips around the world as

early film topic (1896–1914)

antonio costa

A trip around the world in 16 months: this is the project undertaken by the operators commissioned with promoting the Lumière *Cinématographe*. Following the first screening at the Salon des Indiens of the Grand Café in Paris (December 28, 1895), the Lumière brothers had decided against selling their camera and for making use of it themselves. In January 1896, they began using the commercial network they had developed for selling their photographic products to send operators around the world. Their task was not simply to organize film screenings, but also to shoot films, since the *cinématographe* functioned as both a camera and as a projector.

The Lumière operators reached Cologne, Madrid, and Amsterdam within the first months of 1896. Charles Masson travelled through Germany and then passed through Austria-Hungary. Marius Sestrier headed for Australia and then passed through India (Bombay). Alexandre Promio reached New York, and Gabriel Veyre arrived in Mexico. By the end of 1896 and the first few months of 1897 Constant Girel had arrived in Indochina and then in Japan. Other Lumière operators reached Latin America and China.[1] The *vues* they produced according to rules established by Louis

Lumière were regularly sent to headquarters in Lyon, where some were selected to become part of the Lumière catalogue. In this way, the first film archive, which documented the Lumière operators' "trips around the world," was created. On May 1, 1897, the Lumière brothers began to allow the sale of their camera: the operators' production of *vues* slowly decreased, eventually stopping altogether; the last films to be found in their catalogue are dated back to 1905 (Aubert and Seguin, 1996).

Georges Sadoul has characterized the *vues* that constitute the Lumière catalogue as "a prodigious symphony of the world."[2] Rémy de Gourmont, one of the first European intellectuals to give the cinema any attention, wrote in the same year: "I love the cinema. It satisfies my curiosity. Through it, I make a trip around the world, and I stop as I wish in Tokyo or Singapore. I follow the craziest of itineraries. I go to New York—which is not beautiful—passing through the Suez—which is hardly any better—and travel through the forests of Canada and the mountains of Scotland, all within the same hour. I go up the Nile to Kartoum, and, a few seconds later, I contemplate the deep and dark expanse of the ocean from the deck of a transatlantic cruiser."[3] De Gourmont defined the cinema as "a big magic lantern requiring only a screen, a source of light and a projectionist" (39). The definition recalls the landscape views of the pre-cinematographic optical shows and, therefore, implicitly highlights the characteristic attractions of early cinema.[4]

The trip around the world is a theme which has held the attention of both the European literary and scientific imagination since the appearance of the first travel writings: from those of Antonio Pigafetta which chronicle Magellano's second journey,[5] to the German Georg Forster's decidedly more scientific account of James Cook's second expedition (1772–1775).[6] The development of the technique and methods for travel continually reduced the travelling time of these mythical trips, eventually breaking the 80-day record established by Phileas Fogg and his helper Passepartout in the well-known novel by Jules Verne. What is more, the close link between the development of the means of transport and the reproductive *media* (photography, cinema) created a new concept of space, time, and distance. These changes had enormous consequences for systems for representing landscape, social space, and geographic-anthropological phenomena.[7]

With film, landscape, understood as the synthesis of the geographic-anthropological features of a territory, could be reproduced with an unprecedented objectivity that now included duration as well as movement. Yet, even the most neutral of shots always involves the adoption of a point of view, the presence of interpretative models and attitudes that belong to culture, ideology, and the world views of both filmmakers and viewers. Thus, landscape shown in the cinema is never a pure or simple *reproduction*. Rather, it is a technical, economic, cultural, and semiotic (discursive) production.[8]

In this chapter, I will consider the theme of the trip around the world in early European cinema, concentrating on three examples: (a) Italian documentary cinema pioneer Luca Comerio's *Dal Polo all'Equatore*, as seen through Yervant Giankian and Angela Ricci Lucchi's interpretative "remake" of it; (b) the cinematographic and photographic documentation called "Les Archives de la Planète" promoted by the banker and philanthropist Albert Kahn; and (c) *Le avventure straordinarissime di Saturnino Farandola* (Ambrosio, 1914), a film made in Italy by the actor and director Marcel Fabre and which was inspired by author and illustrator Albert Robida's parody of Jules Verne's *Voyages extraordinaires*.[9]

## a two-hour trip around the world: the cinema meets the world's fair

*Il giro del mondo in due ore* (*A Trip Around the World in Two Hours*) is the title of a documentary produced by Pasquali & C. of Turin in 1912. This film, as we learn from a description in *The Bioscope* (London, 14 March 1912), focused on "the various gardens and other places of resort" in Hamburg, Germany. It was possible at the beginning of the 1900s to make such trips around the world by simply tracing a route through the urban space of almost any large European city and visiting various "ethno-geographical" and "zoological gardens" where typical features of every part of the world could be seen: "a temple in Tibet, an Indian garden, groups of Eskimo in typical dwellings, elephants, camels, etc."[10] Pasquali's film simply depicted scenographic installations of exotic places, giving the audience the impression of going on a trip around the world while sitting in their seats, as if they were real visitors of the Hamburg parks. The film illustrates the meeting, or interweaving, of the World's Fair model for exhibition with an apparatus of spectacular vision as analysed by Walter Benjamin in his writings about Paris as "the capital of the nineteenth century."[11]

A similar interweaving was successfully staged at the Paris World Fair in 1900. There, the Lumière brothers' magnificent apparatus, the *Cinématographe Géant*, set up at the Salle de Fêtes on the Champ-de-Mars, had allowed some 25,000 people to experience a most amazing spectacle. For each screening, a winch system in the centre of the immense pavilion lifted a screen measuring 21 × 18 metres from a pool in which it was kept immersed. (The goal was to keep it wet in order to guarantee transparency and ensure vision of the images from both sides). Fifteen moving pictures and as many coloured photographs were projected in sequence. Lighting was made possible by the development of electric lamps (a 150-amp light was used).[12] With this installation, the Fair's labourers reproduced the immensity of the nineteenth century panorama. Above all, the projection of images was integrated into a striking architectural apparatus. Altogether, the screen, the beam of light from the projector, the images in sequence (still and moving images in alternation) took the form of an architecture of light inserted into a large steel and glass construction, therefore creating new and spectacular scenographic effects.

If one now considers what was filmed around the world by the Lumière operators and shown at these screenings, one can understand how the shows themselves offered a kind of *mise-en-abyme* of the Fair's own trip around the world. At the 1900 World's Fair, the cinema still coexisted with panoramas and dioramas, which, even though based on different technology, represented analogous and complementary forms of attractions: their function was to propagandize for the Third Republic's politics of colonial expansion by means of the attraction of exotic panoramas and costumes. Most were stationary panoramas of the traditional type, such as the Panorama of the Mission Marchand, the Panorama of the Congo, the Panorama of Madagascar, and the Saharan Diorama. There were also more complex apparatuses, including the mobile Stéréorama, which was installed in the Algerian pavilion and offered images of a voyage along the Algerian coast that began at sunrise in Bona and ended in Orano at sunset (Toulet, 189). In addition, Raoul Grimoin-Sanson's Cinéorama provided a view of landscapes filmed from an air balloon. To better simulate the effect of a journey, the spectators sat in a space which resembled an actual capsule containing all the equipment of a real air balloon. From within they would see the landscapes that had been filmed from an actual air balloon, projected onto a circular screen by 10 projectors. However, the apparatus was apparently not safe and, after a few projections, providential intervention by the police cancelled the show (Toulet, 194–196).

The World's Fair not only included simulated journeys through space, it also provided journeys through time as well. Among the filmed views offered, there were two of the *Vieux Paris* taken from a boat on the Seine. They reproduced the visual experience of the visitors who, from a boat navigating along the river, could see a scenographic reconstruction of medieval Paris designed by Albert Robida, the famous illustrator and writer of adventure science fiction novels.[13] With this exhibit the Fair not only integrated the Seine River into its own space, it also offered an early example of "river vision" motion picture. E. S. Porter, who shot Edison's *A Trip Around the Pan-American Exposition*, adopted a similar filming strategy for the 1901 Pan-American Exposition of Buffalo (NY). This film offered comfortably seated spectators views of the Exposition's pavilions much like those seen by visitors travelling in boats along an artificial canal. (Among the attractions of the Pan-American Exposition documented by the Edison production was a reconstruction of Venice with bridges, squares, and even gondolas.)[14]

The meeting of cinema and the World's Fair thus afforded multiple possibilities for embarking on journeys to faraway countries, and even into the past, all at little cost. It also pointed toward the intermedial tendency of the new century, dominated by the cinema during the first half, and by television during the second—a tendency foreboded by Albert Robida with his futuristic novel *Le XX^e Siècle*.[15]

## luca comerio: from the pole to the equator

The Lumière catalogue is a precious repository of images filmed in faraway countries. It is the first motion picture archive to embody the idea of a journey across the whole world. A similar idea was also developed by Luca Comerio (1878–1940), a pioneer of documentary cinema in Italy.[16]

Comerio loved travelling, risk, cars, and speed with a spirit that in many respects resembles that of the Futurists. He photographed and filmed the war in Libya, the First World War, the Italian Colonial conquests, and the Fiume exploits of the poet and soldier Gabriele D'Annuzio. As official photographer of the Royal Family, Comerio made several films about the kings and queens of Italy. Moreover, he had the exclusive rights to film the various fronts of the First World War. He was also able to film in distant countries. Unfortunately, as with many other cinema pioneers, Comerio did not understand the evolution of the film industry nor how the public's taste can change over time. During the years of his sad decline, Comerio stopped almost entirely his activities as a documentary filmmaker, in spite of his attempts to get assignments from the fascist regime. He began dedicating himself instead to his archive (where he had collected both his own films and those of other operators). In this way, he was able to make a set of compilation films about the war: *Sulle Alpi riconsacrate* (*On the Reconsecrated Alps*), *Al Rombo del cannon* (*To the Roar of the Cannons*), and *Perché il mondo sappia e gli Italiani ricordino* (*So that the World Knows and the Italians Remember*). As their titles suggest, these films were largely rhetorical works created in compliance with the wishes of the ultra-nationalist politics of the fascist regime. *Dal Polo all'Equatore* (*From the Pole to the Equator*) is the only film that has survived. Unlike the others, it was not projected in theatres and was probably never completed.

Made toward the end of the 1920s, *Dal Polo all'Equatore* remained unheard of until, in recent years, it was discovered by Yervant Gianikian and Angela Ricci Lucchi, two Italian avant-garde filmmakers. Using images taken from this and other works of Comerio's collection, Gianikian and Ricci Lucchi made a film bearing the same title—*Dal Polo all'Equatore* (1986)—which became one of the most noted and appreciated avant-garde Italian films of the 1980s.[17]

Due to the bad condition of the prints, Gianikian and Ricci Lucchi had to re-photograph each frame, making continual adjustments to what they called their "analytical camera," a device which permitted the film to run in spite of the fact that the sprocket holes on the side of the film and many of the frames had deteriorated.[18] In this way, the two filmmakers not only made the material of Comerio's archive visible, but they also offered, so to speak, a reading or a critical interpretation of the original material.

By re-proposing Comerio's title, Gianikian and Ricci Lucchi recapture the idea of a journey. The film is divided into 10 sections, which correspond to different geographic-anthropological spaces. The following is the list, which uses the titles given by the filmmakers, even though they do not appear in the final version. (Gianikian and Ricci Lucchi's film has no comments or intertitles.)

1. Topography on the borders of the Austro-Hungarian Empire: images of the Tyrol, shot in the years before World War I along the mountain railways.

2. The White Sphinx: images of various origins shot in the North Pole, beginning with the Duke of the Abruzzi's expedition in 1899.

3. Shots taken before 1920, in the Caucasian region of the Russian-Persian border: "the elements given in the new form are the panorama, the geometry of the parades, the portraits, the movements of the dance, the faces of the Caucasian crowd later described by Joseph Roth."

4. The Black Sphinx (shot by Comerio in Uganda in 1910, while following the Baron Franchetti, Mussolini's future secret agent, in Africa).

5. Battles—Contrast among the operators in India: film-postcard to be sent to the West about various aspects of colonial life, marked by exoticism and soldierly rhetoric.

6. "Mystic" postcard from Indochina: images from the beginning of the century before the pillage of Indochina, which document the rituals of religious life of the Bonzi.

7. Exotic postcards from France and overseas: films shot in Tangiers around 1910 (the date is not certain, however) which represent a typical exotic repertory and contain pictorial and literary references that range from Delacroix to Flaubert.

8. Gondar, East Africa, 1910: a parade of men and animals set in an exotic landscape among the ruins of colonialism, with parallels established between the head of the village's entrance on horseback and Mussolini's 1926 entrance into Tripoli.

9. "The Black Sphinx" of Baron Franchetti: the Baron's exploits while big game hunting, emulated by Comerio who is filmed with a captured lion cub.

10. The First World War seen by Comerio: shots reprinted both from the original negatives and the positives, with a final aerial shot showing an open space in which a flock of sheep form the words W IL RE (Long Live the King).[19] (Gianikian and Ricci Lucchi, 53–56)

For a more precise idea of the working method and the type of shooting, let us examine some of the sections of the film. With the first, "Topography on the borders of the Austro-Hungarian Empire," the opening material is made up of shots of trains moving along the Tyrolian landscape: there are 5,044 frames for a total of 97 metres (318 feet) of film. After Gianikian and Ricci Lucchi's editing and manipulation, the section is at least three times longer: the original sense of time is altered by slow-motion and frame duplication.

The slow repetition of shots and the insistence on the "fading to black" effect produced by the images of the train going into and out of the tunnel, greatly transform the original material, which was characterized by a certain taste for the picturesque typical of "mountain" films. The obsessive repetition of the train's journey along the rails produces the impression of a network of straight lines superimposed upon the landscape. Gianikian and Ricci Lucchi's editing and picture manipulations give us the impression of a romantic landscape which is defined, penetrated, and circumscribed by the intervention of technological will-to-power.

The idea of a penetration of the landscape is resumed and further explored in the section about the Arctic Pole, which begins with images of the polar ice taken from the deck of an icebreaker. The movement is linked to the idea of conquering a territory: from the shots taken from aboard the ship (subjective camera) we go immediately to matte shots that reproduce a gun barrel shooting at some polar bears (the mother is killed, and the cub is captured). This hunting theme, with its images of the captured cub and of the dead mother, reappears in the African images about the lions.

The fourth section, "The Black Sphinx," best makes clear perhaps the function of the "analytical camera" as a critique of colonial ideology. While the selection and editing of the source material serves in part to highlight the chromatic contrast between the white of the colonizer's clothes (soldiers, nuns, missionaries) and the sometimes dull and sometimes shiny black of the natives' bodies, it also serves to challenge the idea of colonial domination. The natives' powerful limbs, their supple and elegant movements, the forces of nature—everything is regulated by the training of the colonizers who impose their agenda of civilisation upon the multiform variety of daily life, through gestures of prayer (the sign of the cross), military marches, and gymnastic exercises. The colonial world (its nature and its natives) is conquered and then shaped and regulated according to rhythms imposed by its colonizers. Gianikian and Ricci Lucchi alter the projection rate and make selections within the frame, thus questioning not only the realistic illusion of these moving pictures but also the taste for the exotic that informs them. The violence inflicted on what is often called "the state of nature" emerges unequivocally.

Though we are still waiting for a "philological" restoration of Comerio's original film that would make it possible for us to see it and judge it on its own terms, Gianikian and Ricci Lucchi allow us to appreciate the fascination which such images likely exerted on the spectators of the period and make us aware of the consequences of the colonial ideology that inspired them. Both filmmakers, of course, were acutely aware of this aspect of Comerio's work for, as they declared, "the main subject was that of a journey, an exotic journey; of exploration, of a conquest, of a cultural plunder; a subject concerning violence particularly as a sign of preparation for the First World War" (Gianikian and Ricci Lucchi, 41–42). And yet, Gianikian and Ricci Lucchi's work both retains and exalts the high quality of the original materials, and especially the mobilization of the camera, which enhances the power of attraction of the images. As Gentili maintains, "Comerio is one of the fathers of the cinema, not simply of documentaries: he is the pioneer of action cinema: of the camera + the train, of the camera + the car, of the camera + the airship, of the camera + the cablecar" (40).

Significantly, the filmmakers chose to begin and end their trip around the world in Europe. The first section is dominated by the presence of the trains that pass through the woods of the Tyrol. The last section shows the same mountainous landscape, which became a theatre for military operations during World War I. Here an aerial view (by airplane or cablecar) shows us the inscription "LONG LIVE THE KING," obtained opportunely using a flock of sheep. Between the first and second sections, the use of negative images for the war scenes is a clear allusion to the hidden side of the visible. The travelling shots (train, ship, aerial, or cablecar) become a further element of attraction in addition to other "attractions" such as landscape, architecture, animals, habits, and customs.

Gianikian and Ricci Lucchi's montage and visual effects change the film's speed, alter the perception of events, and isolate certain details within the frame. In this way, they uncover the non-equivalence or discrepancy, between real time and film time; they denounce the limits of realistic illusion. Objects, faces, and places are given back their original polysemy. Raymond Bellour rightly proposed an interpretation of Gianikian and Ricci Lucchi's montage in light of Deleuze's theory of the interval: the *affection-image* which occupies the interval "without filling it...somewhere between a perception that is in some respects disturbing and an action that hesitates."[20] In particular, Bellour interprets Gianikian and Ricci Lucchi's "suspended" frames in terms of Deleuze's *affection-image*, that is, the image which stands in suspended time once the sensorial and motor automatisms of perception-action have broken down (Deleuze, 125–144).

In my opinion, Gianikian and Ricci Lucchi's work can be usefully linked to what Lyotard called "the unrepresentable of representation."[21]

Not only do they alter the film speed, but they also allow one to perceive the conventional nature of cinematographic time. Their work opens cinematographic time to another dimension in which different relations are perceivable, removing the object from the automatisms of the so-called "realistic" perception, and allowing hidden and repressed meanings to emerge.

## from the multi-scene garden to "les archives de la planète"

A utopian ideal lies at the base of the "Autour du Monde" project of the Alsatian banker and philanthropist Albert Khan (1860–1940).[22] This ideal is fostered by the conviction that universal peace depends on a knowledge of all the places and populations of the world. When visiting l'Espace Albert Khan[23] on the outskirts of Paris, one gets the impression of being confronted with a highly original work, a life's work, made up of a singular combination of garden and archive. L'Espace Albert Khan is in fact a perfectly well-managed, large compound made up of a multi-scene garden and an audio-visual archive consisting of 72,000 photographic plates and 172,000 metres (107 miles) of film. The management of the Albert Khan Foundation is perfect in all details. Walking through various types of gardens, one can experience concretely different kinds of landscape revealing the manifold relationships between nature and culture. In addition, one can access an audio-visual archive equipped with efficient reference tools, which puts the extraordinary documentation within reach of the specialist, the educated public, or the simply curious.

Albert Khan arrived in Paris from Marmoutier (Bas Rhyn), where he was born and raised in a small Jewish community. He was barely 20 years old when he was hired in the Goudchaux Bank, of which he became the owner a few years later. Before becoming one of the most important financiers of Europe, Khan finished his studies and achieved his "bac ès lettres" and then "ès sciences" under the guidance of an exceptional private teacher, Henri Bergson, with whom he had a long and fraternal relationship.

An internationalist and cosmopolitan ideal guided all Khan's activities. Everything started in his home in Boulogne-Billancourt, where, between 1894 and 1910, he built a multi-scene garden with the advice of the landscape architect Achille Duchène that included Japanese, French, and English gardens; the marsh, the Blue Forest, the Golden Forest, and the Vosges Forest; and an orchard and rose gardens.

The multi-scene garden was by no means invented by Albert Khan. Edmond de Rothschild's park in Boulogne, the Ile de France and Maryland villas in Saint-Jean, Cap-Ferrat, Leonardsau's park in Obernai, the Chamfleuri villa in Cannes, and the Compton Acres country house in Pool, England, are only some of the other multi-scene gardens contemporary with Albert Khan's.[24]

As Marie Bonhomme writes, the different geographic reference points that serve for the various gardens assembled by Albert Khan make us reflect on the main tendencies that dominated imaginary and visual culture between the end of the eighteenth and the beginning of the nineteenth centuries: "Concerning his choices, Albert Khan is then a man of the XIX Century. His gardens are a kind of assemblage of the different tendencies of his contemporaries: the English garden harks back to a landscape style which still has its devotees. The French garden of the Grand Siècle was then coming back into fashion along with the 'japonisme' of the Japanese garden; the naturalism of the marsh, the meadows and the forests of the Vosges; the pictorialism of the Blue Forest and the Gold Forest; the exoticism of the gardens of Cap Martin" (105).

What is extremely interesting is the way in which Albert Khan arranges the transitions from one type of garden to another, from one scene to another: "a rosebush which seems to come from a rose garden is perched on the slope of the Japanese garden; a curtain of golden fir trees between the Blue Forest and the Vosges Forest, a very intuitive way of unconsciously harmonizing and uniting antagonisms by means of almost subliminal representations" (Bonhomme, 105). One spontaneously thinks of a typical cinematic process, the cross fade or dissolve, which operates a kind of "magical" fusion between spaces and different contexts when passing from one scene to another. This is one of the characteristics which makes it possible to draw together the garden and the film even on a methodological level.

Individual models of reference and aspirations to a "universal" prospect are both deeply rooted in turn-of-the-century culture. In this sense, it is difficult not to think of the models of the World's Fair, and in particular of the Paris Fair of 1900. However, we shall also see that there are substantial differences between the colonial ideology which characterized the 1900 World's Fair and Khan's pacifist and philanthropic ideas.

The 1900 World's Fair combined the visual tendencies of the *fin de siècle* with those of the new century. Thus, it not only made the taste for the exotic triumphant (as best illustrated by "japonisme"), but it also systematically used the attractions of a more or less exotic landscape, scenographically reconstructed and reproduced through cinematic and photographic means (as seen in the Lumière brothers' *Cinématographe Géant*). It seems important to me that in his plans for the "Archives de la Planète," Albert Khan envisaged the systematic use of precisely the two means which were used by the Lumière brothers in that apparatus of theirs which occupied the Salle des Fêtes at the 1900 Paris Fair: the cinema and the *autochromes*.

The realisation of a multi-scene garden was only one step in a wider project which included a programme of document and data acquisition (above all photographic and cinematographic) and of study aimed at deepening one's knowledge of the world. This project was divided into the following phases:

(a) 1898: Establishment of the "Autour du monde" scholarships for graduates (both men and women) to travel and to gather information about different countries.

(b) 1906: Founding of the "Autour du monde" Circle, within which the scholarship holders present and discuss with qualified listeners the results of their study trips.

(c) 1910–1930: Constitution of a cinematic and photographic document archive, called "Les Archives de la Planète."

(d) 1910–1930: Series of initiatives centred in Boulogne-Billancourt were to be developed with the aim of deepening knowledge of human geography and of fostering cooperative projects among the populations of the earth.

Albert Khan was a great traveller. Before and after his famous trip of 1908–1909, he went to Tonkino (1884), Spain and Ireland (1886), South Africa (1884 and 1888), England and Venezuela (1890), Egypt (1895), Russia (1897, 1906, and 1912), Germany, London, and Amsterdam (1898), and Sweden and Norway (1910). But it was during a trip around the world in 1908–1909 that Khan first produced a set of cinematic documents and came up with the idea for his Archives of the Planet project. It was inspired by the idea of circumnavigation, of travel along a circular route.[25]

Before leaving, Albert Khan made his young driver, Albert Dutertre, follow a brief and to the point training programme in photography and cinematography, which enabled him to master the various aspects of photographic shots, filming, and sound (Mattera Corneloup, 60). (It should be noted that the Lumière *autochromes*—an incomparable colour shooting device whose versatility and pictorial results still awe us today—were marketed starting in 1907.)

For our purpose, two aspects of this trip need to be singled out. The first concerns the need for adopting an exhaustive and rigorous method of research and recording. Attempts at obtaining reproductions of reality as exact and life-like as could be were made possible by using specific technologies: the stereograph, which creates the effect of 3-D images; the *autochromes,* which yield colour images; the cinema, which reproduces movement and yields "duration"; and the cylinder phonograph-recorder, which allows the reproduction of sound (Mattera Corneloup, 68–69). The second important aspect is Kahn's constant interest in gardens: "the Japanese garden in San Francisco, private gardens belonging to Khan's interlocutors, the Arsenal garden and the botanical garden of Tokyo, gardens in Peking and Shangai, botanical gardens of Singapore and of Penang" (Mattera Corneloup, 70). Clearly, Albert Khan's idea of a connection between the garden and archives of visual and sound documents takes shape during this trip. After its completion, Khan began work on the "Archives de la Planète" project. On the advice of geologist Emmanuel de Margerie and close friend and mentor Henri Bergson, Jean Bruhnes was called in to direct this project. At the Collège de France, Bruhnes established the professorship of "human geography" inaugurated through the financial intervention of Khan.[26]

In certain respects, the cinematic and photographic documents collected in this archive from 1912 to 1930 seem to constitute an extension of the Lumière brothers' initiative, who, as mentioned earlier, had completely ceased producing cinematographic documents since 1905. In addition, the adoption of the *autochrome* technique, developed and marketed by the Lumières, constitutes another significant connection between Albert Khan's project and the Lumière brothers' company in Lyon. However, the differences between the documents collected in the Lumière catalogue and those of the "Archives de la Planète" may very well be more significant than any similarity, particularly where landscape is concerned.

One glance at the Lumière catalogue is sufficient to show that what prevails in those films is the notion of landscape as attraction.[27] On the other hand, the documentation concerning the landscape that we find in the "Archives de la Planète" points instead toward an idea of landscape as *production*,[28] both in relation to the referent (the landscape is a result of interactions between nature and culture which characterize different societies) and in relation to the technique of documentation (more than a pure technological attraction, the mechanical nature of the photographic and cinematographic reproduction now presupposes a truly dialogical production). Naturally, Jean Bruhnes's scientific project is at the centre of what distinguishes both approaches.

Bruhnes gave operators working for Kahn's project specific directions regarding what sort of events required documentation. Operators were asked to document (1) events concerning the nonproductive occupation of the land (houses, pathways); (2) events concerning the control over vegetation and animal life (pets, fields, and gardens); and (3) events concerning destructive economy (destruction of animals and vegetation; the extraction of minerals) (Hervé, 190). The operators then had to follow very precise rules for classifying the images that were shot. For each image (whether a stereoscopic plate, *autochrome*, or film), they had to complete a form giving exact indications of the date, setting, and subject that was filmed (191–192).

Naturally, this documentation program reflected Bruhnes's conception of human geography. He had articulated the latter according to a four-fold division: (1) the geography of man's foremost vital necessities (man's principal needs: food, clothing, sleep, and refuge); (2) the geography of the earth's exploitation (the move from the immediate use of resources for exploitation based on interventions, forecasts, explorations, etc.); (3) economic and social geography (all the changes linked to associational life: family, society, the division of land, legislations, etc.); (4) political geography and geography of history (showing how the most complex of human activities, even those most distant from elementary geographic conditions, have their roots in the reality of terrestrial materials). It follows, therefore, that the documents in the "Archives de la Planète" are of two types: (a) documents concerning environment and habitat and (b) documents concerning economic and social geography on the one hand, and political and historical geography on the other (Hervé, 194).

At this point it is interesting to compare the classification of the subjects in the Lumière catalogue with those in the Albert Kahn collections in Boulogne. Classification of the Lumière catalogue appears to be quite casual. Furthermore, it is strongly linked both to the specific circumstances in which the operators sent to the various countries filmed and to the promotional purposes of the *Cinématographe*. For a precise overall idea of the sort of things found in the Lumière catalogue, the taxonomy used by Michelle Aubert and Jean-Claude Séguin is useful: (a) arts and shows (comedies and genre scenes; dance, circus, and cabaret performances; bull fighting); (b) official events; (c) expositions; (d) daily life (entertainment, popular festivals, intimate scenes, work); (e) cities and landscapes; (f) military views (army, navy, fire brigade) (Aubert and Seguin, 27).

Khan's Boulogne collections use a completely different and more systematic approach to documentation, which, as we have seen, reflects the concepts and methods of Bruhnes's human geography. The themes classified include the following:

- Economic life (agriculture, breeding, commerce, etc.)
- Daily life (rural, urban, traditions)
- Religion (religious practices, the religious)
- Arts and culture
- Political and social events (included in this category are images which were not shot as part of Bruhnes's program as well as those bought from Pathé, Gaumont, Métro, etc.; these are mainly newsreels, etc.)
- Social and political life (festivals, ceremonies, parades, teaching, public health)
- Habitat and architecture
- Customs
- Natural environment
- Transport[29]

Here, however, I am not interested in examining how much of Bruhnes's research program was actually carried out by the recordings which can be consulted today at l'Espace Albert Kahn in Boulogne. The documents, of course, are worth mentioning if only because they constitute an exemplary case of an audio-visual archive placed at the disposal of scholars from all disciplines. Furthermore, apart from their scientific quality, I feel it is important to highlight the extraordinary beauty of the landscapes that were filmed by operators working for the "Archives de la Planète" project, especially those from the Far East. The *autochromes* are just as beautiful, because of both the technical quality of the photographic colour process invented by the Lumière brothers and the choice of subjects.[30]

What concerns me instead is understanding the relationship between this type of documentation and the other aspects of Albert Khan's project, which perhaps may be seen as anticipating something still more complex and ambitious. More specifically, I am referring to the biology laboratory which Khan installed in Boulogne (1926). Its direction was entrusted to Jean Comandon, who made films which are an integral part of Khan's plan. At this laboratory, and in collaboration with Pierre de Fonbrune, Comandon perfected a new micro-cinematographic filming device and made a series of films on the movement of vegetation: the blossoming of flowers, the movement of climbing plants, the germination of seeds.[31] Even though these documents did not arise at Bruhnes's impetus, they still belong to the photographic and cinematographic service Kahn and his collaborators called the Documentation Center (Hervé, 197).

Keeping this in mind, Kahn's conception of the archive and of the role cinematography was to play in it becomes clear. It seems obvious that, within the microcosm of Boulogne, Kahn's intention was to reproduce a sort of scale model of the unceasing process of transformation, of the evolution of life, from the infinitely small to the infinitely big. In fact, in light of this intention we can begin making sense of Kahn's continued efforts at bringing together his interest for gardens with his interest for the cinema. On the one hand, then, there is the idea of a garden as a reproduction of a type of intervention made by man upon nature, which by the same token mirrors different historical and cultural concepts of "nature." On the other hand, there is the idea of a cine-photographic documentation, which was intended to record, by means of still and moving images, the entire complex system of relationships through which bodies (the human body and the social body) interconnect in space (physical space and social space). Both fascinatingly come together in the "Archives" project.

### *saturnino farandola:* a trip around the world in more than eighty days

*Le Avventure straordinarie di Saturnino Farandola* (*The Extraordinary Adventures of Saturnino Farandola*; Ambrosio, 1914), written by Guido Volante and directed and interpreted by Marcel Fabre[32] (he directed it in collaboration with Luigi Maggi, who went uncredited), is the film version of a famous novel by Albert Robida with the very long title: *Voyages très extraordinaires de Saturnino*

*Farandoul dans les 5 ou 6 parties du monde et dans tous les pays connus et même inconnus de M. Jules Verne* (Saturnino Farandoul's most extraordinary trips in the 5 or 6 parts of the world and in all the known and even unknown countries of Mr. Jules Verne).[33]

Robida's novel is a very strange adventure book, halfway between a copy and a parody of Jules Verne's novels (as well as a satire with regards to their ideology of industrial progress and colonial expansion). The film version drew widely from the book's many illustrations, especially their caricatural deformation of and cheerful impudence toward the rules of naturalism and verisimilitude.

Albert Robida collaborated with the *Journal Amusant*, with *Paris Comique*, and with *La vie Parisienne*, and he founded *La caricature*. He was the author of various works, which he illustrated himself, including *Le Voyage de M. Dumollet* (1883), *le XX^e Siècle, roman d'un Parisien d'après demain* (1883). He was also one of the intellectuals who emceed the cabaret evenings of Le Chat Noir, famous for its Shadow Theatre.[34] At the Chat Noir, Robida directed *La nuit des Temps ou L'Elixir du Rajeunissement* (1889), which has a scene that is rightly considered an *incunabulum* of science fiction cinema, and depicted the destruction of Paris during air warfare.[35] This air warfare theme had already been developed by Robida in 1879 in his *Saturnin*, where he had described and illustrated an air battle between Phileas Fogg and Saturnin. In *La nuit des Temps*, the only original subject that was staged at the Chat Noir (the others were all based on literary sources), Robida has his characters drink a magical potion that makes them first return to prehistoric times and then launches them into the twentieth century. This imparted to his work the typical science fiction features of Verne's novels.[36] Finally, Robida did not simply imagine the destruction of Paris: he also imagined its reconstruction. I am alluding here to his role as director and set designer for the *Vieux Paris*, prepared for the 1900 World's Fair, as mentioned earlier.

In *Saturnin*, Robida's hero goes on a trip around the world, from Oceania to Asia, Russia, Africa, and America, eventually reaching the North Pole. But at the same time, he goes on a kind of "intertextual journey" through Jules Verne's novels and has the opportunity to meet the latter's most famous characters, including Captain Nemo, the hero of *20,000 Leagues under the Sea*, and Phileas Fogg, the protagonist of *Around the World in Eighty Days*.

According to Antonio Faeti, an Italian writer and an expert in children's literature, Robida's novel

> is a frenetic epos which leads the reader into a whole library, in which the protagonist navigates in seas that allude to almost all writers of novels about voyages of his time, mentioning all the myths, violating symbols, constructing the maddest of plots which are continuously interwoven with rapid allusions to different lit-

erary territories, drawing out characters, stereotypes, situations. Naturally Verne is the one who is most often targeted: his Captain Nemo comes to life again in Robida's pages, but as he has lost his impenetrable pride, he joins forces with Saturnino and a pack of monkeys in order to fight the Maltese pirates. Phileas Fogg, who here is general of the Southern troops in the war of secession, falls asleep with all his army, hit by chloroform bombs. Ettore Servadac travels astride a flying minaret, while Michel Strogoff travels through Manchuria on the back of a white elephant.[37]

In *Saturnin*, Faeti sees "a funny anti-Darwinian controversy" and discusses "the regressive implications of Farandola's anti-evolutionistic journey." The novel begins with Saturnin who is raised by a community of monkeys. The monkeys become desperate because the small four-handed being does not succeed in developing a tail, in spite of the interventions of a venerable "wizard" monkey who treats him without success, but also because he is not able to acquire the abilities and elegance of his "foster-brothers." The novel ends with Saturnin's return to the island of the monkeys from his childhood, "founding a republic in which all his numerous friends and followers accept to live with equal rights and duties in a village of monkeys" (Faeti, 172).

Robida's novel has many rich illustrations showing the reader the most fantastic and exaggerated inventions of literary texts. Therefore, it is at the same time a literary source and an iconographic model for Marcel Fabre's filmic adaptation. Robida's illustrations, which offer ironic and exaggerated revisions of the illustrations produced for the Hetzel Edition of Verne's *Extraordinary Travels*, are not, however, the only source of Fabre's film. He was also inspired by the unrestrained imagination of Méliès's fantastical cinema, which, according to the influential opinion of Georges Sadoul, had in turn been inspired by...Robida's iconography!

Originally, Fabre's film was a four-part serial the total length of which was 3,660 metres (12,000 feet). Obviously, it was impossible to conserve all the narrative material of an abundant novel in a film of this size, and it was even more impossible to conserve the vast system of intertextual references that supported Robida's writing (and iconography). The copy that can be seen today is a reduced version of 1,612 metres (5,289 feet). This abridged copy almost totally preserves the episodes summarized in the synopsis published in Martinelli and Bernardini's list of films[38] and allows one to fully appreciate the whirl of inventions of a film in which literally everything happens. Presented in 1997 at an important retrospective of Turin's cinematographic productions during the 1910s, in which many scholars from around the world participated,[39] Fabre's film was characterized by Kristin Thompson as one of the most important "discoveries" of the whole collection, despite the fact that it had been screened on various occasions at international silent films shows.[40]

From the wild islands of the Pacific Ocean to the steppe of Asia, from equatorial Africa to Australia, from the mysterious Far East to America, the film presents a repertoire of exotic landscapes. Filming, however, never took place in the real settings. They are instead simulations produced through scenographic preparation and cinematographic trickery. The result is approximate at best. For instance, the numerous scenes in which exotic animals appear—the monkeys of the first part, the elephant, the lions—all seem to have been shot in a circus. The Italian audience of that period had learned to appreciate this sort of trickery, however, in part because of films such as those produced by Luca Comerio or even Pasquali's *Il giro del mondo in due ore.*

In fact, with respect to Comerio's *From the Pole to the Equator,* discussed above, Fabre's film proves to be a parodic version of it in several ways. Indeed, with its taste for exaggeration and its decidedly grotesque and comical tone, *Saturnino Farandola* scoffs at trips of exploration and conquest. This is precisely why it becomes so interesting next to the various films we have examined so far, all of which are marked by a strong ideological dimension, whether it is the ideology of colonialism or the documentation of evolution. Freed from the requirements of documenting and recording the world by the sheer play of its fictional narrative, one could paradoxically argue that, in debunking the theme of the trip around the world, *Saturnino Farandola* is closer in some sense to Gianikian and Ricci Lucchi's reworking of *Dal Polo all'Equatore* than it is to Comerio's original film project. The paradox lies in the fact that Fabre's film relies in good measure on its initial public's acquaintance with the various projects then seeking to use the cinema to document the world, such as those we have discussed earlier. And if *Saturnino Farandola* does not possess the inventive richness of Robida's novel, it does have something similar to the ironic spirit and the paradoxical strain of the original due in part to the novel itself, but also thanks to a very different source to which we alluded earlier. For indeed, in its best parts, the film manages to recapture the ingenious and poetic taste for journeys first encountered in the impossible and fictional travels of Méliès's cinema.

## at the end of the trip

261

In Italy, Marcel Fabre's film was released on the eve of World War I, in that momentous year of 1914 that marks the end of an epoch—precisely, the *Belle Époque,* which not only had witnessed the remarkable growth of cinema but also the apogee of European expansionism.

We have already pointed out that Rémy de Gourmont had precociously established the relationship between the cinematograph and the trip around the world. The combined action of rapidly developing means of transportation and reproductive media—such as photography and cinema—had generated a new "culture of space and time" (Kern, 1983). The trip around the world reached out to the horizon of possible events, even if what it really offered, in fact, was a simulated experience taking place either within the system of "monstrative attractions" ("système des attractions monstratives" [Gaudreault and Gunning, 1989]) or that of the World's Fairs' itineraries.

As we have seen, the use of the cinematograph in the exhibition areas of the World's Fairs offered a sort of *mise en abyme* of the real-life experiences of the visitors themselves, who embarked on travels through time (Robida's *Vieux Paris*) or space (the exotic sights of Venice, which had been rebuilt for the benefit of visitors in the 1901 Pan-American Exposition of Buffalo, NY). Material shot by the Lumière brothers in the first case and by E. S. Porter in the second case was displayed in the same exhibition areas, and staged the perceptual experiences of the visitors, who thus found themselves "elevated to the level of commodities" (Benjamin, 1999).

Through an investigation of the "interpretive restoration" carried out by Yervant Gianikian's and Angela Ricci Lucchi's "analytical camera," we have seen the emergence of the colonialist ideology informing the corpus of images from all the world gathered by the Italian explorer Luca Comerio, and afterwards edited for the unfinished film *Dal Polo all'Equatore*. What Gianikian's and Ricci Lucchi's work lays bare is the same sort of ideological discourse production theorized by Gaudreault and Gunning with their system of monstrative attractions, and which unmasks the illusion of cinematographic realism through the "unrepresentable of representation" (Lyotard, 1978), that is to say, through the laying bare of all those aspects of filmic representation that are *normalized* or concealed in the cinematographic apparatus.

As for Albert Kahn, we have seen that his work offers a totally different perspective on the relationship between the trip around the world, the process of staging, and the archive. As is the case with the World's Fairs, Albert Khan's garden with multiple scenes suggests the idea of a journey through different cultures and different interpretations of the relationship between culture and nature. However, we are no longer confronting a mere spectacular display and reification of the exotic and the picturesque. In Khan's project, which places the scenographic function of the park side by side with the cognitive function of the archive, the notion of travel is strictly associated with the adventure of learning, in all the countries of the world and in all the fields of knowledge. We have pointed out that "Les Archives de la Planète" include as many films as they do sheets of *autochromes*. Developed by the Lumière brothers, the autochromes were used in the *Cinématographe Géant* of the 1900 Paris World Fair and there are obvious affinities between the technique and the aesthetic value of the Lumières' and Khan's productions. Yet it is also clear, as we have seen, that the project of Albert Kahn and his collaborators and inspirators—among whom we find the philosopher Henri Bergson—has an altogether very different purpose and meaning.

A different approach to the theme of the trip around the world can be found in Marcel Fabre's film *Le avventure straordinarissime di Saturnino Farandola*. Adapted from a novel by Robida that in turn parodies the work of Jules Verne, and especially his exaltation of technical and scientific progress, Fabre's film parodies the trip around the world's implications in terms of adventure, knowledge, and conquest. Resulting from a late revisitation of the techniques and narrative strategies of Méliès's cinema, Marcel Fabre's film signals the passing of an era and shows that the sun had now forever set on the cinema's *age of innocence*.

From the Lumière catalogue, to Comerio, Gianikian and Ricci Lucchi, Khan's "Archives de la Planète," Fabre's adaptation of Robida, and a few others only briefly mentioned, ours then has also been a journey of sorts through some of the various *topoi* of early film landscape, a trip around the world if you will, but of a different nature. What our own travel illustrates is that there is no single or unique landscape-function in early cinema; instead, various functions are distributed along several paths: the colonial domestication of the exotic, the contemplative, the scientific, but also the ironic critique and the poetic. Understanding the meaning of the various filmed landscapes of early cinema implies adopting a methodological gaze that goes beyond the films themselves so as to encompass the different settings where they were produced and exhibited as well as the different discursive networks that both legitimated them and were being legitimated by them.

## notes

1. M. Aubert and J. C. Seguin, eds., *La Production cinématographique des Frères Lumières* (Paris: Bibliothèque du Film-Editions Mémoires du Cinéma, 1996); hereafter cited in text.
2. G. Sadoul, *Lumière et Méliès*, ed. B. Eisenschitz (Paris: Lherminier, 1985), 56.
3. R. de Gourmont, "Epilogues: Cinématographe," *Mercure de France* (September 1907): 124–127, quoted in J. Prieur, *Le spectateur nocturne. Les écrivains au cinéma: une anthologie* (Paris: Éditions de l'étoile/ Cahiers du cinéma, 1993), 36–39; hereafter cited in text.
4. On the concept of attraction in early cinema, see A. Gaudreault and T. Gunning, "Le cinéma des premiers temps: un défi à l'histoire du cinéma?," in *L'Histoire du cinéma: nouvelles approches*, eds. J. Aumont, A. Gaudreault, and M. Marie (Paris: Publications de la Sorbonne Nouvelle-Colloque de Cerisy, 1989), 49–63.
5. See Antonio Pigafetta, *Il primo viaggio intorno al mondo con il trattato della sfera*, ed. Mario Pozzi (Vicenza: Neri Pozza, 1994).
6. G. Forster, *Reise um die Welt*, ed. G. Steiner (Frankfurt am Main, 1983).
7. S. Kern, *The Culture of Time and Space, 1880–1918* (Cambridge, MA: Harvard University Press, 1983).

8. For the distinction between landscape as *attraction* and landscape as *production*, see my introduction to the issue of *CiNéMAS* devoted to landscape and film, vol. 12, no. 1 (Fall 2001): 7–14.

9. A. Robida, *Voyages très extraordinaires de Saturnin Farandoul (dans les 5 ou 6 parties du monde et dans tous les pays connus et même inconnus de M. Jules Verne)* (Paris: Librairie illustrée M. Dreyfous, 1879–1880).

10. A. Bernardini, *Cinema muto italiano. I film "dal vero" 1895–1914* (Gemona: La Cineteca del Friuli, 2002), 273.

11. W. Benjamin, *The Arcades Project* (Cambridge, MA: Belknap Press of Harvard University Press, 1999).

12. E. Toulet, "Le cinema à l'Exposition Universelle de 1900," *Revue d'histoire moderne et contemporaine* 33 (April-June 1986): 179–208; hereafter cited in text.

13. Ph. Brun, *Albert Robida (1848–1926) Sa Vie, son oeuvre suivie d'une bibliographie complète de ses écrits et dessins* (Paris: Editions Promodis, 1984).

14. See Ch. Musser, *The Emergence of Cinema. The American Screen to 1907* (Berkeley: University of California Press, 1994), 317–319.

15. On the intermedial perspectives of the novel *XXᵉ Siècle*, see Jurgen E. Muller, "L'Intermedialité, une nouvelle approche interdisciplinaire: perspectives théiques e pratiques à l'example de la vision à la télévision," *CiNéMAS* 10, nos. 2-3 (Spring 2000): 105–134.

16. Besides being a photographer and a documentary filmmaker, Comerio was also a producer of fiction films (amongst others, he founded Milano Films, the production company which, in 1911, made the first feature film of the Italian cinema, inspired by Dante's *Inferno*). See C. Manenti, N. Monti, G. Nicodemi, eds., *Luca Comerio fotografo e cineasta* (Milano: Electa, 1979); L. Sardi, "Luca Comerio, pioniere del cinema milanese," in *Un secolo di cinema a Milano*, ed. R. De Berti (Milano: Il Castoro, 1996), 62–70; A. Farassino, *Fuori di set. Viaggi, migrazioni, nomadismi* (Roma: Bulzoni, 2000), 37–42.

17. See M. Gentili, "Dal Polo all'Equatore. Nel regno dell'immagine tra esplorazioni e violenze," *Cineforum* 28, no. 1-2 (Jan.-Feb. 1988): 4–44; hereafter cited in text; S. MacDonald, "From the Pole to the Equator," *Film Quarterly* 42, no. 3 (Spring 1989): 33–38; P. Mereghetti and E. Nosei, eds., *Cinema anni vita. Yervant Gianikian e Angel Ricci Lucchi*, bilingual ed., Italian/English (Milano: Il Castoro, 2000).

18. Y. Gianikian and A. Ricci Lucchi, "Our Analytical Camera," *Cinema anni vita. Yervant Gianikian e Angel Ricci Lucchi*, *op. cit.* 49-58; hereafter cited in text.

19. I have summarized the contents of the 10 sections, based on the analytical *précis* given by the two filmmakers.

20. R. Bellour, "Il retromondo/Retromondo," in *Cinema anni vita. Yervant Gianikian e Angel Ricci Lucchi*, *op. cit.*, 81; G. Deleuze *L'Image-mouvement*, (Paris: Ed. de Minuit, 1983), 96; hereafter cited in text.

21. See J. F. Lyotard, "L'Acinéma," *Cinéma: théorie, lectures* (numéro spécial de la *Revue d'esthétique*), ed. Dominique Noguez (Paris: Klincksieck, 1978), 357–369; hereafter cited in text.

22. See Jeanne Beausoleil and P. Orly, eds., *Albert Khan, Réalités d'une Utopie* (Boulogne: Musée Albert Khan, 1995). This is the most complete and up-to-date collection of information and studies on the life and the scientific and cultural enterprises promoted by Albert Khan.

antonio costa

264

23. J. Beausoleil, ed., *Espace Départemental Albert Khan. Jardins et Collections* (Paris: Musée Albert Kahn, 1990); hereafter cited in text.

24. See Marie Bonhomme, "Les Jardins d'Albert Khan: une héterotopie?" in *Albert Khan, Réalités d'une Utopie, op. cit.*, 102–104; hereafter cited in text.

25. Marie Mattera Corneloup, "Albert Khan autour du monde," in *Albert Khan, Réalités d'une Utopie, op. cit.*, 59–72; hereafter cited in text.

26. Flore Hervé, "Les Archives de la Planète," in *Albert Khan, Réalités d'une Utopie, op. cit.*, 188; hereafter cited in text. With regards to Khan's project, see also Paula Amad, "Les Archives de la Planète d'Albert Kahn (1908-1931): archives ou contre-archives de l'histoire?", *Les Cahiers de la Cinémathèque*, no. 74 (December 2002): 19–33; and Sam Rohdie, *Promised Lands. Cinema, Geography, Modernism*, (London: British Film Institute, 2001).

27. See footnote 8.

28. *Ibid.*

29. Beausoleil, *op. cit.*, 10-11.

30. The best place to see this material is, of course, l'Espace Albert Khan Boulogne-Billancourt, especially if one can go there while visiting the gardens. However, it can be extremely useful for those who have not been able to visit l'Espace to see the videotape distributed by the Khan Foundation, which contains a rich selection of the material of the archives. It is edited by Claude Hidelot, Jean Kargayan, and Michel Hivert and made in close collaboration with the team of the Musée Albert Khan, directed by Jeanne Beausoleil.

31. Isabelle Do O'Gomes, "L'oeuvre de Jean Comandon," in *Le Cinéma et la science*, ed. A. Martinet (Paris: CNRS Editions, 1994), 85.

32. This actor, of Spanish origin (his real name is Marcel Fernàndez Peréz), who went from the circus to the cinema, became well known in the comedies made by Pathé and Éclair. Hired by the Turin-based production company Ambrosio in 1911, he created, in competition with Cretinetti, the character of Robinet, which made him famous all over the world (in some films Robinet appears beside Robinette, interpreted by Nilde Baracchi). In 1913 he also directed some comedies of the Fricot series, besides, of course, *Saturnino Farandola*, which, together with *Amor pedestre*, is usually considered among his best work. He then immigrated to the United States, where he did various things: he tried to make his character, Robinet, come alive again; he worked for various production companies (Psha, Sanford, Arrow); he also directed some westerns with Pete Morrison. He had to have his leg amputated after an accident at work; and he then became a script writer for Universal. He died in 1929, forgotten by everyone. See A. Bernardini and V. Martinelli, "Robinet," in *I comici del Muto italiano*, eds. P. Cerchi Usai and L. Jacob (Pordenone: Le giornate del cinema muto, 1985), 116–123.

33. See footnote 9.

34. Founded by Rodolphe Salis in 1881, the Chat Noir got its name from a story by Edgar Allan Poe. Various artists worked at the Chat Noir, including Caran D'Ache, the author of *L'Epopée*, an epic representation of Napoleon's Russian campaigns. *La tentation de Saint Antoine* is another famous Shadow Theatre show produced in 1887 by Henri Rivière, inspired by Gustave Flaubert's work: see J. Remise, P. Remise, and R. van de Walle, *Magie lumineuse du theatre d'ombre à la lanterne magique* (Paris: Balland, 1979), 302–311.

35. See J. P. Bouyou, *La Science-fiction au cinéma* (Paris: UgdE, 1971), 31.

36. See M. Oberthür, ed., *Le Chat Noir* (Paris: Réunion de Musées Nationaux, 1992), 49. It should be noted that Jules Verne had already written a novel entitled *Paris au XX$^e$ Siècle* in about 1863, which was not published by Hetzel. It has, however, been recently published, ed. P. Gondolo Della Riva (Paris: Hachette, 1994).

37. A. Faeti, *Guardare le figure* (Torino: Einaudi, 1972), 171–172; translated by the author, Antonio Costa; hereafter cited in text.

38. See V. Martinelli and A. Bernardini, *Il cinema muto Italiano 1914*, vol. 1 (Torino: Nuova ERI, 1993), 52.

39. See P. Beretto and G. Rondolino, eds., *Cabiria e il suo tempo* (Torino-Milano: Museo Nazionale del Cinema-Il castoro, 1998).

40. See K. Thompson, "Colloque: I giorni di Cabiria/La grande stagione del cinema muto torinese," in *Domitor. Bulletin de Liaison* 12, no. 1 (January 1998): 13–14.

# a walk through
# heterotopia

peter greenaway's

landscapes by numbers

bridget  elliott  and  anthony  purdy

## grids, games, and maps

In *Fear of Drowning / Règles du jeu*, published in 1988 shortly after the release of
the feature film, *Drowning by Numbers*, Peter Greenaway offers a numbered
series of 100 speculations about a film he is "still happy to contemplate."[1]
Sections 90 to 99 describe the nine episodes of a projected television series
to be called *Fear of Drowning*: "Each episode would increase in length, starting at twenty minutes and increasing by five-minute increments until the
115-minute *Drowning by Numbers* was reached" (Greenaway, 1988a, 125).[2] The
main characters were to be Cissie Colpitts, her blind mother, Sadie, and
her father, Cribb, a quixotic ferryman on the banks of the River Humber in Yorkshire. The nine episodes were to relate Cissie's childhood from
her birth in 1876 to her 18th birthday on May 10, 1895, "the same day that
Lumière patented the cine-camera. Cissie anticipates the language of the
cinema before it is born" (Greenaway, 1988a, 127). Like Madgett in *Drowning by Numbers*, Cribb is an inveterate game player and in episode 1 "plays

a solo Christening-Game on the wide tidal foreshore of the river. Part hopscotch, part Japanese sand-garden, part quoits, the game-board is fifty yards square and scratched and shaped into the gritty sand of the river beach among the prints of crabs, dogs and sheep" (Greenaway, 1988a, 127). Episode 2 enacts the Lobster-Quadrille, a game devised for 30 players—fishermen, ferrymen, boatmen, their wives and children—to be played on the river foreshore: "The game is nautically mapped out on the beach in a giant square.... A flooded pit in the South represents the Antarctic Deeps, an upturned boat in the East represents the Great Wall of China, a bonfire in the North represents the Aurora Borealis, a grease-bath in the West stands in for the Sargasso Sea" (Greenaway, 1988a, 129).

While Greenaway's stated prime visual intertexts—the Yorkshire photographs of Frank Sutcliffe and John Tenniel's original illustrations for Lewis Carroll's "Hunting of the Snark" (Greenaway, 1988a, 127)—clearly inform and colour the imagined scenes, we might also suspect other landscape practices of motivating the imposition of a 50-yards square game-board, "scratched and shaped into the gritty sand of the river beach among the prints of crabs, dogs and sheep" in episode 1, or the presence of a giant square nautically mapped out on the beach in episode 2. The influence of the British Land Art movement of the 1960s and 1970s is unmistakable, especially the geometric patterns enacted by Richard Long (Figure 11.1) in the course of his many solitary walks in remote parts of the world.[3] By the time we reach the "grand landscape game" called Vertical Features described in episode 8, Greenaway seems well on his way to fashioning his own Land Art paradigms:

> The river estuary and the land around it for a good six square miles is flat—very flat, and landscape features like brick factory chimneys, windmills, lighthouses and church towers stand out very clearly. Cribb has mapped the surrounding landscape for its verticals and has made a table top model set up under a stretched tarpaulin on the beach out of reach of the tide.... Players in the landscape game are tagged according to whether they live in the prescribed areas, and by boat, bicycle, horse or on foot, they travel as fast as they can from landscape vertical to landscape vertical.... Cribb has built himself his own "Vertical"—a rickety tower of ladders and driftwood that marks his house and puts him in mathematical line with the other landscape features. (1988a, 143)

The End Game of episode 9—played on the occasion of Cissie's 18th birthday, for which she will receive a battered camera as a gift—will lead to Cribb's death as the culmination of a series of increasingly metaphysical

Figure 11.1

Richard Long, *A Line Made by Walking, England* (1967). Tate Gallery, London (Courtesy of Art Resources).

games that have come to occupy his entire waking life: "They now involve the Elements with people as minor participants. Cribb pits the movement of the tides with the movement of the clouds, wind direction with shadow length, the flocking of birds with rainfall—devising complex systems of advantage, bonus and handicap, keeping scrupulous scores, notes, checks and counts in numerous ledgers whose crinkly pages and stained covers suggest that they've been dredged from the river. The ledgers are illustrated with Cribb's spidery drawings and Tom's photographs" (Greenaway, 1988a, 145). While this last description anticipates in more than one respect the waterlogged books and elemental magic of Greenaway's next-but-one feature film—*Prospero's Books* (1991)—it is to two of his early short films, both made in 1978, that we must turn if we are to understand the particular relation to landscape that emerges in episodes 8 and 9 of the projected *Fear of Drowning*.

The Vertical Features game in episode 8, that sees Cribb mapping the surrounding landscape for its verticals, is a direct allusion to *Vertical Features Remake*, a 44-minute mock documentary made around the time when Greenaway parted company with the Central Office of Information, a publicity branch of the British Foreign Office. Greenaway had worked there since 1965 as an editor and director of thinly veiled industrial and commercial propaganda films about life in Britain made for overseas distribution. Deeply sceptical about the truth claims of British documentary in particular and contemporary film culture in general, Greenaway uses his knowledge and personal experience with both the Central Office of Information and the British Film Institute to parody the genre and satirize the establishment. The film's starting point is the fictional discovery of some very patchy records of a film project undertaken by Tulse Luper, part magus, part game player, a more dashingly cosmopolitan precursor of the parochially quixotic Cribb and Madgett, a romantically elusive Greenaway alter ego who flits in and out of a number of early works and has only recently reappeared in a more central role after a long absence.[4] Initially commissioned under a State Landscape Programme codenamed "Session 3," Luper's lost or destroyed *Vertical Features* had apparently sought to draw attention to sinister goings on in the landscape; *Vertical Features Remake* purports to present four attempts by the Institute of Reclamation and Restoration (IRR) to reconstruct the missing film. The four short films thus framed are in themselves beautiful examples of structuralist/Land Art examinations of verticals (posts, poles, trees, etc.) in a rural landscape. Trained as a painter in the 1960s and apparently still sharing his contemporaries' deep distrust of the tradition of English landscape art, Greenaway relies on cartographic conventions and arithmetic progressions—the filmmaker's equivalents of the painter's grids and tables—to hold any residual "expressive" or affective impulses carefully in check. As Paul Melia argues: "Shots of the vertical features are arranged so that each successive section of film is one frame longer than its predecessor. In the second film within *Vertical Features*, 11 sections of film, each composed of 11 images, are edited so that each successive section is 11 frames longer than the preceding one.[5] By such means Greenaway was able to produce an elegy to the landscape in full confidence that he was doing so using a non-Romantic, distinctly contemporary vocabulary."[6] However, taken together and interwoven with a voiceover pastiche of theoretical debate involving intellectuals, academics, and members of the IRR, the four films progressively deconstruct their own premises and methods and generate a pointedly absurdist critique of contemporary avant-garde film culture and theory, including the fashionably posthumous figure of the author/auteur.

Bringing its tactic of radical scepticism to bear on the institutions and imperatives of experimental cinema, *Vertical Features Remake* paradoxically allows the landscape to float free of the competing discourses and the meanings they seek to attach to it, making it available for ever new investments and reenchantments that flow directly from the pathos of human failure to contain and circumscribe the natural world in cultural codes and scientific systems. Gridded, mapped, and numbered, appropriated

bridget elliott and anthony purdy

and disputed, the land persists, its mute impassivity a perpetual reproach amidst the all-too-human chatter. In fact, as Amy Lawrence observes, Greenaway's early shorts "uncover a surprising depth of feeling" as they "weave idyllic, nostalgic images" of the English landscape into "a witty exposé of man's attempts to 'read,' interpret, and order nature with a series of grids, maps, and narratives."[7] She continues: "The charm of Greenaway's short films comes from the coexistence of a high-spirited playfulness and a lingering emotional effect. In Greenaway's work, both wit and feeling are produced in the same way: the inclusion of blissfully irrelevant detail, the development of character through throwaway lines and non sequiturs, a sense of resignation when confronted with the universe's lack of meaning balanced by a taste for the absurd" (Lawrence, 14). This is particularly true of *A Walk Through H, or The Reincarnation of an Ornithologist*, a film made a matter of months before *Vertical Features Remake* and shortly after the death of Greenaway's father, himself a devoted ornithologist. It is this film that is reprised in the End Game in episode 9 of *Fear of Drowning*, in which the ill-fated Cribb fails in his attempt to pit "the movement of the tides with the movement of the clouds, wind direction with shadow length, the flocking of birds with rainfall" (Greenaway, 1988a, 145).[8]

*A Walk Through H* begins in a picture gallery in which are hung 92 of Greenaway's drawings (Figure 11.2), which the voice of the dying narrator-protagonist—Colin Cantlie's brisk, authoritative voice of British documentary—will present in sequence as maps arranged for him by Tulse Luper "one Monday afternoon when he heard that I was ill." "Tulse Luper suggested my journey through H needed 92 maps. Anticipating my question, he suggested the time to decide what H stood for was at the end of the journey and by that time it scarcely mattered." These maps will guide the narrator on an allegorical journey into death, or a walk through H: "I finally left on the Tuesday morning early at about a quarter to two."[9] The filmic journey begins at this point as the camera pans and cuts from map to map and we become absorbed in the narrative that unfolds, taking us simultaneously forward on the narrator's journey through H and backward through the events and relationships of his past life that marked the provenance and circumstances of acquisition of each map. In the process, a complex web of family relations, friendships, and enmities is spun into shadowy existence, the insubstantial stuff of the narrator's rapidly disappearing life. His growing confusion and feeble grip on life are belied by the unwavering self-assurance of the tone—if not the content—of his own narrative voiceover, but underscored by the behaviour of the maps themselves which fade not only with use but also after the allotted time for their use is exhausted. As a result, the narrator is forced to run in order to cover the territory represented by one map before the map disappears. However, after looping nine times through the same point on another

271

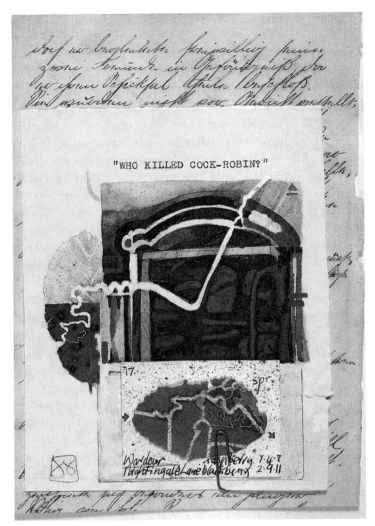

Figure 11.2

Peter Greenaway, *Who Killed Cock Robin?* A map from *A Walk Through H* (1978). (Courtesy of Peter Greenaway.)

map, he realizes that the time allowance for each map stretches forward as well as backward and that it is possible to walk (or run) too fast.

The journey through the maps also intersects in curiously proleptic and self-referential ways with Greenaway's own professional life and artistic projects—collapsing time frames and levels of representation as in the case of map 59, which "ostensibly is the floor plan of a gallery, where I had once arranged an exhibition on the subject of flight. The red line was an instruction for a tracking film camera. It now served me as a track to the sixtieth map." (In fact, the first recorded exhibition to focus on the subject of flight is *Le Bruit des nuages* [*Flying Out of This World*], mounted in 1992 in the Louvre, some 14 years after *A Walk Through H* was made; it would be followed in 1997 by *Flying Over Water*.) References to birds multiply as the maps are more and more frequently intercut with short sequences of migrating birds in flight, the filmic representation of real movement contrasting eerily with the inevitable stasis of the maps, animated only by the displacements effected by the camera. This point is underscored by the narrator as we near the end of the journey: "A map that tried to pin down a sheep trail was just credible. But it was an optimistic map that tried to fix a path made by the wind. Or a path made across the grass by the shadow of flying birds. The usual conventions of cartography were now collapsing. Either that or the route itself was becoming so insecure that mapping it was a foolhardy occupation."

The narrator walks the last half-mile "across a nearly featureless landscape, guided by a few stains and some distant pencil lines": "I had arrived. It was Tuesday morning early at about a quarter to two. I had used 92 maps, and had travelled 1,418 miles." We pull out of the last map and back into the "reality" of the picture gallery, which we see again as a whole as at the start of the film. We see the curator get up from her desk and leave the room, turning out all the lights except the desk lamp. The camera moves in on a book whose illustrated cover, with its photograph of a flock of birds, is framed by the light. The film's last shot is a close-up that shows the author's name to be Tulse Luper, the title *Some Migratory Birds of the Northern Hemisphere*. The typeface is that used for the film's credits. The book contains 92 maps and 1,418 birds in colour.

What then do we make of this complex and condensed artefact that is *A Walk Through H*? To understand better what Greenaway is doing here, we might start with the numbers in the film's closing shot. "92" is a Greenaway favourite, taken initially from the 90 one-minute sections of John Cage's *Indeterminacy* that the filmmaker claims to have miscounted. Along with the division of the film into five parts corresponding to five types of landscape—urban, agricultural, wooded, frontier, and wilderness—the aleatory structure imposed by the 92 maps was the only direction given to Michael Nyman for his independently produced musical score. The number will be repeated often in Greenaway's subsequent work, for example, in the 92 biographies of *The Falls* (1980), the 92 gold bars that animate the 101 stories of *Gold*, the 92 conceits of the Minotaur in *Prospero's Books*, and the 92 suitcases of the most recent Tulse Luper project. Through its different incarnations, it comes to embody the principle of an abstract, arbitrary structure imposed on the author's fertile imaginary world. In *A Walk Through H* it serves more particularly to unify and reinforce the aleatory structure by creating parallels between Tulse Luper's book with its 92 maps of migratory routes, Greenaway's 92 drawings on the gallery walls, and the 92 maps of the ornithologist's story/journey. Both the film's explicit intermediality and its metaleptic play of levels of narrative and representation are further underscored by the number "1,418," used referentially to measure the length of the fictional journey in miles, and self-referentially to measure the length of 16 mm film in feet (Berthin-Scaillet, 20).

Through the typeface used on the book cover, we are referred back to the film's opening credit sequence, to the filmmaker's name, now retrospectively associated with that of Tulse Luper, and to the title, *A Walk Through H*. If, as Tulse Luper suggests at the start of the ornithologist's journey, it now "scarcely matters" to him what H stands for, we as viewers might nevertheless be tempted to reflect further, as this is not Greenaway's first walk through H. *H is for House*, a short film made in 1973 and reedited in 1978, is in essence a home movie that shows Greenaway's wife, Carol, and young daughter, Hannah, engaged in everyday activities on a sunny day around a house in Wiltshire. The soundtrack features both the familiar dialogue between a father's prompts—*A is for...? B is for ...?*—and a daughter's enthusiastic answers, accompanied by Colin Cantlie's more disturbing voiceover recitation of words that begin with H. At first, as Amy Lawrence has pointed out, the words form series or semantic fields whose organizing principle is easy to grasp: *H is for hawk, hoopoe, hawfinch, heron, harrier, hawthorne, heather, hemlock, holly, hellebore, and hazel* (Lawrence, 14). Soon, however, order gives way to chaos as the logic grows uncertain; the series start to shift and flow, principles multiply and interfere with one another, generating noise in an already precarious system: *H is for health and happiness, hearse, hepatitis, heretic, heaven, hell, horror, holocaust, and His Holiness...H is for hat, hue, hatchet, hammer, and Hitchcock...H is for handicap, handicraft, handiwork, handkerchief, and handle...H is for cigars, Havana cigars...H is for hopelessness, happiness, homelessness...hesitation...H is for bean, haricot bean, and has-been.*

The impression of dissipation and breakdown produced by the film's self-decomposing lists recalls Foucault's account of certain aphasiacs who struggle to organize into a coherent pattern different coloured skeins of wool on a table top

> as though that simple rectangle were unable to serve in their case as a homogeneous or neutral space in which things could be placed so as to display at the same time the continuous order of their identities or differences as well as the semantic field of their denomination. Within this simple space in which things are normally arranged and given names, the aphasiac will create a multiplicity of tiny, fragmented regions in which nameless resemblances agglutinate things into unconnected islets; in one corner, they will place the lightest-coloured skeins, in another the red ones, somewhere else those that are softest in texture, in yet another place the longest, or those that have a tinge of purple or those that have been wound up into a ball. But

no sooner have they been adumbrated than all these groupings dissolve again, for the field of identity that sustains them, however limited it may be, is still too wide not to be unstable.[10]

This account is part of Foucault's discussion of the by now famous passage in Borges's essay on the analytical language of John Wilkins, which quotes "a certain Chinese encyclopedia" and its wondrous taxonomy of animals, presented in no apparent order, not even alphabetical, but listed arbitrarily as categories (a) through (n). Foucault argues that the disconcerting quality that runs through Borges's enumeration has little to do with the categories of animals evoked and everything to do with the fact that they have been brought together in a single space, "the non-place of language" (1970, xvii): "What transgresses the boundaries of all imagination, of all possible thought, is simply that alphabetical series (a, b, c, d) which links each of those categories to all the others" (1970, xvi). What is lacking is the common ground, the site, on which such a juxtaposition would make sense: "Yet, though language can spread them before us, it can do so only in an unthinkable space" (1970, xvii). This is the space that, in *The Order of Things*, Foucault calls a heterotopia, by definition unlocatable and unrepresentable as a space or site outside language: "*Heterotopias* are disturbing, probably because they secretly undermine language, because they make it impossible to name this *and* that, because they shatter or tangle common names, because they destroy 'syntax' in advance, and not only the syntax with which we construct sentences but also that less apparent syntax which causes words and things (next to and also opposite one another) to 'hold together'" (1970, xviii). In Greenaway's world, H may well stand for hawk, house, and Hitchcock, but, first and foremost, H is for heterotopia.[11]

We might then conclude that *A Walk Through H* recounts a journey through Heterotopia, a territory that exists only through its maps, just as the places on the cinema screen exist only through the projection of light through sequenced images set in motion at 24 frames a second: "Perhaps the country only existed in its maps, in which case the traveller created the territory as he walked through it. If he should stand still, so would the landscape. I kept moving." This setting in motion—and simultaneous narrativisation—of a series of static images is one of the techniques that Greenaway uses in the film to explore the vocabulary of cinema, first drawing us into the story/landscape through the interaction of "maps" and camera, then expelling us from it as we are returned to the gallery or museum space. In this sense, we might think of the narrator-protagonist's journey as taking place in the nonspace (and the nontime) of the language of cinema: the narrator arrives at his destination, which is also his point of departure, at the same time as he leaves; a distance is apparently traversed but no time elapses.

There is, however, a second occurrence of the term *heterotopia* in Foucault's work, this time used to designate real rather than purely discursive spaces. In a talk given to an architects' group in 1967 and later translated and published under the title "Of Other Spaces," Foucault offers one of his more developed reflections on space, which he sees as the great obsession of the twentieth century as opposed to the nineteenth century's preoccupation with time or history.[12] Not the medieval space of emplacement, or the Classical space of extension, but a space that takes the form of relations among sites, relations that can formally be described as "series, trees, or grids" (1986, 23). In particular, Foucault is interested in certain "real places" that are "something like counter-sites, a kind of effectively enacted utopia in which the real sites, all the other real sites that can be found within the culture, are simultaneously represented, contested, and inverted" (Foucault, 1986, 24). These places that are "outside of all places, even though it may be possible to indicate their location in reality" (1986, 24) are what Foucault here calls heterotopias. Without providing a theoretically adequate definition of the concept, he offers instead half a dozen more or less unrelated principles that serve as a description, or heterotopology, and discusses a number of examples. Some of these principles can help us to think about *A Walk Through H*.

If the heterotopia, in this second sense, is an *other* space, we might hypothesize, according to Foucault's fourth principle, that it exists in or opens onto an *other* time, a *heterochrony*: "The heterotopia begins to function at full capacity when men arrive at a sort of absolute break with their traditional time" (Foucault, 1986, 26). What we see in *A Walk Through H* is what Foucault's first principle calls a crisis heterotopia (1986, 24), a place which allows for the transition or rite of passage from one state to another; here the space-time in which the narrator traverses 92 maps and 1,418 miles is outside all real times and all real places; it is the threshold between life and death. (There is another sense in which the film itself functions as a crisis heterotopia: as a representation of the crossing of the threshold between life and death, it serves also as a site of mourning. Like much of Greenaway's work, it is elegiac.)

According to Foucault's third principle, the heterotopia has a curious ability to juxtapose "in a single real place several spaces, several sites that are in themselves incompatible" (1986, 25). In *A Walk Through H* such heterotopias abound. At the level of the gallery, we have the drawings that serve as maps; the museum or gallery space that holds and frames them and to which access is, in accordance with Foucault's fifth principle, controlled (represented in the film by the curator's ritual gestures of closure); and the book jacket with its promise to map the migration patterns of 1,418 birds of the Northern Hemisphere. At the level of the narrator's discourse, we have the maps themselves, with their unlikely geographies, as well as some of the places evoked in the stories of their acquisition, such as the

Amsterdam Zoo; more important, we have H itself, the place outside of all places, the vanishing point of representation, the black hole into which all things disappear, and, metonymically, the ordered space of language and knowledge, the dictionary and the encyclopedia, their meanings and references eternally deferred: "the time to decide what H stood for was at the end of the journey and by that time it scarcely mattered." But it is at the level of the film itself that the heterotopia manifests itself most fully, for it is here that all the levels and media intersect and interact, setting static artworks in motion with the aid of camera and discourse, and importing the disruptive typologies of Borges's Chinese encyclopedia into the heterotopian spaces of gallery and map.

It is a reflection on film that lies behind the narrator's complaint that the map is being asked to do something it is not designed to do: "to fix a path made by the wind. Or a path made across the grass by the shadow of flying birds." On the one hand, the enterprise is reminiscent of some of Richard Long's Land Art activities—the making of a path in a field of grass by walking back and forth for several hours, or the inscription of a giant X in a meadow achieved by picking daisies according to a prescribed pattern.[13] On the other, the map is being asked to register not so much shape or pattern as pure movement, the most ephemeral changes of light over the territory it represents. In effect, the narrator's complaint brings to mind Jacques Aumont's claim that "after Lumière had filmed the impalpable, the immaterial, the play of light in clouds of vapour, there will no longer be any naïvely painted clouds. They will become ironic, in the hands of Dali, or parodic in the hands of Magritte."[14] Neither map nor painting can capture the play of light, wind, and clouds in the way that cinema can. *A Walk Through H* is not so much an illustration of this truism—with its intercutting of static shots of framed drawings or paintings in a gallery and nature documentary footage of birds in flight against cloudy skies—as a wry yet strangely touching exploration of the heterotopian possibilities of a new avant-garde intermediality. In 1992 Greenaway would take this a step further and mount an exhibition in that most venerable of art institutions, the Louvre, that would try to capture "*le bruit des nuages*"—the *sound* of clouds—entirely through the paintings and drawings of the museum's collection.[15]

## painting by numbers

One of Peter Greenaway's least discussed feature films, *Drowning by Numbers*, addresses ideas not easily summarized even by its filmmaker. After outlining in a 1988 interview the essayistic impulses underpinning both *The Draughtsman's Contract* and *A Zed & Two Noughts*, Greenaway goes on to claim he would need a further two years to adumbrate "in simple words" the theoretical concerns that inform *Drowning by Numbers*.[16] Mobilizing games and number counts in a darkly comic exploration of relations between the sexes and childhood rites of passage, the film might be seen as another of Greenaway's "crisis heterotopias" that also offers an extended meditation on the English landscape and its representation in both painting and film. Before we explore its landscape in detail, a short plot summary will provide some bearings.

The film revolves around the story of three related female characters, all named Cissie Colpitts, who murder their husbands by drowning them one at a time. The first Cissie (Joan Plowright) is married to Jake, a philandering gardener. Her daughter, the second Cissie (Juliet Stevens), is married to Hardy, the sexually inadequate manager of a fireworks factory. The third and youngest Cissie (Joely Richardson), the granddaughter of Cissie One and niece of Cissie Two, marries Bellamy, an unemployed plumber who cannot swim and does not fulfil her expectations. Each Cissie in turn is saved from criminal charges by the coroner, Madgett, who hopes to secure sexual favours in return for falsifying the death certificates. Each time he is disappointed. As the narrative unfolds, the friends and relatives of the drowned men meet by night under the community water tower (forming what the Cissies call the Water Tower Conspiracy) to plan their revenge. Eventually, the three Cissies, Madgett, and his son, Smut, challenge the water tower conspirators to a tug of war with seven players on each side. If the Cissies win Madgett will be left in peace; if they lose, he will explain to the water tower conspirators what really happened. When Smut abandons his post, the Water Tower Conspiracy wins and the three Cissies and Madgett flee in a rowboat just before a storm arrives. At the end of the film, as the weather deteriorates, the Cissies tell Madgett that they will swim away, leaving him, as another nonswimmer, to drown alone in the boat. The last scene shows the three Cissies swimming siren-like around the boat while Madgett prepares for his watery death. Throughout the film, the audience counts a visible sequence of numbers from 1 to 100 dispersed throughout the landscape. The series ends with a shot of the sinking rowboat, which bears the number 100 on its bow.

Instead of the highly controlled spaces of the seventeenth-century country house and garden of *The Draughtsman's Contract* or the artificial confines of the zoo in *Z&OO*, *Drowning by Numbers* returns to the more chaotic contemporary English countryside of the early shorts and *The Falls*. Unlike mainstream Hollywood directors, Greenaway never relegates his landscapes to the role of background against which the film's characters and narratives are made plausible. More in the spirit of cubist paintings, Greenaway's films abandon the tyranny of single-point perspective by employing a number of strategies that upset the usual binary relationship between figure and ground. Before considering these strategies, it is important to note that, because Greenaway is trying to draw his viewers into a filmic world that is idiosyncratic and eccentric, his illusions of both "real" and "fictional" filmic places need to be compelling. This can be achieved in part by presenting successive viewpoints that produce a recognizable sense of place. In this respect, Greenaway was especially gratified when viewers of *The Draughtsman's Contract* were able to re-create exactly the geographical location using information taken solely from the film. As he stresses, in most cases when one works "backwards" trying to re-create a location from a film, one finds a landscape "full of voids and blanks, and grossly ill-fitting details."[17] He is also concerned to capture the *genius loci*, or that which distinguishes one place from another, and the physical and conceptual links between places. Clearly, Greenaway is not interested in representing the sort of nonplaces which, according to Marc Augé, increasingly characterize our contemporary cultural experience— those generic and impersonal hotel chains where the best surprise is no surprise, franchised cappuccino bars which reappear on every other city block, and airport lounges where travellers wait en route to their destination. For Greenaway, it is important for each location to be "always 're-created' by the film to make its own sense of geography, topography and space, whether it be of a Continent or a cupboard, whether it be complex or simple" (Greenaway, 1994, 77). As we shall see, in *Drowning by Numbers* the representation of the English countryside is both complex and highly loaded, as Greenaway employs a variety of strategies to evoke multiply layered senses of place that function in different registers.

Although on the surface Greenaway seems to shift from the more conceptual preoccupations of Land Art in the early structuralist films to the more pictorial aesthetic of landscape painting in feature films such as *The Draughtsman's Contract* and *Drowning by Numbers*, the boundaries between these two artistic practices quickly become blurred. Certainly there are many quotations (both direct and indirect) from landscape painting in *Drowning by Numbers*, some of which Greenaway lists in *Fear of Drowning by Numbers*. These range from the magic night paintings of Henry Fuseli, Samuel Palmer, Joseph Wright of Derby, Vincent Van Gogh, and Van Est (Greenaway, 1988a, 31) to mid-Victorian landscape painting in the period from 1850 to 1860, a decade that spans the heyday of the Pre-Raphaelite painters, John Everett Millais, Holman Hunt, John Brett, and Arthur Hughes, as well as artists such as John Ruskin, Ford Maddox Brown, and William Dyce (1988a, 33). For good measure, Greenaway throws in a number of children's illustrators, singling out Arthur Rackham, Alfred Bestall, Winsor McCay, and Maurice Sendak as particularly influential (1988a, 47).

Of course, the landscape is not the only thing framed by paintings, since they also play a role in shaping the narrative. Pieter Brueghel's *Children's Games*, which hangs on the wall behind Madgett's bed, is emblematic of the coroner's game-playing (Greenaway, 1988a, 43), while the reproduction of Rubens's *Samson and Delilah* that so intrigues Smut foreshadows and directly influences the child's clumsy attempt to circumcise himself, a symbolic castration that sums up both his uncertainty in relation to the

279

Skipping Girl he so admires and the inadequacy that characterizes all the men in the film (1988a, 118). The Skipping Girl wears a dress inspired by Velasquez's *Las Meninas* (1988a, 16), while the dead Hardy is stretched out in the pose of Mantegna's *Dead Christ* (1988a, 112). (Greenaway notes that his cinematographer, Sacha Vierny, had told him that "in France, such a dramatically foreshortened composition is called a 'mantegna'—a rare direct painting allusion in film language" [1988a, 111]. We might deduce that Hardy's death pose has more to do with the intermediality of the shot than with any Christian allegory, while the allusion to *Las Meninas* sends us inevitably back to Foucault's famous discussion of the painting in *The Order of Things*, and thence to the notion of heterotopia.) These are just some of the sources that Greenaway chooses to identify. As we shall see, there are other intertextual references to painting that he does not discuss.

We are offered a glimpse of Greenaway's unorthodox conception of figure–ground relations in *Drowning by Numbers* when he explains that he originally intended to model his interior spaces on those of the nineteenth-century French painter Vuillard:

> I had long been intrigued by his heavy, dark, domes-
> tic, bourgeois interiors where the figures—through the
> use of texture and patterning—almost entirely disap-
> pear into their surroundings—into the furniture, the
> wall-hangings, the upholstery, most especially into the
> wallpaper. The houses of both Cissie One and Madgett
> were to be stuffed with objects—mainly vegetable in
> the first and scientific in the second—where their occu-
> pants would come and go among their possessions—
> mingling with them, being made insignificant by them,
> identifying with them so completely that at times—in
> the early morning and in the late evening—they would
> become interchangeable. (Greenaway, 1988a, 41)

Although Greenaway abandoned this plan because he wanted their domestic possessions to be more readily legible, he generates a similar effect by merging figure and ground in certain landscape scenes in the film. The instance of Madgett and Smut collecting blackberries is a case in point. The Cissies discover the two of them leaning against a tree in a field at dusk in a scene reminiscent of the fairytale sensibilities of an Arthur Rackham. The old gnarled tree seems as alive as the figures disap-pearing into the shadows of its trunk.[18] The diffuse, golden evening light casts a unifying glow over the scene, inviting nostalgia for a rural idyll that was a staple of early and mid-Victorian landscape painting. By this point in the film, we also associate this golden glow with the domestic interior of Madgett's rustic cottage and the tender though unsentimental relationship between father and son. However, the illusory nature of this rural idyll is soon exposed when the Cissies arrive and the mood of reverie is abruptly broken as the conversation turns to Bellamy's death, and we realize that Madgett and Smut have been sitting in front of a field that is on fire, where, as Smut observes, everything is dead. The golden glow is not as innocent as it initially appeared.

Lighting effects so preoccupied Greenaway during the making of *Drowning by Numbers* that "many scenes were filmed some ten times or more, as the natural light faded or brightened, to be certain that the location was appreciated well enough." Even in the cutting room the choices remained painful, with the filmmaker not wanting to sacrifice any of the natural effects: "I wanted to use all ten takes, which would make nonsense of the narrative drama" (Greenaway, 1994, 80). The tension between capturing the rich nuances of the location, which involved filming outside under tricky lighting conditions, and the relentless forward pull of the narrative evidently frustrated Greenaway at points, revealing film's limitations as a genre capable of adequately representing the complexities of landscape. One senses that the emphasis on the highly contrived nature of the landscape in *Drowning by Numbers* is, at least in part, a way of drawing the viewer's attention to the filmmaker's dilemma. Throughout the film we are made aware of the fact that the landscape is theatrically staged, a fact that is underscored by the many artificially lit night scenes featuring, in no particular order, the Skipping Girl with the fluorescent stars on her dress and skipping rope; Cissie One's garden with its fruit and vegetables illuminated like stage props in the footlights; the floodlit water tower seen dramatically from below; Madgett's car with its strangely glowing interior; Smut's nocturnal forays into the undergrowth armed with flashlight; and the final view of the sinking rowboat silhouetted against the exploding fireworks in the night sky. In daylight scenes, Greenaway stresses the artificiality in darkly humorous ways by making death in the natural world seem absurdly larger than life, for instance when Bellamy and Cissie Three crash into two dead cows or when the three Cissies and Madgett discover hundreds of dead herring on the shore. In both cases, the theatrical nature of the "props" is pointed out by the characters, who find the items already counted, painted, and tagged by Smut. In another scene at Madgett's house, Smut counts what look like artificial leaves on a walnut tree while his father explains to the three Cissies that he keeps sheep in order to count them on sleepless nights. The subject of counting leads Madgett to ask the Cissies if they have ever wondered how many hairs are on their head or how many fish are in the sea, to which they respond with a chorus of No's. It would seem that such counting is a peculiarly male obsession. Interestingly, while the artificial leaves are part and parcel of the film's self-conscious staging of the landscape, they also reference the actual conditions of shooting the film just after a series of hurricanes swept through Suffolk in the autumn of 1987. Somewhat perversely, these storms forced Greenaway's film crew to "flood the landscape with artificial light and fill barren trees with artificial leaves."[19] In a twist of fate that Greenaway must have relished, the unexpected weather conditions made the filmmaker into a land artist.

A dangerous undertow concealed beneath beautiful surfaces is one of the hallmarks of Greenaway's feature films and repeatedly reminds us, like the *memento mori* motifs in Dutch still life painting, that over time everything is subject to death and decay. In *Drowning by Numbers* Greenaway draws our attention to this theme through allusions to William Holman Hunt's *The Hireling Shepherd* (1851–1852; Figure 11.3), a Pre-Raphaelite work which Greenaway first encountered in his art school days in the early 1960s as an example of "bad painting" and therefore not to be imitated. As Greenaway explains, the works of the Pre-Raphaelites "have been, and are still, considered to be too literary. Some consider them 'overwrought' and to have 'an excess of sentiment'" (1988a, 35). And yet Greenaway cannot help admiring their sensitive depiction of the play of light, shifting weather conditions, and tiny details of the natural world. He takes great pleasure in the way Hunt's *Hireling Shepherd* appeals so powerfully to the senses with its "strong sensations of warmth, shade, 'stuff' and substance. The sleeping sheep is heavy, the green apples are bitter, the grass in the ditch is wet, the woman's feet are palpable. With no trouble at all you can walk about a landscape—there is enough evidence to name all the plants" (1988a, 39). But what makes the painting even more interesting for Greenaway are its complex layers of allegory. As he notes, beyond its superb surface, the painting reminds us of death and decay in the Death's Head moth that

Figure 11.3

William Holman Hunt, *The Hireling Shepherd* (1851–1852), oil painting. Manchester City Galleries.

the shepherd shows his sweetheart, the apples of temptation that the girl feeds the lamb, and the fact that the sheep have strayed into the corn. Furthermore, the Shakespearean lines that accompanied Hunt's first exhibition of the painting reminded Victorian exhibition goers that the Church of England risked being led astray by muddle-headed pastors who did not sufficiently appreciate the threats of factional infighting and the temptations of Catholicism.[20] As we read Greenaway's commentary, we sense that he sees something of his own aesthetic strategies in this painting's elaborately worked surface and complicated layers of allegorical meaning which, like his own films, have not always fared well with English critics who have frequently considered them to be "too literary."

In *Drowning by Numbers*, there is no simple restaging or direct exhibition of *The Hireling Shepherd*, as there is with the Rubens or the Brueghel. Instead, Greenaway quotes indirectly from this painting by scattering fragmentary references to it throughout the film. For instance, shortly after Jake's death by drowning, there is a shot of a Death's Head moth that seems to function as an allegorical signature of this first death (Figure 11.4), which in turn sets in motion a mechanism that will bring about the deaths of Hardy, Bellamy, and Madgett. The apples of temptation are scattered across the floor and fill the second bathtub which Nancy drags into the house. Hunt's rows of trees are evoked in the scene where Cissies One and Two push the sleeping Nancy in a wheelbarrow down a lane back to her own house, while the sheep and rustic costume appear in later scenes at Madgett's house and through the figure of Sid, the digger, who appears at intervals throughout the film. In other words, Greenaway looks at Hunt's picture through an avant-gardist lens, breaking it down into a series of cubist clues or inorganic fragments rather than offering it to the viewer as an organic whole or reconstituted tableau vivant. The implications of this

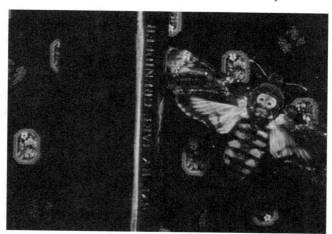

Figure 11.4

Peter Greenaway, the Death's Head moth from *Drowning by Numbers* (1988).

gesture are significant in at least two respects. Using a painting in this way to generate narrative meaning reverses the typical Hollywood practice of making the landscape serve the narrative by situating it, authenticating it, and reflecting human emotions and psychological states.[21] Furthermore, Greenaway transposes a pictorial language of landscape painting into a cinematic one of montage in much the same way that, according to Peter Bürger, the historical avant-garde, starting with Cubism, used montage to recast the meaning of things by tearing them from their original contexts and putting them to new allegorical uses.[22] Paradoxically, Greenaway revitalizes Hunt's painting by dissecting it and scattering its *membra disjecta* in a signifying process *non verbis sed rebus*.[23]

Another way in which Greenaway dismembers the landscape in *Drowning by Numbers* involves a return to the sort of counting, plotting, and measuring associated with the Land Art movement. The obsessive numbering from 1 to 100 that is the most obvious structuring device of *Drowning by Numbers* is echoed in Smut's equally obsessive enumeration of insects, birds, leaves, and corpses, all of which drives Cissie Two to distraction, as she admits to Madgett when she refuses to go blackberry picking with the two of them because Smut would have to count the berries. Bellamy is similarly annoyed by Smut's body count, dismissing him as "a little ghoul" when he and Cissie Three discover that the dead cows they have hit with their bicycles are covered in red paint and not blood, indicating that Smut has already been there. Smut is ideally paired with the Skipping Girl who counts 100 stars at the beginning of the film, explaining to Cissie One that once you've counted 100 all the others are the same, thereby anticipating the premise of Greenaway's 1992 exhibition, *One Hundred Objects to Represent the World*. We inevitably associate her with the filmmaker, not only because her counting from 1 to 100 sets the film in motion by anticipating its larger structure but also because some of the stars she counts bear the names of Greenaway characters such as Spica (*The Cook, the Thief, His Wife and Her Lover*) and Kracklite (*Belly of an Architect*).

As in the case of *The Draughtsman's Contract* (Elliott and Purdy, 30–41), the plot of *Drowning by Numbers* is ritualistically played out in space, much like a chess game where the pieces move according to fixed patterns. Here, though, the film's isolated places take on a mythical or archetypal quality undoubtedly influenced by the world of children's books so present in the film. There is the Water Tower where the conspirators meet to plan their revenge; the Trysting Field where Madgett propositions the three Cissies, moving closer and closer to the water as a mark of his spiralling failure; and the pavement in front of the White House where Smut returns to visit the Skipping Girl, showing her photographs that will later be misconstrued by the policeman who misreads Madgett's elaborately coded world of games as evidence of possible child abuse. On another level, the games frequently function like plot maps, foreshadowing the unfolding story as in the game of Deadman's Catch played on Cissie One's lawn after Jake's death (Figure 11.5). While the three Cissies play on in a spirit of camaraderie, the men drop the skittle one by one and are relegated to the winding sheet in the same order that they will die in the film.

Just as the imaginary filmic landscape is narratively, thematically, and intertextually traversed and plotted, so are individual scenes carefully composed to illustrate these relations visually, as Greenaway explains in the account he gives of Deadman's Catch in *Fear of Drowning by Numbers*. As with some of Richard Long's Land Art projects, Greenaway envisions the scene as a series of intersecting geometric shapes: "seven players are hung in a geometrical cage of the triangle, the circle and the square which is hung on the nail of the water tower" (1988a, 93).[24] The square is the white winding sheet encircled by the players throwing the skittle to each other. The water tower in the top centre of the composition forms the apex of an invisible triangle, one side of which is formed by the diagonal trajectory of the coffin carriers leaving Cissie's house and moving in the direction of the water tower. As the men are relegated to the winding sheet, the three women move closer together, now forming "an inner triangle pressing closer around the square." In the spirit of El Lissitsky's constructivist *Tale of Two Squares* (1920/1922), a children's story that Greenaway does not cite as a source of inspiration, the filmmaker renders the narrative in visual terms instead of relying on words.

Despite its propagandistic function of promoting the new communist regime in Russia, El Lissitsky's visual parable provides an intriguing precedent since it is told through a new abstract and universal geometric language that children could decipher by simply looking at the pictures. The story contrasts two different ordering systems represented by two squares hurtling toward a circular earth—the bad black capitalist square and the

Figure 11.5

Peter Greenaway, Deadman's Catch from *Drowning by Numbers* (1988).

good red communist square. The black square is unable to impose any meaningful order on its earth, which is depicted as a tangled jumble of geometric shapes, while the red one fosters a sense of unity and harmony that resembles a well-ordered city skyline. One suspects that when his work was rediscovered in Western Europe during the 1960s, El Lissitsky must have intrigued artists such as Richard Long and Peter Greenaway, given their similar interests in ordering systems, geometric patterns, and children's games.[25] Like El Lissitsky's reader, Greenaway's filmgoer is given a map of the different factions and alliances that structure the plot, but in Greenaway's case the schematic spatial representation does not refer outward to events in contemporary history with an immediate recognition value, but simply prefigures the singular events of the film's idiosyncratic plot. After discussing in detail the geometric pre(con)figuration of plot in *Drowning by Numbers,* Greenaway concludes: "[a]ll this takes many clumsy and inexact word-descriptions to describe—but if we read paintings like we read books—it would not be such a hidden language for painting can effortlessly produce such elegant solutions" (1988a, 95).

Greenaway's approach to film and to landscape is, in the first instance, that of a painter. His response to the English landscape, in particular, is rich and deep, coloured by a lyrical melancholy that is highly personal and mediated by a long tradition of landscape painting and book illustration that he knows well. But Greenaway is not just a painter. He is also an allegorist, and a literary one at that, and this has sometimes set him at odds with both the art and the film worlds, where the complexity of his cultural engagements and the multiple layering of his artefacts have seemed to some pretentious and to others incompatible with the single-minded sense of purpose required of an artistically responsible exploration of a specific medium, be it painting or film. Making few concessions to his critics, Greenaway has pursued his own goals and found his own solutions to the problems of his practice.

A fundamental tenet is that the landscape, like the built environment, is never a neutral backdrop; nor is it relegated to a subservient role in relation to character or plot construction or the creation of atmosphere. The landscape, in films like *Drowning by Numbers* and *The Draughtsman's Contract,* is a performance that might be applauded in much the same way that Kracklite leads the company in applauding the architecture of Rome in *The Belly of an Architect.* Not that it is there simply to be looked at and admired—far from it. The landscape is an actor in its own right, with an active role to play in the construction of plot, character, and theme through its allegorizing presence; and if the viewer fails to work with the landscape on the terms it sets, much will be lost. This respect for the landscape, this willingness to work in and with it, is something that Greenaway takes from Land Art. But the influence of Land Art does not stop there, for Greenaway also adopts and adapts some of Richard Long's strategies of intervention or interaction—especially the inscription of elementary human codes such as numbers and geometric shapes, often barely perceptible in Long but magnified and amplified in Greenaway—to produce alienation effects capable of restraining or containing any emotional or aesthetic response the landscape might elicit. The relentless counting, gridding, and measuring serves to block any naïve surrender to the seduction on offer and to remind us that there is nothing innocent in the beauty of the English landscape. In *The Draughtsman's Contract*, power relations involving class and gender are constructed and deconstructed through the meticulous plotting and drawing of a house and gardens, while in *Drowning by Numbers* the omnipresence of death in the midst of life is allegorized through an absent painting—*The Hireling Shepherd*—that is at once anatomized and atomized, its mortal remains scattered through the landscape like so many clues in a Land Art treasure hunt.

Greenaway's landscapes are intrinsically intertextual, brimming over with quotations from literature, history, mythology, and painting. They are also, to a very high degree, self-consciously intermedial, the overdetermined, heterotopian site of conflicts not only between codes, discourses, and other organizing principles, but also between media. Placed under erasure by the strictures of a structuralism pushed to comic lengths, they yet contrive to slip through the gaps created by film's undercutting of painting and painting's undercutting of film to float free as a place outside of all places. This, patently, is not a landscape. And yet, patently, it is.

## notes

1. Peter Greenaway, *Fear of Drowning by Numbers / Règles du jeu* (Paris: Dis Voir, 1988a), 1; hereafter cited in text.
2. Greenaway is the first to admit that his math skills are not his strong point. In fact, only one 30-minute documentary would be made in 1988 with the projected title *Fear of Drowning*.
3. The foreshore holds a special attraction for Richard Long on account of the surprising effects that can be produced by tides, as he notes with reference to "Half-Tide" made in Bertraghboy Bay in 1971: "We'd camped on the foreshore when we came to that place in the evening. And the tide was out, and there was this beautiful bed of wet, soggy, bubbly seaweed on this stony beach, and I made a cross of stones on the seaweed…. When I woke up the next morning and unzipped the tent and looked out over the bay, the tide had come in, and instead of seeing my cross of stones, I actually saw the image of my work suspended on the surface of the water, because the stones were keeping the seaweed down. So that work was made miraculously a lot better by the tide coming in and covering it." Richard Long, *Richard Long. Walking in Circles* (New York: George Braziller, 1991), 52–53.
4. For the ongoing multimedia project, *The Tulse Luper Suitcases*, see http:// www.tulselupernetwork.com/basis.html. Peter Greenaway, *The Tulse Luper Suitcases: A Personal History of Uranium by Peter Greenaway* (accessed on June 1, 2005).

5. Apart from being the number of players in a soccer team, 11 is mimetically remarkable in that it juxtaposes two verticals, i.e., constitutes a "vertical feature remake." As Agnès Berthin-Scaillet points out, it is also a palindrome, as are all its multiples up to 121. Agnès Berthin-Scaillet, "Peter Greenaway: Fête et défaite du corps," Special Issue of *L'Avant-scène du cinéma* 417/418 (décembre 1992/janvier 1993): 22; hereafter cited in text.

6. Paul Melia, "Frames of Reference," in *Peter Greenaway. Artworks 63–98*, eds. Paul Melia and Alan Woods (Manchester: Manchester University Press, 1998), 14; hereafter cited in text.

7. Amy Lawrence, *The Films of Peter Greenaway* (Cambridge: Cambridge University Press, 1997), 6; hereafter cited in text.

8. Cribb is one of the first of Greenaway's Icarus figures. Pulled into the sky by the kite he is carrying, he falls into the river where, reproaching himself for over-reaching his capabilities, he lets himself drown (Greenaway, 1988a, 147). *Flying Over Water*, Greenaway's exhibition around the Icarus story, would be mounted in Barcelona in 1997.

9. Some of Greenaway's play with time in *A Walk Through H* echoes certain Land Art preoccupations. Witness Richard Long's response to a question posed by Richard Cork about the relationship between movement, distance, and time in his work: "Yes, time is the fourth dimension in my work, and I am interested in using it in a very particular way. So I have made walks about pace, walks about time only, and also certain geometries, for example, walking between a hundred Tors on Dartmoor in a hundred hours, or walking a thousand miles in a thousand hours. So it is possible to use time almost in a very classical way, as a very formal, geometric thing." Richard Cork, "An Interview with Richard Long by Richard Cork," in Richard Long, *Richard Long, Walking in Circles, op. cit.*, 251.

10. Michel Foucault, *The Order of Things: An Archaeology of the Human Sciences* (London: Tavistock, 1970), xviii; hereafter cited in text.

11. Foucault's discussion of Borges's Chinese encyclopedia has become an established topos of Greenaway criticism. See, for example, Bridget Elliott and Anthony Purdy, *Peter Greenaway. Architecture and Allegory* (London: Academy Editions, 1997), 29; hereafter cited in text; "Skin Deep. Fins-de-siècle and New Beginnings in Peter Greenaway's *The Pillow Book*," in *Peter Greenaway's Postmodern/Poststructuralist Cinema*, eds. Paula Willoquet-Maricondi and Mary Alemany-Galway (Lanham, MD, and London: Scarecrow Press, 2001), 261–262; Lawrence, *op. cit.*, 20–21; Melia, *op. cit.*, 16–17; Alan Woods, "Field of Play," in *Peter Greenaway. Art Works 63–98, op. cit.*, 20; and Bart Testa, "Tabula for a Catastrophe. Peter Greenaway's *The Falls* and Foucault's *Heterotopia*," in *Peter Greenaway's Postmodern/Poststructuralist Cinema, op. cit.*

12. Michel Foucault, "Of Other Spaces," trans. Jay Miskowiec, *Diacritics* 16, no. 1 (Spring 1986): 22–27; hereafter cited in text.

13. The projects date from 1967 and 1968, respectively. We might also be reminded of Long's own fleeting recorded presence in his work. As Anne Seymour writes: "Occasionally we catch a glimpse of his shadow, rucksack or boots, but otherwise we identify with the traces of his passing, the spiral furrowed with the heel of his boot, the line on the map, the number of miles walked, the splash of the stone hitting water, the list of trees, the line of arrows marking the direction of the wind as it buffets his body." Anne Seymour, "Walking in Circles," in Richard Long, *Richard Long. Walking in Circles, op. cit.*, 7. Long started to make serious attempts to

map the patterns of wind over land in the so-called wind line works of the mid-1980s.

14. Jacques Aumont, *L'œil interminable. Cinéma et peinture* (Paris: Librairie Séguier, 1989), quoted in David Pascoe, *Peter Greenaway. Museums and Moving Images* (London: Reaktion Books, 1997), 25.

15. See also the ironic banter in *The Draughtsman's Contract* around Neville's inability to render pictorially the song of birds or a human whistle.

16. Vernon Gras and Marguerite Gras, eds., *Peter Greenaway: Interviews* (Jackson: University Press of Mississippi, 2000), 53.

17. Peter Greenaway, *The Stairs, Geneva: The Location* (London: Merrell Holberton, 1994), 77; hereafter cited in text.

18. The motif of the man swallowed up by (or trapped within) a tree is reminiscent of the enchanted animism of Tolkien's Middle Earth landscapes and had previously been used by Greenaway in one of the "Green Man" or *genius loci* sequences in *The Draughtsman's Contract*, later developed through Caliban's backstory in *Prospero's Books*. Here, in *Drowning by Numbers*, the register seems idyllic rather than menacing, the surface pastoral and untroubled. And yet, as Smut and Madgett well know, death is never far away. For a green approach to the Green Man figure in *The Draughtsman's Contract*, see Paula Willoquet-Maricondi, "The Greening of Cultural Studies: Peter Greenaway's Contract with Nature in *The Draughtsman's Contract*," *Green Letters* 6 (Winter 2005): 9–23.

19. Steven Goldman, "Dead Reckoning," *Guardian* (September 2, 1988): 21; Greenaway 1988a, 77.

20. Greenaway, 1988a, 39–40; Tim Barringer, *Reading the Pre-Raphaelites* (New Haven: Yale University Press, 1998), 11; Tate Gallery, *The Pre-Raphaelites* (London: Tate Gallery/Penguin Books, 1984), 94–96; hereafter cited in text.

21. Another instance of a landscape painting shaping the narrative appears in the film script but not in the final version of the film. When Madgett arrives at the house of Cissie Two to view Hardy's body, Cissie Two takes the clippings of Hardy's hair and places them under the roots of a geranium in a large flowerpot. Peter Greenaway, *Drowning by Numbers* (London: Faber & Faber, 1988b), 79. Having already spotted numerous references to Pre-Raphaelite paintings in the film, the art history informed viewer immediately realizes that Cissie's gesture echoes that of the heroine in John Everett Millais's painting *Isabella* (1848–1850), who buries the head of her murdered lover Lorenzo in a pot of basil (Tate Gallery, *op. cit.*, 68–70). Nagiko's gesture with the bonsai at the end of *The Pillow Book* reprises the same art history reference in a different register.

22. Peter Bürger, *Theory of the Avant-Garde*, trans. Michael Shaw (Minneapolis: University of Minnesota Press, 1984); hereafter cited in text.

23. Bürger, *ibid.*, 68–80; Julian Roberts, "Melancholy Meanings: Architecture, Postmodernity and Philosophy," in *The Postmodern Arts*, ed. Nigel Wheale (London: Routledge, 1995), 139. Our understanding of Greenaway's technique of allegorical montage owes much to Walter Benjamin's *The Origin of German Tragic Drama* (1928). See our discussions in *Architecture and Allegory*, *op. cit.*, 19–24 and in "Peter Greenaway and the Technologies of Representation. The Magician, the Surgeon, their Art and its Politics," *Art and Film. Art and Design Profile* 49 (1996): 16–23.

24. Greenaway had intended to set the film in the flat landscape of East Yorkshire along the River Humber, so that the landscape could be "trav-

elled from vertical to vertical back and forth across the river in a series of zig-zags that may well form a revealing geometrical figure to be manufactured as a gaming-board" (Greenaway, 1988a, 75).

25. Like many avant-garde artists during the 1920s, El Lissitsky was particularly interested in exploring the utopian possibilities of creating a universal visual language.

# landscape and perception

t w e l v e        on anthony mann

t o m    c o n l e y

In the rich and dense pages that inaugurate *L'énonciation impersonnelle ou le site du film* (1991), the deeply regretted Christian Metz takes up some of the spatial paradoxes that inhabit the language of cinema.[1] A medium that offers great vistas where there are few, that thrives on producing illusions of extension in closed confines, cinema owes its charm to the fantasies it elicits of worlds subjectively encountered. Viewers of cinema live a virtual adventure of space and place that resembles what we imagine when we follow the tracks of heroic *personages* roaming about the Mediterranean in the *Iliad* or the *Odyssey*. The languages of cinema, perhaps because they are not really languages in any strict sense, include spatial expression located at the edges of words and in the lagoons of printed letters.

No wonder, then, that Metz, an enthusiast of classical cinema, revisits the master directors in his late work of 1991. Great films become a field for the study of a "geography of enunciation," a space and time in which the positions and voices of ostensibly "living" subjects are called into question. Metz claims that deixis, the process that indicates the space in which interlocution takes place, is weak in film. For a reader not trained in linguistics (such as the author of this chapter, who depends on the concept of the *deictics* that Emile Benveniste develops in his *Problèmes de linguistique générale*[2]), the general sense of deixis includes the process by which subjectivity is gained when "positions" or places are obtained or lost in the act of enunciation. Through interlocution a speaker grasps coordinates locating how and where he or she is situated in the give-and-take of dialogue. *Deixis* "shows the very instance of discourse; it shows us that *discourse is taking place*. It is a way that discourse can make reference to its own eventfulness."[3] When speakers in a dialogue use terms denoting who and where they are, they employ *deictics*: "pronouns or demonstrative adverbs…that are only identifiable within the context of the speech-act."[4]

But film, Metz argues, baffles any sense of space or identity that would derive from enunciation. In watching a movie we never attach a voice on the soundtrack to a body seen on the image track; unless a narrative suspends our disbelief, we hardly identify a sound with an ostensive origin either in or outside of the frame; nor does a musical accompaniment convince us that a "mood" prevails in a given story. Metz claimed that for this deceptively simple reason cinema lends itself to psychoanalytical interpretation. Its modes of enunciation do not refer to real things or people, but to symbolic processes grounded in our imagination of them. It makes eventful the ongoing labor of subjectivity. In cinema, the spectator's consciousness produces an imaginary space that taps into the memory of other films. Cinema awakens feelings whose origins are not easily located. Further, it leads perception to creative diversions or to associations, thanks to inattention, that are not subject to the control of reason.[5] In film, Metz argued, we do not discover,

> like the speaker and the person addressed, fictive people. Nor are they really things, but rather, vectors or directions inside of the geography of film, orientations that the analyst is able to detect. It is indeed there, in a sense, that the activity of cinema is played out between two poles or plots since, effectively, no matter what name is assigned to them, there are those who made [the film] and those who gaze at it. But when the [plots] are marked at a specific point in the film, it is crucial to describe the itinerary of *these tracks henceforth depersonalized and turned into the condition of a landscape.* (34)[6]

Metz sustains that deixis, however much it seems present in the discourses of film, does not cement into place any readily identifiable subject-positions. Deictics can be located neither among *personages* in the film, nor in any palpable space in its audition. Metz notes that at certain privileged points the orientation of the filmmaker and the viewer seem to meet. The point of their encounter, he says, pertains to a condition of landscape, what by extension might be called an area where a *mobility of positions* can be perceived.[7]

Metz carefully delineates the subjective movements in both the narrative of a film and the spectator's attention that defines its space. From the cardinal points that delineate its "plots" and the virtual rhumb lines they trace he discerns a "mobile topography" (36) that characterizes "landscapes of enunciation" of cinema in general. But, at the same time, the critic also concludes that deixis, dramatically weakened by virtue of the technology of cinema, has a richly *textual* character (214). He engages a paradox that identifies a coextension of the lexical and pictorial character of language. It is implied that an iconic quality of oral and written signs becomes visible in a visual field, such that onto the surface on which language seems to be uttered in a film there is also embedded visible signs.

The paradox confirms what Michel de Certeau once stated about the confusion of textual and iconic registers in the cinematic image. "The image," he noted in an interview about cinema, "is basically the truth of the text. It is a multiplication of texts and of their readings upon a single surface. From this point of view there is an intimate relation between the image and the landscape. A landscape is a stratification of texts that allows for a multiplicity of readings.... I believe that there exists no fundamental difference between an image and a text, a text having been for ages perceived as an image."[8] If we set de Certeau's relation of a figure and ground of discourse in the context of Metz's words about the landscape of cinema enunciation, then it becomes something akin to a process of writing, a writing both inscribed on and melded into the landscape of the image. Therefore, the "mobile" geography he discovers in cinema is based on a textual material of enunciation essential to our imagination of filmic space. Enunciation, which is part and parcel of the landscapes on which speech and action take place, are "stratifications" of texts, sedimentations of words and images vital to perception in general.

What Metz proposes is tantalizingly rich for the western, a spatial genre par excellence, especially Anthony Mann's western phase, that depicts an epic geography of America in which are conflated the 1870s and the post-World War II years.[9] Through his westerns, films on which Metz and an entire generation of theorists were weaned, we can ask what indeed happens in the realm of enunciation in these features: when and how does speech become textual? Are mute signs embedded in the landscape of Cold War America seen through the filter of a classical genre? Do subjects begin to dissolve into or grow out of landscapes that betray the menace of the Bomb Culture and the memory of the concentration camps? To broach these questions I would like to keep in view the concept of the textual and mobile character of space that Metz claims to result from the weakening of subject-positions. At the same time, I would like to test the concept through what the clinical analyst Guy Rosolato calls the *perspectival object*, a point that brings together the subjective experience of viewing, the perception of the textual nature of the landscape, and the position of the viewer in relation to the unknown, a relation that the analyst calls a pervasive force vital for life. The perspectival object resembles that indiscernible point situated between the two "plots" of film and spectator that Metz evokes when advancing his case for the impersonal quality of cinematic enunciation.

## the relation of the unknown and the perspectival object

For Rosolato, the task of psychoanalysis entails the exploration of our perception of the unknown.[10] Without being grounded in the unknown, life would not be. We are haunted by the unknown, we thrive on it, we erect barriers of language to insulate ourselves from it. We spend our lives moving toward and away from it. We chart our relation with the unknown by way of perspectival objects, "plot points" that conjoin the visible and the invisible or what can be discerned wherever language fails to say what it would wish to mean. Landscape painting, he adds, tells us why. The genre that has so much inspired the western owes the success of its tradition to the way it blends the visible and the invisible. In Claude Lorrain's landscapes, a founding subjective relation, an enigma at the basis of all life, fuses space with everything that symbolic forms have as their objective to localize or to demarcate.[11]

The artist translates them into palpable form through a perspectival depiction of the four elements. The *sky* opens onto the unknown by confusing with Lorrain's great cerulean backgrounds, "the infinite spaces that we contemplate, day and night, whenever we raise our eyes skyward" (Rosolato, 1986, 309). The *earth* stretches out beyond the limits of our sight, offering thus, in its "telluric density," the horizon inspiring our desire to travel "anywhere out of this world" (the title of Baudelaire's poem in *Tableaux parisiens* is cited in English in the text). The environing *sea* at the edge of the forests and ports in the paintings becomes the invitation to travel, to "board a ship for a perilous and exalting voyage" (Rosolato, 1986, 310). And the soft *fire* of the sun stands as a point toward and away from which our eyes are constantly drawn. Lorrain conveys a "symbolic latency" (1986, 307) that all viewers—both the learned patrons for whom their mythic narratives were prepared and ourselves, untrained spectators in a different age—can savor. The landscapes offer a sense of relation that leads us to discover the mental and somatic pleasure of attaching ourselves to "secrets," set before our eyes, that inspire imaginary voyages at once into the classical world and the inner folds of our memories.

> In a landscape we recover *the greatest concrete space* that we can obtain through the faculty of sight. Far from the crowd, from restrained and cramped spaces, from pro-

miscuity, and away from the *territory* marked by property relations, influence, and protection, we perceive
the distance that transforms our *relation* to the world
and things. No longer do we fret over our immediate
needs and our having to use instruments to do what
we must do; we behold a change in scale, a staging of
perspective. Our reflection is unconsciously drawn
to its pluridimensional character...such as we could
experience it in our childhood, and such as it is recovered in the development of our spatial relations: affective points and surfaces affronted, depths of view and
containment, moral and aesthetic values. The play of
things becomes especially subtle when our contemplation of nature, with the symbolic implications of our
exceeding and surpassing ourselves when our eyes look
further and further away, and it is such that we discover our being fortuitously contained by immensity,
with even an oceanic feeling of exaltation, in the most
maternal sense, all the while we *embrace* the latter with
our gaze. (1986, 307)

The sublime force of the landscape is built on an erotic, maternal object
emerging into visibility and perception in general.[12]

What Rosolato says of Lorrain and the ideal conditions of a contemplation of nature focalized on the scenery of the painting itself is spelled out
in greater detail in "*L'objet de perspective dans ses assises visuelles*" (Rosolato, 1993,
29–52), in which the perspectival object designates or occludes points
where representation opens onto the unknown. The visible replaces
something that lacks, and "reveals the force of the unknown" (1993, 40).
With Lorrain it is situated at the vanishing point of the landscape, but the
point can also multiply and proliferate when we realize that the visual
attraction of the vanishing point is linked to our own mental activity
plotting the voyage that leads our eyes to travel in different directions
across the surface of the painting. But the itineraries, that can be likened
to the lines that link Metz's two "plots" of the film and the spectator, are
no less textual. Spatial organizations that make the object perceptible are
understood as being situated "between the three poles of language, representation, and the referent" (Rosolato, 1993, 50). Perception is thus liable
to scatter about the material of both discourse and images, in areas both
unnamed and, no less, "unnameably."

Rosolato's remarks on the indexical quality of the perspectival object
and what it elicits about the limits or interdictions of representation are
pertinent on at least two counts. First, our mental images are aroused by
way of archaic narratives that "recruit the associative proliferation" (1993,
50) of perspectival objects. Second, the sacred quality of *writing* in these

narratives becomes a perspectival image "in the material sense" (Roso-lato, 1993, 51), in the way that writing is *seen* as much as it is heard or read. Classical works, especially founding epics (the grist of the western), seem especially rich in the relation that perspectival objects hold with language and landscape.

The perspectival object locates the coincidence of pleasure and the dilemma of the unknown, both in clinical treatment and in the analysis of film. One of the most decisive moments in the former occurs at the point, Rosolato has argued elsewhere, where the patient realizes that he or she has no real reason to be alive. No fiction or logic, we discover in the course of analysis, can paper over the fact that we do not belong in the landscapes we inhabit.[13] An overwhelming sense of atopia, in which we feel no sense of being in space, time or history, has to be countered by a slow and painful remotivation of everything that otherwise underscores the arbitrariness of our relation to the world. A new "relation with the unknown" must be initiated through the creation of subjective geogra-phies, whose plotting consists in attaching names or figures not to real places, but to imaginary areas (basic to autobiography) that can assure a vital play of identity.

Invention of space is basic to the dynamics of subjectivity. A sense of autonomy is gained when individuals glimpse in the passage of their discourse visible fragments of writing that belong to the silent and per-sonal alphabet of their own, of near-originary impressions that, when remembered, strengthen the foundation of a sense of being alive.[14] These impressions are grounded in memory but perceived only by quick starts, glimpses, or, as Sophie de Mijolla-Mellor reports about the labor of anal-ysis, in infrequent surprises when discourse and visual shapes become identical to, or explode into, each other.[15] The conflations become *events*, they are experience itself, or "perceptions of perceptions," that allow the patient to move back into the past through material couched in the pres-ent (or vice-versa), and to turn utterances into transitional objects that mobilize the process of transference.

## the perception-image and the landscape

The same holds for a successful viewing of cinema. Psychoanalysis and cinema meet at points where spatial and visual components in the pro-cess of subjectivation and film-work share a common ground. When the viewer can use the weakened deixis or the "mobile geography" of the film to create imaginary spaces that bind cinema to the creation of subjective space, an active and selective relation develops. In glimpsing a perspectival object an analysand also reestablishes a "relation with the unknown." Vis-ibility and invisibility are momentarily confused. Visible, all of a sudden, are discourses that make tangible a broader ground or landscape in which "we discover ourselves being fortuitously contained by [an] immensity"

(Rosolato, 1993, 3–4). Speech or symbolic expression is imagined as a great surface on which, suddenly, visible shapes appear and disappear. Inner and outer surfaces of memory and perception, both the evident and the concealed dimensions of our experience, are projected from a mobile landscape of memory, but also onto vistas that extend before our eyes.

In a different context, in his taxonomy of cinema, Gilles Deleuze makes points that bear on what Rosolato and Metz have put forward in their studies of visibility and enunciation. In his redefinition of the three primary styles of "image" that make up the classical lexicon of cinema set forth in *L'image-mouvement* (1983), Deleuze appeals indirectly to the rapport that geography and landscape hold with psychogenesis, the continuous birth and experience of subjectivity.[16] Three styles of image characterize cinema that affects the body of the viewer. The action-image, approximated to the medium shot, conveys narrative or the conceptual design of a film. The affect-image, likened to the close-up, is emotively charged, and tends to center on the geography of faciality. The long-shot engages psychogenesis, rehearsing the origins of vision and space whenever we suddenly notice that in the space before our eyes we are *seeing* and, further, in what we see, in areas we sense are unknown to us, we fear the fate of getting lost.

The same space also yields the pleasure of vision itself, or of our continuous birth in the greater expanse of the environing world. The sensations are indicative of perception itself. Hence Deleuze speaks of the "perception of perception" (Deleuze, 98), the staging of a space where no immediate center can be discerned, and where, effectively, the atmospheric qualities of the sensory world stretch before our eyes. When, in a long shot, in an indeterminate area or a "center of indetermination," things come into view but are not yet or quite known (or resist being named), the visible field becomes a perception-image. We relive the birth of visibility itself, we get lost in space, and we refuse to ascertain any causes, effects, or other linkages between the elements floating before our eyes.

When it frames a zone that brings forth points that appeal to our perception of the origins of sight the long-shot stages the emergence of a perspectival object. For Deleuze the classic western is composed not so much of action-images (stagecoach robberies, hold-ups, shoot-outs) but of an almost pure perception-image, "a drama of the visible and invisible as much as an epic of action; the hero acts only because he sees first, and wins only because he imposes upon action the interval or the second of delay that allows him to see everything (*Winchester '73* by Anthony Mann)" (Deleuze, 102). Deleuze implies that the "interval" is a gap opened between a received movement and an executed movement, an infinitesimal gap between an "action and a reaction" (291), or a moment between variable and totalizing views of time (50, 72). It has hieroglyphic trappings in that two different modes of expression are nascently held within it.[17]

Now, apposing Deleuze to de Certeau's and Metz's remarks on the textual character of the landscape of enunciation in cinema, we might say that the interval would be discerned as that which brings a form of legibility into the field of visibility. Scattered about the perception-image are lexical shards that concretize many of the unconscious tensions articulating the greater lines of the narrative. Sometimes they are perceived, sometimes not; sometimes they inhere in the landscape but are never consciously seen, read, or deciphered; sometimes, in a sudden start, the spectator glimpses points where perception and language conflate, elide, or explode and disappear.

Thus, when we experience the birth of visibility in the perception-image we discern the "interval" where the visual surface of the film is liable to be *read* or at least to carry multifariously legible and visible components.[18] In these instants a perspectival object flashes into view and no sooner evanesces. The unknown that it conveyed becomes known, but only in order to reveal something else, unknown, that becomes manifest in disappearing, in an infinite scatter of sight that moves all over the landscape. Shards of language are glimpsed *visibly incrusted in the image*. They may come into view as calligraphic traits, rebuses, or merely points that cue the difference between the discourse of the film and the psychic drives that produce its invisible tensions.

## a critical heritage

Deleuze selects *Winchester '73* (1950) to test the hypothesis that the long shot can be a "perception-image" rehearsing the birth of visibility. In doing so he appeals to the contested privilege that Anthony Mann has enjoyed in different critical circles. For many viewers, his westerns, because they come so late in the classical phase of the genre, are signs of the fatigue of an industry and a tradition, and remain unworthy of the praise that proponents of *auteur* theory have bestowed on them.[19] For the American film historian Jeanine Basinger the cycle beginning with *Winchester '73* and ending with *Man of the West* (1958) becomes a complex permutation of classical drama and themes of revenge and retribution.[20] Comparing the lines of tension between a protagonist, a villain, an adjudicating character, and a chorus or community, she uses structural analysis (built to a strong degree on what Lévi-Strauss had inaugurated in the *Mythologiques*[21]) to detect the signature of an *auteur*.

Her view offsets a persisting existential and "territorial" feature of the French critical heritage summed up in two related studies by Raymond Bellour and Jacques Rancière.[22] For Bellour, the Mannian western pits a hero who acts for the sake of action against malevolence. The protagonist, outside of history, is destined to thrive on the solitude and alienation of his own situation which floats between a future that "draws him forward" and a "captivating past" that entices by virtue of an almost primal nostalgia. But, argues Bellour, the language of the epic drama *textualizes* the great landscapes in which the enunciation takes place. The camera conveys the linear logic of the story, "but suddenly, dream-like, literally taking over the field, in a caress, holding a bit long, rises up or closes in, settles, takes on a life of its own: these are the fortuitous movements, almost always outdoors, at given points of the landscape" (Bellour, 271).

Rancière projects similar observations about the movement of the landscape into the nomadism of the Mannian hero. The protagonist is "singularized," he directs and defines the action, places, and other players of the drama. The community, if any, is marked not by family or institutions but by ever-renewed *encounters*. Action is constructed in an infinitesimal gap between the moral dimension of the screenplay and the logic of the hero's itinerary. "In the name of a communal or familial effusion the Mannian hero is forbidden to forget the task he first set out to accomplish: to conduct action itself, to be, in his gaze and in his gestures, the pure incarnation of the very risk of action" (Rancière, 33). Rancière historicizes the existential pathos that Bellour had seen in the hero. The period (1950–1958) was one in which the old western could no longer be "converted in time for an urban morality and a psychological melodrama" (Rancière, 39).

Both critics concur by remarking that in the westerns, all the episodes have the same density. All are equally saturated with infinitesimal events, gestures, or foibles reflective of broader tensions. The films summon the very regime of visibility they celebrate in on-location photography. For Rancière, Mann evades both the "scopic regime" that would confer a truth of visibility upon the western and "the perceptive contracts" that the power of the merchandise, the genre as it was received in the 1950s, confuses with the spectator's gaze (Rancière, 41). According to Bellour and Rancière alike, the viewer is an active participant, but Mann's innovation consists in obstinately foiling the spectator's desire to see. They imply that decor, action, perspective, and even occluded forms of *writing*—in the landscape—comprise much of the substance of the films. The protagonists have a contractual obligation to perceive and to decipher the spaces through which they pass. The consubstantial relation of the landscape, the action of the protagonist, and the viewer confirm how the existential persona (usually played by James Stewart) becomes a complex agent that invents different types of space.

The relation of landscape and perception indicates a quasi-identity of language and visibility. Metz had plotted a similar coextension through his treatment of enunciation. From the overlay of interpretations it can be deduced that the perspectival object, a point spotting the visibility and invisibility of what is known and unknown, is made manifest wherever the decor is both a landscape *and* a field of textual images which both the hero and spectator are impelled to decrypt. When Basinger maintains that

Anthony Mann revolutionized the landscape in the American western by placing his characters "*within* the landscape that brings meaning" (86), or that a "constant shifting and revising of backgrounds" produces a geography and a "landscape that is not static" (86), she implies that what we see in the perception-images is comparable to a Greek chorus that includes the spectator.[23] The viewer is summoned to translate the textual quality of the decor insofar as Metz's "weakened deixis" allows enunciation and landscape to mix. Two films can test the hypothesis.

*winchester '73*

In *Winchester '73* the decor of the arid desert is alien to the humans who move through it. Its relation with the human figure begins prior to the apparent beginnings of the narrative. The credits display a smoothly undulating hillside outlined by the soft light cast on the horizon in the evening. The crepuscular setting makes the bright characters of the title follow the contour of the hills behind them. On the slope of the top of the letters and the hillside two riders on horseback—the hero and his faithful confidant—are discerned crossing the landscape. The moving forms steer their way between the landscape and the ciphers of the title; they literally conjugate the language of the credits and landscape by crossing between the legible and visible areas of the image.

Insofar as the film deals with an intrepid individual's quest to avenge a cruel deed of parricide, the landscape becomes no less important than what will be his objective. Similarly, the title of the film turns into the problematic object that will become at once mantra (it is "a repeatin' rifle"), an almost magic form (a prime number), and even a caduceus (a gun carrying its bearer to unknown places). The title of the film is embedded in the gun that changes hands and thus crosses the landscape. In the first shot following the title sequence, children (who would be median spectators equated with the viewer) ogle at the "unique copy" of the Winchester '73 through the reflective glass of a shop window on a founding day, the Fourth of July, being celebrated in Dodge City.

Yet from the first sight of the credits the weakened condition of enunciation confuses the title with the men on horseback: was one of them—the hero—the bearer of the Winchester '73? Is the gun in the scabbard by his saddle a mystical concretion of the man-in-the-landscape? The relation that is implied between the credits and the first shot underscores the *perspectival* issues at the basis of the film. From the beginning it is asked how the gun figures in the landscape. Which the narrative quickly confirms: a shooting contest in Dodge City puts the hero, Lin McAdam (Stewart), and his nemesis, Dutch Henry Brown (Steve McNally), whom we later discover is McAdam's enemy brother, in competition for the rifle.

Much of the film follows at once the destinies of the hero and the Winchester. In the greater course of the diegesis the landscape is defined as what threatens the white man who dares to inhabit a space owned by Apaches. The hero and his confidant (Millard Mitchell) travel by night to evade the common enemy. A decor of western grazing lands, like the shots of the hillside in the credits, alternates with human space that is carved out in protection against the surrounding tribes. Familiar subplots include an Apache raid; a botched marriage of a barroom singer, expelled from Dodge City, with a timorous fiancé who happens to be caught up in gunrunning; his murder, at the hands of a sleazy outlaw, Waco Johnny Dean (Dan Duryea), who "spells trouble" (notes the hero's confidant) for everyone in his midst; the robbery of a stagecoach; moments of confession and attraction between the itinerant singer and the hero.... The plot sets the crowning event, the duel of McAdam and Dutch Henry, on a rocky mountainside.

At the climax of *Winchester '73* the landscape acquires a new visual intensity that corresponds to the hieroglyphic aspect of the opening credits. A drama of vision is mobilized, one in which, as Deleuze notes, the hero is the agent imposing "upon the action the interval...that allows him to see everything" (102). But the landscape supposedly granting a privilege of vision to the hero is no less invested in the energies of the spectator. The hero remains "blind" to himself and others, but the spectator is able to decipher the landscape in ways the hero cannot. It is not he, but *we* who *see* the relation of visibility that ties the hero to the landscape at the instant he chases over it. The moment of realization is in fact the interval or hieroglyph that multiplies the perspectival object by scattering the sign of the repeating rifle.

In a graphic sense McAdam seeks both revenge and the gun he won. The latter, however, is the paradoxically "original copy" both of a lever-action rifle and the title of the film. It is now carried in his brother's arms, through an unremitting decor of Arizona cactuses, rocks, crags, and jagged shapes of such *accidental* character that the topography seems to be fate itself. The route from the town to the cabin is defined in a volley of quick takes of McAdam galloping over the landscape, on the heels of his enemy, who barely but surely eludes him. The shots that register the action can be classified as "perception-images" that situate McAdam, in long-shots in extreme deep focus, crossing a landscape spiked with cactuses.[24]

We begin to *read* the landscape—since it fails to speak or to position itself as an interlocutor—as an agglomeration of perspectival objects. McAdam is dwarfed by the desert trees as he rides toward the villain's cabin nestled in the hills behind Tascosa (Figure 12.1). The cactuses may be qualified as a residue of the romantic aura of "pathetic fallacy" in which the plants behold the drama below them with a "familiar gaze" (as Baudelaire stated) of detached interest. As a rebus the cactuses textualize the landscape by causing their literal shape as a quasi-alphabetical sign to collapse the romantic heritage of the western. On closer inspection it is clear that the shape of each cactus resembles a rifle stuck into the earth, its trunk having affinity with a stock, its main branch a barrel, and each curved branch that bends outward and upward as if it were the giant triggers or lever of the Winchester's patented loading mechanism. We see a world of spiked and spurred "gun-cactuses" that proliferate the very enigma that inhabited the film since the inscription of the title on the hillside. Winchester '73s are frozen everywhere in the landscape, but the hero, bent on finding the object of his quest, gallops forward, entirely blind to its presence. Thus the "interval" of which Deleuze wrote in respect to *Winchester '73* is not the gap in the exchange of gunfire between Dutch Henry and McAdam, but the scatter of perspectival shapes stippling the entire image-field. The landscape seems to vibrate when its vegetation resembles the rifle on which the children and the adults had earlier fixed their gaze.

The psychoanalytical dimension of McAdam's crazed pursuit of his brother in the landscape is familiar and clear. The scatter of the desired gun, both visible and invisible, in the texture of the landscape yields a fetish-object on which the gaze of the two enemy rivals, McAdam and Dutch Henry, is aimed.[25] The landscape is so pocked with objects catching and reflecting the hero's drives that he can only remain lost in an unrelenting pursuit. No more than a dozen shots record the hero riding after his brother from the site of the holdup to the rocky hills over the hideout. The space that McAdam crosses, then climbs, does not serve as a decor "over" or "against" which he moves. Like an image and a text, the protagonist and landscape are coextensive, indeed, they are mirrored translations of each other. The protagonist invents space by dint of encountering it, but it does the same in forcing him to betray his own obsessive, crazed, almost sadistic character.[26] It inflects his condition, it spurs and drives

Figure 12.1

Still from *Winchester '73*.

him onward, it even envelops him in its own maze of fragments that multiply the presence of the lever-action rifle (Figure 12.2).

At the same time, when we see the implicitly ideographic "writing" of the cactus in the field of vision, a literal spell is cast on the landscape. The pictogram "cactus" sums up in literal ways, visibly and linguistically, the anal drive that the Winchester had so obviously elicited in the interval between the narratives of retribution and circulation. The vegetation of the desert becomes a field of hardened, spiny, almost fossilized dejections that locate the bodily zone toward which all the hero's energies are directed, making manifest many of the prevailing contradictions about visibility and invisibility. The landscape is pure, without language, but at the same time, as a character or a chorus, it speaks with uncanny legibility.[27]

The pictogrammatical confusion of the gun, the vegetation, and the countryside extends into the adjacent mountains. When the enemy brothers engage battle the maze of boulders is conveyed in deep focus photography that sets the antagonists in extreme counterpoint. One brother alternately serves as a minuscule target and sighting point for the other. The horizontal trajectory of the gunfire seen earlier in the shooting contest at Dodge City is now thrown into extremely tilted perspective, begging the spectator to treat the most minuscule details as elements that make both the landscape and the drama coextend (Figure 12.3). Each of the enemies aims at a moving point, a blip or a dot, between the sky and the rocks. To gain an advantage (or to narrow the gap between himself and his brother), McAdam tosses frangible stones into the air to lure Dutch Henry into consuming his ammunition and thus to fail to heed—McAdam is sure to remind his brother of the fact when he yells out into the landscape—their father's childhood lessons about thrift.

Figure 12.2

Still from *Winchester '73*.

Using words that George W. Bush would later borrow in declaring that he would capture Osama Bin Laden from his lair on the parched stretches of Afghanistan, Dutch Henry tells his brother that he'll "smoke him out" of the rocky landscape.

In this unlikely arena of struggle, the decor inflects the name of the hero. The landscape, that had correlated the protagonist's character with its own attributes, now begins to identify who he is and even to decline his name. "McAdam" connotes a multiple or reproducible "originarity," a Mc-Adam, a make-Adam, the trademark that complements the unique copy that is Winchester '73 (that both Rancière and Leutrat and Liandrat-Guigues underscore).[28] But now, in the rocks and the desert, "McAdam" also echoes the pictogram of the road paved by crushing, pulverizing, and grading stones into narrow earthen beds. The trail he follows up the hillside to the hideout and the hills bears his own name (Figure 12.4). When such a degree of immanence of language and landscape is reached—when the name becomes figured by and in the landscape at the same time the hero defines its latent traits—a condition of total visibility and invisibility, of blindness and insight is reached.

*the man from laramie*

The landscape of *Winchester '73* becomes a map of relations that the film designates as unknown. In most westerns the decor lends an aura to a field of action. Here an unuttered language is incised into the field of vision in order, it appears, to define a perspectival character in the grounding violence of human relations. In few films does the landscape ever become so *literal* or productive of the overall drama. Can the same be said of the other films? Does Mann find in *Winchester '73* a "unique" landscape, like

Figure 12.3
Still from *Winchester '73.*

Figure 12.4

Still from *Winchester '73.*

the rifle, that matches the action, or does he attempt to repeat the coincidence of shapes and forms in other features of the western phase? *The Man from Laramie* (1955) locates the drama of visibility in the areas where the landscape, because its site of enunciation cannot be specified, is also inhabited by language.

In this film textual signs and decor do not immediately explode into hieroglyphics that reveal in the blitz of cactuses the rapport of the hero with his world as had the western of 1950. In *The Man from Laramie* the epic quest is embroiled in a family romance, in which signs of kinship ties, incest, and xenophobia are rampant. The credits place roughly hewn beams of wooden letter-struts, painted in red, over a gray parchment ground traversed by a barbed or sutured line. They fade into black, and the film emerges into a broad, hard, arid, sensuous landscape of a desert. Under an infinite expanse a blue sky is riffled with patches of flattened clouds. The cinemascope lens displays an almost Greek world of beginnings set in New Mexico. From left to right, in the middle field, entering into the landscape, three wagons are driven by two men and drawn by teams of six mules (Figure 12.5).

The landscape refuses to reveal a language legible to the hero who crosses through it. What had been located in the *cactus* in *Winchester '73* is now invested in the *wagon*. The narrative moves ahead to show how the wagon is a secret, later to be discovered in the landscape, that rolls over its surface. What enters into the first shot will be visually linked to the mode of transport that ferries forbidden objects, boxes of repeating rifles, to bands of Apaches who are said to be responsible for marauding the countryside.[29] The wagon becomes the most insistently visible and legible

305

object of everyone's desires. Written in and by the landscape, it concretizes the relation with the unknown.

Standing by a window giving onto an endless expanse of mesa, the cattle baron Alec Waggoman (Donald Crisp), an aging patriarch succumbing to blindness, bemoans the irony that he owns 10,000 acres of range without being able to see 10. Fumbling about the papers and letters on his desk (the ciphered space of paperwork representing what he cannot see), he learns that one of his wagons is "missing." As he ferrets about, Waggoman is driven to fail to see his proper name in the landscape of braided relations. For both spectator and patriarch secret names are branded in ruts, tracks, and occluding shapes. They all constitute a kind of Braille that the eye touches when it contemplates the countryside. When on the verge of discovering that his surrogate son is responsible for betraying him, Waggoman utters, "Dave, we've got to find that wagon!" Ironically, it is his biological, miscreant son who displays the contents for the spectator before he lights a fire that sends into the sky smoke signals that will attract the Apaches to obtain the contraband. In a close-up, the only shot that brings writing into the landscape at large, the network of contradictions at play is encrypted into the space in a textual way. The stenciled words that designate the *barbed* wire for fencing destined for the *Barb* Ranch are below the name of the father, Alec Waggoman, the name that recalls the hero's unfortunate encounters at the local salt flats, where his wagons had been burned and many of his mules exterminated. So arresting is the close-up of the letters on the wooden crate that the film itself seems determined by its own glyphic aspect (Figure 12.6). Familial relations are so enmeshed in the overall writing of the landscape that the nubile female to whom the stepson Vic (Arthur Kennedy) is betrothed—but who prefers Will Lockhart (James Stewart)—is named Barb Waggoman (Cathy O'Donnell). Barbed wire delineates space, but the duplicitous quality of writing itself (it circulates in the film as whatever catches its victim, its essence being barbed) is close to what distinguishes it from *barbarity*, or the "natural" language of the Apaches. Even the director's name is written

Figure 12.5

Still from *The Man from Laramie.*

into the drama. The credits identifying the director recur in the narrative when it is implied that A(lec) Waggoman(n) carries the name of the grounding "acteur" or "auteur" of the narrative.

Textual tatters eventually inform what is patterned almost unconsciously in the first shot. The wagon is confused with the name of the patriarch, and is connoted when the first shot displays a "wagon" (a *vehicle*, if I. A. Richards's definition of a metaphor is recalled) driven by a "man" (that would be its *tenor*). But the determining conundrum either has to remain invisible or else lend clues to the ways that the image-field will display other components that define the interval of the visible and invisible. The moving wagons are equipped with the reins and blinders that turn the environing space into an enigma. After the first shot the team continues to descend the hill on which they were first descending. The retinue stops when Stewart tells his mate, "we'll camp here," whereupon the hero moves to examine the remains of the wagons recently burned in a Native massacre. In descending from his perch from the top of the wagon the hero is seen, albeit briefly, through a skein of leather reins. He is virtually "blinded" or striated by the abstract configuration of lines interposed between the lens and the view of the hero contemplating the death of his compatriots (Figure 12.7).

As with the reins, so too the blinders: throughout the story the camera records the immutable reactions of the mules to their surroundings. Like the members of a chorus, the beasts of burden serve as visible ciphers in the field of action. Time and again the camera cues on their bridles in order to place them adjacent to the eyes of the human players, most often in shots where characters are looking at what they cannot have or see (Figure 12.8). The leather patches underscore the presence of human blindness. The mules are yoked to a stylistic feature, gaining particular resonance in *The Man from Laramie*, that equates perspective with enigma. Throughout the film "blinders" cue and sustain the relation of the personages to the unknown.

Figure 12.6

Still from *The Man from Laramie*.

Figure 12.7

Still from *The Man from Laramie.*

All the bridling and concealing apparatus is remotely visible in the first shot, what might be called the initial "perception-image" of *The Man from Laramie.* Included among the array of visual enigmas is the seed of a Quixote-Panza relation of the hero and his confidant, a mirror of sorts, who aids the protagonist in his actions. The relation of the hero to his servant figures in the vistas whenever the couple nestles into the landscape and exchanges words over cups of coffee, the elixir that in both *The Man from Laramie* and *Winchester '73* seems to be a universal solvent of communication. At one point they wonder about their past lives. Lockhart (Stewart) confesses that he has only known a military life and has eaten, refectory-style, in mess halls. He insists that he is from "Laramie," to the north, the toponym that Stewart's twang agglutinates as a memory of the Second World War and Korea, in "L'army." When he utters the name, whatever he touches becomes marked by a relation to a familial absence (but not a loss) or to a desire to renew an oral rapport with the war, by which he had been attached to the world. He puts his lips to the nipple of a canteen while responding to the voice of the grizzled interlocutor who has called into question the hero's nomadic virtue. The hero slakes

Figure 12.8

Still from *The Man from Laramie.*

Figure 12.9

Still from *The Man from Laramie*.

his thirst at a point when old Charlie, his sidekick/helper, tells him he is detached from his world (Figure 12.9). The material object-relation of the canteen in the landscape emerges through this detachment, a visibility of a nourishing object, and the surrogate figure of the confidant who had, like the names and things displayed in the first shot, concretized the various networks of forms that the film explores all over its surface. While Lockhart avows that he is from a historic place in Wyoming, the toponym recedes to the collective memory of trauma. He and thousands of others are from a disbanded "army."

Because of what the first shot of the film reveals after being wound through the plot, the landscape of *The Man from Laramie* becomes more intricately complex, but also more immediately evident, than what was evinced in *Winchester '73*. In the film of 1955 networks of familial relations are tied to the space of the film. The landscape-object is less partial, less fragmented, less jagged or destined than what the hero crossed in the work of 1950. The mythic character of a point of impossible fusion is seen when the wagons are indeed *not* under the purview of Waggoman, or when the "barb" of the ranch of that name and the barbed wire that passes for repeating rifles are contrary to the receptive majesty of the New Mexico plateau. A different, almost welcoming relation is engaged, but it is in every event defined by a *textual character* that, in moving toward a conclusion, we can say owes its wealth and force to what Christian Metz discovered in the geography of enunciation and space.

309

## conclusion

At the outset Metz's concept of weakened deixis was seen animating a geography of cinema in which language and space are indefinite but forcibly mixed. It was also surmised that Metz's study of enunciation brings together issues that pertain to the ways that *perspectival objects* can be located in filmic space. The concept informs some of the ways that language, space, and desire can be discerned in the viewing of cinema. In Deleuze's taxonomy the concept defines how visibility is born in the "perception-image." In the paragraphs above the latter has been equated with the extreme long-shots that portray the landscape in Anthony Mann's western cycle (1950–1955).

The existential and classical traditions that inspire Mann's westerns concern not only the displacement of classical poetics or myth into a film genre, as is well known, but also—and especially, at least for the context of the cinematic landscape—broader relations of language and space. They are concretized in the dialogue of the landscape, narrative, and characters in *Winchester '73* and *The Man from Laramie*. In both films the drama of learning to see or of gaining insight comes through trials of blindness underscored by the irony of the multiplication and scatter of linguistic and pictorial fragments in the image-field. In the process of glimpsing the perspectival objects (Guy Rosolato) in the "textual landscape" of these films, we discover the "site" of cinema that Christian Metz had studied so carefully in his last published work on enunciation and film, but also, by contrast, Deleuze's concept of the "interval," vital to the *movement-image*, that is built from a crucial and vital relation with the films of Anthony Mann.

## notes

1. Christian Metz, *L'énonciation impersonnelle ou le site du film* (Paris: Méridiens Klincksieck, 1991); hereafter cited in text.
2. Emile Benveniste, *Problèmes de linguistique générale, Vol. 1* (Paris: Gallimard, 1966).
3. Wlad Godzich and Jeffrey Kittay, *The Emergence of Prose* (Minneapolis: University of Minnesota Press, 1987), 20; italics added.
4. Philippe de Lajarte, "The Voice of the Narrator…," in *Critical Tales: New Studies of the 'Heptameron' and Early Modern Culture*, eds. John D. Lyons and Mary B. McKinley (Philadelphia: University of Pennsylvania Press, 1993), 187.
5. One of the finest studies of the imagination, memory, divided attention, and cinema is Jean Louis Schefer, *L'Homme ordinaire du cinéma* (Paris: Gallimard/Cahiers du cinéma, 1982), a work that Gilles Deleuze sums up in the following way: "[Schefer] says that the cinematographic image, as soon as it assumes its aberration of movement, effectuates a *suspension of the world*, or *stirs up* the visible that, far from making thought clearly visible, as Eisenstein wanted, to the contrary addresses what cannot be permitted to be thought in thinking, just as it shows what cannot be seen in vision," in *L'image-temps* (Paris: Minuit, 1985), 219." (Here and elsewhere all translations from French sources are mine.)
6. Italics added. Original text: "[Foyer et cible d'énonciation ne sont pas] comme l'énonciateur et l'énonciataire, des personnes fictives, ce ne sont même pas exactement des choses, ce sont des directions intérieures à la géographie du film, des orientations décelées par l'analyste. Car il [est] vrai, en un sens, que l'activité du film se joue tout entière entre deux pôles, ou deux 'plots', puisqu'il y a nécessairement ceux que l'on fait et ceux qui le regardent, quel que soit le nom qu'on leur donne. Mais lorsqu'ils se marquent en un point précis du film, l'important est de décrire le tracé de cette empreinte désormais dépersonnalisée et passée à l'état de paysage.

7. Michel de Certeau observes that the emergence of the landscape in Western painting has much to do with the mobilisation of subjectivity that comes with the dislocation and rearrangement of speech and visibility. "Mobility of positions" is taken from Michel de Certeau, "The Gaze: Nicolas of Cusa," *Diacritics* 19, no. 2 (Summer 1987): 18. Anticipating some of the conclusions of this chapter, we can say that Metz's point is adduced in the overall effect of the landscape in *Bend of the River* (1951). Behind and above the site of the narrative of founding a society is a great mountain on a landscape in Oregon. All the action turns about where the mountain is and how the antagonistic parties must negotiate crossing over the space between the utopian community inland and the world outside along the coast. But the pervasive mountain is as omnipresent on the image track as the quasi-deictic that the characters utter over and again: Where is…, How do we get to…, Where to ford the waters, etc., at "the bend of the river." They must get to and about the "bend of the river" so often that the title of the film gets lost in its enunciation, and to the degree that the epic space that grounds the narrative also gets concealed. For the sighting point of the mountain, the location where *Bend of the River* was shot, melds into the spectator's association of its shape with the rival logo of Paramount studios. The condition of a local but general, historical but also economic, landscape emerges from the weakening of the sense of place in the very area where location is emphasized.

8. Michel de Certeau, "Entretien avec Alain Charbonnier et Joël Magny," *Cinéma*, no. 301 (January 1984): 19–20.

9. Gilles Deleuze shows how the "American cinema has endlessly made and remade a same fundamental film, that was the Birth of a nation-civilization" cast in organic terms. Gilles Deleuze, *L'Image-mouvement* (Paris: Minuit, 1983), 205. A future study might coordinate the collapse of this birthplace in the postwar years to Mann's epic phase (after 1957), especially if Kaja Silverman's treatment of post-holocaust masculinity—taken up in a study of *The Best Years of Our Lives*—is kept in view. Kaja Silverman, *Male Subjectivity at the Margins* (London: Routledge, 1992), chapter 1.

10. Guy Rosolato, *Eléments de l'interprétation* (Paris: Gallimard [Coll. de l'inconscient]), 1986); hereafter cited in text; and *Pour une psychanalyse exploratrice dans la culture* (Paris: PUF, 1993); hereafter cited in text.

11. "Claude Gelée: Un espace de sérénité dans son secret symbolique" first appeared in *Psychanalyse à l'Université* 34 (1984) to commemorate the exposition of the painter's work at the Grand Palais (Paris, February-March 1983); it is reproduced in Rosolato, 1986, 305–316.

12. To say that the maternal object *is* the reassuring quality of the landscape is tantamount to retrieving a gendered tradition that codes the perceiver as male and the countryside as female. By underscoring the relation with the unknown Rosolato is not aligned with the ideology of psychogeography that Gillian Rose studies with acumen through the optic of Lacan and others. Gillian Rose, *Feminism and Geography: The Limits of Geographical Knowledge* (Minneapolis: University of Minnesota Press, 1993), 86–112.

13. The observation is ratified in literature. Montaigne's *L'Apologie de Raimond Sebond* (Paris: Aubier, 1978), a text that serves as a negative ground for Cartesian philosophy, argues that God's best creation would be one in which man, if not absent altogether, would be best relegated to a rung below all other creatures on the ladder of being. And Baudelaire, in an essay

on landscape painting in his time, shows that our subjective relation to the vista before our eyes attests to the frailty of any link between man and nature. Landscapists who refuse to insert *staffage* that would make the world the measure of man are praised. The very frailty in question is crystallized in the first sentence: "Si tel assemblage d'arbres, de montagnes, d'eaux et de maisons, que nous appelons un paysage, est beau, ce n'est pas par lui-même, mais par moi, ma grâce propre, par l'idée ou le sentiment que j'y attache." Charles Baudelaire, *Oeuvres complètes. v. 2*, ed. Claude Pichois (Paris: Gallimard-Pléiade, 1976), 660. [If such an arrangement of mountains, waters. and houses, what we call a landscape, is enthralling it is not because of itself but because of myself, my own grace, because of the idea or the feeling I attach to it.] In fact a pictogram betrays what Baudelaire puts forward. In one draft of the essay, he wrote, "Oui, l'imagination *fait* le paysage" (Baudelaire, 665) [Yes, the imagination *makes* the landscape]; but in another, published in *La Revue Française*, he stated, "Oui, l'imagination *fuit* le paysage" (Baudelaire, 1046) [Yes, the imagination *flees* the landscape].

14. Admirers of Christian Metz here might feel a sense of pathos. For in *L'énonciation impersonnelle*, Metz wrote a work whose truth may have been symptomatic of a condition that fueled depression. The crushing feeling of atopia that comes with impersonal enunciation, that his writing sought both to reveal and struggle against, is mapped out from its beginning to end. The book constructs a critical and autobiographical space, despite an effort to demarcate its boundaries that remains uninhabitable. On the other side of the coin, Michel de Certeau offers the formula of a "pictogrammar" that invents the fiction of a space that a subject can inhabit and traverse, in his remarks on place-names that one chooses for self-mapping. Michel de Certeau, *L'invention du quotidien 1: arts de faire*, ed. Luce Giard (Paris: Galimard/Folio, 1990), 156–157.

15. Sophie de Mijolla-Mellor, "La travail de pensée dans l'interprétation," *Topique: Revue freudienne* 46 (1991): 201–203.

16. Gilles Deleuze, *Cinema 1: The Movement-Image*, trans. Hugh Tomlinson and Barbara Habberjam (Minneapolis: University of Minnesota Press, 1986 [1983]); hereafter cited in text.

17. See also Marie-Claire Ropars-Wuilleumier, *Écraniques* (Lille: Presses Universitaires de Lille, 1992), in which interval and hieroglyph are associated (chapters one and two).

18. In the first chapter of *'image movement*, Deleuze notes that the image is not merely given to be seen. "It is as legible as it is visible" (Deleuze, 24). The correlation is an unstated axiom in his theory of film.

19. David Bordwell, Janet Staiger, and Kristin Thompson, *The Classical Hollywood Film* (New York: Columbia University Press, 1984), chapter 1.

20. Jeanine Basinger, *Anthony Mann* (Boston: Twayne Publishers, 1979); hereafter cited in text.

21. Claude Lévi-Strauss, *Mythologiques, 4 Vols., Le cru et le cuit; Du miel aux cendres; L'origine des manières de tables; L'homme nu* (Paris: Plon, 1964–1971).

22. Raymond Bellour, "Anthony Mann," in *Le western* (Paris: Union Générale d'Editions [10/18], 1966); hereafter cited in text. Jacques Rancière, "Poétique d'Anthony Mann," *Trafic* (1993): 29–41; hereafter cited in text.

23. Basinger notes how Jean-Luc Godard was captivated by the same problem, and how two earlier treatments do justice to the theme: H. Reid, "Mann and his Environment," *Films and Filming* 8, no. 4 (January 1962), 11–

12; and J. H. Fenwick and Jonathan Green-Armytage, "Now You See It: Landscape and Anthony Mann," *Sight and Sound* 34, no. 4 (Autumn 1965): 186–189.

24. In a certain way the protagonist rides through and among the desert trees as if here were a western version of Baudelaire's originary "man" who moves through the woodlands of "Correspondences." He passes through a "forest of symbols" that behold him in a world in which he does not really belong. The acclaim of French readers for Mann's westerns might be related to the heightened awareness of synesthesia and animism that Baudelaire brings to poetry and paintings of landscapes.

25. As spectators we find ourselves in the very position of the hysteric patient whom Freud recalls at the end of "The Unconscious," who encounters so much difficult pleasure in donning his stockings. The fetish-object of his gaze is so ubiquitously woven about his legs that he cannot see through things enough to get dressed in the morning. Sigmund Freud, *The Standard Edition of the Complete Psychological Works*, vol. 24, ed. and trans. James Strachey (London: Hogarth Press, 1955 [1915]), 200.

26. Andrew Sarris and other critics have shown that the James Stewart "persona" is actualized in the actor's collaboration with Anthony Mann. Andrew Sarris, *The American Cinema. Directors and Directions, 1929–1968* (Chicago: University of Chicago Press, 1985), 99. It should be recalled that Mann's Stewart is in no way that of Hitchcock or other directors. In the westerns Stewart resembles many of Fritz Lang's almost pathological heroes who almost share the evil of the characters they wish to bring to trial. In this way McAdam (or later, Will Lockhart) bears affinities with Dave Bannion (Glenn Ford) in *The Big Heat* or Vern Haskell (Arthur Kennedy) in *Rancho Notorious*.

27. The relation of the landscape to the Greek chorus is both traditional and etymological. We can say that the "chorography" of *Winchester '73* includes in its range of denotation the local areas (Dodge City, the landscape by night, the circle the cavalry defends, Riker's tavern, the fiancé's family's home, Tascosa, the hideout) of the film's imaginary geography. These sites could be related to the partial, "derived worlds" in which a character, inspired by fetishistic or regressive impulses, blindly refuse to recognize the "originary" worlds or the wholes in which they are located. An almost unconscious association in this sequence would align the word-sign *cactus* with *cacke*, the signifier of the anal drive that compels the hero to murder his brother.

28. Jean-Louis Leutrat and Suzanne Liandrat-Guigues, *Les cartes de l'ouest, Un genre cinématographique: le western* (Paris: Armand Colin, 1990), 47.

29. In this respect, if a sociohistorical view is taken of the film's "secret," the wagon of rifles delivered to the Apaches are likened to the American "secrets" of technology that Alger Hiss was to have given to Russian Communists, the man who was said—to children in the 1950s—to have inaugurated postwar evil. The allegory thus confirms lessons that were told to American children, viewers of *The Man from Laramie*, throughout the age of paranoia that characterized the postwar years and the period of the Korean "conflict." The relation of the allegory to the discovery of the camps is taken up in Tom Conley, "A Fable of Film: Rancière's Anthony Mann," *Sub-stance* 33.1 (2004): 91–107.

# the cinematic void

desert iconographies in michelangelo antonioni's *zabriskie point*

m a t t h e w   g a n d y

> The mode of expression in the cinema of Antonioni
> is characterized by a layering of mystery and indeter-
> minacy in which there is a blurring of any distinction
> between objective and subjective dimensions to visual
> perception.
>
> Céline Scemama-Heard[1]

## introduction

On a warm summer evening in Berlin one can occasionally see a vast
desert landscape shimmering beneath the blinking lights of the Alexan-
derplatz Fernsehturm on the city's skyline. The *Freiluftkino*, or "open-air
cinema," has now become something of a shrine to one of the oddest yet
most enduring movies to emerge from the late 1960s, bathing its mildly
intoxicated audience in a visual phantasmagoria of billboards, bodies, and

bleached gypsum. The release of Michelangelo Antonioni's *Zabriskie Point* (1970) was met with a mix of adulation, incredulity, and outright animosity, not least because of the enormous expense and mystery surrounding its production. The Italian filmmaker's excoriating yet obtuse critique of American society has subsequently acquired something of a cult status in its guise as existential desert drama rather than in its originally intended role as counter-cultural representation of impending social and political revolution. Part psychedelic passion play and part neo-Marxian road movie, the film *Zabriskie Point* is mostly set in the extraordinary desert landscapes of Arizona and southern California.

One of the most distinctive features of Antonioni's cinema is the depiction of a "dialogue" between the actor and the landscape in which the representation of space is of equal if not greater significance than the presence of the human figure.[2] This dialogue is in no sense a cultural ecology of place, as articulated within the traditional idioms of landscape studies, but is an emphasis on the experience of landscape in human consciousness. The modern idea of landscape that Raymond Williams succinctly characterized as one of "separation and observation" has in the cinematic space of Antonioni been reunited within the psycho-geographic realm of his cinematic protagonists.[3] Antonioni's engagement with the power of modern spaces to provoke fear, anxiety, and disorientation has become significant within philosophical attempts to delineate (or unbound) our understanding of place as a corporeal experience that cannot easily be contained or categorized within modernist conceptions of rationality or spatial order. The most powerful of these interactions between the human figure and the landscape is provided by Antonioni's fascination with those desolate spaces that have the power to evoke deep unease or catharsis. Even his earliest and now largely destroyed documentary film *Del gente del Po* (1943/1947), which explores the landscape and people of the Po estuary in northern Italy, contains many of the distinctive elements of an "Antonionian landscape": the use of slow and lingering tracking shots; the deployment of cloud, mist, and other natural elements to add complexity to the *mise en scène*; and the exquisite attention to aesthetic detail.[4] We can trace a shift within Antonioni's films from the neorealist "urban deserts" portrayed in earlier features such as *La notte* (1960) and *L'eclisse* (1962) toward a gradual engagement with real deserts as powerful metaphors for social and cultural redemption in *Zabriskie Point* (1969) and *The Passenger* (1975) (Figure 13.1).[5] The desert is for Antonioni not only a concrete space to be conveyed in all its aesthetic complexity but also an allegorical and metaphorical realm through which we can explore different facets of human consciousness and experience. Such a formulation is, as we shall see, deeply flawed in its largely nondialectical and universalist conceptions of relations between nature and culture, but it is nonetheless

316

Figure 13.1

Production still from *Zabriskie Point*.

a powerful tableau for the enactment of a particular form of cultural critique framed within the teleological discourses of modernist thought.

Despite the classic insights of film critics such as Béla Balázs, André Bazin, and Siegfried Kracauer, the cinematic landscape remains an underexplored and somewhat enigmatic dimension of modern culture. This may in part be due to the perpetual uncertainty surrounding the relationship between abstract and allegorical representations of space within the development of popular culture. In recent years, however, the neglect of the cinematic landscape may also have been underpinned by a theoretical distrust of the visual tableau associated with the emergence of modern cinema. The very idea of the cinematic landscape as an object of critical inquiry consequently faces a degree of "dislocation" in which the cultural and historical coordinates behind the production of film may be occluded from critical analysis or theoretical discussion. This chapter attempts to redress this balance through a close engagement with the cinematic landscape as a cultural artefact which is deeply embedded in wider social and cultural processes but which is not in the final instance reducible to these external influences. In relation to *Zabriskie Point*, for example, the desert landscape introduces a medley of intersecting themes ranging from the role of nature in modernist conceptions of space to the cultural resonance of "primitivism" as an implicit riposte to the perceived artificiality of the urban landscape. Yet, as this chapter seeks to show, Antonioni's use of these arid landscapes as a political metaphor reveals a series of limitations to the director's attempt to use ideological motifs drawn from nature in order to articulate a wider critique of American society.

317

Following the resounding critical and commercial success of *Blow-Up* (1967), set amid the vibrant cultural scene of 1960s London, Antonioni secured an unprecedented degree of financial and artistic freedom from Metro-Goldwyn-Mayer studios for the making of his first American feature, *Zabriskie Point* (1970), named after a remote desert outcrop in Death Valley, California. His strong bargaining position emerged at a unique juncture in the history of U.S. cinema when many of the top grossing films were being made outside of the Hollywood studio system. This combination of circumstances allowed Antonioni to bring in key personnel, such as the cinematographer Alfio Contini from Italy, to the chagrin of the Hollywood studio unions. No editing was to be carried out in the United States (an unprecedented departure from the usual Hollywood practice), and the two lead roles were to be filled by unknown nonprofessional actors. Location shoots were consistently used in preference to MGM's own studios: for a five-minute sequence, an extra floor was added to the Mobil Oil headquarters in Los Angeles, for example, to be used instead of a cheaper studio simulacrum; major logistical challenges were posed by the extended location shooting in remote, arid, and inhospitable desert environments; and for the explosion sequence at the end of the film an elaborate building complex, constructed in the American modernist style of architects such as Frank Lloyd Wright and Bruce Goff, was built on a desert hillside surrounded by 17 cameras in specially prepared concrete silos.[6]

The eagerly awaited *Zabriskie Point* became increasingly pivotal to MGM's attempt to reverse its dwindling profits through the establishment of a successful foothold in the growing market for youth culture.[7] In his occasional interviews Antonioni declined to give any clear indication of what the film would be about, yet MGM had already committed over $3 million dollars to the project (a figure which would be quickly exceeded as production dragged on). Antonioni suggested somewhat obliquely that the film would be "tied to current events" and emphasized his fascination with the dominance of billboards in the American landscape. "The story I want to tell," declared Antonioni, "is typically American, not only in its setting and atmosphere, but also in its deeper psychological and sociological meaning."[8] "*Zabriskie Point*," explained Antonioni, "was not intended as a documentary about America, even though several of the basic incidents were taken from actual events."[9] Antonioni certainly strived toward some measure of cultural authenticity through, for example, the deployment of Sam Shepard (the up and coming young playwright) and Fred Gardner (the former *Ramparts* editor) to assist with the screenplay and perhaps also to act as counterfoils to accusations of an establishment sellout through his contract with MGM.

When *Zabriskie Point* was finally released in early 1970, the level of critical hostility incurred was unlike anything Antonioni had experienced since

L'Avventura was booed at Cannes in 1960. A number of leading U.S. critics clearly resented Antonioni's attempt to represent the contemporary cultural and political upheaval facing American society. Elliot Morgenstern of *Newsweek*, for example, considered that the film was "bad enough to give anti-Americanism a bad name"; Pauline Kael in the *New Yorker* lambasted the film as "a crumbling ruin of a movie"; and Vincent Canby, writing in the *New York Times*, derided the film's "stunning superficiality."[10] Parts of the underground press were also hostile to *Zabriskie Point*, along with a spate of other general release political films appearing in 1970 such as *The Activist*, *Getting Straight*, and *The Strawberry Statement*: it was felt that these films failed to deliver any coherent or credible political message (Bodroghkozy, 2002). But other U.S. reviewers revelled in the film's structural complexity and technical excellence (the vivid landscape photography, for example, was enhanced by Antonioni's first use of Panavision). Larry Cohen, for instance, writing in *The Hollywood Reporter*, found Contini's photography to be "uniformly brilliant" and defended the unorthodox use of nonprofessional actors.[11] Outside the United States the representation of landscape featured far more prominently in the film's critical reception but there was a lingering unease over the beguiling aesthetic power of the film and the clumsy handling of political themes.[12]

Part of the awkward complexity of *Zabriskie Point* is derived from Antonioni's attempt to convey so many different aspects of American society simultaneously: the political dynamics of the American youth movement; the economic realities of American capitalism; the iconographies of the American landscape; and the psychological experiences of his main protagonists as they struggle to make sense of their situation. The tense interplay among these different elements is underpinned by, for example, the intermingling of real and fictitious events within the narrative structure of the film, the use of real historical figures to play themselves within the context of dramatized reconstructions, and the use of historical footage of incidents such as civil unrest interspersed with imaginary representations of these events. Though the political import of *Zabriskie Point* and its associated critical opprobrium have waned since the early 1970s, the film remains a significant point of departure for the exploration of allegorical portrayals of the American landscape.

## the logic of disintegration

The title sequence for *Zabriskie Point*, like Antonioni's *Red Desert* (1964), uses a series of out-of-focus images to signal a kind of aesthetic and political disorientation. The blurred faces, yellow filter, and fragments of dialogue are accompanied by ethereal psychedelic music to induce a trip-like feel to the beginning of the film before we fade into a raucous student meeting. The frame now fixes on individual faces caught in the midst of debate to evoke a documentary *cinéma vérité* style in stark contrast with the diffuse

and abstract opening sequence. The political poignancy of the film is signalled from the start by Kathleen Cleaver, the wife of the Black Panthers
leader Eldridge Cleaver, shown at the centre of a tense gathering of radical
student activists (Figure 13.2).[13] Cleaver and the few other Black activists
attending the meeting mock the revolutionary pretensions of their white
comrades. Amid demands to close down the university, a middle-class
female student asks what "would make white people revolutionary," but
Cleaver warns that "the whole point is that the enemy are invisible." The
discussion turns to the question of direct action and the risk of death for
the student activists. We encounter one of the film's principal protagonists, Mark (played by Mark Frechette), who has been standing listening
to the discussion all along and suddenly announces that he is willing to
die too. The crowd turns toward him, and he leaves the room. His exit
provokes an angry reproach from another student who dismisses Mark's
utterance as "nonsense" and adds that if he wants to be a revolutionary
then "he has to learn to work with other people." But anger and confusion quickly turn to farce as another student quips laconically to scattered laughter that he remains "resolute in his struggle against bourgeois
individualism." The American political stage of the late 1960s is presented

Figure 13.2

Production still from *Zabriskie Point.*

as a fractured and chaotic melee of differing opinions in which no clear course of action can be discerned.

In the next sequence Mark embarks on a brief tour of Los Angeles in a red pickup truck. Our first encounter with the world outside the university is marked by a series of immense roadside billboards painted with idealized landscapes of the American Southwest. Beyond these imaginary landscapes the real city is depicted as an alienating jumble of office buildings, factories, and advertising hoardings set to discordant electronic music. This "jarring of the senses" denotes a Simmelian reading of the urban landscape as one that is dominated by commerce, abstract human relations, and, of course, a "blasé" outlook. Perhaps in a reference to his earlier depiction of industrial Ravenna in *Red Desert*, we are confronted by a sequence of red signs set to the clanking reverberations of mechanical music. "The billboards are an obsession of Los Angeles," reflects Antonioni. "To us the billboards are so contrary, but for the people who live there they are nothing—they don't even see them."[14] The visual representation of Los Angeles as a threatening and alienating city is interwoven with social and political themes derived from the urban crisis of the 1960s. In one understated yet powerful sequence, Mark and a colleague buy a gun from a firearms store. They manage to obtain a weapon without a license on the pretext that they live in a "borderline" neighbourhood. As they leave the premises the proprietor reminds them to drag anyone they shoot into the house. An implicit urban topography of fear and racism is clearly evoked where the use of extreme violence can be casually justified in the defence of property.

Another crucial dimension to the early part of the film is the role of a real estate company in the unfolding drama. We first encounter the film's other principal protagonist Daria (played by Daria Halprin) by the security desk of what is represented as a dynamic property company in downtown Los Angeles. We see her adopting a somewhat coquettish demeanour with her new boss, the successful real estate attorney Lee Allen (played by Rod Taylor), in the air-conditioned sterility of the company's reception area. In a later scene we find Allen promoting his scheme for a luxury desert development complex called "Sunny Dunes" to a room of potential investors. The promotional films for the project depict an array of water features in a clear intimation of the centrality of water to wealth and power in southern California. Grinning mannequins populate a synthetic utopia of model golf courses, manicured lawns, and state-of-the-art kitchens.

In the final scene, which takes place on the university campus, violence erupts between large crowds of students and heavily armed police during which Antonioni intersperses some documentary footage of campus unrest at Berkeley.[15] Mark witnesses a situation in which an unarmed Black student is shot; moments later the police officer who carried out the fatal shooting is also shot. Mark reaches for his own gun after the incident in an ambiguous moment which leaves us unsure who shot the police officer before he flees into the city. After "borrowing" a light plane from a Los Angeles airfield, he takes off over the city and heads east. Mark's aerial ascent provides a succession of exhilarating panoramas which play on the technological vistas associated with Italian Futurist traditions: first, we encounter a seemingly endless expanse of homes, swimming pools, and parking lots; then, as we gain altitude, we observe vast freeway intersections set against the LA skyline; and finally, the city dissolves into the distant haze of the desert beyond.

The film then cuts abruptly to a ground level view of the rolling dunes and ridges of the desert as seen through the window of Daria's green Buick. While she heads for Phoenix through the desert landscape, the film returns us briefly to the real estate office in Los Angeles where the development project is being negotiated over large-scale maps and plans with talk of "water table deficiencies" and "contingencies." These scenes powerfully juxtapose the serenity of Daria's encounter with the real desert and the remote commodification of land and nature being undertaken in downtown Los Angeles. She interrupts her journey through the desert with a stop-off in a godforsaken place called Ballister where she meets some elderly men reminiscing over the past. The dusty town is a locale of fading memories where intensified "small town values" hold out against the combined threats of displacement and redevelopment. The main street is littered with the debris of former prosperity. Rusted upturned cars lie lifelessly under the full glare of the mid-day sun as if to emphasize the sense of a redundant community facing both social and physical disintegration. Daria later abandons a stroll through the poverty-stricken town after being pestered by a gang of street kids and hurries back to her car. We are left with a final image of a lone man in profile sitting at an empty bar; the sense of torpor is emphasized by cigarette smoke curling languidly toward the ceiling.

## the beautiful void

The flight from the city into the desert marks a turning point in the film away from the overt political conflict depicted in Los Angeles toward an exploration of more abstract themes. In this sense *Zabriskie Point* marks a continuity with Antonioni's earlier explorations of spatial voids, wastelands, and landscapes of estrangement, which he developed in films such as *L'avventura* (1959) and *Red Desert* (1964). As we leave the last vestiges of human settlement behind, the American desert landscape unfolds into a "decentred" or unbounded space in which any distinction between real and imaginary perceptions of place becomes progressively eroded.

Recent philosophical explorations of unusual spatial forms have played a significant role in reinterpreting the critical legacy of Antonioni and moving beyond narrowly formalist or one-dimensional responses to his work. Gilles Deleuze, for example, has identified the changing landscapes of Antonioni between the 1960s and 1970s as emblematic of a shift in cinematic space from the "movement-image" to the "time-image."[16] Deleuze attempts to break free from the Metzian legacy of structuralist cinematic theory by exploring the emergence of cultural forms or images within the medium of cinema that do not correspond with any *a priori* conceptual schema. He is not interested in the identification of any putative visual syntax but in an engagement with filmmaking as a form of philosophical and cultural innovation.[17] It is difficult, however, to subsume Antonioni's intellectual project within a poststructuralist philosophical framework because his cinematic vision originates within a largely teleological, dualistic, and hierarchical conception of modern culture.[18] His depiction of relations between nature and culture, for example, remains resolutely nondialectical in its neoromantic emphasis on primal origins that lie outside of history.[19] During the production of the film, Antonioni referred to the landscapes of *Zabriskie Point* as "primitive" in a clear intimation of his search for a primordial aesthetic to juxtapose with the perceived artificiality of modern urban culture (1968/69, 29).

The German cultural critic Tom Holert has recently suggested that Antonioni's desert landscapes share important similarities with the development of North American Land Art exemplified by the work of artists such as Robert Smithson, Michael Heizer, and Walter De Maria.[20] Whilst Holert is right to identify the late 1960s and early 1970s as a crucial juncture in the development of desert iconography and its extensive appropriation within popular culture, he tends to elide different strands of landscape aesthetics by overextending his analysis of the intellectual complexity behind Land Art. He treats it as if it corresponded with the kind of increasingly abstract desert vision articulated by Antonioni. The critical difference between Antonioni's representation of nature and leading Land Artists such as Robert Smithson is that in Antonioni's conception of primal or "first nature" relations between nature and culture remain essentially pre-given rather than socially constructed. While Antonioni and Smithson both enjoyed an ambivalent relationship with contemporary forms of social and ecological critique, they nonetheless stem from very different intellectual traditions: the presence of nature in the work of Smithson, for example, has a distinctively dialectical quality, whereas for Antonioni, the perceived antinomy between nature and culture is never seriously challenged. In this sense, Antonioni's depiction of the American landscape does not form part of the rupture in modernist cultural practice that art historians such as Rosalind Krauss have ascribed to the emergence of Land Art in the late 1960s.[21] Antonioni uses "nature" in *Zabriskie Point* in its broadest sense as a metaphor for something that resides outside of "history": something which is unchanging and ever-present as a deeper layer of human consciousness and experience. Yet within this discourse of historical erasure lurks the "ghost of colonialism" in which pre-European influences are either erased or elided with the imaginary projections of Western culture.[22] This is reflected, for instance, in Antonioni's use of Native American motifs such as Daria's buckskin clothes at the close of the film to indicate his attachment to a highly romanticized conception of cultural authenticity in the American desert. Antonioni's engagement with the creative energies of nature lies closer to teleological conceptions of modernist abstraction than the dialectical impulses of North American Land Art.[23] The role of nature within the development of abstract expressionism, for example, emerged within the critical discourses of "high modernism" as a twentieth-century extension to the romantic sublime and as an effective means to convey pure aesthetic experience. The issue, then, is the relationship between cinematic abstraction and the history of cultural modernism within which the postwar move toward abstraction played a significant yet historically specific role.

The juxtaposition of desert landscape with a "primal" conception of nature is most strikingly evoked in *Zabriskie Point* by the eroticization of landscape. This is gradually developed in the film by the powerfully anthropomorphic representation of the arid landscape as a series of undulating flesh-coloured human forms. When we eventually arrive at the remote desert promontory after which the film is named, we are confronted by an expanse of deeply dissected and folded hills bathed in a luminous rosy light. The framing of the two figures in the landscape induces a sense of aesthetic rapture in which the landscape itself seems to acquire its own agency. In one sequence, Daria runs out of the frame, but the camera hovers over the "empty" space and draws back to depict the hillside in stunning clarity and detail. The bleached landscape appears to listen and respond to the human figures, creating its own echo of spatial intimation. The culmination of this depiction of "corporeal space" is reached with the love scene between Daria and Mark that develops into a panoramic expanse of lovers across the arid hillside (played by members of Joe Chaikin's Open Theatre). The desert orgy sequence is clearly an imaginary projection of Daria—like the film's violent finale—and can be interpreted as a means to represent her sexual pleasure through a temporary loss of identity. The scene of desert ecstasy can be read as a play on the pastoral theme of an "earthly paradise," yet transposed without irony to the arid badlands of Death Valley. However, the bleached colouration of the desert sex scene (in contrast with the vivid pink hues deployed on the arrival of Mark and Daria in the desert) also implies a morbid juxtaposition of eroticism with death. As Mark and Daria make love there is a momentary depiction of Daria's sleeping yet very pale face so that her orgasm is represented as a kind of *petite mort*. The use of the desert as the locus for a modern fable of love and death, a cinematic combination of *eros* and *thanatos*, shares parallels with the synthesis of Marxian and Freudian ideas developed by social theorists such as Herbert Marcuse in the 1960s who sought to interpret sexual freedom as a form of political action.[24] But Antonioni's representation of sexuality is more ambiguous than this since the expression of sexual desire in *Zabriskie Point* is suffused with a deep sense of melancholy. This is suggested by the abrupt representation of an empty expanse of rocks at the end of the love scene in which the sound of music is replaced by the roar of a jet engine overhead and the slamming of a car door to invoke a sudden disenchantment of the desert landscape.

## spectacle and denouement

After the desert love scene Mark returns the now gaudily painted plane to the airfield in Los Angeles and is quickly surrounded by armed police. Moments later we see his body slumped across the control panel of the aircraft. Daria continues her journey to meet her boss at an elaborate meeting complex in the Arizona desert and hears of Mark's death on the car radio (Figure 13.3). In a moment of forlorn contemplation, she stands by her parked car as if to abandon her journey but resolves to continue. The imposing desert building provides a striking contrast with the dissected and frangible landscapes of *Zabriskie Point*: its gleaming angular structure abuts the arid hillside in defiance of nature. Daria enters the landscaped atrium of the building complex with its elaborate water features and presses her body against a water-covered rock in a moment of grief and heightened awareness of her physical surroundings. The camera pans back to depict the entire complex with its intricate patterns of reflections accompanied by the sound of wind chimes in the desert breeze. We can observe Allen and his business associates debating over the details of the planned real estate scheme through large plate glass windows: only

Figure 13.3

Still from *Zabriskie Point*.

momentary segments of dialogue are audible but the faces are closely depicted in their intense negotiations. After briefly meeting with her boss, who appears surprised yet delighted at her arrival, Daria wanders through the strange building. She encounters a Native American domestic servant in a stairwell, and they exchange knowing glances in a clear intimation of her political awakening. She then flees the building and runs back to her car. She drives a short distance away, gets out of the car and stands with her back toward us so that we face the desert real estate complex with her (Figure 13.4). The camera pans back to the building. The pages of a copy of *National Geographic* flutter in the breeze; an abandoned cigarette slowly burns; Allen and his business associates discuss a model of the planned development (their faces oddly refracted through a glass table top). The camera pans back again repeatedly to our shared vantage point with Daria, and there is a momentary stillness. Then the entire building explodes; not once, but repeatedly, and from different angles. A fiery mushroom cloud extends far above the hillside with burning debris thrown in every direction.

Following the dramatic and repeated representation of the exploding building, there is an extraordinary shift in tempo toward the elegiac depiction of floating debris. Slowed down images of exploding items such as a television set, rows of bookshelves, a clothes rail, and a fully stocked refrigerator are shown. The clothes move through space like jellyfish pulsating beneath the water, unable to determine their trajectory. The screen is filled with a spray of pieces of white electrical goods set against a pale blue sky followed by an array of undamaged objects such as apples, fish, sausages, whole cuts of meat, and black balloons. The strange assortment

Figure 13.4

Still from *Zabriskie Point.*

of moving objects resembles a drop of pond water or some other micro-scopic world magnified many times to reveal a menagerie of unfamiliar organisms. The drifting detritus of consumer culture is reminiscent of the garbage-strewn industrial landscapes in *Red Desert* and represents not just a disavowal of avaricious consumption but also suggests the release of things from the "prison of their existence."[25] The meaning of waste is a recurring preoccupation in Antonioni's cinema that we can trace back to his striking documentary, *Nettezza urbana* (1948), about the street sweepers of Rome. Antonioni is clearly fascinated by the "ornate wastefulness" of bourgeois society and its casual disregard for everyday objects.[26] He builds on a well-established critique of American society developed, for example, in F. Scott Fitzgerald's depiction of the decadence and transitory gratifica-tion of the "roaring twenties" before the Great Crash and the emerging postwar critique of mass production and built-in obsolescence developed by Vance Packard. Waste is for Antonioni not simply a question of mate-rial loss but is also a complex aesthetic and philosophical problem integral to the experience of modernity and the perpetual forces of entropy and disintegration.

It is clear, however, that the explosion only occurs in the mind of Daria. Her destructive fantasy is both a political mirage and also an imaginary attempt to avenge the death of her lover. It can also be read as a symbol of her politicization driven by a new awareness of the interconnections between the different events she has experienced. The splintering debris of the modernist citadel marks a simultaneous coalescence of abstract ideas around the need to act and brings the narrative back to the opening student debate. As with any utopian discourse, however, the new politi-cal form must be imagined within the context of existing reality: hence the cathartic aspect of the film as a repudiation of American society in the face of the death of her lover and the wider injustices alluded to dur-ing the duration of the film. At one level, the fantasy of violent retribu-tion for Mark's death also represents a confrontation with the rapacious transformation of the semi-arid landscapes of Arizona and southern Cali-fornia. The explosion can be read as a disavowal of the violence that is implicit not only in the cultural and political origins of commodities but also in their effect on society. "In *Zabriskie Point*," suggests Antonioni, "the material wealth of America, which we see in advertisements and on bill-boards along the roads, is itself a violent influence, perhaps even the root of violence" (1970). At another level, however, the eschatological theme also connects with the menace of cold war nuclear destruction, the cen-trality of desert space to the testing and development of military hard-ware and the idea of a redemptive "industrial-technological apocalypse." The explosion of the real estate complex is an apposite metaphor for the intersection between cinematic space and the development of military spectacle.[27] The compound-like structure of the desert building edifice certainly shares some similarities with the kind of cell-like architectural spaces associated with the U.S. atomic testing program with its mixed emphasis on defence and observation. Desert space emerges in *Zabriskie Point* as an apex of technological, political, and aesthetic extremes through which new kinds of landscapes are created and destroyed. Yet the desert retains an "intact silence" in the words of Jean Baudrillard, even after its complex geological structures have encountered human violence.[28]

## conclusion

By the early 1970s, the cinematic desert had become a kind of *tabula rasa* around which countercultural discourses could develop in opposition to the perceived hegemony and cultural inauthenticity of industrial capitalism. In the case of European and North American cinema the shifting relationship between landscape and popular culture combined with the cinematic legacy of the classic western to produce a new sensitivity toward the philosophical and political possibilities of desert space as a locus for cultural critique.[29] The desert represented a kind of cinematic frontier that could enable the exploration of new kinds of imaginary spaces. Consider, for example, Werner Herzog's ghostly depiction of the Sahara in *Fata Morgana* (1971), Nicolas Roeg's mystical evocation of the Australian outback in *Walkabout* (1970), or Pier Paolo Pasolini's use of location shoots in Yemen to represent a mythical precapitalist realm in *Arabian Nights* (1974).[30] In these and other exemplars, desert space serves as a dramatic stage for cultural redemption through a confrontation between different belief systems either explicitly presented within the films themselves or implicitly, as in the case of Pasolini's search for different forms of premodern cultural "authenticity." For Antonioni, however, the desert motif is deployed not simply to assert the continuing cultural salience of the premodern but to explore the existential dilemmas that underpin modernity itself through the confrontation between his cinematic protagonists and the looming emptiness or incomprehensibility of these extraordinary landscapes. As we move from the city to the desert, the depiction of landscape becomes an exploration of pure form as roads, vapour trails, and rock formations become part of a larger canvas: there is a double movement here as Antonioni blurs nature and human artifice, thereby lending an anthropomorphic quality to the eerie stillness of the desert. At the same time, he retains a profound sense of an underlying "nature" buried beneath the complex stratification of modern culture. The mysterious qualities of the American desert are deployed to reveal a preexisting symbolic realm that has been obscured by utilitarian rationalism and the advance of consumer capitalism. Yet Antonioni's neoromantic attachment to the human subject is belied by his framing of the human figure within the landscape to produce an intense confrontation between human consciousness and the indifference of inanimate nature. Many critical responses to his cinematic legacy have tended to take these universalist themes at face value and not sought to disentangle Antonioni's cinematic abstraction from its cultural and historical context. Or, more recently, his work has been simplistically appropriated within a putative postmodern cinematic canon on account of its complexity and indeterminacy, thereby flattening and truncating any cogent historiography of cultural modernism and its cinematic expression.[31] In contrast, this chapter has sought to engage with the cinematic landscape in *Zabriskie Point* as a distinctive historical moment reflected in the disparate encounters between different strands of environmentalist and political critique ranging from the Marcusian repudiation of consumer capitalism to the contemporary "rediscovery" of non-European and premodern cultural forms.

The film *Zabriskie Point* seeks to evoke a vivid sense of place—the specific cultural and political milieu of Vietnam-era America—and at the same time develop a more abstract experience of space through the juxtaposition of Los Angeles with the vast desert landscapes lying beyond the urban fringe. Antonioni uses the American landscape as a powerful metaphor for intellectual uncertainty by indicating a different rhythm of time, a geological space outside of modernity, and also as a means to develop a "primitivist" critique of the perceived artificiality of consumer capitalism. In this sense, the film signals a far more ambitious intellectual project than his depiction of London in *Blow-Up* (1967) because he tries to convey both an accurate portrait of late 1960s America and also uncover a "structural truth" about the nature of reality.[32] The sharp if somewhat caricatured political delineations of *Zabriskie Point* are in part reflective of the deep political schisms of postwar Italy which characterized the development of Italian cinema even if Antonioni had himself moved further away from neorealism than many of his Italian contemporaries. In this sense, the mixed reception experienced by the film testifies to the different cultures of political filmmaking which developed in Italy during the 1950s as distinct from those in the United States where the political legacy of McCarthyism served to suppress the direct cinematic representation of class antagonisms. Though widely regarded as a failure, *Zabriskie Point* remains one of the most interesting attempts to explore the allegorical and aesthetic power of desert landscapes within the specific context of the social and political upheaval facing 1960s America. For Antonioni political themes are often played out in terms of individual psychological dramas rather than straightforward allusions to political movements or ideas; in *Zabriskie Point* we encounter a mix of representational strategies ranging from the documentary style of the opening to the destructive fantasy sequence that closes the film. The significance of cinema for modern conceptions of landscape stems from the malleability of the cinematic medium as a locus for changing interpretations of space in which the relationships between inside and outside, between film and audience, and between cinema and the wider development of philosophical ideas are engaged in a perpetual process of renegotiation and reformulation. It is within this fluid context that the cinematic legacy of Antonioni allows so many different conceptual vantage points from which to explore the changing relations between space and modern culture.

## notes

1. Céline Scemama-Heard, *Antonioni: le désert figuré* (Paris: L'Harmattan, 1998), 83. My translation.
2. See, for example, "Michelangelo Antonioni: Interview with Charles Thomas Samuels" in *Film Heritage* 5, no. 3 (1970): 1–12.
3. See Raymond Williams, *The Country and the City* (London: Chatto and Windus, 1973).
4. See Noa Steimatsky, "From the Air: The Genealogy of Antonioni's Modernism" in *Camera Obscura Camera Lucida: Essays in Honor of Annette Michelson*, eds. Richard Allen and Malcolm Turvey (Amsterdam: Amsterdam University Press, 2003), 183–214.
5. See Nuria Bou, "Deserts, Deserts Urbans" in *El Segle del Cinema*, ed. J. Balló (Barcelona: Centre de Cultura Contemporània de Barcelona, 1995), 88–92.
6. Bruce Davidson, "Antonioni v. Hollywood," *Sunday Times* (25 January 1970).
7. Aniko Bodroghkozy, "Reel Revolutionaries: An Examination of Hollywood's Cycle of 1960s Youth Rebellion Films," *Cinema Journal* 41, no. 3 (2002), 38–58; hereafter cited in text.
8. Michelangelo Antonioni, quoted in Robert Joseph, "Billboards, Bears and Beads," *Cinema* 4, no. 4 (December 1968).
9. Michelangelo Antonioni, quoted in Guy Flatley, "'I Love this country': Antonioni Defends *Zabriskie Point*," *New York Times* (February 1, 1970); cited hereafter in text as *Antonioni/Flatley*.
10. See Vincent Canby, "Screen: Antonioni's 'Zabriskie Point,'" *New York Times* (February 1970); Vincent Canby, "No Life in Antonioni's Death Valley," *New York Times* (February 1970); Joseph Morgenstern, "Death Valley Days," *Newsweek* (February 16, 1970).
11. Larry Cohen, "MGM's *Zabriskie Point* Fine Artistic, Commercial Film," *The Hollywood Reporter* (February 10, 1970). See also Stephen Handzo, "Michelangelo in Disneyland," *Film Heritage* 6, no. 1 (1970): 7–24.
12. See, for example, Guido Aristarco, "Il mestiere del critico: evoluzione di Antonioni in *Zabriskie Point*," *Cinema nuovo* 23, no. 205 (May/June 1970): 205–210; Jean-Louis Bory, "Le vol d'Icare," *Le Nouvel observateur* (27 April 1970); Michel Capdenac, "Faire sauter la baraque," *Lettres françaises* (22 April 1970); Wolf Donner, "Visionen vom schlimmen Amerika," *Die Zeit* (11 September, 1970); Else Goelz, "Antonioni entdeckt Amerika," *Stuttgarter Zeitung* (18 September 1970); Julian Jebb, "Intimations of Reality: Getting the Zabriskie Point," *Sight and Sound* 39, no. 3 (1970): 124–126; Derek Malcolm, "Uneasy Rider," *The Guardian* (12 March 1970); David Robinson, "Antonioni's America," *The Financial Times* (13 March 1970); Marie Seton, "Antonioni Excels Himself," *Film World* (India) 6, no. 4 (August/September 1970): 14–15; Giulio Schmidt "Zabriskie Point," *Rivista del Cinematografo* 11 (November 1970): 574–576; and Philip Strick, "Zabriskie Point," *Monthly Film Bulletin* 37, no. 436 (1970): 102.

13. The involvement of the Black Panthers and other radical groups in the making of *Zabriskie Point* involved complex negotiations over how their participation might assist in their political aims. See Soren Agenoux, Interview by Sam Shepard, *Inter/view* 1, no. 3 (1969): 6–7.

14. Michelangelo Antonioni, Interview by Marsha Kinder, *Sight and Sound* 38, no. 1 (Winter 1968/1969): 26–30; hereafter cited in text.

15. Documentary footage is also used to striking effect in *The Passenger* (1975), where we see jarring images of the military execution of political opponents in Nigeria.

16. See Gilles Deleuze, *Cinema 2: the Time Image*, trans. H. Tomlinson and R. Galeta (London: Athlone, 1989 [1985]). See also Tom Holert, "Strudel und Wüsten des Politischen: 'Zabriskie Point', 'Spiral Jetty' und die Grammatik der Entgrenzung" in *Jahresring 48: Jahrbuch für moderne Kunst. Kunst / Kino*, ed. Gregor Stemmrich (Köln: Oktagon, 2001), 94–119.

17. See John Rajchman, *The Deleuze Connections* (Cambridge, MA: MIT Press, 2000).

18. See Matthew Gandy, "Landscapes of Deliquescence in Michelangelo Antonioni's *Red Desert*," *Transactions of the Institute of British Geographers* 19, no. 2 (2003): 218–237.

19. See Matthew Gandy, "The Heretical Landscape of the Body: Pier Paolo Pasolini and the Scopic Regime of European Cinema," *Environment and Planning D: Society and Space* 14, no. 3 (1996): 293–310.

20. See, for example, Holert, *op. cit.*

21. See Rosalind Krauss, "Sculpture in the Expanded Field" in *The Anti-Aesthetic: Essays on Postmodern Culture*, ed. Hal Foster (Port Townsend, WA: Bay Press, 1983). See also the interesting commentary provided by Emily Scott in her M.A. thesis, *The Birth of the Atomic Desert* (Los Angeles, University of California, 2003).

22. Patrick Werkner, *Land Art USA* (München: Prestel, 1992).

23. See Matthew Gandy, "The Heretical Landscape of the Body: Pier Paolo Pasolini and the Scopic Regime of European Cinema," *op. cit.*

24. Alberto Moravia, "È esplosa pure l'arte di Antonioni," in *Zabriskie Point*, Michelengelo Antonioni (Cappelli Editore, 1970), 11–16.

25. Michael Althen, "*Zabriskie Point*: carte blanche," in *Antonioni: die Kunst der Veränderung*, ed. Rolf Schüler (Berlin: Berliner Filmkunsthaus Babylon, 1993), 70.

26. Michelangelo Antonioni, quoted in Philip Strick, *Michelangelo Antonioni* (London: Motion Publications, 1963), 8.

27. See, for example, Paul Virilio, *War and Cinema: the Logistics of Perception* (London, New York: Verso, 1989).

28. Jean Baudrillard, *America*, trans. Chris Turner (London, New York: Verso, 1988), 123.

29. See Holert, *op. cit.* On the cultural resonance of desert landscapes in modern culture see also Reyner Banham, *Scenes in America Deserts* (London: Thames & Hudson, 1982) and David Jasper, ed., *The Sacred Desert: Religion, Literature, Art, and Culture* (Oxford: Blackwell, 2004).

30. See, for example, Gandy, *op. cit.*

31. Critics who seek to enlist the work of Antonioni within a post-structuralist or post-modern cinematic canon include Peter Brunette, *The Films of Michelangelo Antonioni* (Cambridge: Cambridge University Press, 1998); Angelo Restivo, *The Cinema of Economic Miracles: Visuality and Modernization in*

*the Italian Art Film* (Durham, NC: Duke University Press, 2002); and Sam Rohdie, *Antonioni* (London: British Film Institute, 1990).

32. On Antonioni's privileging of his depiction of "structural truth" over "naturalistic truth" in *Blow-Up* see Restivo, *op. cit.*

# contributors

**Jacques Aumont** is professor of film aesthetics at the Université de Paris III (Sorbonne nouvelle) and heads the Collège d'histoire du cinéma at the Cinémathèque française. He once worked as a critic for *Cahiers du cinéma* (1967–1974) and was on the editorial board of *Iris*. He supervised the French translation of S. M. Eisenstein's writings and is the author of several articles and books, including *Montage Eisenstein* (Albatros, 1979), *L'oeil interminable* (Séguier, 1989), *L'image* (Nathan, 1990), *Du visage au cinéma* (Editions de l'étoile, 1992), *À quoi pensent les films* (Séguier, 1996), *De l'Esthétique au présent* (De Boeck et Larcier, 1998), *Amnésies* (P.O.L., 1999), *Dictionnaire théorique et critique du cinéma* (with Michel Marie; Nathan, 2001), and *Les théories des cinéastes* (Nathan, 2002).

**David B. Clarke** is senior lecturer in human geography at the University of Leeds. His research focuses on the geographies of consumerism and the media, particularly film. He has edited *The Cinematic City* (Routledge, 1997), authored *The Consumer Society and the Postmodern City* (Routledge, 2003; Chinese ed., Laureate Books, 2005), and co-authored *The Consumption Reader* (with Marcus A. Doel and Kate Housiaux; Routledge, 2003).

**Tom Conley** is professor of French in the Department of Romance Languages at Harvard University. He has translated into English works by Deleuze and de Certeau, and is the author of several articles and books on literature, film, and theory, including *Film Hieroglyphs: Ruptures in Classical Cinema* (Minnesota, 1991), *The Graphic Unconscious in Early Modern French Writing* (Cambridge, 1992), *The Self-Made Map: Cartographic Writing in Early Modern France* (Minnesota, 1996). His latest book, *A Map in a Movie: A Study of Cartography and Cinema*, is forthcoming in 2006 (University of Minnesota Press).

**Antonio Costa** is professor of film history and theory at the University IUAV of Venice. He has published books on early cinema in Europe (*La meccanica del visibile. Il cinema delle origini in Europa*, La casa Usher, 1983); Georges Méliès (*La morale del giocattolo*, poi Clueb, 1989); the relations between the cinema and the fine arts (*Cinema e pittura*, 1991; *Carlo L. Ragghianti: i critofilm d'arte*, Campanotto, 1995; *Il cinema e le arti visive*, Einaudi, 2002); and literature (*Immagine di un'immagine*, Utet, 1993). His latest book, *Marco Bellocchio. I pugni in tasca*, was published in 2005 (Lindau).

Marcus A. Doel is research professor of human geography at the University of Wales Swansea. He has written widely on poststructuralism, social theory, and critical human geography. He is the author of *Poststructuralist Geographies: The Diabolical Art of Spatial Science* (Edinburgh University Press/Rowman & Littlefield Publishing, 1999); and the co-editor of *Fragmented Asia* (Ashgate, 1996), *Dynamic Asia* (Ashgate, 1998), and *The Consumption Reader* (with David B. Clarke and Kate Housiaux, Routledge, 2002). He is currently preparing a book on *Spaces of Consumption* (with David B. Clarke; Sage, 2006).

Bridget Elliott is professor of art history in the Department of Visual Arts at the University of Western Ontario, where she teaches in the areas of nineteenth- and twentieth-century art history, theory, and criticism as well as in film and media studies. With Jo-Ann Wallace she is the author of *Women Artists and Writers: Modernist (Im)Positionings* (Routledge, 1994) and, with Anthony Purdy, *Peter Greenaway: Architecture and Allegory* (Academy, 1997). She recently co-edited, with Janice Helland, *Women Artists and the Decorative Arts: The Gender of Ornament* (Ashgate, 2002). Other publications include articles in the following refereed journals: *Art & Design, Art History, Feminist Art News, Feminist Review, Genders, Oxford Art Journal,* and *Victorian Studies.* A book, *Specular Spelunking: Cross-Dressing and Looking in the Late Victorian Music-Hall,* which considers the visual spectacle of late Victorian music-hall entertainment, is near completion. Her current research project considers how and why various Decadent ideas and forms from the 1890s were revived in Deco art, architecture, and film during the 1920s. She currently serves as a member of the editorial board of the *Oxford Art Journal.*

Matthew Gandy is reader in geography at University College London. He has published widely on cultural representations of nature and landscape. His work on cinema includes articles on landscape in the films of Antonioni, Herzog, Haynes, and Pasolini. He is the author of *Concrete and Clay: Reworking Nature in New York City* (MIT Press, 2002). His current research is focused on nature, technology, and the production of urban space.

Martin Lefebvre is Concordia University research chair in film studies at the Mel Hoppenheim School of Cinema, where he teaches film theory. He has published a book on Alfred Hitchcock's *Psycho* (*Psycho: de la figure au musée imaginaire. Théorie et pratique de l'acte de spectature,* L'Harmattan, 1996) and co-edited a collection of essays on S. M. Eisenstein (*Eisenstein: l'ancien et le nouveau,* Publications de la Sorbonne, 2002). He has published articles in several journals including *Screen, New Literary History, Poétique, Semiotica, Protée, CINéMAS,* and *Visio.* Since 1996 he has served as editor of *Recherches sémiotiques/Semiotic Inquiry.* A member of the Peirce/Wittgenstein research group at Université du Québec à Montréal, his current research focuses on

American cinema, pragmatism, and the semiotic philosophy of Charles S. Peirce. He also heads The Research Group on the History and Epistemology of Film Studies at Concordia University.

**Laura U. Marks** is a theorist, critic, and curator of independent and experimental media arts. Her current research interests are independent media in the Arab world, and formal and historical links between classical Islamic art and new media art. She is the author of *The Skin of the Film: Intercultural Cinema, Embodiment, and the Senses* (Duke University Press, 2000) and *Touch: Sensuous Theory and Multisensory Media* (Minnesota University Press, 2002), as well as dozens of essays. She has curated programs of experimental media for festivals and other venues worldwide. Dr. Marks is the Dena Wosk University Professor in Art and Culture Studies at Simon Fraser University, Vancouver.

**Jean Mottet** is professor in the département d'arts plastiques et sciences de l'art at the Université de Paris I (Panthéon-Sorbonne). A specialist of American and early cinema he has organized, in collaboration with New York's MoMA, a D. W. Griffith retrospective that was held at the Centre Georges Pompidou, along with an exhibition. The proceedings were published as *D. W. Griffith* (Publications de la Sorbonne/L'Harmattan, 1984). In 1999 he won the Jean Mitry prize for his book on landscape in American cinema (*L'Invention de la scène américaine. Cinéma et Paysage*, L'Harmattan, 1998). He has since edited *Les paysages du cinéma* (Champ Vallon, 1999) and, more recently, *L'arbre dans le paysage* (Champ Vallon, 2002).

**Maurizia Natali** is currently adjunct faculty at the Rhode Island School of Design. She holds a PhD (Doctorat Troisième Cycle) in Film Theory and Aesthetics from the Université de Paris III (Sorbonne Nouvelle, D.E.R.C.A.V.). She is the author of a book on landscape in film (*L'Image-Paysage. Iconologie et cinéma*, Presses universitaires de Vincennes,1996), as well as several articles published in European and American journals. Her areas of expertise are film aesthetics and theory; art history and film; cinema and painting; visual culture and media.

**Heather Nicholson** is research fellow in the Manchester Centre for Regional History and North West Film Archive at Manchester Metropolitan University. She has taught, made presentations, and written widely on diverse aspects of sociocultural and landscape-related change in relation to the interpretation of visual evidence and the politics of representation within British and international contexts. She is editor of *Screening Culture: Constructing Image and Identity* (Lexington Books/Rowman and Littlefield, 2003) and serves on the editorial boards of the *British Journal for Canadian Studies*, the *London Journal of Canadian Studies*, and *Landscapes*.

Anthony Purdy is professor of French at the University of Western Ontario, where he also teaches in the graduate programs in Comparative Literature, Visual Arts, and the Centre for the Study of Theory and Criticism. He works in the fields of French, English, and comparative literature and visual studies with special emphasis on the relations between literature and other discursive formations. Drawing on the disciplines of sociology, economics, anthropology, cultural geography, archaeology, and art history, his current research focuses on constructions and critiques of modernity—especially as they relate to time, place, and memory—in literature, film, and museology. He has been vice president (1994–1996) and president (1996–1998) of the Association des professeurs de français des universités et collèges canadiens; a founding member of the board of the Research Institute for Comparative Literature at the University of Alberta (1986–1995); board member (1994–1995) and executive board member (1995–1996) of the Canadian Federation for the Humanities; and on a number of editorial and evaluation boards and committees. In addition to eight books and 25 book chapters, he has published in numerous refereed journals, including *Art & Design, La Licorne, Mosaic, Nineteenth Century French Studies, Poetics Today, Recherches Sémiotiques/Semiotic Inquiry, Revue des Sciences Humaines, Revue d'histoire littéraire de la France, Strumenti Critici, Style, Textual Practice,* and *University of Toronto Quarterly.* A book on Michel Tournier is in the final revision stage. Dr. Purdy is currently working on a book project titled, *The Presence of the Past: On the Representation of Cultural Memory.*

Peter Rist is professor in film studies at the Mel Hoppenheim School of Cinema, Concordia University. He has had numerous articles published on East Asian cinema and has edited books on Canadian and South American cinema. Areas of special interest include silent American film; Brazilian, Cuban, Korean, and Chinese (including Hong Kong and Taiwan) cinemas; the films of John Ford; experimental cinema; and the history of film style.

Catherine Russell is professor in film studies at the Mel Hoppenheim School of Cinema and Director of the PhD programme in Humanities at Concordia University. She is a member of the editorial boards of *Cinema Journal* and *CINéMAS,* and book editor for the *Canadian Journal of Film Studies.* She has published several articles in journals such as *Cinema Journal, CinéAction, Camera Obscura,* and *Asian Cinema;* and is the author of *Narrative Mortality: Death, Closure and New Wave Cinemas* (University of Minnesota Press, 1995) and *Experimental Ethnography: The Work of Film in the Age of Video* (Duke University Press, 1999). She has recently edited an issue of *Camera Obscura* on "New Women of the Silent Screen: China, Japan, Hollywood" (*Camera Obscura* 60, Vol. 20 no 3, 2005). Her research interests include the western and melodrama genres, experimental cinema, and Japanese cinema, as well as the work of Walter Benjamin. She is currently finishing a book titled, *The Cinema of Naruse Mikio: Women and Japanese Modernity* (forthcoming, Duke University Press, 2007).

# index

# H